COPY-EDITING

Judith Butcher

COPY-EDITING

The Cambridge Handbook
for Editors, Authors and Publishers

Third Edition

CAMBRIDGE
UNIVERSITY PRESS

Published by the Press Syndicate of the University of Cambridge
The Pitt Building, Trumpington Street, Cambridge CB2 IRP
40 West 20th Street, New York, NY 10011 – 4211, USA
10 Stamford Road, Oakleigh, Melbourne 3166, Australia

First published 1975
Reprinted with corrections 1976
Reprinted 1978, 1980
Second edition 1981
Reprinted 1983, 1986, 1987, 1989
Third edition 1992
Reprinted 1993, 1994, 1996

Printed in Great Britain at the University Press, Cambridge

British Library cataloguing in publication data

Butcher, Judith 1927–
Copy-editing: The Cambridge handbook. – 3rd. ed.
1. Typescripts. Copy-editing
I. Title
808.027

Library of Congress cataloguing in publication data

Butcher, Judith.
Copy-editing: the Cambridge handbook/Judith Butcher. – 3rd ed.
          p.   cm.
Includes bibliographical references and index.
ISBN 0 521 40074 0
1. Copy-reading – Handbooks, manuals, etc.
2. Proofreading – Handbooks, manuals, etc.   I. Title.
PN162.B86   1992
808'.02–DC20   90–47567 CIP

ISBN 0 521 40074 0 hardback

Contents

Contents

Illustrations

Preface to the first edition

Copy-editing is largely a matter of common sense in deciding what to do and of thoroughness in doing it; but there are pitfalls an inexperienced copy editor cannot foresee. Some years ago I wrote a handbook for use within the Cambridge University Press, so that new copy-editors could benefit from the accumulated experience of their predecessors rather than having to learn by making their own mistakes; and it has now been suggested that such a book might be of use in other firms.

It is impossible to write a handbook suitable for every publisher or every kind of typescript. This book is based on my experience at Penguin Books and the Cambridge University Press, where copy-editors work on the premises and see a book through from the estimate stage until the proofs are passed for press. Freelance copy-editors and others working to a more limited brief – or commissioning editors who wish to do their own copy-editing – will be able to make use of the parts relevant to their own job; the things to be done remain the same, although the same person may not do them all.

As I am not writing primarily for authors, I have not, for example, explained the reasons for choosing one system of bibliographical references rather than another. By the time the book reaches the copy-editor the system is chosen, and the copy-editor's job is to make sure that it works efficiently, by eliminating certain faults in it. Publishers now realize more and more, however, that authors must be briefed early and adequately. If your publisher does not already have a good set of notes on style for its authors, do prepare one: not all authors will be prepared to follow your instructions, but many of them will be grateful for any guidance you can give.

It is difficult to decide how to arrange a book of this kind, but it seemed best to cover first the things that are common to all books, and to leave the more complex material until later, rather than to adopt a more strictly logical order. Chapter 1 outlines the copy-editor's function. Chapters 2–5 cover this in more detail in relation to the three stages at which the copy-editor works on the book: the preparation for an estimate or the setting of specimen pages; the main copy-editing stage, at which the text and illustrations are prepared for the printer; and the proof stage. Chapter 6 discusses some difficult points of spelling, capitalization and other things collectively known as house style. Chapters 7–9 treat the various parts of the book in more detail: preliminary pages, headings, tables, notes, indexes and so on. Chapters 10 and 11 cover more complex material such as bibliographical references, quotations, poetry and plays; chapter 12 books with more than one author or in more than one volume. Chapters 13 and 14 deal with specialized subjects: science and mathematics, classical books, books on law and music. The final chapter gives some points to look out for when preparing reprints and new editions.

Many people have given me good advice during my years in publishing; and it would take too much space to thank them all individually. I am especially indebted to those who have written parts of this book: Michael Coles compiled the chapter on science and mathematics, Gillian Law wrote the section about books on law, and Jeremy Mynott the one on classical books; Mrs M. D. Anderson made the index.

Authors of this kind of book lay themselves open to the charge of not following their own precepts. Alas, both my copy-editor and I are fallible, and I should be grateful if you would let me know of any errors, omissions or better ways of doing things.

Preface to the second edition

I have taken the opportunity to include the new British Standard proof correction marks and to revise the information about US copyright legislation. Innumerable smaller changes have been made throughout the book.

Preface to the third edition

I was delighted to be asked to prepare this new edition. In the second edition the amount of resetting and repaging had to be kept to a minimum; but this edition has been entirely revised and reset.

I have, however, kept the original coverage, even though most copy-editing is now done by freelance editors or copy-editors who may work to a house style and a standard design, and at only one stage of the book or journal's production. Since they work on their own, they need written guidance both on copy-editing in general and on how their own work fits in with what other people may be doing to typescripts at different stages.

As before, the book is a collaborative effort.

Lynn Hieatt has written a section on typescripts produced by the author on disk (1.2); there is a section on unbiased, non-sexist writing (6.2); and there are five new appendixes: those on Hebrew, on Arabic, and on Islamic and other calendars were written by Roger Coleman, Susan Moore and Iain White respectively.

Christopher Scarles has revised his material on copyright and permissions; Sheila Champney has masterminded and co-ordinated the revision of chapter 13, with the help of Michael Coles, Karin Fancett and Jane Holland (geology), Jane Farrell (medicine), Peter Hammersley (computing), Sandi Irvine, Jacqueline Mitton (astronomy) and Mairi Sutherland. Susan Moore has revised the section on classical books, Gillian Law her section on books on law, and many people have given me expert advice.

I was asked to include more examples, and have done this, particularly in chapter 10, where I have also altered the layout to try to make the information easier to find.

I did consider whether to say more about US and other alternatives to the British style and practice that I have outlined in the book; but style and practice vary so much, both within Britain and throughout the world, that it seemed best to keep the book simple – listing the problems the copy-editor faces and giving one or two possible solutions. I have found that it is more difficult for inexperienced copy-editors to recognize a potential problem than it is for them to discover the appropriate solution.

The index is fuller and therefore easier to use; it was made by Michèle Clarke.

In addition to those already mentioned, I should like to thank the following: Henry Hardy and Sandi Irvine sent me long and very helpful lists of suggestions based on the second edition; Susan Moore, Robert Campbell, Gillian Clarke, Nicola Harris and Lesley Ward commented in detail on the whole of the draft of the third edition. Janet Mackenzie provided advice on Australian practice and Mike Agnes on American practice. John Trevitt read much of the draft and answered innumerable questions about production and design. Lynn Hieatt and other people at Cambridge University Press and elsewhere have gone to immense trouble to comment on parts of the draft and answer my questions. Mary Piggott of the Society of Indexers commented on chapter 8. Victoria Cooper and Penny Souster advised me about the music section (14.3) and provided the music examples. I am very grateful to them all, and to my copy-editor, Jenny Potts. I did not follow all the advice I was given; and the book, except in the sections written by other people, expresses my own views.

Despite all our efforts, there may well be errors, omissions or better ways of doing things; and I should be very grateful if you would let me know of any, so that I can continue to improve the book.

① Introduction

WHAT COPY-EDITING IS

There are three kinds of editing.

1 *Substantive editing* aims to improve the overall coverage and presentation of a piece of writing, its content, scope, length, level and organization. The editor may suggest improvements for the author to make, or may (by agreement with the author) rewrite and rearrange the material, suggest better illustrations, and so on. The editor at this stage will normally look out for legal problems such as libel and plagiarism.

2 *Detailed editing for sense* is concerned with whether each section expresses the author's meaning clearly, without gaps and contradictions. It involves looking at each sentence, the author's choice of words, the punctuation, the use of abbreviations, comparing the data in tables with the relevant text, checking text against the illustrations and their captions, and so on. The editor will at this stage look out for any quotations or illustrations that may need permission from the copyright owner, and will also look out for other legal problems.

3 *Checking for consistency* is a mechanical but important task. It may to some extent be done at the same time as 2. It involves checking such things as spelling and the use of single or double quotes (see section 3.6), either according to a house style or according to the author's own style; checking the numbering of illustrations, tables and notes, and any cross-references to them, and also the consistency of bibliographical references.

'Copy-editing' usually consists of 2 and 3, plus 4 below.

4 *Clear presentation of the material for the typesetter* involves making sure that it is complete and that all the parts are clearly identified: for example the grade of each subheading, which pieces of text (such as long quotations) should be distinguished typographically from the main text, and where tables and illustrations should be placed. The copy-editor may also size the illustrations, mark type sizes, and so on.

The same person may do all four of these things, or they may be split in various ways. Those who do the substantive editing may be called editor, commissioning editor, journal editor, developmental editor, and so on; those who carry out the jobs in categories 2–4 may be called editor, desk editor, production editor, subeditor or copy-editor. For the sake of simplicity I have called the latter copy-editors, and the people who brief them commissioning editors.

The main aims of copy-editing are to remove any obstacles between the reader and what the author wants to convey, and also to save time and money by finding and solving any problems before the book is typeset, so that production can go ahead without interruption.

Different publishers work in different ways, according to the kinds of material they publish. This book is based on the most complicated kind of publication, where the design and house style are not standardized and the copy-editor has to make decisions about stylistic conventions and obtain advice on points of design; when I say 'ask the designer' I mean that you should ask someone who has the necessary technical knowledge, if you do not have it yourself. I have also written as though the copy-editor is directly in touch with the author, though in some cases this will not be so.

For simplicity's sake I have used British examples, but copy-editors working in other countries can substitute their own conventions, such as proof correction symbols. The problems remain the same, even if the solutions may be different.

In book publishing, copy-editors may be involved at three stages. Soon after the book has been accepted for publication, they should look at the typescript to see whether the author's word processor might be used to correct some recurring faults of consistency, style or layout (see section 1.2) before copy-editing starts, and whether there are other general changes which the author should be asked to approve in advance (see section 3.3). At this stage the copy-editor can also brief the designer and production department as to any complications to be taken into account in designing the book and planning its production (see chapter 2).

After working through the typescript and illustrations in detail (see chapters 3 and 4), the copy-editor may read a proof or collate the author's proof with a proofreader's, ensuring that the author's corrections are comprehensible and consistent with the existing material, and that they can be incorporated without great difficulty or expense. The copy-editor tries to see that the cost of corrections is allocated fairly between author, typesetter and publisher, and to ensure that any additional material, such as an index, is legible, well organized and consistent (see chapters 5 and 8).

The good copy-editor is a rare creature: an intelligent reader and a tactful and sensitive critic; someone who cares enough about perfection of detail to spend a long time checking small points of consistency in someone else's work but has the judgement not to waste time or antagonize the author by making unnecessary changes.

Copy-editors are not usually experts on the subject of the work, but they must be able to interest themselves in it in order to try to put themselves in the position of the intended readers. Authors are so familiar with their subject, and may have written a book over so long a period, that they cannot see it as it will appear to someone else; and the copy-editor will often see where an author has been repetitious or ambiguous, has omitted a step in the argument or failed to explain a point or spell out an abbreviation.

Although the copy-editor's main interest is likely to be an editorial one, the job involves production considerations too. Knowing the book in detail, one can make the author's intentions clear to the designer and typesetter; and realizing the constraints within which the typesetter has to work, one can explain to authors why it may be impossible to carry out their wishes in exactly the way they propose. It is this joint role which gives the job its fascination.

1.2

TYPESCRIPTS: HARD, ELECTRONIC AND CAMERA-READY

In this book the word 'typescript' is used to describe the material that the copy-editor works on, whether it is word-processor printout, typewriter-produced copy or electronic files. Most material that reaches a publisher will be in one of the following forms:

1 *Hard-copy typescript* (see section 1.2.1): word-processor printout, typewriter-produced copy or even handwritten manuscript copy, the copy-edited version of which will eventually be keyed by a typesetter; often called simply 'manuscript'.

2 *Electronic typescript* (e.t.s.) (see section 1.2.2): electronic files pre-

pared by the author and submitted on disk or tape, which may be dealt with in any of several ways:

- processed by a typesetter as they are, with little or no copy-editing or design
- copy-edited and designed on a hard-copy printout, then corrected by the author before being processed ('output') by a typesetter (see pp. 14–23)
- copy-edited and designed on a hard-copy printout, then corrected by a typesetter before being processed (see pp. 13–14)
- copy-edited, corrected and possibly even designed on screen before being processed by a typesetter (see p. 24)

3 *Author-generated camera-ready copy* (c.r.c.) (see section 1.2.3): camera-ready copy prepared by the author to the publisher's specifications, which may be dealt with in one of two ways:

- sent for making film and printing after minimal copy-editing and design (there may have been copy-editorial and design comment at a preliminary stage)
- fully copy-edited and designed on a first draft, after which a final version is submitted by the author.

Some so-called camera-ready copy may be material that is presented to the publisher as electronic files produced on a desk-top publishing system or a specialized typesetting package, which often require no further intervention before being output. These electronic camera-ready copy files are usually accompanied by a hard-copy printout for the typesetter's reference.

1.2.1 Hard-copy typescript

A hard-copy typescript ('hard' in that it is presented on the hard medium of paper) will be keyed by a typesetter from copy that has copy-editor's marks and corrections throughout and that is accompanied by a design specification for founts, layout, and treatment of tables and illustrations (see chapters 2 and 3).

Most hard-copy typescripts are prepared by authors using word processors. When authors use their systems knowledgeably and their printers provide clear and unambiguous output, and when the authors have followed any publisher's specifications for general layout and style, there are many respects in which typescripts prepared in this way are easier for the copy-editor to work with than typewriter-produced copy.

The major benefit of typescripts prepared on word processors is that, if the copy-editor has an opportunity to look carefully at the typescript at an early stage and can request corrected pages from the author, some of the traditional copy-editorial headaches and problems of presentation can be eliminated before copy-editing begins. For instance, one can ask authors to provide double-spaced copy for notes or bibliography, if they were originally single-spaced, to amalgamate several subsections of a bibliography or to subdivide an unacceptably dense one. Authors using their word processor's search-and-replace facility carefully can eliminate many inconsistencies. One can also ask an author to remove such things as *op. cit.* references from the notes and replace them by author–short-title references (see section 10.1). Similarly, if you can define at an early stage the (seemingly inevitable) problems of inconsistent or inappropriate hyphenation, spelling and capitalization, the author can be asked to search for the terms and change them as agreed throughout the text and send a new printout before you begin work on the typescript in earnest. It would be a relatively simple task for an author, for example, to apply an '-ise' style consistently (though this must be done carefully, since otherwise one could end up with 'size' becoming 'sise', or 'seize' becoming 'seise'), to correct a habitual misspelling of a word or name, or to locate all author–date references to a specific year and effect an alteration. By using the word processor's facilities, a careful author should be able to find *all* instances of a given characteristic – something that very few copy-editors can guarantee they have done. If the author is going to be asked to make some changes of this sort and to provide an entirely new printout before copy-editing begins, you can ask, for instance, that inappropriate italic or bold face be replaced by normal roman, or that other basic changes be made throughout.

Once copy-editing has begun, however, tell the author not to generate and send updated pages to be substituted, since the copy-editorial work already done on the original sheets would then have to be transferred to the new ones. Also, this new copy might contain other subtle changes, changes that could be discovered only by reading the entire page a second time – which is not an efficient way of proceeding. If you want, say, a revised bibliography or note section, the author can be asked to produce this and send it while the copy-editing of the text proceeds; however, once work has begun on a given section, any new pages sent to the copy-editor must have clearly marked on them (perhaps in a bright colour) exactly what has been altered. Explain this to your authors as early in the copy-editing process as possible, and ask that, once copy-editing has commenced, they simply provide a list of the page and line numbers of any further changes or additions they wish to make to their text, for you to alter on the top copy, or at least indicate clearly on any new pages what has been changed from the original version so that you can locate the passages and make the changes by hand.

You might find it useful to send the author a list of words on which decisions have to be made and, once a final list of spellings, hyphens, capitals and the like has been agreed between you, ask the author to search for these words and tell you where they occur, so that you can make them consistent. For a typescript in need of heavy correction, however, this method would prove extremely cumbersome. This approach would obviously be most useful at a much earlier stage, before the author has begun final keying. Some publishers send style sheets to authors for them to follow in preparing their material, especially for series and in journal work.

There are pitfalls in working with typescripts prepared on word processors, as every copy-editor knows. The biggest problem for the copy-editor is the quite natural assumption that a beautifully produced and printed word-processed document is 'correct' – the power of the printed image can assert itself to everyone's disadvantage here. For the same reason, a professional-looking printout carrying no handwritten corrections may not have been checked thoroughly by the author after having been printed; the copy-editor must be alert to this. Authors may try to make it look as much like a printed product as they can, which can be unhelpful; everyone concerned can work more efficiently and easily on clear, conventional double-spaced copy. For example, if quoted extracts are printed by the author in type of a smaller size than the text type, and if the copy-editor decides to run-on a given quotation within the text, or the design specifies text-size type, a note will need to be added to tell the typesetter to ignore the smaller-size type. The minuscule superscript note numbers produced by some printers are difficult to see and therefore time-consuming to locate and check; authors whose printers cannot produce legible superscript note numbers could be asked to use normal text-size numbers instead, or to go through the typescript and clarify the note numbering by hand instead of trying to produce a more finished look to what is, after all, an ephemeral document.

Remember that, when authors have reworked their text in light of what you have decided between you, their software will probably automatically renumber the pages, so be careful, when quoting page and line numbers in your communications with the author, that both of you are referring to the same material.

The typesetter who will key the copy-edited typescript will also have a search-and-replace facility – much more powerful and sophisticated than the author's – and if at the last minute a change *must* be made to a spelling, or to hyphens, capitals or dates, you can write a general note to the typesetter, asking for such changes to be made during keying or asking for global changes to be made after the job has been keyed. This might add to the keying costs, so it should not be used as a final copy-editing correction stage; but it is a useful procedure to keep in mind for all material sent for keying, because anything done at the keyboarding stage is cheaper than the equivalent change made at proof stage.

1.2.2 Electronic typescript

Publishers and authors realize a number of benefits from using authors' disks or tapes. Firstly, the keyboarding time is saved and the proofing-out period is shorter. The proofs themselves should be clean and free of literals (except for material rekeyed by the typesetter; see below), which can eliminate the need for revise proofs and thus shorten production time later in the schedule. Some publishers make it a condition of acceptance that typescripts be provided on disk or tape, and many authors much prefer to key the material themselves – especially when it is complex and when they have already spent a great deal of time carefully keying and checking their work. Some typesetters specialize in dealing with electronic typescripts and have reduced their straight keyboarding staff as a consequence. Finally, publishers can realize some cost savings in producing work in this way.

The keys to successfully handling electronic typescripts lie in providing a full and clear brief to author, copy-editor and typesetter, and in judging each project on its merits at an early stage.

Sometimes it is decided, for the sake of speed or because the author is known to be competent and has been well briefed, not to have a formal copy-editing or design stage on an e.t.s. Material suitable for this treatment might include certain kinds of journal work and proceedings from conferences that need to be published quickly if they are to have maximum impact and, therefore, maximum sales. There should always be a thorough discussion by the interested parties of the merits and shortcomings of this method of publishing, and the author should be told that the material will be produced without copy-editing or even careful reading if this is the case. Some publishers give copy-editors and designers the opportunity to look through an initial printout of such material, to make comments about presentation and suggest necessary changes, before the final e.t.s. is accepted.

Most material accepted in electronic form – just like most of that accepted in hard-copy form – *will* need full copy-editing. Just because it is presented as already keyed files does not, obviously, mean that it is necessarily well written, or free of stylistic inconsistencies or capitalization problems. Depending on the circumstances and the market for the published material, a publisher will require the same standard of copy-editing for electronic typescripts as for material produced in other ways. The author should understand from the beginning that a good many changes will probably have to be made to the keyed files to make them conform to house style or simply good practice.

It must be determined at the very beginning who will make the copy-editorial corrections to the e.t.s.: author, copy-editor or 'typesetter' (the typesetting firm or 'interfacing house' who will process, or 'output', the disks/tapes). As the copy-editor, either you will be marking up the printout and asking the author or the typesetter to make the corrections on the disks or tapes, or you may be keying the corrections yourself on screen after you have agreed with the author what needs to be done (see p. 24). Publishers vary in their procedures; make sure you understand exactly what your role will be before beginning work on an e.t.s.

When you are copy-editing on the hard-copy printout of the author's disks or tapes, it is vital that the printout is the very latest version – time and effort are wasted and frustration results if the author has made changes to the e.t.s. that are not recorded in the printout you are working on. In your very first letter to the author you should stress this point and, if there seems to be any doubt at all whether changes have been made on the e.t.s. that are not reflected on the printout you have been given, wait until you are confident that you have the final version before beginning work in detail. Many a copy-editor and author have been surprised at proof stage to find that whole paragraphs have been deleted in error, or passages mistakenly turned into italic – things that were not spotted at copy-editing stage simply because they were not reflected on the printout.

Finally, the typesetter has to know what material will be received for outputting, when it will be received and what will need to be done to it. Appendix 12 contains an example of the kind of information a production department will need from the author of a proposed electronic project before it can be assessed. The typesetter making the assessment may make comments or suggestions on how the e.t.s. should be prepared or altered; and these will need to be passed on to the author.

Viruses

Serious problems in dealing with electronic material, such as corruption of the data or even, in extreme cases, complete system failure ('crashing'), can develop because of the presence of 'viruses' on the disk or in a computer system. Most typesetters' equipment will have some form of 'gate-keeping' package to protect against any damage that could be caused by viruses. If you use your own equipment, it would be prudent to install one of these packages yourself. Authors may know about the danger of viruses and take precautions at their end, but this should not be assumed.

Fortunately, problems with viruses are rare. But if you notice any persistent errors on the printout or if the typesetter reports faults or problems when the e.t.s. is first examined, the possibility of viruses should be considered and taken very seriously.

Prelims
If there are any preliminary pages, most of these will almost certainly be keyed afresh by the typesetter, even if the author has included them in the e.t.s. Such things as the title page, contents list, lists of illustrations and abbreviations will need to conform to the publisher's design for spacing and layout, which means that the typesetter may find it simpler to rekey at least some of this material accordingly – unless the author has been extremely well briefed and is very skilful. The obvious exception to this would be prefaces or other 'text-like' material in the prelims, which will probably not need to be keyed again. The copy-editor will need to mark up all preliminary pages on the final printout as for a hard-copy typescript for the typesetter's reference (see chapter 7).

Tables
Tables in an e.t.s. are sometimes keyed with the text by an author who is able to handle the complexities of tabs and general layout. If so, authors should be asked to put all the tables together at the end of the relevant section or chapter or in a separate file, and indicate on the printout where they should appear in the text ('Table 2.3 near here' or 'TB' – see p. 19). Tables are more often – and perhaps appropriately, because they are complicated to key – submitted as hard copy, keyed by the typesetter, and added to the e.t.s. or even stripped in as repro on to the final camera-ready copy in the same way that illustrations might be. Most of the time the typesetter, without specifically telling the publisher, will rekey tables and other complex material even if they are on the e.t.s., because rekeying is often much simpler (and thus cheaper) than adjusting the spacing or alignment on the author's files. It is right that typesetters should decide whether to use or rekey some files, of course; they should, however, be encouraged to tell the publisher what material has been rekeyed, so that it can be checked at proof stage. Publishers who send typesetters samples of disks or tapes at an early stage often ask for a written report on just such matters, urging the typesetter to indicate what material might need rekeying later. This possibility of tables and sometimes other material being rekeyed is a strong reason for having e.t.s. output proofread in the usual way.

Illustrations

In an e.t.s. that is to have illustrations, the copy-editor will usually need to indicate on the final printout where the illustrations should come, in the usual form (e.g. 'Fig. 5 near here' or 'IL' – see p. 20), so that if there is not a design paste-up to refer to, the typesetter can place them as near as possible to where the author wants them. The usual illustrations checklist indicating placement in the text (see p. 80) should also be completed by the copy-editor, and the usual work done to have illustrations drawn and accurately sized to the final design specifications.

Authors with good graphics software may be able to produce line illustrations in readable form on the e.t.s., but caution should be exercised before accepting that this is the best way illustrative material should be generated for a given project. Perhaps a better overall approach is for authors to submit their e.t.s. illustrations as camera-ready artwork, having output it themselves on a high-resolution printer or imagesetter. (If from the former, the output should be at one-and-a-half times or twice the size it is to appear in print, in order to produce the clearest image.) Such illustrations would then be reduced and incorporated by the typesetter. If the illustrations are submitted on the e.t.s. itself, the typesetter should be asked for a sample printout to determine the quality of the output before the publisher decides to go ahead with producing them by this method. Very complex illustrations will probably need to be commissioned separately from professional studios.

Captions or legends should be put into a separate file, unless the typesetter has requested otherwise.

Footnotes and endnotes

Ask the author to put any note material into a separate file, if it is convenient and simple to do so (with some software, this would be inappropriate). The typesetter's report should tell you whether any alterations need to be made to the note material itself, or to the text indicators keyed to the notes. (Typesetters often report that note numbers in the text are indistinguishable from ordinary numbers, and need to be coded in some way (see p. 16) so that they can be turned into superscript numbers of a smaller size.)

Special sorts

If special sorts – Greek or Hebrew characters, mathematical or musical notation symbols or unusual accents – are wanted and they cannot be keyed, the author will have dealt with this on the e.t.s. in one of two ways: (a) blank spaces will have been left that you can see on the printout, probably filled in later in handwriting by the author; or (b) some specific key or keys will have been used to indicate where special sorts are required.

If the author has used the first method, you can leave the filled-in blanks on the final printout and add a marginal mark to draw the typesetter's attention to them. Be sure all the special sorts are legible and that the typesetter will know what they are; include a printed list of them if you can. It is more helpful to the typesetter, however, if the author keys visible codes in place of the sorts that cannot be produced. So long as the author uses certain keys exclusively for the missing sorts and provides a conversion chart of what has been keyed and what is wanted, the typesetter can make global searches and add the special sorts required. The author may use a set of generally accepted codes, but, as mentioned above, it does not matter so long as they are used consistently and a list of them is provided for the typesetter.

Dashes (en rules or em rules – see sections 6.12.1, 6.12.2) are a common occurrence in most texts. If you want en rules instead of hyphens in spans of numbers and the author has keyed hyphens, you need only give the typesetter a note that all hyphens between numbers should be changed to closed-up en rules. If you want spaced or unspaced parenthetical dashes in the final text, tell the typesetter what unique keys the author has used for these features and what they should be changed to. Some publishers recommend three closed-up hyphens for closed-up dashes, two for spaced dashes (as in the list below). However, any keys used uniquely and consistently for these features will do, so long as the typesetter knows what they are.

Something such as the following would do:

<&> = Greek theta
<**> = Russian 'soft' sign
<H2O> = cap H/subscript 2/cap letter O
<-> = minus sign (if this must look different from a hyphen)

<- - -> = closed-up en rule
<- -> = spaced en rule (parenthetical en dash)

Emphasize to the author that, as in all coding work, these particular combinations of keys must not have been used for anything else in the typescript, or the typesetter's global change will be rather more dramatic than you had anticipated, and the result may be gibberish. The typesetter will need to know whether these sorts occur in text-size type only or in any other sizes. Appendix 12 shows one way of laying this out. Any similar list will do, so long as it contains all the necessary information.

Watch for superscripts and subscripts, which sometimes cannot be read by the typesetter; and highlighting or visible codes (e.g. <4>) may need to be added on the printout to indicate where they should occur. The typesetter should have reported any problems of this sort in the original written analysis of the e.t.s.

(a) Disks or tapes that will be corrected by the typesetter

If the author is unable or unwilling to make copy-editorial changes to the e.t.s., your publisher may decide to set the typescript conventionally from the printout, since most of the advantages of e.t.s. projects can be realized only when authors provide material that needs no further editorial work. However, there may be overpowering economic, logistic or political reasons for deciding to proceed with an e.t.s. and have the typesetter input all the copy-editorial changes, even though typesetters' charges for correcting on screen can be high. If you proceed this way you will, as usual, need to tell the author what changes you are planning to have made, communicating your general and specific queries during copy-editing. Mark the necessary changes, once they have been agreed, directly on the printout (see p. 17).

Even if it is not your usual practice, send a photocopy of the pages with changes marked on them, or even the entire printout, to the author once copy-editing has been completed, so that all the alterations can be approved at this stage and proof correction thus minimized. Once you have the approved copy-edited printout ready, with all your usual marks indicating fresh pages, levels of subheading, where poetry extracts occur, etc., pass it, along with the disks/tapes and any general notes for the typesetter about required style, global changes and the like, to the production department. You may already have marked design features on the printout, or it may be seen by a designer or united with a set of design specifications at this stage.

The typesetter will produce proofs and probably send them to the author or publisher in the usual way, with the marked-up printout to check against. At this point, the author (or professional indexer) will prepare or finalize the index, if one is required (see p. 26). A proof-reader should now read the proofs, since there may have been 'transmission errors' when the disks/tapes were converted to the typesetter's system, or, as described above, the typesetter may have rekeyed some material without specifically identifying it for the publisher to check. Second proofs will probably not be needed, as there should be very light correction.

(b) **Disks or tapes that will be corrected by the author**

Some authors are eager to keep control over their material and are therefore willing and able to correct their own e.t.s. after copy-editing. Some publishers actually require e.t.s. projects to be corrected by authors, having found that jobs proceeding in this way with competent authors are relatively trouble-free (and often less costly). Also, publishers have found that including authors in most of the stages up to producing proofs gives them a better understanding of the publishing process as a whole, and this can increase goodwill all round. The decision as to who will correct the e.t.s. may be made before you receive the typescript to work on, but if you have reason to believe (from what you see on the printout) that the author is not a particularly careful keyboarder you may want to discuss the wisdom of this procedure with your publisher.

Before beginning your copy-editorial work on an e.t.s. that the author will correct, make sure both that the author realizes the amount of work that will be involved in this correction and that the author can do the work competently. Sending the author a few sample folios of copy-edited text with clear markings on them, either from the printout in question or from another typescript that has copy-editorial (and possibly design) marks, is a good way of indicating the kind and amount of work you will be asking for. Some authors, when they see how much detailed manipulation will be involved, decide they will not be able or willing to undertake it. The laborious job of searching for and replacing every instance of an inconsistent capital or spelling, or of making all mathematical variables italic, may not appeal to them.

If this happens, or if the printout shows that the author has not keyed the material competently and there are many editorial changes that need to be made, discuss the correction procedure with your publisher. There is little point in asking an author who is not a very accomplished keyboarder to make corrections, if this results in a poorer e.t.s. for the typesetter to work with. Your publisher may decide to have the material keyed conventionally, using the printout as the typescript, rather than proceed with the e.t.s. Typesetters' charges for intervening in the files and correcting can be high; there is also the obvious problem that every time the typesetter enters the e.t.s. and rekeys, there is the chance of introducing error.

Marking copy-editorial changes for the author
If the author agrees to make the changes required and you have confidence that this can be done accurately, begin copy-editing directly on the hard-copy printout. Determine first what alterations need to be made throughout — whether spellings, use of hyphens and capitals need to be made consistent, whether *op. cit.* in the notes needs to be changed to author and short title, whether the amount or lack of space before and after equations needs to be regularized, and other similar points. Keep a list of these, accompanied by your comments or suggestions for change, and send it to the author for consideration, either at this early point in your work or when you send the c.t.s. for the author to correct, depending on how much discussion or persuasion you think will be necessary.

You will not need to indicate on the printout every place in which one of these problems occurs — a mark at the first instance plus your clear note indicating what you suggest or what query you have about usage will result in the author's making a global search and change, thus altering the particular elements throughout the whole e.t.s. Obviously, this can save you a great deal of time and effort. The author may have the typescript in more than one electronic file — in fact, especially for books, authors will usually use a number of different files to hold the text; one file for each chapter is common (and may have been recommended by your publisher or the typesetter). The searching and changing may therefore involve some work for the author, but is still a relatively simple task.

The author can make similar global changes to matters of presentation and layout. If the typesetter has reported, for instance, that the text note indicators cannot be distinguished from other arabic numbers in the e.t.s. (see p. 11), ask the author to find all these indicators and key them differently, perhaps by putting angle brackets around them (e.g. <4>).

It is worth emphasizing here that there may be hidden problems with the keying, ones you cannot see on the printout and which the typesetter may not have noticed on the initial perusal of the sample e.t.s. (This is why the author should, at the initial feasibility stage, send sample e.t.s. files that are comprehensive enough to show the typesetter examples of all the material, and thus the quality of keying and possible faults that need correction.) This includes such things as paragraph 'hard' returns having been keyed inappropriately at the ends of some but not all lines, or the letter 'O' keyed when the number 'o' was wanted. It is also possible that the author has used spaces or tabs to achieve paragraph indents or visual positioning of lines: this sort of thing cannot usually be dealt with by a global search by the typesetter, so it can cause problems. The author should key headings and other features simply, using upper- and lower-case letters instead of all capitals, and should not, for example, use tabs and returns to centre a two-line heading: the typesetter would have to remove them again for the heading to output properly. (The actual text of a feature may, however, be usefully coded by the author for italic or bold, for example; see p. 19.) If the typesetter has recommended corrective action on points such as these, ask your author to make a separate check to eliminate them. If the typesetter has not given any special instructions, assume that no problems exist that cannot be dealt with at outputting stage.

The copy-editor must have confidence that all these marvellous global changes will be made carefully and accurately. It is no good having the author give too general a command which might result in, say, turning all the hyphens and all the minus signs into en dashes, or making spelling changes no one had intended, such as turning 'Colorado' into 'Colourado'. By the time you begin your copy-editing work in earnest you should have some idea of your author's keying ability and degree of sophistication in these matters. Do not ask an author who has what you think are marginally acceptable skills to do anything too complicated; any such things would be better left to the typesetter at a later stage, even if this might increase costs.

Proceed with copy-editing on the printout as you normally would for a conventional typescript. When working on the printout, use a bright-coloured ballpoint or fine-tipped felt pen for your changes and marginal queries, so that the author can spot them easily. You will probably have to spell out to an author things that you could take for granted that a professional typesetter would know. Use the British Standard proof correction marks (see appendix 13) or a similarly widely known system for marking the corrections, and ensure that the author has a copy of them for reference. Explain in a note to the author any other abbreviations or technical terms you may have used.

When working on any kind of typescript material, most copy-editors consult their authors about proposed changes before making them. This is where your method will be different when working with an e.t.s. that the author is going to correct, since after it is copy-edited the printout will be sent back to the author for corrections to be made. You can be bolder in marking suggested changes on an e.t.s. printout, because the author will see precisely what you have done and, if there is a strong objection to a particular change, the author will not have to implement it. Before beginning the work, however, you should already have communicated and determined what the level of copy-editing will be and what strong ideas the author may hold. You cannot empha-size too firmly to an author that all changes must be made *consistently*.

'Coding' added by the author: control codes and generic codes
Some typesetters prefer to receive disks/tapes with all the copy-editorial changes made to the text and accompanied by a final printout marked up as usual, but with no extra 'coding' added by the author for typographical and design features. This results from their experience with authors who have entered the wrong codes, or the right ones inconsistently: either of these faults can cause headaches for the type-setter. If the author is not thought competent or is unwilling to add any

coding, proceed next with the steps described in the sections below. (In this case, you may have to mark on the final printout such things as where italic or bold occur, or where spaced en dashes are required, if the typesetter has reported that these features cannot be read and your author is unable or unwilling to mark them.)

However, in some cases you may want to ask an author whom you have come to recognize as competent to make all the copy-editorial changes *and* to undertake some 'coding' work of one sort or another as well, depending on the quality of the e.t.s. and the typesetter's requirements. The amount and type of the coding work required will vary, and some typesetters, as already mentioned, prefer completely un-coded files – no two jobs are likely to be exactly the same. The information in this chapter is given only as a general guide; be sure to liaise with your publisher before asking an author to do any coding work, and make sure that any codes that you use or ask the author to add will be acceptable to the typesetter.

The typesetter's report may have indicated that some features cannot be read on the disks/tapes – such things as the paragraph return, the tabs, or the putting of characters into bold or italic, sometimes fall into this category. (For special sorts, see p. 12.) The author may think that these features have already been effected simply by keying the software 'control codes' (also called 'function calls' or 'function codes') or by using the pull-down menus or windows on the word processor. However, these features on some authors' systems may not be able to be read by the typesetter's system, and you may need, therefore, to ask the author to highlight them in some way throughout the e.t.s. This high-light coding, which one can see on the screen and on the printout, is often called 'generic' or 'visible' coding.

If you have been told that the typesetter cannot read the *italic* control code, for example, you might ask the author to key some simple abbreviation before and after each instance of italic in the text. (It should not be too difficult for the author to locate all these instances, since whatever keystrokes were used initially can be searched for.) You may suggest the use of one of the codes described in an existing, formulated system such as SGML (Standard Generalized Mark-up Language), or your publisher's preferred codes, or you or the author may invent a simple code such as the following:

<i>word needing italics<i*>
<bf>word needing bold-face type<bf*>

Similar devices can be used for other elements that the typesetter indicates cannot be read.

No matter what keystrokes you ask the author to use, the typesetter will need a list of them, so that they can be searched for and replaced by the typesetter's own control codes for the particular features. Make sure that this list is prepared and accompanies the e.t.s. when you have finished your work.

The author's coding work may end here. But if you have, again, a competent and willing author, you can greatly increase the value of the e.t.s. if you go one step further and ask the author to key some visible indications of the document's structure, showing where chapter titles, subheadings, poetry extracts and all the other features of the e.t.s. occur. If the author does this consistently and well, the typesetter can simply search for the codes used and replace them with the relevant typesetting codes. Here, too, either a standard system or something like the following could be used:

main heading	<MH>	
chapter number	<CN>	
chapter title	<CT>	
text begins on new line, full out	<TX>	
text begins new paragraph	<NPTX>	
first-level text heading	<A>	
second-level text heading	<B>	
third-level text heading	<C>	
first-level heading in notes, bibliog., etc.	<X>	
second-level heading in notes, bibliog., etc.	<Y>	
quoted prose extract begins	<EXT>	
extract source begins	<ES>	
quoted poetry extract begins	<PTY>	
poetry source begins	<PS>	
table	<TB>	(keyed near where you want the table to be placed)
table body	<TBB>	(keyed at the beginning of the table)

illustration	<IL>	(keyed near where you want the illustration placed)
illustration body	<ILB>	(keyed at the beginning of the illustration)
illustration caption	<ILC>	(keyed by the caption)
bibliography or references	<BIB>	(keyed at the beginning of the section)
footnote	<FN>	(keyed at the beginning of the separate FN file)
endnote	<EN>	(keyed at the beginning of the separate EN file)

It is worth emphasizing once again that material with no author-introduced codes will always be preferred to inadequately or inconsistently coded material, which has to be corrected by you or the typesetter, often painstakingly (and therefore expensively). The copy-editor does not need to understand the implications of all the coding required by the publisher or typesetter. One might in some cases ask an author to send some sample passages of coding work, to see if the principle has been grasped. The copy-editor must make sure that the author is provided with clear and unambiguous instructions as to how to perform the additional work. Your publisher may have some prepared documentation on this for sending to the author. Any problems should be discussed straight away with the production department.

Design
The typesetter will follow the design specification sent with the e.t.s. or stored on disk from previous similar projects (common in journal work), translating the author's codes or interpreting your written marks to effect the printed design of the work. Usually you and the author need not do anything beyond what has been described above.

There may be times, however, when the author will need to alter the e.t.s. if it contradicts the design decided on. For example, the author may have keyed headings in all capitals when the design specifies upper and lower case, which means the typesetter will have the job of altering these and may make errors in judging what should be capitalized and what should not. Discuss any such matters with the person responsible for the design of the finished work and tell the author what needs to be changed.

Small capital letters will sometimes be required in an e.t.s., for the usual reasons – either because the design calls for non-lining (old style) figures, which look much better with small capitals (see p. 144), or because passages occur within the text in full capitals that would look enormous if produced at full capital height (see p. 132). If e.t.s. authors cannot key small capitals on their system, and if they are doing some visible coding, ask them to code for small capitals by using, for example, <sc> at the beginning of the material, going back to text type afterwards by keying an 'end of small capitals' code such as <sc*>. Most typesetters prefer all the characters to be keyed as lower-case letters instead of capitalized ones, so ask the author to do this, too. Thus:

<sc>god said, let newton be! and all was light<sc*> is one example.

If you want any of the characters to be full capitals within these small capitals, ask the author to type these as capitals (as perhaps God and Newton in the example above), and emphasize them in coloured pen on the printout.

If small capitals appear in complex equations that would therefore involve the author in a great deal of fiddly coding, or if the author is not doing any coding at all, mark where the small caps. are needed on the printout with a coloured pen and tell the typesetter what you have done.

Some publishers send authors standard printed design details indicating what needs to be done to the e.t.s., especially in journal work, where the design will usually be the same, or for book work where a standard design will be used. Others provide some kind of package – variously called electronic design templates, macro packages or pre-formatted disks/tapes – which require only that the author key the text straight on to the pre-formatted but otherwise blank disks/tapes supplied, or transfer design information to their own e.t.s., according to the accompanying written set of detailed instructions. In this way, the e.t.s. ends up with the desired design features and layout, and the typesetter's outputting work is greatly simplified.

This way of proceeding requires more basic word-processor knowledge and interest than many authors will have, but can be very successful if they are keen and competent.

After copy-editing is finished

Once you have completed copy-editing, send the author any disks/tapes that you may have been keeping (perhaps the ones the author submitted initially) along with the printout marked up by you, flagged if appropriate with coloured stickers or notes, and with your list of general and detailed notes and queries. The author will then make the corrections and make a final, up-to-date printout of the corrected e.t.s. Ask the author to check this new printout carefully against the original one, to see that all the changes have been correctly keyed and that nothing has gone wrong (for example, whole passages converted to italic, or wiped out altogether). Undoubtedly, the author will find a few further errors, or decide to rephrase a sentence or two (or more) during this stage, and alter the e.t.s. further. The copy-editor cannot emphasize too strongly to the author that the final printout sent back must truly be the *final* one, with all late changes printed out and highlighted for you to copy-edit. The author must not be tempted to make any other changes once the final printout has been produced, without printing out the affected folios again. Many an author and copy-editor have been surprised to find at a later stage that an anomaly has crept in which can be explained only by the author's having entered the e.t.s. just to make one last-minute correction without having printed out the new folio for someone to check.

Having made all the corrections, the author should send you the final version of the e.t.s. and the final printout, together with the original (now 'foul') printout. This stage resembles the traditional first proof stage because, unless you have been given different instructions by your publisher or you have some reason to be entirely confident about the author's equipment and competence, you (or someone) will need to collate the foul and the final printouts and confirm that all the corrections have been properly made and that the author has not created further need for alteration – the thoroughness of this check will depend on how reliable your author is and how heavily corrected the first printout was.

You may find that the author, without notifying you, has decided not to implement some of the changes you suggested. If this occurs, you will have to decide whether it is best to leave things as they now stand, communicate with the author again and discuss the matter, possibly asking the author to make the changes now, or mark the changes yourself on the final printout. Similarly, you may find a few copy-editorial points during your collation that you missed the first time round and that still need correcting. The typesetter will probably be asked to make these final changes, unless they involve something basic to the whole text that has not come to light until now.

Who will make the final changes depends on whether the authors are nearby or on the other side of the world, whether they have methods of conveying the material quickly to you, and whether they have the capacity, the time and the good nature to do further work. If the typesetter is going to make any editorial changes, these should be marked clearly on the final printout and accompanied by marginal marks and a general note about any global alterations.

Final stages

Once the final printout has been thoroughly checked and you are satisfied with it, prepare the preliminary pages copy for keying by the typesetter, unless the author has already keyed these pages on the e.t.s. in your publisher's correct style and design (see p. 10). Pass the printout, the disks/tapes and any of your usual briefing forms to the production department. A designer may then set out a design in the traditional way, or a specification will be provided for the typesetter's reference during the final processing. The typesetter should be sent clear, unambiguous notes and marks on the hard-copy printout.

When sent to the typesetter, the e.t.s. should always be accompanied by the up-to-date printout of the data for the typesetter's reference. Without this reference copy a typesetter is handicapped, and time can be lost and confusion result.

(c) **Copy-editing on screen**

Some publishers ask copy-editors to correct electronic files on screen, adding editorial and design changes themselves. This has many advantages and may be entirely appropriate for material such as reference texts or school books, where the work is collaborative and there is not an easily identifiable 'author' of the work with whom to discuss changes. It may also suit journal work where the style is strictly applied by the publisher to the author's text. Before the copy-editor begins work on screen, there should be a thorough discussion with the commissioning editor, the production department and the author about the procedures to be followed. Good communication about copy-editorial change is particularly important when working in this way, because the copy-editor will have control of the material in a way that one does not have with a hard-copy typescript. Once a change has been made to the e.t.s., there will be no record (except an earlier version of the disks/tapes or an unrevised printout) of what has been changed. This could lead to misunderstanding as well as simple human error. The copy-editor should ensure that the publisher's procedures are known and agreed to by the author before altering the e.t.s. One could use one of the flagging (sometimes called 'redlining') systems of some editing packages, through which the alterations are highlighted on the e.t.s. for the author's attention, assuming the author will get a final look at the e.t.s. before processing (which will probably be more common in book work than in journal publishing). Once again, the general principle of keeping your author informed about what will be done to the text should be stressed, even if you are implementing a well-established and strict journal style in a short article.

In addition to the copy-editorial changes you will be making, you must know exactly what coding additions or changes, if any (see section on coding, above), are to be made by you on screen, and whether you are to mark the e.t.s. for design as well.

(d) **Electronic transfer of data**

Sometimes publishers receive electronic typescripts from authors by capturing electronic data sent by modem or other electronic-delivery method, often for reasons of speed or because of the difficulty of reaching the author. The material can be copy-edited on a hard-copy printout made on arrival at the publisher's or sent separately by the author. This printout is then either copy-edited on screen (see above) or sent to the author for the copy-editorial (and possibly coding) changes to be inserted, and the author then sends the material back to the publisher electronically once the final version is ready. After this, a further copy-editorial check against the latest printout should be made, since electronic transfer is not foolproof – and therefore should not necessarily be encouraged. Again, some written record should be kept of the changes and decisions made jointly by author and copy-editor in case any questions arise at a later stage.

(e) **Proofs**

Proofs will be provided by the typesetter in due course. Theoretically, there will be none of the usual 'typesetter's errors'; proofs should be needed only for confirmation of layout, pagination, appropriate line breaks, and for placement of illustrations and preparation of the index. However, the typesetter may have made errors in keying or coding, 'conversion errors' do occur, and viruses (see p. 9) in the typesetter's equipment or the author's disks/tapes can cause major upsets. It should not be assumed that proofs produced from electronic files that seemed error-free after copy-editing do not contain problems that occurred during the outputting process. Also, as every copy-editor knows, errors are often spotted in proof that were not seen at an earlier stage. Proofs of an e.t.s. should be proofread carefully as a matter of course.

As mentioned earlier, if the typesetter found some material difficult to design or read, it may have been rekeyed, often without your knowing it, and may therefore contain the usual typesetter's errors. (If you discover that the typesetter has rekeyed material that was not meant to be touched without alerting you so that you could check it, be sure to tell the production department about it.) Sometimes typesetters want to please their customers and not be seen to have problems with electronic typescripts, and often undertake rekeying as a more efficient use of staff time than adjusting material already keyed but deficient in some way. This may well be a legitimate way of proceeding, but the typesetter should highlight such passages on the proof so they can be carefully read for errors.

(f) **Index**

The index is usually prepared or finalized at this 'proof' stage, and then either sent by the author (or other indexer) on disks/tapes or submitted in hard-copy form, to be keyed conventionally by the typesetter from a copy-edited version. Time is precious at this stage and copy-editorial changes are often quite considerable on index copy, which often makes it more sensible, especially in book work, to follow the latter course. The same procedures employed for the copy-editing and correcting of the text apply to the index and any other appendix material dealt with at this stage. Again, index proofs should be carefully proofread regardless of how they were prepared.

1.2.3 **Author-generated camera-ready copy**

A word about nomenclature. The term 'camera-ready copy' (c.r.c.) should be reserved for material that is truly ready for the camera, with no modifications to be made to it. Different forms of c.r.c. should be described in the plainest and clearest way, to avoid confusion. Most 'camera-ready copy' is that produced on bromide paper or film by a typesetter; there is also 'author-generated c.r.c.' (discussed in this section), a stage in the processing of which is 'draft c.r.c.'. (The confusing term 'camera-ready typescript' should be avoided.) For material that is camera-ready in the main but which is to be added to by the publisher (through the provision of typesetter-produced preliminary pages, running heads and the like), the term 'text c.r.c.' may be appropriate.

Most publishers provide guidelines and patterns for authors preparing camera-ready material. If the author's printer is of the right quality and the author is willing and able to manipulate the e.t.s. files, the final appearance of the material can be of a high standard and can be truly ready for the camera. This procedure has always been suitable for material with complicated (and therefore expensive) typesetting requirements, for conference proceedings and journals, and for projects of various kinds with restrictions on their production budgets. It is also becoming increasingly attractive to a generation of technically literate authors who want to have complete control over their material.

In the past, author-generated c.r.c. was accepted by publishers largely because of the convenience and the cost savings of having the author act as the typesetter, sometimes with little regard to the quality of the design or the resolution of the output. It would not take a very experienced eye to spot the less-than-happy results of some of these early 'camera-ready' publications, which have brought the method into some disrepute.

There is no longer any reason for the standard of author-generated material to be low. Most reputable publishers will have a policy on quality, accepting author-generated c.r.c. only when it meets a specific standard of readability and good basic design. Preliminary discussion of the merits of and reasons for accepting a particular author's offer to provide c.r.c. should always be held, with a sample of the output being seen and assessed by copy-editorial, design and production professionals.

Author-generated c.r.c. may not always be thoroughly copy-edited, because of limitations of time or cost, but it should always at least be proofread for possible libel, safety, etc., for sense, and for literals, and be looked at by someone from a design viewpoint to see if the presentation needs to be improved.

If the draft c.r.c. material is to be thoroughly copy-edited before the final camera-ready version is submitted for printing, discuss with your publisher how much more in addition to copy-editorial changes you should ask the author to do in the way of rearranging layout, altering typefaces, spacing and the like. Often an author will not have followed the publisher's initial specifications in some respect that, if not put right, can spoil the look of the printed result or make it inconsistent with other works in the same series.

Sometimes publishers proceed as follows: the author submits a sample of the material at an early stage for preliminary copy-editorial and design comment, after which a full draft of the c.r.c. incorporating the suggested changes is submitted. The draft is copy-edited, marked for design and returned to the author, who effects the changes and submits the final c.r.c. The copy-editor compares the original draft with the final c.r.c. to ensure that all is well, and may send back part or all of the material if changes still need to be made. Finally, the c.r.c. may be sent straight for printing, or the publisher may have the preliminary pages, running heads, etc., set by a typesetter for stripping into the text c.r.c.

Some publishers accept so-called 'camera-ready copy' that comes not in hard but in electronic form, produced by technically sophisticated software such as the widely used T_EX. T_EX (pronounced 'tek') is a typesetting programming language used among academic authors and is designed to enable them to key complicated mathematics. A preview mode displays on the screen exactly what their work will look like when it is output. T_EX is widely used on desk-top and mainframe computers. There are other, truly WYSIWYG ('what you see is what you get') packages in common use, such as Quark Xpress, Ventura and PageMaker, usually described as 'publishing programmes'. Sometimes the copy-editor is not involved in work of this sort, and sometimes a full copy-edit is required.

It is always worth a publisher's time to have at least a proofreading stage, if not a full copy-edit, for all material before it is printed – if for nothing more than libel and safety – even when it is produced by competent authors on sophisticated systems.

② Estimates and specimen pages

It may be necessary to obtain an estimate of the production cost, or even to have specimen pages set, before (or while) the typescript is copy-edited. You will anyway find it useful to have a typographical specification, so it is sensible to go through the typescript when you first receive it, looking for design and production factors. You can also look out for things you will need to settle with the author as soon as possible (see section 3.3), including any missing or unsatisfactory illustrations, captions or text.

If there is any doubt, ask whether the copy you have is the one that will be sent for setting, so as to avoid duplication of marking if possible. If you want to be able to start copy-editing before the estimator returns the typescript, make a photocopy after you have marked it up (see section 2.2), and send the photocopy for estimate, together with photocopies of the illustrations and captions, marking these clearly 'For estimate only'.

See that the typescript is clear enough for you and the typesetter to work on, particularly if there are unfamiliar words in it; is it single-spaced or faint; are there illegible or confusing alterations? If so, now is the time to ask the author for a better copy.

If you are not sure whether the typesetter will have problems in interpreting, say, handwritten Greek or a complex layout, ask the production department to ask the typesetter at this stage, so that better copy can, if possible, be obtained before you copy-edit.

You may notice other faults, such as unsatisfactory bibliographical references (see chapter 10), which the author should, if possible, be asked to remedy before copy-editing begins.

Before going any further, I should explain the sense in which I shall use certain words:

folio: a sheet of typescript

page: a page of a proof or a finished book or journal, for example p. 83 of this book

leaf: two pages which back on to one another – a 'recto' (right-hand page) and its 'verso' (left-hand page) – for example pp. 85–6 of this book

The distinction between 'page' and 'folio' is a useful one, because a page and a folio will contain a different amount of material: an index that is ten A4 or quarto folios long will (if it is typed double-spaced and single column as it should be) occupy only two or three pages when it is printed.

part: a group of related chapters with a part number or title or both
section: a subdivision of a chapter
subheading: a heading to a section of a chapter or of a bibliography

The other kinds of headings are called part headings, chapter headings, table headings and running heads. A running head – also called a head-line or pagehead – is the heading that appears at the top of every page (with some exceptions) in most non-fiction books and journals and some novels (see section 9.2).

2.1

BRIEFING THE DESIGNER

The designer needs two kinds of information: first the suggested page size and general appearance, the kind of reader for whom the book is intended, and the desired production cost or selling price; and second-ly what the book consists of, which parts of it should be distinguished typographically, and so on – the individual items in the designer's specification (fig. 2.1). This section deals with the second kind.

Look at every folio of the typescript, to ensure that you see all the things you need to tell the designer, who will probably not have time to look at every folio and might not notice an extra grade of subheading in chapter 10 or unusual characters wanted in chapter 2.

List factors that might affect the choice of typeface or typesetter. It is not necessary to point out something that will be obvious to anyone glancing at the typescript, for example mathematics in a mathematics book, though it may be useful to point out that it contains a particular complication such as superscripts to superscripts. Mention things that occur occasionally, for example special sorts (see below) or passages containing words in capitals for which one might want to use small capitals. Say approximately how many folios contain these complica-tions, and give folio references to examples. Even if a foreign language

CAMBRIDGE UNIVERSITY PRESS

Typesetter (initials) GO (DTP) Setter Quark Ex 3.0
Printer (initial) UPH Sub-ed JP

Author BUTCHER
Title Copy-editing The Cambridge Handbook for Editors, Authors and Publishers:
Third edition Revised and updated   4007049

Trimmed size 228 x 152 mm   Back margin (per page) (R) 8½picas: (L) 3½picas
Head margin (trimmed) 2 picas to cap height r/head ... line feed from trim 30 pts to baseline of running head
Type area Measure (picas) 24 picas × 37 text lines   81pts from r/head to 1st text line
Texttype Adobe Garamond 10½pt/13½pt with +1 tracking 1/space throughout
Extracts (Ext) 10 pt unjustified indented 12pts left with ½ line space above and below
Poetry (Pry) as ext line for line
Sources for Ext (ES) and Pry (PS): 8½pt ranged right

Table type 9½/11pt   Lists 10½/13½pt
Running heads 10½pt A.Garamond U/lc with 7½pt Syntax black numerals with 81 pts line feed   between firs text line
Left (verso) Chapter no. plus chapter title
Right (recto) A]heading plus number   (new section, new title)
Drop folio at foot 10½pt A. Garamond os figs 27pt below last 1 ne
Para indent 1 em   Figure style Old style   Word spacing 60 75 80
Bibliography (Bib) 10/12pt   Indent turnovers 1 em
Appendices (App) 10/12pt   Index 8½/10pt unjustified double column

SUB-HEADINGS
A] Syntax black caps 9½pt 1/space +10 tracking, hangs outside de measure by 3 picas turnovers indent 3 picas ie text left   nextline full out
line feed above 24 pts to no./19½pt to title,6 pica rule between, 24pts line feed below to text
B] Syntax black U/lc 9½pt ranged text left with numbers in Syntax roman hanging in margin em space away   nextline full out
line feed above 33pts /   line feed below 21pts /
C] Syntax bold U/lc 9½pt ranged text left with lc letter in parentheses set in Syntax roman hanging outside measure em space away   nextline full out
line feed above 23 pts   line feed below 17½ pts /
D] Syntax italic U/lc 9½ pt ranged text left   nextline
line feed above 27 pts / 17½pt below B line feed below 13½ pts /
Break-in text   line space   full out

PART TITLE ...

CHAPTER (with new page):
Chapter Number (CN) Syntax black 1½pt numbers reversed out of circle 5mm diameter solid
hangs outside measure on 3 pica alignment, 115pts line feed below trim
Chapter Title (CT) Adobe Garamond 18/20pt U/lc align text left 115pts line feed below trim
turnovers f left

Main Heading (MH) Adobe Garamond 18pt Italic U/lc hangs outside text measure aligned left
on 3 pica alignment 115 pts line feed below trim
Chapter text begins: U/lc full out left 36pts below last MH or CT line of lines on chapter opening page varies

SORTS (or see attached list) All specials plus some Arabic, Hebrew and Russian
Use the Adobe Garamond Expert set throughout and all standard ligatures
ILLUSTRATIONS 19 line drawings
CAPTIONS Syntax roman 7½/10pt X 24 picas unjustified
ADDITIONAL SPECIFICATION (BUL) Bulleted lists: set bullets at this size • with turnovers
aligned left under first word otherwise set as UL for size etc.
Ex (example) 10/12½pt X 23 picas unjustified align left on 12pt indent, with ½ line space
above and below

Cols (columns) 10½/13½pt unjustified indent 1st col 12pts, then max 2 picas gap between cols.
En Cols 10/12½ unjustified
Headings in endmatter: (x) Syntax black caps 1/space +12 tracking) 9pt hangs outside
measure on 3 pica alignment, with 31pts line feed above and 19 pts line feed below
(y) Syntax black U/lc 8½pt aligns text left with 25pts line feed above and 12½pt if below
Appendix main headings: (AM) 15pt A.Garamond U/lc 115 pts line feed below trim align
text left. (AT) Adobe Garamond ital. U/lc 17pt 20pts line feed below AM hanging outside
measure on 3 pica alignment
NB When filling out page depth always run pages short to avoid widows etc. never deep.

PRELIMS allow 12 pages. Index allow 26 pages.
Other copy to follow allow   pages for
SIGNED for estimate Dave Tomlinson Date
for setting Date 25·2·91

Fig. 2.1 Designer's typographical specification

does not use a different alphabet, it may need a typesetting system that can position floating accents accurately or a typesetter who has experience of setting that language; so mention any languages used, unless they involve only half a dozen phrases or book titles.

Mention also any additional costs that will not be included in a typesetter's or artist's estimate, for example a large number of cross-references to pages (see section 2.1.4). If the commissioning editor has not already done so, list any material that will be provided later, giving an estimated length in printed pages: 'Not yet available: foreword 2 pp., index 8 pp.'

If the book is to be set in the same style as an earlier one, warn the designer of any differences that will affect the typographical specification. The new book might be more complicated and include one or more of the following: an extra grade of subheading, tables, bibliography, appendixes, the contributor's name below each chapter title; bold, Greek or mathematical characters in text or headings. It might have much longer or much shorter headings. It might be less complicated and might not need running heads; or for economy one might decide against separate leaves for part titles.

2.1.1 **Special sorts**

I use the term 'special sort' to mean a character that a typesetter may not have available or may have to add by hand, for example phonetics, Hebrew, Greek, unusual accents or letters with dots or dashes above or below them. If they are not very clear, ask the author now to provide clearer versions, so that the typesetter knows exactly what is required. If the author uses an unusual convention, ask the designer whether this would cause problems; and if it would, ask the author whether it is essential, or whether something else could be substituted.

It is useful if you can tell the designer whether each special sort is used a great deal throughout the book or only once or twice; and give folio references to examples.

If you plan to use something not yet marked on the typescript (for example bold italic for vectors), say so now, so that the typesetter can take this into account.

2.1.2 **Headings**

Say whether part headings are to be on separate leaves (often called part titles); see section 3.5.3.

Try to limit subheadings in the text to three grades. This should be ample, except in a reference book, and it is difficult for the designer to specify more than three kinds that will be sufficiently distinct from one another and from table headings, running heads, etc.

The headings should be coded in the margin, by a ringed letter or number, according to their place in the hierarchy (see section 9.3.3). If you know which passages are to be set in smaller type (e.g. the bibliography), code those headings differently from the ones in text type, because the designer's specification will give the size as well as the style appropriate for each code letter. Tell the designer how many grades there are in the text and endmatter, and how they are coded: for example 'three grades in the text, labelled A, B, C; one grade in the bibliography, labelled X'. Mention any factors that might affect the typographical style, for example that the headings are extremely long or short or include numerals or italic or Greek; or that grade A appears only in chapter 5. If headings or notes must appear in the margin, point this out.

2.1.3 **Footnotes and endnotes** (see section 9.4)

Tell the designer whether the notes are to be footnotes or endnotes; whether any footnotes should be keyed by number or symbol, and, if by number, whether the numbering may continue through each chapter or must start afresh on each page. If there are an exceptionally large number of footnotes per chapter, or many very long ones, discuss with the commissioning editor whether they should become endnotes. If they are to remain footnotes, mention the number and length in your brief to the designer, as this may affect the design and will also warn the production department to expect a higher production cost because of possible problems with paging.

2.1.4 **Cross-references**

Unless the book is written to fit a page layout, cross-references to pages cannot be completed until the book is typeset and paged, so each one involves a proof correction. Exact cross-references may be necessary in reference books, but other authors may include a page reference when all they mean is 'I've already dealt with this point in detail.' Often a chapter or section number is enough, because most readers will not want to turn immediately to the passage referred to. If cross-referencing by page is essential, tell the production department the approximate number, so that the cost can be estimated.

2.1.5 **Passages to be distinguished typographically**

I use 'small type' to mean a size between text type and footnote type. Say whether it is necessary to distinguish long quotations (see section 11.1), exercises, etc., typographically from the main text, leaving it to the designer to decide whether small type, indention or unjustified setting – or perhaps a different typeface – should be used to distinguish them. If there is a particular advantage or disadvantage in using text type, small type or italic, say so. Give folio references to isolated or particularly complicated examples.

Appendixes are usually set in small type, but may be in text type if, for example, they contain mathematics or long quotations that are to be displayed in smaller type. Point out any relevant factors.

2.1.6 **Tables** (see section 9.5)

Tables may be set in small type or in footnote type, or the type size may vary according to the size of the table. Give folio references for any complicated tables, and say whether very large ones may be split or turned to read up the page to avoid having a fold-out.

2.1.7 **Illustrations** (see chapter 4)

If you are not certain, ask the designer whether the author's artwork and lettering, and also any photographs provided for the halftones, are suitable for reproduction, so that better alternatives can be provided if necessary.

The author may have sent some information with the illustrations, and it is helpful if you can at this early stage tell the designer which illustrations must be reproduced same-size or at a particular reduction; which illustrations must be reduced by the same amount as one another or reproduced at the same scale; which drawings or photographs have been borrowed and must not be lettered; whether any coloured originals are to be reproduced in colour or black and white. If your publisher uses an illustrations checklist (see p. 80), fill in what you can now.

Halftones

Say how many there are. If they are not to be printed in the text, the commissioning editor will say whether they are to be grouped, scattered or pasted in individually to face the relevant page of text; the last option is much more expensive, and may have to be vetoed on grounds of cost. If you already know that the halftones cannot be trimmed without losing some essential detail (and therefore cannot be bled, i.e. run off the page), or that there are editorial factors affecting sizing, say so. If you do not yet know which of the photographs will be used, make this clear and provide a simple hypothetical basis for the estimate.

Line drawings

Say how many there are, counting numbered figures as one each; if some are made up of more than one part, show this on your illustrations checklist. Mention any points about style and size (maps and large diagrams may sometimes affect the page size).

Possible fold-outs

Say whether each illustration, when unfolded, must be visible even when the book is not open at that page; also whether the fold-out must face a particular page or may be bound in at a place that is more convenient for the binder (e.g. between two folded sheets – 'signatures' – of the text). Give figure numbers and ask the designer whether there is a cheaper way of dealing with the material.

Possible artwork

Things other than illustrations may require artwork as well as typesetting, for example genealogical tables with many rules (lines), music, chemical formulae containing diagonal lines, crossed-out letters, tables with complex ruling, etc. Give folio references unless they occur throughout the book.

Illustrations not yet available

Give as much information as possible. Printers can estimate the cost of printing a half-page or whole-page illustration; but it is impossible to estimate for drawing without knowing how complex the illustration is likely to be. Say, for example, 'Estimate 1 complex whole-page map, 5 simple half-page diagrams.'

If the captions are not yet available, give their probable length: 'Estimate captions as 1 line each.'

2.2

MARKING THE TYPESCRIPT FOR AN ESTIMATE

See that the typescript is complete: check the folio numbering and also any other numbering schemes such as sections, tables, equations, figures and plates. The folios should be numbered in one sequence (see section 3.5.2), though the preliminary pages may be numbered separately. As you will have to provide complete copy for the preliminary pages at some stage, it is probably worth doing so now (see chapter 7).

Write 'fresh page' or 'recto' at the top of the appropriate folios, including those for preliminary matter, bibliography, etc. Write 'verso blank' on part-title folios.

Code the subheadings (see above and section 9.3.3). If the author wants space left between sections that have no headings, use a space mark (see appendix 13).

Identify all material that is not straightforward text. If the designer will use your codes on the design specification, each will indicate a type size as well as a style, so distinguish, for example, between displayed prose and poetry (e.g. 'ext' and 'verse ext') and also between quotations displayed in the text and those displayed in a note ('verse ext' and 'N verse ext'). Show the extent of the passage by a line in the margin, if it is not obvious.

If the tables are not typed on separate sheets, it may be helpful to mark their extent (see fig. 9.1, p. 216).

Footnotes need not be marked if they are clear in the typescript. See that any endnotes are conveniently placed for the reader (see section 9.4.4).

If you are sending a duplicate typescript for estimate, label it clearly on the first sheet: 'Duplicate. Not for setting.'

2.2.1 **Illustrations** (see chapter 4)

Now is the time to ask the author for captions, typed lists of names for maps, clearer roughs, improved artwork and better photographs for halftones.

See that the illustrations are identified by author's name, short book title, figure number and, if possible, folio number. Unnumbered illustrations may be identified by the folio number, plus 'top', 'middle', etc., if necessary. Mark the approximate position of each illustration in the margin of the typescript, if you can do this without first reading the text; if you cannot, say which chapter the figures belong to. (This will, of course, be clear if they are numbered by chapter: 1.1 etc.) If you can at this stage make a checklist of illustrations (see p. 80), this will help the designer and estimator.

If you send photocopies for an estimate of cost, mark them 'For estimate only'.

Originals for line drawings
The illustrations should be separated from the text, by photocopying if necessary.

If the author is likely to need more than the standard time to check any redrawn or relettered artwork, warn the production department, so that they can allow for this in the production schedule.

Originals for halftones
It is essential that photographs are treated with the utmost care, as any marks may be reproduced. They should be handled as little as possible

and never folded; keep them between pieces of stiff card a little larger than the prints, so that the corners do not become dog-eared. Do not use paperclips or mark the face of the prints; any marking on the back should be done very lightly, with a soft pencil or china marker. Do not use a felt-tip pen: the ink dries slowly and may mark the front of another photograph.

If the photographs are the author's, label each print with the author's name, short book title and illustration number. This information is best typed or written on a self-adhesive label which is then attached to the back of the photograph. The top of the picture should be identified if there is any possibility of confusion, as there may be with aerial photographs or electron micrographs, for example.

If the prints are borrowed from, say, a picture library, they must not be marked; mark up an overlay (see p. 87) or a photocopy.

2.2.2 **Revised estimate**

If the typescript is returned to the typesetter for a revised estimate (e.g. on a different format or pattern) and you can definitely say that the copy has not changed since the last estimate, or alternatively how it has changed, it will save the estimator from having to go through the whole typescript in detail again.

2.3
_____

SPECIMEN PAGES

Specimen pages are intended to show solutions to all the general typographical problems in a book or series. A specimen may consist of as little as one page to show small, recurring problems such as those in a dictionary, or as many as eight for exceptionally varied and complicated material. Four pages should usually be enough, because parts of two or more folios may be combined on one page.

The specimen should show a full page including running head and page number, a chapter opening, all the grades of subheading, footnotes or endnotes, and long quotations (or other passages distinguished from the main text). Do not include a table unless they are an important feature of the book or unless the specimen is to be used as a guide for authors. There is no need to show a problem that occurs only once; this, with its folio reference, can be mentioned to the designer, who can mark up the relevant part of the typescript accordingly.

Choose folios which show the recurrent problems, and photocopy them, listing the items to be included on each specimen page, and giving the wording for the running head and the page number to be set. (It is quite convenient to use the folio number, changing it to odd or even as necessary to make it suitable for a right-hand or left-hand page, so that one can easily refer back to that folio.) As a rough guide, allow two folios of double-spaced A4 or quarto typescript for each page of the specimen, unless you are compressing an extravagant typescript layout, perhaps into double-column small type.

On the chosen folios mark up spelling, capitalization, punctuation, abbreviations, etc., in the editorial style you propose to follow in the book.

Illustrations are not usually included in specimen pages unless there is some problem of sizing or of style (e.g. the use of a second colour).

Incomplete typescripts
Specimens based on small parts of the book may turn out to be unsatisfactory unless they are well planned and prepared early enough to be used as a model by the author: a sample, particularly of a multi-author work, is often not typical, and illustrations that are not yet available may have some influence on the page size. Find out whether there are likely to be more kinds of subheading, more complicated mathematics, etc., in the rest of the book, and what the illustrations will be like. The more the designer can see the better, so three sample chapters and a few illustrations are better than one of each; and give what information you can about what is still to come.

Specimen for a series
Ask how typical the present book is: whether others are likely to contain more mathematics, subheadings, Greek, complicated tables, diacritical marks, etc., and pass this information on to the designer.

When the specimen is set, and you have discussed it with the designer, send the author a copy, explaining any specific problems and the reason for any departures from the layout in the typescript.

If there are small amendments to the specimen, it is sufficient to mark these on your own reference copy and on the copy that will go to the typesetter with the copy-edited typescript. If larger amendments are needed, a revised specimen will probably be necessary.

③ Preparing the typescript for typesetting

3.1

VARIOUS LEGAL ASPECTS

The copy-editor is one of the few people who read a book or journal thoroughly before publication, and an incidental but extremely important part of the copy-editor's role is to keep an eye open for any legal problems. The main sorts of problem to be aware of are the following.

3.1.1 The right of integrity

Under the UK Copyright Act of 1988, an author has the right to object to derogatory treatment of his or her work, 'derogatory' being defined as a 'distortion or mutilation of the work' or anything that is 'prejudicial to the honour or reputation of the author'. This right of integrity is one of the so-called 'moral rights' recognized by the Act, the other being the 'right of paternity' – the right to be identified as the author. European countries recognize the right of integrity, and at the time of writing there is discussion about the introduction of moral rights in the USA and Australia. In any event, whether the right of integrity is part of a country's law or not, the basic principle can be taken for granted: that all changes to an author's text must be subject to approval. There are legally valid exceptions, however. Where the author is contributing to a newspaper, magazine or periodical, or to an encyclopedia, dictionary, yearbook or other collective work of reference, the right of integrity does not apply, and the publisher has the legal right to cut and edit without the author's permission, though there are, obviously, good reasons to tell the author what changes one proposes, and to obtain his or her approval if possible.

3.1.2 Infringement of copyright

In the main, the most you can do here is to be sure that all necessary permissions have been obtained (see section 3.7.1). If the author has lifted passages from another's work and included them, unacknowledged, as part of the text, you have no way of knowing this unless you happen to recognize a passage; if you do, tell the commissioning editor.

Related to this kind of illegal use of another's work is plagiarism, which in general terms means unfairly using another person's ideas or structures, as against copying directly, word for word, which would be infringement of copyright. Again you would have no way of knowing that the author had plagiarized unless you knew the plagiarized book, but you should be alert to the possibility.

3.1.3 **Libel**

A libel is a published statement tending to discredit a person in the eyes of reasonable members of society; a 'person' in this context includes a group of people, a society, a company, and so on, as well as an individual. Normally the libelled person must be alive (which could mean that, in the case of a society, say, one or more of its members are alive even though the society may be long disbanded), although there is such a thing as 'criminal libel', which can apply to the dead. You must be sensitive to the possibility of libel; draw *any* dubious passage to the comissioning editor's attention. Quite apart from its being very expensive and disruptive for the publisher to deal with, libel can cause an immense amount of unwarranted distress to an individual.

3.1.4 **Negligent misstatement**

A negligent misstatement can arise in advice, information or instructions which it is reasonable to assume will or may be acted upon. It can arise not only out of what is said, but also out of what is left unsaid. The error may originate with the author or may be introduced by an outside editor, publishing staff or the typesetter. The publisher's liability for such misstatement can arise if it can be shown that there is a *prima facie* duty of care incumbent on the publisher, that the misstatement could have been avoided by the exercise of reasonable care and skill, and that the error has led to physical injury or damage to the plaintiff, or to financial loss or damage. The author should be asked, in writing, to confirm that all such instructions, including such illustrations as wiring diagrams, have been double-checked and are accurate from the safety point of view. Any queries about such matters arising during copy-editing or any other pre-publication stage should be referred to the author, again in writing, and all correspondence concerning them should be kept on file, to show that the publisher has taken all reasonable care to avoid negligence in respect of statements contained in the book. (See also section 6.13 on safety.)

3.2

HOW MUCH COPY-EDITING TO DO

Most publishers send their authors instructions about how to prepare their typescripts. These will cover such things as double spacing, subheadings, capitalization, quotation marks, spelling, bibliographical references, tables and illustrations; but even if the author has tried to follow these there may be hidden faults.

When you receive the typescript for copy-editing, the commissioning editor may tell you how detailed a job you are expected to do, or how much time and money has been budgeted for copy-editing. The level aimed at will depend on various things:

- how soon the book must be published
- whether it will have a limited life or market
- the readership
- the method of production: whether the book will be keyed from the typescript after copy-editing or whether the author will have to make any changes either on camera-ready copy or on a magnetic disk

Of course, it will also depend on the present state of the book; and commissioning editors, like other people, can be lulled into thinking that a good-looking typescript implies a well-written book. So it is worth looking at parts of the typescript in detail (some folios of text, notes and bibliography) to get some idea of the problems, so that you can discuss these with the commissioning editor before starting your detailed work. The author may be asked to revise parts of the typescript before you begin; and if a book submitted on magnetic disk needs very many changes that the author cannot easily make, it may be cheaper to ask a typesetter to key the whole book from the typescript, in which case the typescript can be copy-edited in the conventional way.

For the purposes of this chapter I have assumed that you have been asked to do as thorough a job as the book requires, and that the book will be keyed by a typesetter after copy-editing rather than returned to the author for correction on disk. (For books submitted on disk see section 1.2.)

The commissioning editor may be responsible for the general content, organization and style of the book; for picking up any errors of fact or potentially libellous passages; or for obtaining permission to reproduce quotations, illustrations, etc. However, even if all this should have been done by the time you receive the typescript, you should look out for these things yourself, as well as for out-of-date material, bias, parochialisms and problems of safety (see sections 6.2 and 6.13). Your role is to try to ensure that neither author nor publisher has second thoughts at proof stage.

How far one should correct an author's style is a matter of judgement: it will depend on the author's reactions to one's proposals, and on the kind of book and the intended readers. In works of exposition one must change misleading, ambiguous or obscure English and the misuse of words. Consistency of tone is important too: for example, a consistently informal style can work well, but a colloquial phrase or slang word in the middle of formal prose can jar or distract the reader from what the author is saying.

Good copy-editing is invisible: it aims to present the book the author would have written if he or she had had more time or experience – not, as some new copy-editors think, their own improved version. John Gross has written that, leaving aside any large errors of judgement or fact that a copy-editor might commit, the damage they can do 'consists of small changes (usually too boring to describe to anyone else) that flatten a writer's style, slow down his argument, neutralize his irony; that ruin the rhythm of a sentence or the balance of a paragraph; that deaden the tone that makes the music' ('Editing and its discontents', in Christopher Ricks and Leonard Michaels (eds.), *The State of the Language*, 1990 edn (London, Faber & Faber), p. 288).

As copy-editing problems vary from book to book, it is impossible to list all the things you should do. A checklist of the most obvious things appears as appendix 1, but you will want to modify the list to suit the kinds of material you work on. To avoid too much repetition, the present chapter contains only brief references to things treated in more detail elsewhere in the book.

You must provide copy that the typesetter can follow without misunderstanding or delay. The typescript must therefore be complete, legible and unambiguous; passages to be distinguished typographically must be identified, and all subheadings coded; fresh pages and rectos, and the position of all text illustrations (and tables where necessary), must be marked; roughs for any line drawings must be intelligible to the artist; and so on. All these things must always be done, however rushed the book is. See section 3.5.

For the reader's sake you should see that the book is well organized, clear and consistent (see section 3.6). How much you do will depend on the commissioning editor's brief, the level at which the book is written, and whether your publisher has a house style which is implemented in every book. Having such a style means fewer decisions for the individual copy-editor. However, the more changes there are to make, the more likely it is that something will be missed and that the book will be inconsistent; and there are few things that annoy authors more than having an inconsistent system substituted for their own – whether their own was inconsistent or not. If your publisher does not have a rigid house style, it is usually easier and safer to implement consistently the author's own conventions, provided they are clear and sensible.

WRITING TO THE AUTHOR

As soon as you can, write an introductory letter to the author, to introduce yourself and explain in general terms what you will be doing. Say when you hope to send your queries about detailed points, and ask whether the author will be available to answer them then. Authors are pleased to hear that progress is being made; and you may want some missing material or a revised or more legible version, or agreement to some general changes you propose, before you start detailed work on the book.

You may also need to mention points where your house style differs from the author's, or to suggest a system to replace what is inconsistent or unsatisfactory in the typescript. Not all authors want to be bothered with such things as the choice of -ize or -ise spellings; but even authors who are very inconsistent in their typescripts may care a good deal about such things as capitalization; and minimal punctuation may be just as intentional as punctuation according to the rules.

If authors are not consulted about changes at typescript stage, they are likely to object when they see them in the proof, and to insist that their original system is reinstated.

You should mention any general departures from the layout and style in the author's typescript, for example:

- parts and chapters: a decision not to have a separate leaf for part headings; renumbering chapters in arabic; other numbering systems to be changed
- subheadings: changes to improve an overcomplicated or confusing system
- running heads: what is to be used (e.g. chapter title on the left, first-level subheading on the right); ask the author for shortened forms if necessary
- notes: whether the footnotes are to be numbered through each chapter or afresh on each page, or the fact that the notes will be endnotes, not footnotes; the position of endnotes, if the author has placed them where the reader will not be able to turn to them easily
- quotations: the use of single quotes; whether (and how) long quotations will be distinguished; the use of square brackets and three-point ellipses (see section 11.1)
- tables: the need to number them because long ones may not be placed exactly where they are in the typescript (see section 9.5)
- illustrations: where any separately printed halftones will be placed
- bibliographical references: the content and form of references in the text or notes; the organization of the bibliography
- cross-references, if the author has too many or uses forms such as *v. inf.*
- spelling, capitalization, accents, hyphens, form of possessive (see section 6.12)
- italic

- numbers: use of words or figures; elision of pairs; comma or space for thousands
- dates
- bias: any rewriting necessary, e.g. avoiding use of 'he'
- abbreviations: inclusion or deletion of full points
- scientific nomenclature and terminology, displayed formulae, etc.

Explain why you have had to depart from the author's own system; and avoid using jargon such as 'copy' or abbreviations such as 'a/w', 'p/up', 's/s' or 'ts', which the author will not understand.

As you go through the typescript in detail you will find small points not covered in your general letter. It is not necessary to tell authors about every individual change you make, but you should give them one or two examples of every *kind* of change, so that they will have some idea of what you are doing; if there are many changes, offer to send them a photocopy of the copy-edited typescript. Warn them that when they receive proofs they should not alter anything except type-setter's errors, and ask them to let you have any late corrections now.

Tell them the date by which you need answers to your queries. Should a book run into problems – if it turns out to need more work than at first appeared, or if the author does not answer your letters or faxes and cannot be reached by telephone – keep the commissioning editor informed.

If you send authors a photocopy of the copy-edited typescript, ask them to mark small corrections in a distinctive colour, to retype any large ones and list the folios affected, so that you can easily check the new material for consistency with the rest. They need not return any unchanged folios. Ask them *not* to send new versions of folios that contain only small changes, especially if the typescript includes a lot of technical marking, for example of maths, since it is easier to add a small change to the existing folio than to read and mark up a new one.

Record any decisions or agreements with the author on general points. You may need to refer to these at proof stage if the author's memory of what has been agreed differs from your own; or someone else may need to deal with the proofs on your behalf. Similarly, record anything received from or sent to the author. Remember too that other departments will need a note of the author's change of address.

3.4

MARKING UP THE TYPESCRIPT

To work quickly and economically, the typesetter must be able to read straight down each sheet of typescript: flaps of paper will hide what is underneath (and the waxed 'Post-it' variety of note may become detached and get lost); additions written up the margin or on the back will mean turning the sheet to read them; instructions to transpose paragraphs on different folios will also cause delay. If the author has a word processor, ask for tidy, retyped folios. If not, it is worth spending some time retyping any handwritten material and reassembling the text in the right order. An occasional addition is acceptable when headed 'Insert at X on fo. 000', typed on a *full-size* sheet following the relevant folio and keyed into the text by a marginal note 'X insert from fo. 000a'; at the end of the insert write 'back to fo. 000', to remind the typesetter to go back, not straight on. If the author has used some half sheets, paste them on to full-size sheets, or they may be overlooked. If you need to fasten some new material over the lines it replaces, it is best to use paste rather than pins or staples. It is difficult to write on most kinds of sticky tape, so do not cover any wording that will need to be marked up.

See that any handwritten material – especially proper names, unfamiliar words and potentially ambiguous letters – is legible. Identify l and 1, capital O and zero, k and kappa, minus, en rule and em rule, x and multiplication sign, multiplication point and decimal point, etc. Typists sometimes use 'll' to mean 'lines', 'eleven' or even 'roman two'. See section 13.2.4 for possible ambiguities in mathematics and science books.

3.4.1 How to mark the typescript

Whatever you decide to mark must be marked throughout, unless the book is on disk and the author or typesetter can make global changes. On a typescript to be keyed by a typesetter, it is not enough to mark the first few instances, because the book may be keyed by more than one keyboard operator. Nor should your marking be spasmodic (as a reminder): if it is, the typesetter will not know whether you intend a distinction between the cases you have marked and those you have not, and may follow copy.

Use the signs in British Standard 5261, *Copy Preparation and Proof Correction*. Some of these are given in appendix 13. Authors and type-setters overseas – and some British authors – use different marks, now being replaced in Britain by those in the British Standard. The commonest of these alternative marks are the symbol # for space and the abbreviations l.c. (lower case) and rom. (roman). Some tick an end-of-line hyphen that is to be retained. There is no need to change these for the typesetter, provided they are clear; but send the author a list of the BS signs for use on the proofs and to explain your marks on the typescript.

The following should be marked in the left-hand margin. Instructions should be ringed, to show that the words are not to be set.

- 'fresh page' or 'recto'
- codes to identify grades of subheading and other material to be distinguished typographically; also vertical lines to show the extent of such passages if it is not absolutely clear in the typescript
- instructions for the placing of text illustrations (and tables where necessary)
- the identification of an ambiguous letter, if there is no room to do so clearly above the letter, or if the identification applies throughout the folio

All other marks should be between the lines of the typescript if there is room to make them clearly (see fig. 3.1). A typesetter who is keying the book from the typescript is going to read every word; if a correction is marked in the margin, the operator will have to look from the line of text to the margin and then back to the text, which will take more time. (See section 1.2 for marking up typescripts that will be corrected on disk.)

Every note written on the typescript will be read by everyone who handles it, so keep instructions to a minimum, and erase or cross out any comments that the typesetter need not read. If you have to leave queries for the author on the typescript, head them 'Author' and ring them.

(a)

had never entered into such a marriage. I have always been of that
opinion.

'I have no doubt you have,' said my aunt.
Miss Murdstone turns up again as Dora Spenlow's confidential friend — an
ironic term meaning 'paid companion and spy.' She links the two relation-
ships: she is again engaged in being companion to someone 'in all essential
respects a mere child.' having followed David's own childhood, we are now
prepared to see that being a child constitutes a claim on those who are older
and wiser. The child has its own qualities which make it loveable, which
give it its own truth of vision. They also attract predators, whether these
are brutal teachers, or seducers, or confidence tricksters; so that the
child is, as Betsy points out, 'likely to be made unhappy by its personal
attractions' preeminently in marriage to a person who cannot offer support,
or who wants to 'improve' the child, moulding it to his 'firmness.' David is
infatuated with Dora, and marries her. He then discovers that she is a
child, and is taken aback. He had been very tactfully warned by Betsy
Trotwood:

'Oh, Trot, Trot! And so you fancy yourself in love! Do you?'

'Fancy, aunt!' I exclaimed, as red as I could be. 'I adore her
with my whole soul!'

'Dora, indeed!' returned my aunt. 'And you mean to say the
little thing is very fascinating, I suppose?'

'My dear aunt,' I replied, 'no one can form the least idea of what she
is!'

'Ah! And not silly?' said my aunt.

'Silly, aunt!'

Fig. 3.1 Folios of corrected typescript. (*a*) is based on Michael Black, *The Literature of Fidelity* (London, Chatto & Windus, 1975); (*b*) on *The Cambridge Agrarian History of England and Wales*, vol. IV, *1500–1640* (Cambridge University Press, 1967).

(b)

manorial theory, the exact position of Welsh manorial lords under the legislation of 1536-1542. This is one of the major problems surrounding the
development of landownership in our period, and will call for rather closer
attention at a later stage.

Ⓐ   6/ TYPES OF FREEHOLD ESTATE

Up to this point we have been concerned in general terms with the broad
background, in general, and with the principles which alone can explain the
character of the early freehold estate in Wales. The growth and structure
of these estates now call for slightly more detailed consideration; and for
convenience of exposition they can be divided into four categories:

(i) the estate of adventitious origin created by foreign settlers in
Wales;

(ii) The privileged estate established by members of a native official
class;

(iii) the clanland estate of hereditary origin;

(iv) the clanland estate of nonhereditary origin.

Ⓑ (i) Estates of adventitious origin

Estates of adventitious origin were those established outside areas of
Norman settlement by non-Welsh families which, allowing for inevitable cross-
fertilization in an indeterminate borderland, were almost wholly confined
to the hinterlands of English urban foundations in north Wales (see table 5).
The earliest large concentration of this kind, which appeared among clanlands near Conway between 1420 and 1453,[26] was inherited by the Bulkeleys, who,
with a modest cluster of seven burgages of their own in Beaumaris, were at
this time poised for a similar drive into the clanlands of Anglesey[27].

Table 5
near here

Even though whiting-out is the clearest way to cancel an unwanted underlining, avoid using correction fluid: what the author wrote should remain visible, as he or she may not agree with your suggested change and may want the original wording reinstated.

The following do not need a marginal instruction:

- deletion: just delete the letter or word, but make sure it is clear exactly how much is to be deleted. Use a vertical line to delete a single letter; use a horizontal line to delete something longer, with a vertical line at each end if there is likely to be any doubt whether, for example, the punctuation at either end is to be deleted:

    the world, ~~however,~~ if

    If you wish to retain the punctuation that follows a deleted phrase, rewrite it immediately after the word it should follow; otherwise the keyboard operator will have tapped a word space before seeing it:

          talk to him,~~when he returns~~ because he
    not   talk to him ~~when he returns~~, because he

    If you delete a hyphen in the middle of a word, make it clear whether you want the word to be closed up or printed as two words.

    well|nigh   well|nigh

- transposition: use ⊔⊓
- italic: use a single underline
- bold: use a wavy underline
- capital: use a treble underline
- small capital: use a double underline
- lower-case letter: put a diagonal line through the top of the capital letter: Ⱪ. If several letters or words are to be made lower case ring them and write ≢ above them; or you can mark them CHAPTER
- cancellation of underlining: a few straight strokes through the line: never
- a stet mark below an unusual spelling or end-of-line hyphen that is to be retained, e.g. a smal roasted Quince
- ae, oe ligatures: ring or put ⌒ over the pair of letters: ae
- close up: use ⊂ , e.g. over ride
- no space between paragraphs, where an extra line has unintention-

ally been left in some places: use vertical 'close up' mark
- no space to be left where there is extra space in typescript: use wavy horizontal line to fill up a line, a vertical or diagonal line to fill up a page
- new paragraph: use ⌐ where this is not clear in the typescript
- not fresh line, not new paragraph: use ⌒. If several lines are to be run on, or there is very little space between the lines, you may omit the horizontal line joining the curve at either end; but make sure that your marks cannot be mistaken for commas or parentheses:

    England,⌒
   ⌒Ireland,⌒
   ⌒Scotland

- space, e.g. in those items listed on p. 124: if they are closed up in the typescript, put Y where the space is to be inserted, e.g. 8mm
- en rules: write 'N' or 'en' (ringed) above the dash; if the rule is to be spaced (as for a parenthetical dash) put Y both sides if the dash is closed up in the typescript; if the dash is to be unspaced, use a 'close up' mark both sides if the dash is spaced in the typescript. Similarly for em rules

For the marking of mathematics see section 13.2.

Make sure that your marking is unambiguous. When changing double to single quotes, use a *vertical* line; a diagonal one may touch the other quotation mark and lead the typesetter to think you are deleting the quotes altogether. It may be better to cross out the double quotes and write a single one above, if there is room to do this clearly.

When marking space between a person's initials, be careful that it does not look as though you are deleting the points.

Though a line through a capital letter is usually understood as indicating a change to lower case, a line through a single capital, such as the A in 'table 16A', could be thought to be a deletion, so substitute a lower-case letter.

If you want to cancel an underlining for italic, put two or three short lines through it, not a wavy line which may look like an instruction for bold. If you do want to change a straight underlining to a wavy one, do not put a wavy line above or below the straight one, or it will look as though you want bold italic; cancel the straight one.

If you do, by agreement, white something out, be careful not to obliterate descenders in the line above; if you leave the patch to dry, do remember to complete it. Always reread any sentence you have altered, to make sure that the right amount has been deleted or added and that it is correctly punctuated.

If the typescript contains italic (or bold) characters, rather than underlining, and you want to follow the author's system exactly, give the typesetter a clear general instruction to follow copy for italic and bold. If you may want to change some instances, ask the typesetter to ignore the way the words are typed, and underline for italic and bold in the usual way. If you want to cancel just one italicization among many, ring the word and put the appropriate symbol (⎵⟋⎸; see appendix 13) beside it.

Stet all unusual spellings that are to be retained, if these occur only spasmodically. If a book contains a great many unusual spellings, tell the typesetter to follow copy, and make sure you have corrected typing errors (if you yourself can distinguish them).

If you add letters between two foreign words, make it clear whether the added letters are a separate word or should be joined to the preceding or following word, by using 'close up' or space marks.

de ⌒
parcere subjectis et ⟋ bellare superbos

Where two additions or substitutions fall close together, with only a word or two unchanged between them, it is easier for keyboard operators if the whole phrase is written above the line: if they have to look down to the line to see the unchanged words and then up again to the rest of the alteration, they sometimes miss the intervening words.

For good typesetters it is enough to stet the end-of-line hyphens that are to be retained even when the word is not broken (hard hyphens); but it is safest to mark each hyphen to be retained or to be deleted and closed up.

En rules should be identified where a hyphen is not an acceptable alternative.

If a sentence ends at the foot of a folio and it is not the end of the paragraph, it helps the typesetter if you indicate this, perhaps by a horizontal arrow:

if the preceding sentence ended with an almost full line. ⟶

If the author indicates a new paragraph by a line of space rather than indention, it may be sensible to write a general note to the typesetter at the first occurrence: 'Indent all paragraphs and leave no extra space between paragraphs except where specifically marked'; but remember to mark paragraphs that should *not* be indented, and make clear whether sentences starting after a table or figure, or at the top of a folio, start new paragraphs, if the preceding sentence ended with an almost full line.

3.4.2 Marking up photocopies of printed material

There is less room between the lines, so you may need to use more marginal marks, but keep them to a minimum. It may help to make an enlarged photocopy.

The main differences from marking typescript are:

- changing italic to roman: ring the italic word and write ⊬ in the margin. (Alternatively, if there is a lot of italic or bold that is not wanted, say 'Set italic/bold only where marked for it')
- italic: give a general instruction to follow the style of the copy; if extra italic is needed, underline in the usual way
- bold: as for italic
- delete the original running heads and page numbers unless they are to be reproduced exactly as they are

3.5

COMPLETE, SELF-EXPLANATORY COPY

If there has not been an earlier planning stage, go through the type-script and illustrations before starting your detailed work, to make sure that the material is complete and clear enough for typesetting, drawing and/or reproduction (see chapter 2). If you need a typographical specification, brief the designer (see section 2.1); if the specification already exists, check that it covers everything.

Unless the book is urgent, wait to start detailed copy-editing until the typescript is complete. A missing chapter often arrives much later than the promised date, which means that when you go back to copyedit it you will have to remind yourself of detailed points of style; and if the bibliography has not yet arrived, you cannot easily check the bibliographical references in the text or notes.

Similarly, typesetters can work more quickly and efficiently if they receive the whole book at once. They should at the very least receive everything that will appear in the text and footnotes from the beginning of the first chapter to the end of the last one, and preferably also any endnotes, appendixes and bibliography. If some preliminary matter, such as a foreword, cannot be provided before the book goes for typesetting, list that item as 'to come' and give the approximate length, if possible. If its length is not known, the preliminary pages should be paginated in roman, to allow flexibility.

If the author has provided rough drafts of the illustrations, rather than finished artwork, send the roughs for drawing as soon as any queries about them have been answered. Warn the production department if the author will not be able to check the finished drawings quickly.

Any list in the prelims or endmatter that contains a large number of page references – an index, a table of cases or a list of references doubling as an author index – should not be sent for setting until the final page numbers have been added from the page proof. If the typescript includes such a list, return it when you have checked any wording against the text, and ask the author to fill in the appropriate page numbers when page proofs are available. On the other hand, an index that refers to item numbers rather than page numbers should be sent for setting with the text, since the item numbers will not change.

3.5.1 Checking for completeness

You may be the first person to look at the typescript and illustrations closely enough to make sure that nothing is missing. Check the folio numbering and also any other numbering schemes such as sections, tables, equations and illustrations: gaps in the sequence are a warning that part of the typescript may be missing, or that the author has cut the text and has not tidied up afterwards. You should provide those things that the author may not have thought of: *complete* copy for the preliminary pages, including half-title and verso of the title page, lists of captions for the illustrations, and a list of running heads if short forms are to be used.

3.5.2 **Numbering systems**

The folios should be numbered in one sequence throughout the type-script, so that the typesetter can see at once where a folio belongs, though the preliminary pages may be lettered or numbered in roman, to allow for the addition of material not provided by the author. For example, the author will provide the title page, contents list and any preface, and will call these folios 1–3, with the text starting on folio 4. You need to add a half-title, the copy for the verso of the title page, and perhaps a series list to face the title page. So it is simplest to letter the prelims A–F and say on the last folio, 'Text starts fo. 4' or 'Fo. 4 follows.'

If a folio is added after, say, 166, call this extra folio 166a; immediately below the folio number on 166 say '166a follows' and on 166a '167 follows', so that anyone checking the folio numbers knows at once if a folio is missing. If the author cuts the text, or misnumbers, and there is no folio 166, say at the top of 165 'Fo. 167 follows.' If there are many gaps or insertions, or the chapters are paginated separately, re-paginate the whole typescript.

Chapters, appendixes, etc., are best numbered in arabic, since many readers are not familiar with roman numbers, though it may be simplest to retain roman numbers in references to other books and journals. If you renumber chapters etc. in arabic, remember to change the numbers not only in the headings but also in the contents list and in any cross-references.

Chapters are better numbered in one sequence rather than separately in each part, so that cross-references can consist of a chapter number only, e.g. 'see chapter 12' rather than 'see part II, chapter 4'.

Section numbers may include the chapter number:

chapter 6
section 6.1 (first section in chapter 6)
subsection 6.1.3 (third subsection in section 6.1)

Some authors number introductory sections with a zero, so that the introductory section in chapter 6 would be 6.0. If sections are distinguished from subsections by their numbering, it is not necessary to distinguish their headings typographically. If there are many cross-references to section numbers, the chapter and section numbers should be included in the running heads.

Illustrations and tables may also be numbered by chapter.

If authors number (or letter) the points in their argument and refer to them, make sure they refer to them by the right number and that there are no intervening numbered sequences that might be confused with them. If authors do not refer to the points often, you may want to persuade them to remove the numbers: these may just be the remains of the scaffolding on which the book was constructed.

Numbered paragraphs should be laid out like other paragraphs unless they form a list of points that needs to be distinguished from the main text. The distinction will be based partly on the length of the paragraphs and partly on whether the reader is likely to refer back to the items independently of the surrounding text.

Lists of short items may have hanging indention, with the first line starting full out and subsequent lines indented. They may be numbered:

1 Define the topic of the book and draw up a list of chapters needed.
2 Select potential contributors carefully and solicit their participation in a letter that describes the volume and their individual contributions in detail.

Unnumbered items may start with a dash, bullet or other symbol:

- Prepare sketches of all new line drawings; submit them for editing; have them drawn to the publisher's specifications; proofread all final artwork.
- Locate existing illustrations; write for originals and permissions.

Or they may start with a little subheading:

green: typesetter's own marks (corrections and queries)
red: author's or publisher's correction of typesetter's errors
blue or black: author's and publisher's own alterations (including any carried out in response to typesetter's queries)

Whatever the layout, make sure it is clear where the last point ends and the main text resumes.

Punctuation and capitalization of items in displayed lists depends on the length and content of the items; for instance, short items that are not complete sentences are better lower case and with no final punctuation (see the various examples in this section).

3.5.3 **Fresh pages**

Put 'fresh page' or 'recto' at the top of folios where appropriate, including those for preliminary matter, bibliography, etc.

Parts
The chapters may be grouped into parts. Each part may have a part-title leaf, that is, a right-hand page containing just the part number and title, and usually backed by a blank left-hand page; the first chapter heading in that part is placed at the head of the next right-hand page. There is occasionally an introductory note, which may be placed immediately below the part heading or on the verso; or a map may be placed on the verso; but the first chapter should not start there. If the part heading is to occupy a separate leaf, it should be on a separate folio in the typescript, included in the folio numbering and marked 'recto', with 'verso blank' at the foot and 'recto' at the top of the next folio.

If the parts have separate title leaves, the appendixes should have a joint one too, to show that they are not just appendixes to the final part; but there is no need for a joint or separate title leaf for the bibliography and index – or to mention them on the title leaf to the appendixes – because there is no risk that the reader will think that they do not refer to the whole book.

To save space, the part may just start on a fresh page, with the first chapter starting lower down the same page. See that the wording for the part heading is written above the chapter heading; or, if it is given on a separate folio, make clear to the typesetter that it is not to occupy a separate page. The folio should be labelled 'fresh page' (or 'recto' if it is decided to start all parts on a right-hand page).

Chapters

The main text (introduction or chapter 1) always starts on a right-hand page. Later chapters may start on a fresh page, or may run on, separated from the preceding chapter only by a space. If there are to be offprints of individual chapters (in the case of a contributory volume, for example), the chapters will usually start on a right-hand page.

Appendixes

The first appendix to a book always starts on a fresh page; the others may run on from the first or start on fresh pages; it depends on their length and importance. Appendixes to chapters run on at the end of the relevant chapter.

3.5.4 **Subheadings**

Subheadings should be coded to show their place in the hierarchy (see section 9.3.3). Do not code merely by the way the subheadings are typed; see that the system works logically.

3.5.5 **Spaces**

The designer's specification will describe the space wanted above and below headings, tables and other displayed material, but if you want the typesetter to leave space elsewhere you must make this clear.

Space between unheaded sections

Some typists are erratic about the amount of space they leave between paragraphs, and the typesetter may not know whether the extra space is intentional. If the author wants extra space, put a space sign in the margin, and indicate the amount of space if this will not be clear from the design specification. Some publishers place an asterisk in the space: this shows up more clearly than space alone if the section ends at the foot of the page or if the page already has spaces above and below displayed quotations, tables or illustrations.

Similarly a retyped passage may end half way down the folio; and the typesetter needs to know that this space does not indicate the end of a section and therefore extra space: draw a vertical or diagonal line across the empty space to show the typesetter that the space has no significance; but do not do this at the end of a chapter if chapters start fresh pages.

Space within paragraphs
Some authors white-out unwanted words on their working copy of the typescript, and then send the publisher a photocopy, on which the reason for the blanks is not apparent. If the author's revision has resulted in blank patches, draw a line through these so that the typesetter does not think that they have been left for extra material to be inserted at proof stage.

3.5.6 **Footnotes and endnotes** (see section 9.4)

See that every note has an indicator in the text, and vice versa. It is very important to get this right at the typescript stage, and essential if the first proof is to be paged or if the notes are numbered in one sequence through each chapter. A conscientious typesetter who notices that a note is missing may delay paging the book until you can say how much space should be left for the note. A missing footnote indicator would mean guessing which page the note refers to, and this could lead to repaging at proof stage and possibly alterations to the index.

If the notes are to be numbered in a continuous sequence through each chapter, see also that there are no additions (such as 10a) in the numbering.

Move note indicators to follow punctuation, and preferably to the end of the sentence or a break in the sense, unless the reference is to a specific word. See whether very long footnotes, or parts of them, could be incorporated into the text or an appendix.

It helps the typesetter if you say, on the first folio of the typescript, where footnotes can be found, unless, of course, they are typed at the foot of the relevant folio of text. Some authors put them at the end of each chapter, some at the end of the typescript; if they are at the end of each chapter, give the folio number for the relevant notes on the first folio of each chapter (e.g. 'Footnote copy on fos. 43–6').

3.5.7 **Tables** (see section 9.5)

If the tables are on separate sheets, mark their position in the margin of the text (e.g. 'Table 4.5 near here'); if they are not on separate sheets it may be helpful to show their exact extent (see fig. 9.1, p. 216); and those over four to five lines should probably be numbered. See that the structure of each table is clear, and that the units used, date and source are given, where appropriate.

3.5.8 **Other passages to be distinguished typographically**

See that all such passages in the text and appendixes are clearly identified, and that it is obvious whether the sentence immediately following should start at the margin or be indented. If whole passages such as long quotations are to be indented, make this clear either by coding or by marking the layout of each passage.

If definitions, proofs, etc. are not to be distinguished by being set in small type or italic, the end of each one should be indicated in some way, and it may break up the text too much to insert space before and after each one. Consult the designer about a suitable device and mark this clearly in the typescript.

3.5.9 **Cross-references** (see section 6.4)

Check all cross-references to illustrations, sections, tables, equations, etc. If the author has given folio numbers in cross-references to other pages, change the digits to zeros or bullets, to remind the author to fill in the page numbers at proof stage. Although you cannot tell exactly how many digits will be needed, try to see that a reasonable amount of space will be left by the typesetter; for example 'see pp. oo' implies more than one page, 'see pp. ooo–oo' would be better. Write the folio numbers in the margin to help locate the passage at proof stage.

Try to cut down the number of references to specific pages, except in a reference book. If there is a table number, for example, it is not necessary to give a page number as well, if the table is within about twenty folios. As tables may not appear exactly where they are in the typescript, change 'table 5 below' or 'the following table' to 'table 5'. If there are many cross-references to pages, check a few to see whether the passage referred to is something a reader might need to look up at this point, and if they seem unnecessary discuss with the author whether some of them could be deleted. Cross-references to pages are expensive and interrupt the flow of the text. They may also necessitate an extra stage of proof, which will lengthen production time.

3.5.10 Preliminary pages (see chapter 7)

Provide the complete wording, including that for the half-title and title-page verso and any series list. Check the contents list against the text and see that any material not yet available, such as an index, is included in the list. Check any lists of illustrations or tables against the captions or headings respectively.

3.5.11 Running heads (see section 9.2)

If short forms need to be used, in order to fit across the page, provide a typewritten list giving the wording for each running head, including prelims and endmatter, with the correct capitalization, spelling and punctuation. The list should be headed by the author's name and short book title, and may be divided into columns. For example:

Left (or *verso*)	*Right* (or *recto*)
Preface	Preface
[title of part 1]	[title of chapter 1]
	[title of chapter 2]
[title of part 2]	[title of chapter 3]
. . .	. . .
Bibliography	Bibliography
Index of authors	Index of authors
General index	General index

3.6

A WELL-ORGANIZED AND CONSISTENT BOOK

Look at the general organization. Are subheadings and numbered paragraphs used with restraint? If there are too many they will confuse instead of helping. Are some of the illustrations unnecessary; would a map or glossary be helpful? Would tabulated material be better in the form of a graph, or vice versa; would certain passages of running text be better tabulated, or vice versa? Would a particular section of the text be better as an appendix, or vice versa? In a book containing two or more interrelated parts, such as a catalogue with a separate section of illustrations, see that the system of cross-references is adequate.

All abbreviations that may not be familiar to the reader should be explained in a list in the preliminary pages or the first time they occur; a list is more helpful if the abbreviations appear only in footnotes or only rarely in the text.

Bibliographical references in the text and notes should be consistent and full enough to lead the reader unerringly to the right item in the bibliography; if there are many references in the text or notes, the bibliography should not be broken up into several sections through which the reader will have to search to find the relevant book or article.

3.6.1 **Consistency**

If a book is inconsistent in matters of detail, the reader or reviewer may begin to doubt the author's accuracy and thoroughness over matters of fact. In some cases inconsistency may lead to ambiguity: if the author capitalizes a word inconsistently the reader may think some distinction is intended. Watch out for names as well as other words, especially those that have alternative spellings, e.g. Ann(e), Mackintosh or McIntosh. In books on history, authors may inconsistently anglicize proper names, for example Henry/Henri, Frederic/Frederick/Friedrich. Time spans and ages also need checking, and in novels the colour of hair and eyes may vary. To take an obvious example:

> At ten, Anne was a quiet child, whose brown eyes looked at you thoughtfully.
> She first caught sight of Neil seven years later . . .
> There was a faraway look in Ann's blue eyes. She was thinking of herself at sixteen, watching Neil as he . . .

Few readers notice whether dates are written '10th August, 1989', '10 August 1989' or 'August 10, 1989', but inconsistency in style may still distract their attention from what the author is saying – even though they may not be conscious of what has distracted them.

The easiest way to ensure consistency is to make lists, as you go through the typescript, of the author's general style – spelling, capitalization, hyphens, italic – and unusual proper names, with the folio number of the first (or every) occurrence, in case you need to change the style later. If you have a house style that covers systems such as standard spellings, hyphens, capitals, dates and numbers, it may suit you best to use a sheet divided into six or eight alphabetical groups (see fig. 3.2). Otherwise you – and also the typesetter and proofreader – will probably find it easiest to have a list divided into categories (see fig. 3.3).

Remember that quotations and book or article titles should *not* be made consistent in spelling etc. with the rest of the book.

The things which should be consistent are:

- spelling (see section 6.14): watch out particularly for alternative spellings such as -ize or -ise, Basel and Basle; also anglicization of personal and place names
- accents, particularly on semi-anglicized words such as regime, role, naïve, elite, and on transliterated words
- hyphenation/one word/two words, not only in ordinary words but also in such place names as Hong Kong, Cape Town
- capitalization (see section 6.3)
- italic, especially for semi-anglicized words or those very familiar to the author, e.g. Indian terms in a book on India (see section 6.7)
- abbreviations, particularly the use of full points in groups of capitals (see section 6.1)
- dates (see section 6.5.1)
- units of measurement (see sections 6.8 and 13.3)
- numbers, especially elision of pairs of numbers, and the use of words or figures (see section 6.10)
- single (or double) quotes (see section 11.1.2)
- bibliographical references (see chapter 10)
- cross-references (see section 6.4)
- singular or plural verb after group nouns such as 'government'
- 'it' referring to countries

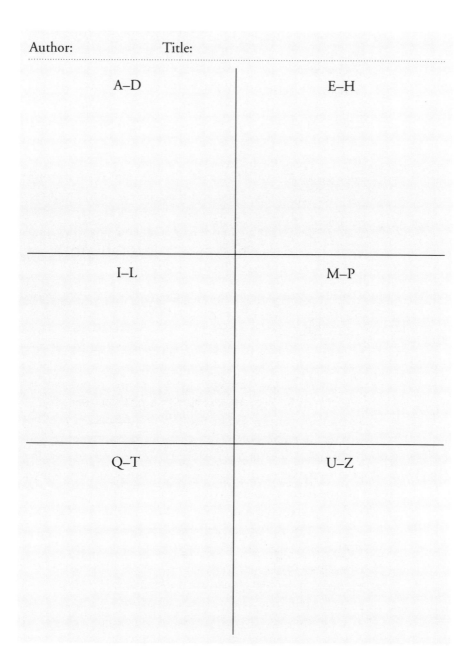

Author: Title:

A–D   E–H

I–L   M–P

Q–T   U–Z

Fig. 3.2 Style sheet divided into alphabetical groups.

```
STYLE SHEET

Author:                    Title:


Spelling
-ize
judgement
Cainozoic
savanna


Abbreviations
all-cap. abbrevs. no points
AD, BC small caps.


One word              Hyphenated            Two words
bridewealth           base-level            hill slope
cottonfield           birth-rate            ice sheet
foodcrop              fish-meal             land mass
floodplain            ice-cap               rain belt
groundwater           palm-oil              salt pans
landform              sea-level             sea water
waterhole             water-table           work load


Caps.                 l.c.
Blacks/Whites         black/white (adj.)
Western, the West
Karoo


Quotation marks
single; none for displayed extracts
punctuation to follow closing quote unless (a) punc. is ? or ! or (b) the
   quotation is or ends with a complete sentence starting with a cap.


Dates
7 July 1988
date-spans within one century elided to 2 digits: 1986-88


Numbers
spelt out up to 100
3- and 4-digit nos.: 2000  20 000
max. elision


Cross-refs.
Chapter 2    Fig. 4.3


Bibliographical references
book titles max. caps.
article titles min. caps. with quotes


Miscellaneous
see back of sheet
```

Fig. 3.3 Style sheet divided into categories.

Some publishers have a house style for all these things; others follow the author's own system, provided it is sensible and consistent. Even the latter group are likely to have a preferred style for some or all of the following. In each case I think the simplest form is the best, for example:

- dates: 1 May 1973, 1970s (see section 6.5.1)
- elision of pairs of numbers (see section 6.10.7)
- omission of points after contractions containing the last letter of the singular (e.g. Dr, St, Ltd) and after abbreviated units of measurement (e.g. mm, lb). Note that the plural of these units is the same as the singular, viz. 5 mm, not 5 mms
- single quotes, except in books where a distinction between single and double is needed (see section 11.1.2)
- placing of punctuation in relation to closing quotes (see section 11.1.2)
- three-point ellipses to indicate an omission (see section 11.1.3)
- low decimal point (as recommended by the Royal Society)
- SI units in science and mathematics books (see section 6.8 and chapter 13)
- thousands indicated either by space in numbers over 9999 (in science and mathematics books) or by comma in numbers over 999 (or over 9999)

Apart from consistency of convention within the text, you should see that the following are consistent. The contents list, lists of figures, plates, tables, etc., must tally in wording, numbering (preferably arabic), spelling, capitalization and hyphenation with the chapter headings, subheadings, captions, etc., that they refer to, though captions and table headings may be given in a shorter form in the list. The list of abbreviations should tally with the text, for example in capitalization, italicization and inclusion of points.

You should check quotations repeated within the book (e.g. in comments on phrases from a longer quotation) and spot-check other quotations, if the source is available, to see whether you need to ask the author to check all of them. Look out also for the occasional British spelling when a British author quotes a US source, and vice versa.

You should also check the alphabetical order of the list of abbreviations, bibliography, glossary, etc.

3.7

COPYRIGHT PERMISSIONS AND ACKNOWLEDGEMENTS

Under the contract, the author is usually required to obtain permission for the use of any copyright material in the work and to pay for it. In complex cases such as an anthology, however, the publisher often does this work for the author. In any event the publisher should see to it that this often rather onerous work is done properly: that there is a proper clearance of the desired rights, enshrined in a businesslike way in an exchange of letters. All permissions correspondence should be lodged with the publisher, so that, when you are going through the typescript and illustrations, you can make sure that all permissions have been cleared and that acknowledgements are in the form required by the copyright owner.

3.7.1 What requires permission

In general, the use of another's work must be subject to written permission from the copyright holder or his or her publisher or agent (the publisher is the best person to write to in the first place). But there are exceptions to this. The most obvious one is where the work is out of copyright. In the main, a work is out of copyright in the UK if its creator has been dead for more than fifty years (to be changed to seventy years from July 1995. From that date, all EU countries will give this longer period of copyright protection.). Two distinct copyright periods apply in the USA, however: if the work was created before 1 January 1978, protection runs for a period of twenty-eight years from publication, renewable for a further twenty-eight years; works completed from 1 January 1978 are in copyright until fifty years after the creator's death. The lengths of copyright periods in all countries are given in *Copinger and Skone James on Copyright* (13th edn, London, Sweet & Maxwell, 1990). In any event there are exceptions which have to be treated on an *ad hoc* basis (the copyright in a new critical edition of the works of an author who has been dead for centuries, for example).

Other exceptions to the general need to clear permissions concern the length of a quoted passage and the context in which it is placed. There is a natural desire in people dealing with permissions to have a tight set of rules, but such rules do not exist and would be difficult to formulate in a way that deals fairly with the multiplicity of different occasions when someone wanted to quote a passage, or use an illustration, from another's work.

As far as UK law is concerned, there are two main circumstances in which permission need not be sought. One is where the quotation is *non-substantial.* In practice, the freedom to quote non-substantial passages seems to be very rarely exercised, owing to the general vagueness of the phrase: there is no definition of substantiality, but it does have to do with quality as well as length. Each publisher must formulate their own policy here, and it would seem reasonable at least for that to allow for quotation of a very short passage without permission. The other exception is where the material (and here it could be illustrations as well as prose) is being included 'for the purpose of criticism or review' either of the work of which the material forms a part or of another work. So a critical study of a major novelist still in copyright can include passages from that novelist's work, and from the works of others still in copyright, without permission, provided it is clearly necessary to include these passages (that is, provided the passages are actually discussed in the critical study). In addition to these two exceptions, the UK Copyright Act does allow certain exceptions to the publisher of collections for the use of schools, and these should be studied carefully by anyone involved in such works.

In US law, a general exception is granted under the concept of 'fair use', and the US Copyright Act of 1976 lays down useful general 'factors to be considered' in deciding whether a use is 'fair' or not:

(1) the purpose and character of the use, including whether such use is of a commercial nature or is for non-profit educational purposes;
(2) the nature of the copyrighted work;
(3) the amount and substantiality of the portion used in relation to the copyrighted work as a whole; and
(4) the effect of the use upon the potential market for or value of the copyrighted work.

In effect, what the US Act is saying here is something that should be borne in mind in general: there are no rules which can apply to all circumstances; most cases have to be judged on an *ad hoc,* subjective basis which intelligently bears in mind the sorts of consideration listed in 1 to 4 above.

In any event, *all* in-copyright material in anthologies, books of readings and the like (works which are essentially compilations of the works of others) is subject to permission, no matter how brief.

Music

A musical composition is protected in the same way as a literary work, and one would normally expect to have to ask for permission for any quotation from a score in copyright, subject to the exceptions given above. Sometimes there are two copyrights involved – in the melody and in the arrangement – so that the fact that its composer has long been dead, or that it is from a traditional folk melody, does not necessarily mean that a quotation is out of copyright. Sometimes there are three copyrights: in the melody, in the arrangement and in the words.

Illustrations and tables

If drawings or photographs have not been made by the author or specially commissioned, and they are still in copyright, permission must be obtained, subject to the 'criticism or review' exception and provided they do not fall within the scope of the agreement between publishers belonging to the International Group of Scientific, Technical and Medical Publishers (STM). If an illustration is used on the cover, or may be wanted generally for publicity reasons, permission for that purpose is necessary even if permission has already been obtained for use in the book.

If the basis of a map or table is a map or table originally appearing elsewhere, then permission should usually be sought, whatever the degree of modification. But clearly this rule needs a sensible interpretation in the case of maps: there is a great difference between copying the outline of South America from an atlas and using, in a modified form, somebody else's map of possible Roman settlements in Norfolk.

An author who wishes to use a photograph of a living person (other than crowd scenes or a photograph of a public figure used for its news or historical value) should obtain that person's permission. In some photographs – for example those used in medical books – the person's identity should be disguised by a patch covering either the eyes or the mouth.

3.7.2 **Acknowledgements**

It is a legal requirement that the sources of all in-copyright quotations (words or music), tables and illustrations should be given, whether or not it was necessary to obtain permission for their use. The 'sufficient acknowledgement' required by the law is made by giving author (composer etc.) and title, but in the normal run of events fuller acknowledgement is given using any special wording provided by the copyright holder, so check the permission correspondence. In some cases this correspondence may continue after the typescript has been sent to the typesetter, so check again at proof stage to see that no additions or changes are needed. Do not try to make the wording of American credit lines consistent: under earlier US law copyright can be lost entirely if the acknowledgement is not given correctly. If you do have to depart from the wording laid down by the American publisher, write to say why and give the wording you propose to use; in most cases it is an explicit condition of use that a certain wording is used, and any deviation must therefore be subject to permission.

The acknowledgement must also be made *in the place* required by the copyright holder, who may say that the acknowledgement should be made immediately below the quotation or illustration, or on the copyright page (verso of the title page). This can sometimes cause difficulty if the instruction about wording and placing is not received until the book is in page proof; again, tell the copyright holder as soon as possible if you cannot do what is asked.

Unless the acknowledgements are given in the text or on the copyright page, it is useful for the reader to have a complete list in the preliminary pages or at the end of the book, even if this means that some sources are given twice. Acknowledgements lists may be in alphabetical order of copyright owner or in numerical order of first (or each) illustration or page number for each copyright holder. If illustrations are identified by page number, a descriptive phrase will of course be needed as well, if all the illustrations on one page were not obtained from one copyright holder; also such a list cannot be completed and sent for setting until the page numbers are known.

If the illustrations are the only copyright material, the acknowledgements may be included at the end of the relevant items in the list of illustrations – if there is one – instead.

In collections of papers, acknowledgements may be in the first foot-note of the appropriate paper, or in a small separate section at the end of it, so that they are included in offprints.

In science books, acknowledgements for illustrations are given at the end of the caption, usually in the form of a short reference to the source – 'From Smith, 1990', or 'After Wilkins & Mayo, 1988' if the illustration is modified or adapted – provided that the full reference is given in the list of references *and the copyright holder has not asked for other wording.*

3.7.3 **Other points**

It may well happen that a quotation needing permission comes from a work published by your own firm. In that event, the original author should be contacted, and it would seem fair that he or she should receive the normal payment.

If the permission covers only one edition or only one printing, note this information where it will receive the attention of anyone dealing with a new edition or reprint of the book. The correspondence with the copyright holders should be kept where it can be consulted by the department dealing with permissions and foreign rights.

3.8

BEFORE PASSING THE TYPESCRIPT ON

Make sure that all the folios are there and in the correct order, that the prelims are complete and any series list is up to date, and that all other material such as illustrations, list of captions, running heads and jacket copy is complete. Tell the designer and production department the length, position and expected arrival date of any copy not yet available.

If a chapter title or illustration number has been altered, have all the necessary consequent changes been made? Should any folio numbers in your brief to the designer be changed? Are there any additional design points to which you should draw the designer's attention?

Provide any style notes a proofreader may need, particularly about any apparent inconsistencies.

3.9

JACKET AND COVER COPY

Some copy-editors provide or check some of the copy for jackets and covers. Here is a list of what may be needed.

Front of jacket and cover
- author, title, subtitle
- possibly series title
- possibly publisher's name, though more usually on the back (or back flap of jacket)
- on a journal cover the ISSN should preferably be printed in the top right-hand corner

Spine of jacket and cover
- author and title; possibly subtitle
- publisher's name or logo (symbol)

Jacket front flap
- blurb
- price
- possibly contents list, though more often on back flap of jacket

Jacket back flap
- piece about author
- photograph of author, plus credit line
- caption and credit for picture on front cover
- name of jacket designer
- name of publisher if not on front or back
- name of country where jacket is to be printed, e.g. 'Printed in Great Britain'
- (the back flap may also be used for the continuation of the blurb, a contents list, reviews of the book, an advertisement of another book, or a list of books in the same series)

Back of jacket
- reviews of this book or advertisements for other books, or list of books in the series

- name of publisher if not on the front
- ISBN and bar code

Back of printed cover *(paperback or hardback that has no jacket)*
- blurb and/or reviews
- caption and credit for picture on front cover
- name of cover designer
- publisher's name if not on the front
- ISBN and bar code

All blurbs, whether for this book or for others, should be spelt in the style of this book; book titles and reviews should, of course, be left unchanged.

④ Illustrations

Printed illustrations are of two kinds: line and halftone.

Line illustrations

These include diagrams, maps and graphs. They are drawn in solid black ink, with no gradations of grey, though shading can be provided by a pattern of dots or lines called a tint, as in figure 4.3. Line drawings may also be needed for some things that are not pictures, that is for things that cannot be keyed by the author or by all typesetters. These may include ringed or crossed-out letters, numbers or words; chemical formulae with rings or diagonals; music; structural diagrams in linguistics books; non-roman characters; and genealogical tables. If the book contains such diagrams or symbols, show the designer samples of each kind as early as possible, and ask whether they can be typeset or will be drawn by the typesetter or an artwork studio.

Documents such as newspaper cuttings may also be used as artwork rather than reset.

Halftones

Halftone reproduction is needed for illustrations such as photographs and wash drawings, which contain gradations of tone between black and white. It may also be needed to reproduce old engravings. Note that not all photographs are halftones: an author may provide photographic prints of finished artwork for diagrams; but these are not halftones, because there is not a continuous gradation of tone.

Illustrations for halftone reproduction are usually broken down into tiny black dots of various diameters to simulate the strength of tone. An examination of a newspaper photograph through a magnifying glass will show this clearly. Different screens, that is different numbers of dots to the inch, are used for different papers: on newsprint a screen of 50 to 85 is used, but one of 150 or more might be used for the best reproduction on a coated paper.

As well as ordinary halftones there are two other kinds which are useful in certain cases: 'cut-out' halftones may be made from photographs of objects such as statues, to eliminate an obtrusive background; and combined line and halftone may be used for a photograph that needs some lettering or a scale.

Halftones are usually printed on the same paper as the text, so that each illustration can appear near its text reference. Alternatively, the halftones may be printed separately from the text, as what was traditionally called a plates section; this means that one can use coated paper to enhance the quality of the halftones without having to use it for the text as well. The halftones may then be printed by a different printer. Separately printed halftones are usually numbered in a separate sequence.

Coloured halftones are printed four times – usually in magenta (red), yellow, cyan (blue) and black – to produce the effect of all the colours in the original. If there are some coloured halftones in a book with a small print number, the publisher may decide to have these printed separately, to avoid the need to print the whole book four times. In that case they should probably be numbered in a separate sequence from the other halftones, because it would be expensive to paste each one in at the relevant point. If you are in any doubt about where the halftones will be placed, discuss this with the designer or production department.

The word 'plate' originally meant a halftone page printed on different paper from the text; it is now used to refer to any halftones numbered in a separate sequence from line illustrations.

After general coverage of illustrations and what the copy-editor needs to do (in this section and section 4.1), this chapter contains separate sections on line illustrations (4.2), particular points about maps (4.3), graphs (4.4) and halftones (4.5). This entails some repetition, but different kinds of illustration do need different treatment to some extent, and many books contain only halftones or only line illustrations.

4.0.1 **Reductions**

Although you may not be responsible for sizing the illustrations, you may find it useful to know a little about it.

Reductions are linear: that is, '50%' or '2 = 1' means that the final version will be half as wide but have only a quarter of the original area.

Reductions expressed as percentages are potentially ambiguous unless expressed as 'reduce to 60%' to show that the illustration should not be reduced *by* 60 per cent. Reductions, especially for halftones, are often expressed in the form of a final width when the illustration is reduced. See figure 4.1, which also shows how to calculate the final depth.

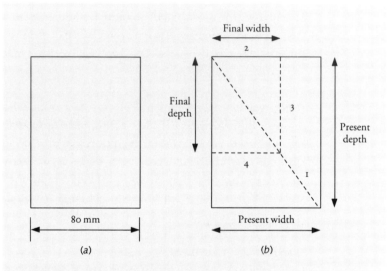

Fig. 4.1 (*a*) How the final size of an illustration may be marked. The vertical lines by the arrowheads show the exact width to be reduced. (*b*) If you wish to know what the final depth will be, draw a rectangle the same size as the illustration, omitting any areas to be masked off; and rule a diagonal line from corner to corner (1). Mark off the final width on the top line of the rectangle (2) and draw a vertical line to meet the diagonal (3). The vertical line will be the final depth; and a rectangle the final size may be obtained by drawing a horizontal line from the point where the vertical and diagonal meet (4). A similar method (but with steps 2–4 in the reverse order) can be used if you know the final depth and want to know the final width.

Line drawings
Reduction tends to improve final quality, provided the line thicknesses are suitable and any shading or lettering is sufficiently open: reduction minimizes slight irregularities by decreasing the thickness of the lines, but it also decreases the distance between them, with the result that closely spaced lines may close up.

The use of the same reduction for all the figures means that the same size of lettering can be used throughout and that the typesetter or printer will be able to photograph several pieces of artwork at a time and will not need to keep resetting the camera – which takes time and is therefore expensive. Maps cannot always easily be drawn for uniform reduction, as the cartographer may find it more convenient to draw them the same size as the relevant maps in an atlas.

Very large originals may contain more details than can be shown on a page, and are difficult to handle; they may therefore have to be redrawn. If the final size will be much smaller than the originals, warn the author; it may be as well to have one original reduced to the final size, to show the effect.

Halftones
If an author provides a photograph that contains fine detail likely to disappear after reduction and screening, ask whether part of the picture may be omitted ('masked'), so that the relevant part need not be reduced so much.

4.0.2 **Large illustrations**

Illustrations that are turned on the page
Illustrations that are to be compared with one another should be printed the same way up. If some halftones in a group have to be turned, try to place them together, so that the reader does not have to keep turning the book.

The bottom of turned illustrations should be at the right-hand side of the page; preferably, no wording on the figure should be upside down when the book is upright, though with large graphs this may be unavoidable.

Although the running head and page number are usually omitted from a page containing a turned figure, one should try not to have more than two consecutive pages without a number; so one may include page numbers where there is a sequence of turned illustrations.

Fold-outs
Fold-outs are large sheets that have to be folded and pasted into the book individually. They are very expensive, cumbersome to use, and apt to tear along the folds, especially if they unfold downwards as well

as sideways. They should be used only if the relationship between the parts of a large detailed map or diagram is very important. Fold-out halftones are rare, but occasionally one may be necessary in order to reproduce an old map at a reasonable size.

If there is to be a fold-out, tell the production department whether the whole of the illustration, when unfolded, should be visible even if the book is not open at the page; this may be necessary if the fold-out is referred to often. See section 5.5.6 for the best position for a fold-out. If there is no list of illustrations, the fold-out should have 'facing p. 000' printed at the foot, so that the binder knows where to insert it.

Double-page spreads

A double-page illustration will have to be printed in two separate halves unless it is in the middle of a signature (a folded printed sheet) of a book with a sewn binding; so it is not suitable for an illustration with important wording across the central area.

Double-page illustrations are usually split into two equal parts, but they may be better split to one side of the centre, to avoid a break at a critical point.

Endpapers

If an illustration printed on the endpapers is referred to in the text, it should be repeated in the body of the book, as the endpapers may be obscured by library labels or because a library fastens the jacket to them; and they will disappear if the library has the book rebound. Remember too that a paperback edition will have no endpapers.

4.1

WHAT NEEDS TO BE DONE

Separate the illustrations from the text, including any symbols or diagrammatic material that will have to be drawn (see p. 36). See that all the illustrations are there. Label each one with author, short book title and illustration or folio number; it helps everyone if every illustration is numbered for identification, even if the number is not to be printed.

It is useful to have a form on which you list each illustration, giving its number and/or text folio number, whether it is line or halftone, how many pieces of copy have been provided for each, and whether these are roughs, lettered or unlettered artwork, or photographs. Such a list can be used by the designer, artist and typesetter to check that no illustration copy is missing; and there should also be space for the designer to add any instructions about placing and reductions. If you keep a copy of the list, it will be easier for you to keep track of which artwork has come to you for checking and which illustrations need correction.

Check all the illustrations against the text. Are they appropriate to the nature and level of the book? Do they show clearly the points they are intended to illustrate? Ask the author to confirm in writing that any potentially dangerous diagrams, such as wiring diagrams, are correct and that photographs show people taking any necessary precautions such as wearing protective clothing.

Is the quality of the photographs, diagrams, lettering, etc., good enough? If you are not sure about this, ask the designer's advice as early as possible, so that the author can be asked to provide better originals; or it may be decided to obtain better photographs elsewhere or to redraw or reletter diagrams or maps.

You may need to provide a typed list of lettering, such as place names for maps (see p. 87). Mark up any new lettering for such things as capitalization and italic; and give any instructions about scale, consistency, masking and so on (see section 2.1.7).

See that permission has been obtained to reproduce all borrowed illustrations, and include the necessary acknowledgements in the caption or in the list of illustrations or a separate note (see section 3.7).

4.1.1   Captions and list of illustrations

Provide a typed list of captions, checked against the content of the illustrations and against the text. Make a list, even if each caption merely says 'Fig. 1' etc. The captions should be typed double-spaced, with the author's name and short book title at the top of the first folio. Keep a copy in case the top copy goes astray, especially if you have had to compile the captions yourself. You or the designer must tell the typesetter whether each caption is to be the same width as the illustration (in which case the appropriate width is written beside each caption) or text measure, and also whether turnover lines should start flush left or be indented or centred.

See that each caption contains all the necessary information, so that the illustration is intelligible without reference to the text; but delete unnecessary wording such as 'Graph showing . . .' Captions usually start 'Fig. 1', 'Map 1' or 'Plate 1', though where there is only one sequence of illustrations in the book – and where the caption consists of more than just the number – 'Fig.' etc. may be omitted. If the figure numbers are not to be printed, ring them on the list of captions.

See that there consistently is or is not a point after the number and at the end of the caption. If there is no point after the number, one needs extra space there, so it may be easier to include a point. Very short captions need no point at the end:

15. The Pitt Building

but if any of the captions consist of more than one sentence, it is probably best to end them all with a point:

15. The Pitt Building. This early engraving shows the original railings and lamp-posts.

Sources

In a book using the author–date system of bibliographical references, the sources will usually be given in that form at the end of the caption or the relevant part of it:

Fig. 2.1. Prehistoric lanes in a downland 'Celtic field' system. Dole's Mill in Puddletown, Dorset. (After Taylor 1979.)

('After' is used when one has revised the borrowed figure.)

Where illustrations may be of interest outside their immediate context, there will probably be a list in the preliminary pages (see section 7.9); if there is only one illustration, for example a map, it can be included in the contents list. The sources may appear in the list of illustrations or a separate acknowledgements list (see section 3.7.2), unless the copyright owner specifies that the acknowledgement must appear immediately below the illustration. For example, the caption might read:

3. A poet and his audience, *c.* 1400, from Chaucer's *Troilus and Criseyde*. Chaucer is reading his masterpiece to a wealthy audience that may have been Richard II's court. With the growth of literacy, such works were intended for reading as well as listening audiences, particularly of nobles.

and the entry in the list of illustrations:

3 A poet and his audience, *c.* 1400, from Chaucer's *Troilus and Criseyde* (Master and Fellows of Corpus Christi College, Cambridge)

Where the source will be of interest to the reader (e.g. the museum where an object can be found), it should be included in the caption. The dimensions and/or date may also be useful.

In the list of illustrations there is usually no punctuation after the number or at the end of the item.

If an illustration, such as an old engraving, already includes a caption, make clear whether this is to be reproduced as part of the illustration or omitted.

4.2

LINE ILLUSTRATIONS

If the author's rough sketches have to be redrawn and checked before they are incorporated in the proof, they need to be dealt with at an early stage so as not to delay the book. So, if you can, send the roughs to be drawn before you have finished work on the typescript. You should not send them before you have checked them against the text and captions, and marked up any lettering; but the text may be held up, perhaps while you wait for the author to answer queries, or while you work through the notes and bibliography, and there is no need for the drawings to wait too, if all your queries about them have been answered.

If some of the illustrations are likely to occupy a whole page, send a copy of the captions with the roughs, as the artist will want to know how much space to allow for them. In certain cases the captions may also help the artist with the drawing.

4.2.1 **Separating the originals from the text**

If the author has drawn the illustrations on folios that also include text, photocopy the folios if you can, and put the photocopy in the text so as to give the artist the best possible original to draw from. On the photocopy, ring the figure and caption and write 'artwork', so that the typesetter knows that these are being dealt with separately and the wording need not be keyed with the text. (The captions are usually set separately, from the list you provide.) On the copy to be used by the artist, ring everything that is not to be included in the artwork, for example lettering that will be incorporated in the caption.

It is important to leave a copy of the folio in the text if there is anything at all on it other than the illustration and the caption: if artwork is needed for a genealogical table, for instance, the heading and any notes may be set with the rest of the text and if so should not be ringed. If in doubt ask the designer.

4.2.2 **Numbering**

Each original should be clearly identified by author's name, short book title and figure number or identification number.

Diagrams that are referred to in the text should usually be numbered in the finished book, and referred to by number in the text, because the typesetter may not be able to place them in exactly the right position: there may not be room at the foot of the page, or it may be your house style to place all illustrations at the top of a page. Warn the author about this. While you are going through the text, change 'is as follows:' to 'is shown in figure 10'. If the figure is in the middle of a paragraph in the typescript, and is followed by a new sentence, mark the new sentence to run on.

Small pieces of artwork occupying less than four or five lines of text are not usually difficult to place exactly where they occur in the typescript; and if they are not really 'figures' they need not be numbered but may be identified for the typesetter by the folio number with, if necessary, 'top', 'middle', 'bottom'. Tell the typesetter, either in marginal instructions or in a note at the beginning of each chapter containing such artwork, that each piece of artwork must be placed exactly where it is in the typescript.

Figures may be numbered in one sequence through the book, or by chapter (figure 6.1 being the first figure in chapter 6). In symposia or other collections of papers, they may have to be numbered afresh in each paper, in which case each original will have to carry the contributor's name as well as the general identification for the book. Where possible, avoid having more than one sequence of numbers for text illustrations; for example, graphs are usually numbered in the same sequence as other diagrams. If, however, the book contains some diagrams relevant only to the immediate context, and also some maps to which the reader may wish to refer several times – and which should therefore be listed in the preliminary pages – they should be numbered separately; but in that case make sure that you always refer to them as 'figure 1' or 'map 1', so that neither the reader nor the typesetter has any doubt as to which one is meant. If halftones are to be printed in the text, they may be numbered in one sequence with the line illustrations, though maps may again be numbered separately. Frontispieces are not usually numbered.

4.2.3 **Position**

See that the place for each figure is given in the margin of the text: the best position is usually near the first or most detailed reference to the illustration. If you think the order of the figures should be altered, suggest this to the author, and if necessary renumber the relevant figures – and of course the captions and any cross-references. The marginal note should be in the form 'Fig. 6 near here' and ringed. It is easy to omit a marginal reference to a figure by mistake, so check that every figure has been mentioned in the margin, and that if there are two series of numbers (e.g. of diagrams and maps) it is clear whether figure 6 or map 6 is referred to.

4.2.4 **Content and captions**

The copy-editor is the last person to see the text and illustrations together while they can both be changed without difficulty and expense. So it is extremely important to check the one against the other.

See that drawings are complete (for example that both axes of graphs are labelled and that the scales are unambiguous), and that symbols and conventions are used consistently in all the figures, as well as in the captions and text. This check is particularly necessary when an author uses someone else's illustrations which may employ a different set of conventions.

See that each figure tallies with its description in the caption and text; it often happens that an author changes the text slightly but forgets to change the relevant diagrams. Check particularly the style for abbreviations and the spelling of proper names.

Any identification letters or unusual symbols or abbreviations should be explained in a key or in the caption or text. In general, remove as much lettering as possible from the drawing into the caption, to keep the illustration uncluttered. However, a key containing symbols that cannot be typeset must be in the figure artwork; and a scale in the figure may be better than a magnification or reduction ('× 1000' or 'half actual size') given in the caption, as these last two would have to be changed if the illustration was reduced for reproduction.

4.2.5 **Shading**

Shading is usually applied in the form of tints, which are patterns of dots, lines, etc., in various densities, that can be applied by the author, the artist or the typesetter. Their use permits the differentiation of several types of area.

4.2.6 **Information for designer and artist**

If you wrote some notes for the designer in preparation for an estimate (see section 2.1), check what you wrote and list any changes. Otherwise make a list of general points now.

If diagrams are to be reproduced in more, or fewer, colours than in the original, state any preference the author may have as to the use to be made of the extra colour, or the conventions to be used to replace colour (perhaps a solid bold line to replace red, and a dashed line to replace green). See that any illustration that must not be redrawn, or any original that has been borrowed and must not be relettered, is mentioned in the list. If graph grids are to be included, say so; if only some are to be included, make it clear which are to be retained.

Warn the designer if, for example, three figures must be fitted into one double-page spread for comparison, or if the drawings must be reduced either by the same amount or in proportion to the size of the objects they portray, or if they must be printed to a certain size (say × 200 or 10 mm to a kilometre).

Provide, or check, a typed list of wording for figures such as genealogical tables and maps which contain a number of unfamiliar words or proper names that are handwritten on the rough.

Ensure that the author's intention for each illustration is clear: the artist has no knowledge of the book, and any queries will cause delay, so any instructions and annotations must be simple, legible and unambiguous. If the author's roughs are not accurate enough to be copied exactly, add your own explanatory notes on individual figures or attach a photocopy of a similar illustration from another book. The notes should include all the points that may not be apparent to anyone who has not read the book: for example, that the line AF in figure 4 should be twice as long as the line AD in figure 1, or that six lines which appear to meet at F actually do meet there. The notes should be written on the roughs themselves, or firmly fastened to them.

If the figures are not to be redrawn, any marking-up of the lettering, etc., should be on a photocopy or overlay. An overlay is a flap of tracing paper fastened to the back of the drawing and folded over to cover the front; take care that it is fastened and folded in such a way that it cannot slip out of position; if there is any chance of movement, the correct position in relation to the drawing should be identified by corresponding marks on overlay and drawing. Any other instructions should be on a separate sheet attached to the original.

Some originals are more elaborate than they need be, because they have been taken from other publications. In that case tell the artist, or draw a rough sketch to indicate, what must be included.

Creative illustrations
The artist may need to be told about – or, better still, shown – appropriate geographical or historical details to be used in the drawings. See that the briefing provided is appropriate and adequate; it may take the

form of detailed roughs, photographs of places or of objects in museums, or drawings and relevant text from other books. If the artist is to consult other books, it is not enough to quote author and title: artists cannot be expected to have access to any but the standard works of reference; nor can they be expected to read through several books to find the information they need. If source books have been recommended by anyone other than the author, make sure the author agrees with the choice: authorities often disagree, particularly about historical reconstructions.

The artist should also be given a duplicate typescript, or at least the relevant folios. Mark the text passages that describe what is to be drawn.

4.2.7 Marking up the lettering

If the figures are not to be redrawn, mark up a photocopy. Ring any material that is not to be included in the drawing. See that lettering is legible; identify capital O/zero, l/1/I, Greek, subscripts, etc.; remove any unwanted full points after abbreviations; and mark capitals, italic, bold, and so on, according to the usage in the text. Keep capitals to a minimum: only the first word of a label – if that – needs an initial capital.

4.2.8 Redrawn and lettered artwork

It is best to ask authors to check any redrawing, and any complicated lettering. Alterations to artwork are caused as often by authors' inadequate or incorrect roughs, or second thoughts, as they are by artists' mistakes.

As original artwork is extremely vulnerable in transit, send the author a photocopy instead. Before sending it, check that no drawings are missing. See that each one is clearly and correctly identified, and, if there is time, check the drawings against the roughs. Ask the author to mark corrections in a colour that will show up on the photocopy, or to give a clear indication in the margin, to make sure that no small change is overlooked. If you have to send the artwork itself, see that it is carefully packed; if possible, it should be packed flat with plenty of padding, and it should never be folded. Ask the author not to mark any corrections on it, as ballpoint – and sometimes even erased pencil – will be picked up by the camera. Pale blue crayon is satisfactory, but very few authors have a pale enough one, so cover each drawing with a transparent overlay, on which the author can mark any corrections, using a soft pencil or crayon in order to avoid damaging the artwork underneath.

Tell the author about any wording you have moved from the drawing to the caption, and explain that areas coloured (usually) blue on the artwork will be covered by a tint.

Make it clear that this is the last stage at which corrections can be made without great expense, and that it is important to check the drawings and lettering carefully. On the other hand, the author must correct only actual errors.

When the author has returned the drawings, see that any corrections are clear and sensible, and that they do not depart from the agreed conventions. If the artwork was sent, see that it has all been returned; although the author need not return photocopies or roughs of illustrations that require no correction, it is useful to have them, if only to verify that no alterations are necessary.

If you did not have time to check the drawings before you sent them, have a general look at them now. If sans serif lettering is used, make sure that l, 1 and I are easily distinguishable. If a dot tint is already laid, ring any dots that come so close to lettering that they will make the letters look deformed. It may also be part of your job to see that the artwork will reduce and reproduce well; that its style harmonizes with the typographical style of the book; and that each illustration is properly sized.

Unless there are very few corrections, tell the designer or production department whether the changes should be charged to author, artist or publisher.

If the book is already being made up into page (or if the author sends a substitute figure at proof stage), check that no change in size is likely, for example because the vertical axis of a graph has been extended or cut; if a change is likely, consult the production department. If the typesetter has already passed the relevant page, decide whether the author should be asked to alter the figure so that it can be reproduced the same size as before, or whether the typesetter should be asked to repage as far as the end of the chapter.

Separate the artwork that needs correction, and list those figures; then pass all the artwork to the designer or production department. Corrected artwork will probably be given to you to check; if the author particularly asks to see it, point out that this may delay the book unless the author can be reached by fax.

4.3

MAPS

Maps should include all the places a reader is likely to look up, but should be free from unnecessary detail. Inexperienced authors may provide copies of printed maps which, through the use of more than one colour or a larger size, include more details than can be shown in a one-page black-and-white map. They may not have stopped to ask themselves: is all the information necessary for the readers of my book? Are the right places shown? Are boundaries or contours needed, and, if so, which? Should any mountains be shown; which seas, bays, etc., should be named, which rivers included? Are roads and railways necessary? Does the map need latitude and longitude lines, a north point, a scale (see below)?

I have already mentioned the disadvantages of fold-outs, double-page spreads and endpaper illustrations. If a map is too crowded or covers too large an area to be fitted on to one page, it can probably be split geographically or by subject – say physical features on one map and density of population on another – or even chronologically. The reader will probably find the maps easier to follow if each contains only the minimum of information. It may be possible to have an inset map, on a larger scale, covering a particularly crowded area.

If only one or two place names are outside the main area of a map, and it would mean making this main area very small if the places outside it were to be shown, it may be more sensible to omit the distant places; one could indicate, by an arrow, the direction in which they lie.

4.3.1 **Briefing the cartographer**

The cartographer will need photocopies of existing maps, or sketch maps; information about the inclusion of boundaries, contours, etc., if this is not clear from the sketch maps; and a typed list showing the correct spelling of the names to be included in each map. See that the briefing is adequate, for example that it is clear exactly which areas should be shaded, how many kinds of shading are needed, whether one particular tint should be a combination of two of the others, or whether all the tints should be graded in density to show, say, different densities of population. See also that the cartographer will know whether to follow the author's neat-looking, but possibly inaccurate, drawings for coastline and placing of towns or archaeological sites, etc. If the map is to show the position of ancient places that no longer exist, the cartographer must be told exactly where to place them.

The list of names should have a column each for countries, provinces, towns, smaller villages or settlements, old sites, rivers and other natural features, ethnic groups, etc., because a different kind of lettering is likely to be used for each. If the lettering is to be typeset, add to this list all the other lettering needed on the map, for example the latitude and longitude numbers, the wording for the scale, key, etc. The designer will specify type size and the use of bold or italic; but if any kind of name needs to be particularly prominent, point this out. Mark capitalization of things that are not proper names: for example, 'Railway station', 'Land above 1000 metres'.

As you go through the text, check place-name spellings against the list. See that all the necessary names are included, and that the spelling does not vary from map to map. Watch out for out-of-date names for, say, African states and towns.

Tell the designer which maps must be reproduced to a certain scale. Maps to be compared with one another should be reproduced to the same scale if this will not mean that they will differ greatly in final size. Ordnance Survey maps are often reproduced to the same scale as in the sheet from which they are taken; make sure that the whole of the required area will fit on to the page with grid numbers added at the edges if necessary (give instructions about this). Maps in school books may be used as the basis for exercises in measuring distance, in which case they must be on a scale where, say, 100 km is an exact number of millimetres, so that the student can measure distances with a ruler.

North points
These are usually unnecessary if north is at the top of the map. If maps are to be compared, north must be in the same direction and preferably at the top unless there is some particular reason for another orientation: for example a map may have the North Pole in the centre, to show the relationship of northern North America and northern Russia.

Scales
Scales may have both metric and imperial gradations. One cannot have two sets of contour lines, or two labels for each line; but, if land over a certain height is shaded, and the shading is explained in a key, the height can be given in both forms. Persuade the author to choose a height shown in an atlas, and if possible one that can be converted approximately to a round number.

Town plans, and maps of a district and of any country except the very biggest, should have scales, because many readers will not be familiar with the distances involved. For larger areas, such as continents, China and Russia, it will depend on the projection used: directions and distances may vary so much across the map as to rule out the use of scale and north point completely. If a north point cannot be used, orientation – and distances – can be made clear by having a marginal indication of latitude and longitude. Maps of a large area are usually drawn with an average north and south orientation on the page. If distances are more important than orientation, say so, so that the cartographer can use the most helpful projection.

Keys
See that the key, or the caption, contains all the necessary information, and that the items in the key are in a sensible order.

4.3.2 **Checking the artwork**

Check the following for consistency from map to map: style of north point, scales, conventions to indicate sea and high ground, etc., comma or space in thousands, full points after abbreviations, capital-ization, spelling and so on.

See that the labelling does not obscure rivers, boundaries or small areas of shading, and that town names are, if possible, placed so that the relevant dot is near one end of the name. All names that must be nearly vertical, because they follow the course of a river or label a very narrow area, should read the same way.

See that there is sufficient distinction between the tints used, and that they are correctly coded in the key. Ring any areas of tint that come so close to lettering that they may make it look deformed when the map is reduced.

4.4

GRAPHS

It is easier for the artist to follow a careful drawing than to make a graph from a list of numbers. The grid is not usually reproduced; tell the artist whether it should be. If artwork for graphs is drawn on graph paper,

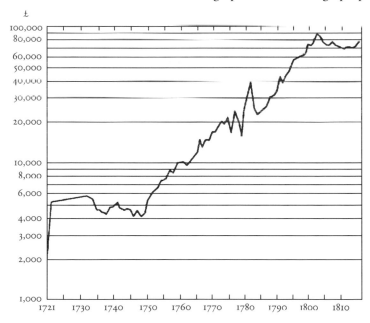

Fig. 4.2 Logarithmic graph.

it must be ruled in a pure pale blue that contains no grey, or the grid will be picked up by the camera. If a graph is to be used for actual measurements and the grid is not reproduced, it helps the reader if horizontal and vertical axes are repeated at the top and right-hand side, respectively.

Graphs are sometimes drawn with one or both axes on a logarithmic rather than a linear scale. A logarithmic scale is one where, for example, the distance between 1 and 10 is the same as that between 10 and 100, 100 and 1000, and so on (see fig. 4.2). This means that a great range of values may be plotted, and also that small changes show up in the lower part of the range and only very big changes in the higher part.

A histogram is a graphical method of illustrating frequency distributions. The graph is normally made up of vertical columns, the heights of which are proportional to the number of observations occurring in the range that each covers; this

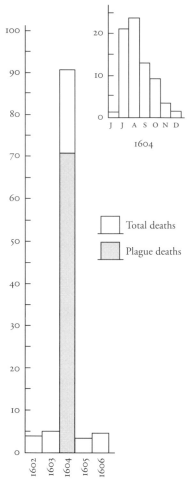

Fig. 4.3 Histogram.

range is indicated on the horizontal axis (see fig. 4.3). Each column may be divided to show constituents as well as total value.

The numbering on the axes of a graph does not always start at zero; and O may mean origin rather than zero, in which case it should be marked to be an italic capital. *O* is usually to be found only in graphs showing positions relative to co-ordinate axes labelled, say, *x* and *y*, where the text probably also contains phrases such as 'the *Ox* axis'. Zero is better on a graph with numbers on the axes.

If the lettering labelling the vertical axes of graphs is too long to read horizontally, it should read upwards.

4.5

HALFTONES

4.5.1 **Originals**

For black-and-white halftones the originals should be sharp, black-and-white glossy prints with clear contrast in tonal values, detail visible in both highlights and shadows, and an uncluttered background. Matt or 'pebble-dash' prints, photocopies or illustrations from other publications (which will already have a screen) will not reproduce well and should be avoided, though screened illustrations can be reproduced 'dot for dot'.

As I have mentioned before, photographs should be handled as little as possible and should be kept between pieces of stiff card so that the corners do not become dog-eared. Do not use paperclips, which may scratch the surface and will almost certainly dent it; such dents tend to cast a minute shadow that has to be eliminated by the typesetter or printer. For the same reason, do not mark the face of the prints, or mark them so heavily on the back as to dent them; any writing should be done very lightly, with a soft pencil. If the prints are not the author's, mark up a photocopy instead.

4.5.2 **Position**

Text halftones
These are placed in the text near the first or most detailed reference, and you should mark the approximate position in the margin of the typescript ('Fig. 79 near here').

Separately printed halftones
The exact position cannot be decided until the book is in proof (see section 5.5.5), but the publisher will decide at typescript stage whether the plates are to be grouped, wrapped round signatures (folded printed

sheets), inserted in the centre of signatures, or pasted in individually. The decision may depend on the desired selling price, and also on whether there are detailed references to the plates in the text. If there are, and it would be too expensive to paste each one in to face the relevant page, it is most convenient to the reader if they are grouped, because it is then easier to find a particular plate.

If there is no list of plates, each pasted-in plate, and the first and last page in each group, should have 'facing p. oo' (or 'frontispiece') printed at the foot as a guide to the binder; and the position of a group can be mentioned immediately after the contents list:

The plates will be found between pages ooo and ooo.

4.5.3 **Numbering**

Each print should be labelled with the author's name, short book title and illustration number. This information is best typed or written on a self-adhesive label, which is then attached to the back of the photograph.

Although all halftones must be numbered for identification, there is no need for them to be numbered in the finished book unless they are grouped or referred to in the text; in any case the frontispiece is not usually included in the numbering.

Text halftones are usually included in the figure numbering. Halftones printed on different paper are more likely to be numbered in a separate sequence, because of the expense of inserting them at the right place in the sequence when the book is bound.

4.5.4 **Instructions**

See that the top of the photograph is indicated lightly on the back of the print if necessary.

Lettering
If a letter, arrow or scale is to be added to a halftone it should be on a photocopy or overlay; see that the position for the letters or arrows is clear, and that the corners of the print are marked on the overlay if there is any likelihood that it may slip.

Masking
If the author has not already done so, mark on a photocopy (or lightly on an overlay) the area that must be included and anything that must be omitted, leaving the designer to decide the actual area as best suits the layout; but where an exact area is required this should be indicated. When photographs are intended to be bled (to run off the page) it is essential that significant details should not come too close to the edge of the print; so one that could only be trimmed on the left and at the top should appear at the top of a left-hand page, and so on. If a photograph can be trimmed to the same shape as the available space, it goes without saying that it will not have to be reduced as much, provided that the caption is not very long.

Retouching
This is very expensive if it is to be done well. Consult the designer if the author wants some retouching done or if you think some is desirable.

Sizing
Halftones may be text-width or bled; in a two-column layout they may be one-column or run across both columns. Detailed sizing may be left to the designer; but if you know the approximate final size, see whether the photographs can be reproduced satisfactorily at that size, taking possible masking and the length of the caption into account.

Avoid turning a halftone on the page, if it can be reproduced upright without too great a reduction. If some halftones in a group must be turned, try to place them together so that the reader does not have to keep turning the book. The foot of a turned halftone should be at the right-hand edge of the page.

Tell the designer if the photographs are to be reproduced at a certain magnification or reduction in proportion to the original size of the objects shown.

4.5.5 **Captions** (see section 4.1.1)

Captions for separately printed halftones are usually kept short, so that the pictures can be as large as possible.

If the caption contains a magnification, this will have to be changed if the halftone is reduced for reproduction; and it may be better to include a drawn scale either on or below the halftone.

4.5.6 Passing the halftones on

Halftones should be passed on to the designer with the other illustrations, either when copy-editing is complete or earlier if some of the other illustrations have to be drawn. A copy of the captions should accompany the photographs.

Separately printed halftones may be sent later, if this is unavoidable. They should in any case be sent in one batch.

⑤ Proofs

One of the copy-editor's main functions is to minimize proof correction, both by eliminating faults at the typescript stage and by going through the author's corrected proof when he or she returns it to the publisher.

Books to be typeset from an author's corrected disk need to be proofread once the author has put in the copy-editor's corrections; other books will be proofread once the typesetter has keyed the material or corrected the author's disk.

Alterations at proof stage are so expensive that they should be restricted to the correction of typesetter's errors; authors receive proofs only to check that the typesetter has followed the typescript accurately. However, when authors see their book again after an interval, and in a new form, they may look at it with fresh eyes and wish to make changes; there may have been new developments in their subject (particularly in the sciences); or they may show the proofs to colleagues, who may suggest alterations. If an author corrects the proof heavily, it will not only be very expensive but may also necessitate another proof stage to check that the corrections have been carried out properly, which will delay the book and may tempt the author to tinker further.

The publisher opts for the minimum number of proof stages appropriate to the complexity of the book and the production method, and both the commissioning editor and the copy-editor should stress to authors, at an early stage, that the typescript or disk sent to the typesetter must represent their final thoughts. If an extra stage of proof is needed, to see that typesetting corrections have been made accurately, this may be checked only by the copy-editor.

When dates for the proof stages are known, the publisher asks the author to keep these free or to say straight away if they are inconvenient, so that the schedule can be rearranged. Any delay in returning proofs to the typesetter may cause an even greater delay in the general production schedule. At this stage the publisher stresses again the need to keep correction to a minimum, and asks the author to correct legibly and in ink, using conventional signs (see appendix 13) and colours (see section 5.4).

The schedule should also allow time for the copy-editor to go through the author's corrected proof before it is returned to the typesetter. Copy-editors can make sure that authors' corrections are clear, feasible and consistent, and that all queries are answered. They can also save money by persuading authors to cancel unnecessary corrections and to make others in a more economical way.

5.0.1 **Proof stages**

If the book contains line illustrations that the publisher is having drawn or amended, the author should be sent a photocopy of the artwork to check before it is incorporated in the page proof, because any later alterations other than a simple deletion may be costly and delay the book.

The text can be typeset in one sequence, with the running heads, subheadings and various sizes of type; but the exact position of complex tables, line and halftone illustrations – and of course running heads, page numbers and footnotes – will not usually be known until the book is divided into pages. If the book is straightforward, the first proof will be paged. This enables the author to see everything in position; the index can be made straight away; and a second proof can often be avoided. For a more complex book the first proof may be what are usually called 'galleys', generally sheets of continuous text that are not divided into pages and do not have the tables, illustrations and any footnotes in their final position; in that case there will be a second, paged proof.

Books with paste-ups
If the layout is complex and the relationship of text and illustrations is crucial – for example in a heavily illustrated book for children – the publisher's designer may prepare a paged layout once the author has checked the galley proofs for typesetting errors. The designer pastes a duplicate set of proofs on to layout sheets (showing a page or a 'spread' – a pair of facing pages), incorporating space for the illustrations and any other material; for example the captions may not be set until the width of each illustration is known, so that they fit neatly underneath. In the paste-up the illustrations may be represented by photocopies,

rough sketches or just empty rectangles, and captions by pencil lines to show how many typeset lines each will occupy. A photocopy of this paste-up is sent to the author to show what size the illustrations will be and where they will be placed in relation to the text. The author will be asked to approve (or provide alternatives to) any deletions or re-wording which the publisher may suggest to improve the layout, and to complete any cross-references. The author or copy-editor should transfer all typesetting corrections to the author's corrected proof, which is returned via the publisher to the typesetter. At this stage the index can be compiled from a copy of the paste-up.

The next stage will be a page proof to enable the author or the copy-editor to check text corrections and any new typesetting (e.g. captions), and to see that the typesetter has placed the text, illustrations, captions, running heads and page numbers as instructed on the paste-up, and also that the illustrations are the right way round. It may be necessary to have a separate proof of the illustrations, to check the quality of their reproduction.

Before outlining what needs to be done to the author's corrected proof, I shall say something about how to read proofs, how to mark corrections and how to minimize correction costs.

I should also explain the term 'marked proof' or 'marked set' (some-times called the 'master set'). This is the copy of the proof on which the typesetter marks any corrections or queries, usually in green (see sec-tion 5.4); and this is the copy the typesetter wants back. As duplicate proofs are usually photocopied after the corrections have been inser-ted, the only distinction between the proofs may be that the 'marked proof' is marked in green and may be labelled 'Marked proof. Please return this set.' The important thing is that all the corrections – the typesetter's, author's and proofreader's – should be combined on one set of proofs and colour-coded correctly.

5.1

HOW TO READ PROOFS

Proofs may be checked in three ways. One may 'read for sense', which means a careful reading, looking at spelling, punctuation, etc., noting queries to be checked against the typescript later. One may read for sense, but in addition check names, dates, numbers, and so on against the typescript as one reads. Or one may 'read against copy', which means checking each phrase, spelling and punctuation mark against the typescript; but in that case one would also need to read the proof quickly for sense, since one cannot do both efficiently at the same time. Some proofreaders 'read against copy' first, and then read straight through for spelling, punctuation and missing words; others prefer to do the general reading first, so that the queries raised then can be checked when they compare the proof with the typescript.

As an ordinary reader one trains oneself to disregard spelling mistakes and to concentrate on the author's meaning; and quick readers take in a whole phrase at a time. To become a proofreader one needs to unlearn these habits. Train yourself to read slowly, so that you see every letter in each word and note the punctuation of each sentence. You may find it easier to notice errors if you place a strip of paper or a ruler across the page, and move it down a line at a time, to isolate the line you are reading from those which follow. It is also sensible to reread any line in which you have found an error. Look particularly to see that no opening or closing quotation marks or parentheses (round brackets) are missing, as this is the sort of thing the author is likely to miss.

You may read a duplicate proof, not the marked set, but even so it is better to use pencil rather than ink for queries or other marks that may be cancelled later. If these can be rubbed out, leaving the proof uncluttered, there is no risk that anything essential will be missed when corrections are transferred to the marked proof.

The commissioning editor's brief at the copy-editing stage will have stated the quality aimed at, and by implication whether, for example, minor inconsistencies the copy-editor missed earlier – and which the ordinary reader will almost certainly miss – should be corrected now.

If you have the typescript or the copy-editor's list of spellings, capitals and hyphenation, it is easy to mark inconsistencies and to note whether they are within a few pages of a correct form and may catch the reader's eye. If you are proofreading a book you did not copy-edit, and you have no list of spellings etc., it may be worth making one as you go along. I myself have found it useful to mark all optional forms by a simple marginal mark until I have discovered what the most usual form of each one is. It is much quicker to run through the proof afterwards, looking at each of these marks and making any essential alterations, than to list all the page numbers for each. Look out also for errors in foreign phrases, discrepancies in names, periods of time and ages, and in novels such things as colour of hair or eyes.

If the various components of the book – text, illustrations, captions and tables – are proofed on separate sheets, it is particularly important to check for discrepancies of fact: if authors cannot easily lay out all the material side by side, they may rely on their memory.

Some dangers:

- If there is a glaring error, one's eye tends to leap over the intervening words; so, when you have marked the correction, read the whole line again.
- Whereas a word that is obviously misspelt is fairly easy to spot, a typesetter's error can change one word to another and this is more likely to slip through: for example, 'causal relationship' can become 'casual relationship', 'ingenuous' 'ingenious', 'unexceptionable' 'unexceptional', 'alternatively' 'alternately'. Watch out also for 'its' and 'it's'; and 'yours' and 'theirs' sometimes appear with apostrophes.
- On the other hand, the author may intentionally not use the obvious word but substitute something similar in look but different in meaning, just to give the reader a jolt; so one must not take it for granted that a slightly different word is necessarily wrong.
- A British typesetter who is asked to retain American spellings may through habit spell some words in the British way. Watch for this specially, because otherwise the British spellings will not strike you as wrong.
- See that you do not alter inconsistent spelling, capitalization and punctuation in quotations.

You should check particularly the things that the author will take for granted: the preliminary pages, headings, running heads, and the numerical sequence of pages, notes (and their text indicators), sections, tables, illustrations, equations, etc. See that illustrations and tables are sensibly placed. Add the missing page numbers to the contents list and any lists of illustrations or tables, checking the titles against the captions or table headings at the same time. Missing cross-references to pages will probably have to be filled in by the author, but put a marginal mark by each one, to alert whoever will collate your proof with the author's, to ensure that none are missed. Check all references to illustrations, tables, section and equation numbers.

Mark wrong founts (letters in the wrong type or size), unequal spacing between words or lines, and inconsistent indentions, for example after headings; and check that there consistently is, or is not, punctuation following a run-on heading. If faulty letters appear to be due to a mark introduced by photocopying, ring the affected area and make a general comment.

At proof stage, word breaks should be left unaltered unless they are actually misleading or startlingly wrong. Misleading breaks are those which lead the reader to think that the word is a different one. This is largely a matter of pronunciation, because many readers 'pronounce' the first half of the word as it stands, even if they are reading quickly. For example, psycho- is a suitable place to break psychosomatic but not psychology, even though the root is the same in both cases; Christian should be broken after Chris-, not Christ-. Three classic examples of bad breaks are read-just, reap-pear and the-rapist. Words should also not be broken in the middle of a syllable. US typesetters usually follow the word breaks shown in Webster dictionaries; some of these breaks are frowned on in Britain, but changes to them are charged as author's alterations in the USA. (For word breaks in foreign languages see *Hart's Rules*.)

If someone else will be collating your corrections with the author's, keep your queries to a minimum. If you do query something, show clearly what you are querying and say why: '? meaning', '? construction', '? see p. 314' (and mark the relevant part of p. 314). Similarly, if you change something that is in itself correct, such as an optional spelling which is not on a list of spellings for the book, say why you are changing it, so that the person collating the proofs knows that the change is necessary for consistency and is not just a matter of your own preference. If something is inconsistent and you do not know which way to make it consistent, mark *all* the instances; no one else will have time to go through to look for them.

HOW TO MARK CORRECTIONS

One corrects proofs differently from typescript, because at proof stage the typesetter just looks down the margin to see which lines contain corrections; a correction that is made only in the text will not be noticed. The correction should be written in the nearer margin and level with the error. If the line of text contains more than one mistake, the corrections in the margin should be written from left to right in the same order, separated by oblique strokes where appropriate. Use standard correction signs (e.g. those in the British Standard on proof correction; see appendix 13).

Keep the marginal corrections short and clear (see figure 5.1): if only one letter is wrong, merely cross out that letter and put the correct letter, followed by an oblique stroke, in the margin. Some authors put a marginal deletion sign for deleting the wrong letter, and an insertion sign for inserting the right letter; do not follow their example, because typesetters charge according to the time they take, and the more they have to read, and the more unconventional the marginal marks, the slower they will be. The whole word should not be written in the margin unless there is more than one group of letters wrong in it, or unless the correct form is unusual. On the other hand, a whole phrase may have to be rewritten in the margin if there is a complicated change in word order; or one may need to show how a complicated piece of layout should look and what should line up with what. Anything other than the actual correction should be ringed.

Ring full stops and colons for clarity. Distinguish a closing quote from a comma, and superscripts from subscripts. Mark corrections to be bold or italic where appropriate.

Treat a letter with an accent as a single character: even if only the accent is wrong, cross out both letter and accent and write the correct form in the margin. Similarly with groups of letters which may form a single character, called a ligature: ff, fi, fl, ffi, ffl (as here). If part of one of these needs correction – say fl changed to ffl – the whole character should be crossed out and rewritten in the margin.

If you delete a letter or letters, make it absolutely clear how much is to be deleted. A carelessly written diagonal stroke through one letter can pass through part of its two neighbours, and the typesetter may not be able to tell whether you are deleting one letter or three.

Even horizontal deletion signs are clearer if they have a small vertical stroke at each end: for example, a horizontal line through a word may extend above a following comma, and it may not be clear whether the comma is to go or to stay.

Where there can be any doubt, make the word division clear by the use of space' or 'close up' marks. For example, if an hyphen is deleted, make clear whether one word or two is wanted instead; if one or more letters are added between two foreign words, show whether the letters form a separate word or are to be added to the preceding or following word. Answer any typesetters' queries briefly/ merely cross out the question mark if you agree with the suggestion; cross out the whole suggestion if you disagree.

5.3

MINIMIZING CORRECTION COST

Proof correction is far more expensive than the original typesetting. Authors are sometimes given a 'correction allowance' of, say, to per cent of the composition cost; but this does not mean that they can correct every tenth word, or even make one correction in every tenth line, without exceeding the allowance: it is more likely to work out at one small correction for every two typeset pages. if the author has made many changes, discuss this with the commissioning editor, who should warn the author if the correction allowance is likely to be exceeded.

If a proofreader has corrected heavily, one should not necessarily transfer all the corrections to the marked proof. Obviously, one must

correct factual errors and passages that do not make sense. Beyond that one should consider the overall number of corrections (excluding type- 3
stage. For example, one should insert a missing quotation mark; but if 3
setter's errors), the readership and expected life of the book, and the 1
standard requested by the commissioning editor at the copy-editing 2
punctuation is wrongly placed in relation to a closing quotation mark

Fig. 5.1 Page of corrected proof.

If you delete a letter or letters, make it absolutely clear how much is to be deleted. A carelessly written diagonal stroke through one letter can pass through part of its two neighbours, and the typesetter may not be able to tell whether you are deleting one letter or three. Even horizontal deletion signs are clearer if they have a small vertical stroke at each end: for example, a horizontal line through a word may extend above a following comma, and it may not be clear whether the comma is to go or to stay.

Where there can be any doubt, make the word division clear by the use of 'space' or 'close up' marks. For example, if a hyphen is deleted, make clear whether one word or two is wanted instead; if one or more letters are added between two foreign words, show whether the letters form a separate word or are to be added to the preceding or following word.

Answer any typesetter's queries *briefly*: merely cross out the question mark if you agree with the suggestion; cross out the whole suggestion if you disagree.

5.3

MINIMIZING THE CORRECTION COST

Proof correction is far more expensive than the original typesetting. Authors are sometimes given a 'correction allowance' of, say, 10 per cent of the composition cost; but this does not mean that they can correct every tenth word, or even make one correction in every tenth line, without exceeding the allowance: it is more likely to work out at one small correction for every two typeset pages. If the author has made many changes, discuss this with the commissioning editor, who should warn the author if the correction allowance is likely to be exceeded.

If a proofreader has corrected heavily, one should not necessarily transfer all the corrections to the marked proof. Obviously, one must correct factual errors and passages that do not make sense. Beyond that one should consider the overall number of corrections (excluding typesetter's errors), the readership and expected life of the book, and the standard requested by the commissioning editor at the copy-editing stage. For example, one should insert a missing quotation mark; but if punctuation is wrongly placed in relation to a closing quotation mark it is probably not worth changing at this stage. Similarly, one may leave inconsistent hyphens and capitals, if the meaning is clear and the two forms do not occur within a page or two of one another; also passages which could be worded or punctuated better but which do convey the intended meaning.

It may be possible to reduce the cost of a correction by rewording a line where something must be added, so that it still contains approximately the same number of letters and spaces. Some typesetters will reset the affected lines and strip them into the camera-ready copy or film; others will correct on the computer and rerun the whole paragraph or page. In the first case the number of lines affected by a correction makes a great difference, and an added word near the beginning of a paragraph may involve resetting several lines. In the second case an addition at the beginning of a paragraph may be no more expensive than any other within the paragraph; but rerunning the paragraph may introduce new and possibly undesirable word breaks at the ends of lines. You will need to ask the production department what the typesetter's correction method is, so that you know how best to minimize the cost of individual corrections. Bear in mind that the typesetter will charge for an author's alteration, even in a line that has to be reset for a typesetting error. If the author, to be helpful, rewords to compensate for, say, a typesetter's omission, make clear that this is the reason for the alteration.

If an *essential* addition or deletion affects the length of a paragraph, it is acceptable for a pair of facing pages to be one line longer or shorter than specified by the designer. If a page contains a number of spaces above and below subheadings or displayed material such as mathematics, quotations and tables, it may be possible to reduce each space very slightly, to make room for one extra line of text or footnote. If you have to move material from one page to the next, see that the following are not split between two pages: a footnote and its text indicator, or a subheading and the text that follows it (there should be at least two lines of text between the subheading and the foot of the page). A page should not start with a 'widow' (a short line which is the last line of a paragraph), if this can be avoided. Remember that a change in paging may affect the index.

If you are not sure what is the best way of reducing the cost of a correction, ask the designer or the production department. If possible, contact the author and explain the difficulties. If you cannot do this before the proofs are due back with the typesetter, you may have to modify the text as you think best and write to the author to explain what you have done. It depends, of course, on the kind of book and author; consult the commissioning editor if there is a real problem.

If an extra proof of all or part of the book will be necessary because of the amount of correction, warn the commissioning editor and the production department, because the extra proof stage will mean delay and extra expense.

5.4

ALLOCATING THE COST OF CORRECTIONS

Typesetters will charge for all corrections which are not their own errors and colour-coded as such. The following is the standard British system of colour-coding:

green: typesetter's own marks (corrections and queries)
red: author's or publisher's correction of typesetter's errors
blue or black: author's and publisher's own alterations (including any
   carried out in response to typesetter's queries), plus the following,
   which the typesetter should be asked to charge as part of the
   composition cost and not as author's corrections: insertion of cross-
   references and any running heads that cannot be written until
   proof stage

Some publishers ask authors to distinguish any publisher's errors (errors of omission or commission made during editing or copy-editing) by marking those in black. Typesetters will not separate the charges for blue and black corrections unless specifically asked to; but without this extra colour, authors may mark all errors by other people (typesetter or publisher) in red, and the copy-editor should see that the colour coding is made fair to the typesetter.

It is not worth checking every correction against the typescript, to see whether you missed the error while copy-editing – though it may be worth checking a few, because one can learn salutary lessons about one's blind spots. You will have to check against the typescript if a proofreader queries a passage that does not make sense, or a quotation or a discrepancy in the spelling of a proper name. If the typescript (or the author's index typescript) does not answer the query, you will have to ask the author by telephone or fax.

If the typesetter does not use the British colour-coding system, explain it on the first sheet of the proof.

5.5

THE AUTHOR'S CORRECTED PROOF

Authors are usually sent their typescript and two copies of the proof: the marked proof and a duplicate to keep for reference or to mark up when making the index. It is sensible for authors to read the duplicate set, which they can annotate as they wish; then, when they have checked the proof, they can eliminate all but the essential corrections, and copy these legibly on to the marked proof.

Some publishers transfer any typesetter's queries and their own to a duplicate set to send to authors, and retain the marked proof to mark up neatly themselves and colour-code when the authors send their corrections.

There may be a second set of corrected proofs, which has been read by a freelance proofreader, the series editor or perhaps the copy-editor.

If the author has made many changes, apart from correcting typesetter's errors, see what proportion of the changes appears essential, desirable or unnecessary, and then discuss the problem with the commissioning editor. One of you should contact the author if the author's correction allowance is likely to be exceeded or if you intend to cancel or modify some of the author's corrections.

As you go through the proof, try to keep the cost of corrections to a minimum (see section 5.3) and see that corrections are correctly colour-coded (section 5.4) and consistent in spelling, capitalization, and so on with the rest of the book.

Make sure that all queries have been answered, and that something has been done about any pages that are too long or too short, though, as I have said, it is acceptable to have a pair of facing pages one line longer or shorter than the rest.

Ask the author about the proofreader's queries concerning content; do not assume that the proofreader is right. (Similarly you may find that a hurried volume editor may make a mistake when correcting a contributor's article.)

See that all the author's corrections have a marginal mark and are correct, legible and unambiguous (see section 5.2), for example that an insertion mark is correctly placed. The extent of deletions must be made clear. Identify ambiguous characters; distinguish quotation marks from commas, and see that commas are not written so large that they look like parentheses. See that the author has used the correct underlining for capitals: some authors use two lines instead of three. If letters are added in non-English material, see that it is clear whether the addition is a separate word or is to be added to an existing one. However, unorthodox corrections can be left, provided they are clear and consistent, for example an accent ringed in the text, with a deletion mark in the margin. If necessary, write a note on the half-title of the proof, or in the margin the first time the correction occurs.

If a correction is not clear, it is probably quicker to rewrite it on a piece of adhesive label, than to use correction fluid, which takes a second or two to dry. If a page is very messy, transfer the corrections to a duplicate proof.

Anything written on the proof will be read by everyone who handles it; so if the author has explained the reason for a correction or written a long answer to a query, ring it and put a line through it to show that the typesetter need not read it.

If lines of text are to be moved from one galley or page to another, do not cut up the marked proof. If the correction is very complicated, cut up and rearrange a duplicate proof or a photocopy and attach this to the marked proof.

If the author alters a heading, see that it is also altered in the contents list and running heads if necessary.

An indexer works from an uncorrected proof, so make a note of any changes in the spelling of proper names, and incorporate them in the index typescript when you receive it. If some corrections may affect page references in the index – for example if a table has to be moved from one page to another – check the relevant page numbers on the second proof and alter the index if necessary.

Only one copy of the proof – the marked set – should be returned to the typesetter; so, if you have more than one corrected copy, see that the marked set contains all the essential corrections. Some publishers keep a fully corrected duplicate set in case of accidents.

5.5.1 **Preliminary pages**

Read the whole prelim proof, as authors tend not to read these pages carefully. Any late material, such as a foreword, list of plates or acknowledgements, should be sent for setting when the first proof is sent for revise.

Watch out particularly for any changes the author makes on the title page. If the book title or form of the author's name is altered, tell the commissioning editor, who may wish to dissuade the author from changing the title at this stage. See that any agreed changes to the book title, author's name and affiliation are sent to the people responsible for the cover, jacket and publicity; and be certain to check these on proofs of the jacket, cover and blocking die (which stamps the hardback binding). If the book title is changed, see that the half-title and, if necessary, the running heads are changed accordingly. If the book is mentioned in other books already in production, for example in a series list, see that its title is corrected there.

Make sure that a translator or artist has been mentioned where appropriate.

Title-page verso (see section 7.5)
Are the publisher's addresses given correctly?

Is the copyright notice set out correctly? Is the date correct? Is the owner given correctly? Should there be a separate notice for the illustrations or translation? Should the notice be omitted or qualified?

Is the publication date correct?

Add or check any CIP data that are to be included.

Is the ISBN correct? Should there be more than one?

Does the printer's address include the name of the country?

List of contents, etc.

Have all the page numbers been correctly filled in? Have the lists been changed in accordance with any changes made in headings and cap- · tions? Do the titles given for the indexes tally with what has now been provided? Are the indexes in an appropriate order? The most general one usually comes last. Should the (first) index start on a left-hand page, in order to bring the book within a multiple of eight pages?

Acknowledgements list

Should any changes or additions be made as a result of recent correspondence or any alteration in the numbering of the illustrations? If the illustrations are unnumbered, the list cannot be completed until the page numbers are known: see the list is sent for setting.

5.5.2   **Page numbers and running heads** (see sections 9.1, 9.2)

It is sensible to check these, as the author is unlikely to. You will need, in any case, to check the page numbering to see that each batch of proofs is complete.

Page numbers should not be printed on blank pages or on the half-title or its verso, the title page or its verso, the dedication and epigraph pages, or pages carrying only part titles. They may also be omitted on pages containing turned tables, turned illustrations, or illustrations extending into the margin where the page number would normally appear; but if there are references to these pages (in the preliminary pages, cross-references or the index), see that not more than two consecutive pages are without a number.

Although the page number will not appear in the printed book, these unnumbered pages of proof or camera-ready copy must carry a ringed page number, to ensure that the typesetter or printer knows where to place each one.

Discourage the author from making any change that will affect the running heads. If an author insists on such a change, see that *all* the relevant running heads (and the contents list) are altered.

Running heads are omitted above headings that intentionally start new pages (e.g. chapter or part headings); above all turned illustrations and tables; above text illustrations and tables which extend beyond the type area (except at the foot) and are not turned. Running heads are included above headings which *accidentally* occur at the heads of pages (including chapter headings in a book with run-on chapters); above text illustrations and tables which fall within the type area and are not turned.

Where section titles are used for running heads and a new section starts a page, the chapter title or an abbreviated form of the section title may be used for the running head, to avoid having identical headings one above the other (see p. 204). Where a new section starts below the top of the page the title of the new section should be used as the running head. Where more than one new section starts on the page, the first or last new heading may be used as the running head, but the same rule must be used throughout.

See that the correct page numbers are inserted in the running heads for endnotes (e.g. 'Notes to pages 25–6').

5.5.3 Footnotes and endnotes

Check the sequence of numbers if no one has already done so, making sure that no text indicators or notes are missing. See that footnotes are placed correctly on short pages, and that rules are included (if required) above the continuation of every footnote that runs on to another page.

5.5.4 Line illustrations

Check that any scale given in the form of a magnification or reduction in a caption has been altered if the illustration has been reduced for reproduction. See that the foot of any turned illustration is at the right-hand side.

If any corrections are essential, list the pages concerned for the designer to look at. The artwork may not need to be returned to the artist, as the typesetter may be able to correct labelling and make other simple amendments. If there are larger changes, provide a photocopy showing the alterations required, for the designer to send to the artist.

If the proof is paged, make sure that any alterations will not increase or reduce the size of the illustration.

If the first proof is in galley and does not include the illustrations, make sure that their position is marked.

5.5.5 **Halftones**

The proofs do not show the final quality of reproduction, and are intended only to show the layout and caption wording. Authors are often worried by the quality, and you may need to reassure them. Where the quality of halftone reproduction is particularly important, the publisher may send the author a separate proof that will show this.

As with line illustrations, check magnifications and scales in captions, and see that the foot of turned illustrations is at the right-hand side. See that each halftone is printed the right way round and has the right caption.

Separately printed halftones
If these have not been proofed by the time the first proof of the text is returned to the typesetter, check with the production department, as these separately printed illustrations are sometimes overlooked.

Once the book is paged, you should insert the 'facing page' numbers in the list of illustrations (if any) or at the end of the contents list (see section 4.5.2). If their position is not given in the prelims, any halftones to be pasted in individually should have 'facing p. 000' (or 'frontispiece') printed at the foot of the page below the caption; and each group, wrap-round, etc., should have 'facing p. 000' at the foot of the first and last page. This helps ensure that the plates are incorporated in the correct position when the sheets of the book are bound up.

The commissioning editor or designer will tell you whether the halftones are to be in a group or pasted in individually. If they are to be grouped between signatures (folded printed sheets), their exact position will depend on the number of pages in each signature and whether the preliminary pages are to be part of the first one. For example, each folded sheet may be thirty-two pages, with the first one containing preliminary pages i–xii and text pages 1–20; the second signature would finish with p. 52, and so on. The production department will be able to tell you about this and say whether the position you suggest for the halftones is feasible.

5.5.6 **Fold-outs**

If a fold-out refers to the whole of the book, it may be best placed after
the index (so that it can lie almost flat) unfolding to the right, and with
the whole of the illustration visible even if the book is open at another
page. The end of the book is also the best position for a figure or table
consisting of two or three fold-outs, as the bulge they form is less
unsightly there and they are easier to handle. If a fold-out refers to only
one section of the book it should unfold to the left at the beginning
of the section or unfold to the right at the end of it. Two large illustrations can be printed back to back on one fold-out if they need not be
compared. If there is no list of illustrations, see that each fold-out has
'facing p. 000' printed at its foot.

5.5.7 **Paste-up** (see p. 100)

If there is a paste-up, check that any corrections on the marked galley
proof will not affect the layout; tell the designer if they will. See that
any corrections marked on the paste-up are incorporated in the
marked galley proof.

5.5.8 **Covering note**

It may be necessary to send a covering note or notes, so that something
important is not overlooked; but essential information or instructions
for the person making the corrections must be written on the first (or
other appropriate) page of the proofs as well.

Any comments or requests addressed only to the designer and the
production department should not be included in a note for the typesetter. A covering note might contain the following:

for the designer: any design points in the text (with page references)
and any queries; any illustrations that need correction
for the designer, production department and typesetter: a request for a
further revise because of heavy correction or new material; any large
corrections for which you think the typesetter should pay

5.6

SECOND PROOF

If the first proof was in galley, the typesetter will now divide the book into pages, inserting running heads, page numbers ('folios' to the typesetter) and illustrations, and moving tables and footnotes to their final position. If footnotes are to be numbered by page, the note numbers and text indicators will be corrected at this stage. In order to avoid a short line at the top of a page, the typesetter may make a pair of facing pages one line long or short.

A second, paged proof is sent to the author, to check running heads, page numbers and the position of tables and illustrations, to complete cross-references and to make the index. Authors should also check that corrections marked on the first proof have been made correctly. They should be warned that they need to check the whole of every line affected, to make sure that new errors have not been introduced, and to read the lines immediately above and below the correction, in case the corrected line has been inserted in the wrong place. They should also be warned if the typesetter has rerun the parts of the book containing corrections and may have introduced new, unacceptable word breaks.

When the author returns the proof, the copy-editor should go through it as before.

Before passing the proof for press, read any recent correspondence between the commissioning editor and author if you can, in case any decisions have been taken that you did not know about.

All queries on the proof must be answered and all cross-references completed. See that proofs of any separately printed halftones and fold-outs are sent to the designer for the typesetter, and that their position is given either in the preliminary pages or on the halftones or fold-outs themselves.

It is worth checking the publication date, copyright notice, CIP data, ISBN and acknowledgements list again. In the contents list check that the correct title and page number are given for each index: it may be that the general index originally intended has been replaced by an author index and a subject index.

If the author returns the earlier marked proof with the revised proof, keep it until any query about correction costs has been settled.

5.7

CAMERA-READY COPY

You may be given camera-ready copy to check, perhaps on its way from the typesetter to the printer. Check that all earlier corrections have been made, that the prelims are in the right order, that the index begins on the page given for it in the contents list, and that any unnumbered pages are correctly placed.

It is worth rechecking the title-page wording, the publication date, copyright notice and ISBNs.

If there are any corrections, mark them on a photocopy, not on the camera-ready copy itself.

5.8

JACKET OR COVER PROOF

Check the ISBN, book title, inclusion or omission of subtitle, author's name and affiliation, series title, etc., against the proof of the preliminary pages; make sure that any changes made on the title-page proof have been incorporated. See that the blurb tallies with the text in spelling and general style, and that any caption or acknowledgement for a jacket or cover picture or design has been included. The jacket carries only the ISBN for the hardback edition, and the paperback cover only the paperback ISBN; the jacket should contain the words 'Printed in [Great Britain]'. Check that the bar code is there. If the spine wording on the jacket and/or cover reads along the spine, it should read downwards not upwards.

If you are asked to check the spine wording for the blocking die, see that the spelling and capitalization of the author's name, book title and publisher are correct and that they are in the right position.

5.9

AFTER PASSING PROOFS FOR PRESS

If the author sends late corrections, ask the production department whether there is time for them to be made, and if so pass them on after making sure they are absolutely necessary and completely clear; they are best marked on a copy of the proof page. If they are too late, tell the author and put them in the corrections file for a reprint. Erratum slips (called 'errata slips' if they list more than one error) are expensive to insert and may make a worse impression on reviewers and readers than the mistakes they refer to. If there is an erratum slip, put a copy in the corrections file, to make sure that the corrections will be incorporated in the text when the book is reprinted.

An erratum slip should be headed by the author's name, book title and ISBNs. Use italic for *for, read*, etc., so that inverted commas can be reserved for use within the quoted phrase if necessary. Spell out 'line' to avoid confusion with 1.

> Smith, *Kafka*
> ISBN 0 521 12345 6 hardback
> ISBN 0 521 65432 1 paperback
>
> *Errata*
> p. 112, line 1, *for* casual *read* causal
> p. 118, line 15, *for* ambiguity *read* 'ambiguity'
> p. 122, fig. 5, *insert* 2 *beside the unlabelled circle*

House style

Except when using an author's disk, some publishers have a fairly rigid house style covering spelling, abbreviations, etc.; others follow the author's own style in most things, if it is sensible and consistent. Each procedure has its advantages and disadvantages. If one is to follow the author's style one cannot always start the detailed marking straight away: one first needs to discover what the style is, which may be difficult if the author is not entirely consistent or if the system is unconventional; and one then needs to evaluate the system. However, a rigid house style may mean altering a perfectly good system; and the more changes one makes the more likely one is to miss some instances and to present authors with an inconsistent version of a system they did not choose. It is obviously best to brief authors *before* they prepare their final typescript, to tell them about the firm's preferences, and to ask them above all to be consistent.

Even if your publisher has a house style, it will not cover every spelling, hyphen and capital. So keep a note of the author's system as you go through the typescript, noting the folio number of each occurrence or making a marginal mark, until you have decided what the style should be. Some of these style points may be incorporated in a style sheet for the typesetter or proofreader.

There are several books that give useful guidance on tricky spellings, hyphenation, capitalization, punctuation and so on, and I list some of them on pp. 443–4. I shall myself just mention the points that seem to cause particular difficulty.

6.1

ABBREVIATIONS

Avoid unnecessary abbreviations, and see that any unfamiliar ones are explained at their first occurrence and possibly also in a list. Make sure that the abbreviations used are not ambiguous: for example spell out 'verse' if v. could be confused with a roman number; spell out 'lines' if the book will have lining figures (see section 6.10.1) and ll. could look

120

like 11; try to avoid the use of ff. to mean both 'folios' (fos. is better) and 'following'.

Use English rather than Latin, where possible: for example 'see above' rather than '*v. supra*'.

Omission of full points

There should be no full point after per cent or abbreviated units of measurement such as mm and lb, though 'in' may have one to avoid ambiguity. Note that the plural of abbreviated units is the same as the singular: 65 lb not 65 lbs. (*Hart's Rules* recommend that the plural s should be retained in hrs, qrs and yds, but it does not seem worth keeping these exceptions; in scientific work, h should be used for hour(s).) Do not use ' and " to mean feet and inches.

Most British publishers omit the full point after contractions – abbreviations that include the first and last letter of the singular – for example Mr, Dr, St. The only common exception to the rule is 'no.' (number, from *numero*). The fact that a plural abbreviation, such as Pss. for Psalms and vols. for volumes, includes the last letter of the full plural form, does not turn it into a contraction; it keeps the full point of the singular, though some publishers omit the point after plural forms.

Some publishers also omit full points after abbreviations such as n. ('note') and f., ff. ('following'), which are unambiguous and appear in heavily punctuated passages such as bibliographical references and indexes.

Sets of initials

One can punctuate all, none, or just those that consist of lower-case letters; or one can distinguish acronyms (sets of initials such as NATO, UNESCO, which are pronounced as a word; these can also be in the form Nato, Unesco). Abbreviations consisting of initials should usually have a point after each initial, or no points at all, for example p.p.m. or ppm, but not ppm. with a single point.

Small capitals may usually be used in place of full capitals for sets of initials; but ask the designer before marking them in passages or headings set in sans serif, bold or italic, where true small capitals may not be available and the simulated equivalent may be unsatisfactory. If there are many proper names (and therefore many initial capitals), or lining figures are used, sets of small capital initials may look incongruous and too insignificant, for example US Library of Congress, AD 1692.

Avoid the use of an apostrophe in the plural: NCOs is better than NCO's. However, some authors may feel that an apostrophe is necessary with a set of lower-case initials, to separate the s from the other lower-case letters; and this is acceptable.

Use lower case for a.m. and p.m., except in US style, where they are usually small capitals.

In translated matter see that the abbreviations are altered where appropriate.

Punctuation after abbreviations
Where an abbreviation that takes a full point comes at the end of a sentence, do not add another full point to end the sentence. One point performs both functions.

See also under 'e.g.' and 'ibid.' in section 6.1.1.

Italic
Italic abbreviations should be used for italic words such as book and journal names. If the author has used roman throughout it may not be worth changing them if there is no ambiguity, but one should keep the roman–italic distinction where both author and work are abbreviated, as in Soph. *OC* (Sophocles, *Oedipus Coloneus*). In any case the abbreviations in the list of abbreviations should be in the same form as in the text. Common Latin abbreviations such as e.g. are roman.

Capitalization at the beginning of a footnote
A few authors and publishers prefer *c.*, e.g., i.e., l., ll.,p., pp. to be lower case at the beginning of a footnote, and *Hart's Rules* recommend this; others treat cf., *ibid.*, *op. cit.* and *loc. cit.* in the same way. If you decide to retain the lower-case forms, and the typesetter is not familiar with this style in your books, explain the system on your style sheet, and stet the lower-case letters.

6.1.1 **Notes on individual abbreviations**

AD, BC: see section 6.5.1

&: an ampersand is often used in the author–date system of bibliographical references. Elsewhere use 'and' except in names of firms, statute references, and where the author is using & to make a distinction

&c. should become 'etc.' except where a document is being transcribed exactly

c., *ca*, approx.: use one of these consistently, rather than a mixture. *c.* is to be preferred to *ca*; both are usually italic

e.g., etc., i.e., viz. are set in roman. In the past, publishers changed them to the longer, English version, unless the text was in note form; but ask the author before changing them. See that the author is consistent in the use (or omission) of commas before and after these abbreviations

et al.: see p. 253

f., ff., *et seq.*: 'pp. 95f.' means p. 95 and the following page; 'pp. 95ff.' or 'pp. 95 *et seq.*' means p. 95 and an unspecified number of following pages; so do not make f. and ff. 'consistent'. ff. is preferable to *et seq.*, but a pair of page numbers is better. Remember that in all these cases one should use pp., not p.

ibid., *op. cit.*, *loc. cit.*, *idem*, *eadem* (see pp. 243–4): all except *ibid.* are best avoided. They may be either roman or italic, but they should all be treated in the same way. The comma is often omitted after the first three, to avoid the spotted appearance given by double punctuation

v.: in references to legal cases v. is roman and the names of the parties are italicized (see section 14.2.4)

is commonly used in American style to mean 'number'; but as not all readers will be familiar with this, it is best to substitute 'no.' The sign is also used as a symbol in linguistics books. As it is also a proof correction symbol for 'space', particularly in the United States and Australia, tell the typesetter when the symbol is to be set, and remember to do this at proof stage too, if the symbol appears in a correction

Names of genera: see section 13.5.1

6.1.2 **Spacing**

Many publishers give their typesetter standard instructions about spacing common abbreviations such as personal initials. For copy-editors who mark the spacing of abbreviations individually, table 6.1 lists some common ones.

Table 6.1 *The spacing of abbreviations*

Closed up

AD	6ff.	a.c.	ECG	kV	μg
BC	6p	b.p.	e.m.f.	kVA	o.d.
B.Chir.	6% (but 6 per cent)	B.T.U.	°F	kW	pdl
D.Phil.	16n.	°C	ft/s	mA	pF
e.g.	1970a	c.g.	GMT	mCi	pH
i.e.	1s, 2s, 3p (quantum states)	c.g.s.	Hb	Mc/s	p.p.m.
Ph.D.	§16	CNS	h.f.	mmHg	RNA
q.v.		CoA	h.p.	m.p.	r.m.s.
		c/s	i.u.	m/s	s.w.g.
		dB	kcal	mV	v.p.
		d.c.	kHz	μA	
		DNA	km/h	μF	

Spaced

AD 1605	initials, e.g. D. H. Lawrence	20 000
at. wt	*loc. cit.*	3 : 8 (ratio: equal space either side of colon)
c. 1800	mol. wt	
cos φ	n. 5	9 ft/s
et al.	*op. cit.*	5 mm
et seq.	p. 22	8 a.m.
fig. 23	6 per cent (but 6%)	400 BC
fl. oz	sp. gr.	25 °C
	vol. 2	15° N
		56 v ff. (v = verso; space about one-ninth of an em in both places)

6.1.3 **List of abbreviations**

If the book contains several unfamiliar abbreviations that appear from time to time, so that the reader may have forgotten the full form, it is probably sensible to compile a list of abbreviations. If the author does this, see that the list contains all the unfamiliar abbreviations, that the abbreviations tally with the usage in the text, and that they are in alphabetical order. Delete any unnecessary items, such as SI units or symbols for chemical elements in high-level works, or abbreviations you decided to spell out.

If the abbreviations are used in both text and footnotes, the most useful place for the list is at the end of the preliminary pages; but some authors prefer to list bibliographical abbreviations at the beginning of the bibliography.

6.2

BIAS AND PAROCHIALISMS

This is a sensitive area and one where strong opinions may be held by individual authors and by publishers. We should be alert to different kinds of bias and parochialism, but should be careful not to impose our own preferences against the wishes of the other parties. Social attitudes and linguistic conventions in this area have changed significantly over recent years and are still evolving, but there is still quite a wide variation in practice. If you discern a major problem, discuss it with the commissioning editor before tackling either the typescript or the author. What follows tries to represent the current consensus in Britain.

6.2.1 **Bias**

Bias can be shown both in the situation portrayed and by the words used (or not used). In particular in textbook writing and certain kinds of creative writing (for example, for children) one should be careful to treat people as people; and no race, class, sex or age group should be stereotyped or arbitrarily given a leading or secondary role. The sort of thing to look out for is:

- Does the text show women, members of racial minorities, disabled people and so on in a wide range of jobs and at all levels, for example as doctors, specialists and managers, as well as nurses, secretaries, shop assistants and unskilled workers?

- Are both girls and boys shown as interested in, say, mathematics, science, mechanical skills, poetry, cooking and sewing?
- Is each person seen and portrayed as a human being, with a full range of attributes, with both men and women showing traits such as sensitivity, logic and initiative? Or are men praised only in terms of job status and money, and women only in terms of looks, number of children or relationship to a man (housewife, working wife, wife of Henry Smith)?
- Do the illustrations avoid this sort of bias, as well as the text?

A good way to look for inadvertent bias in a seemingly neutral statement of fact is to substitute, say, a member of a different race, or a man for a woman, and see whether the statement still reads as neutral:

The new head of the planning department	
is a woman, Mrs Blanche Smith	is a man, Mr John Smith
is Mrs Blanche Smith, whose husband is Professor of Gerontology	is Mr John Smith, whose wife is Professor of Gerontology
is an Asian, Mr Sayed Kasim	is an Englishman, Mr John Smith
is John Smith, formerly Planning Officer with Elchester City Council	is Blanche Smith/Sayed Kasim, formerly Planning Officer with Elchester City Council

Only the fourth of these statements would sound natural, whichever of the three people was involved. Of course the context affects this. It may be that the writer of the first three is celebrating or emphasizing the fact that a woman or a member of a cultural minority has been appointed at this level; to change the text would then be to change the intended meaning.

6.2.2 **Inclusive language**

In their notes for authors many publishers ask authors to use inclusive language and to be careful to avoid bias. Some authors will nevertheless write as they have always written, using 'he' as a neutral pronoun, and in some cases the publisher will not wish to impose a change. If there is a general issue here, it may be better for the commissioning editor to raise the question with the author in the first instance. One should anyway send the author examples of the kind of change one proposes. The author may be willing and able to make the necessary changes, and since rewording is often the best solution, it is obviously best that the author should be the one to do this.

I recommend Casey Miller and Kate Swift's *The Handbook of Non-Sexist Writing for Writers, Editors and Speakers* (2nd British edn, London, Women's Press, 1989), which covers problems that some authors at least may not be conscious of, and suggests solutions.

Inclusive language which draws attention to itself as such will distract the reader; the aim should be unobtrusiveness.

6.2.3 Neutral nouns

See that words that in theory are neutral are used neutrally. Some examples of non-neutral use are:

> Authors usually dedicate their books to their wives.
> My next-door neighbour is a Canadian who is in England for a year with his wife and children.
> woman author, male nurse

'Man' and its compounds can usually be replaced without resorting to 'person-'. The exact choice of word will depend on the context, but here are some examples:

man, Man	*could become*	people, we, human beings, etc.
to man		to staff
mankind		the human race
man-hours		work-hours
man-made fibre		artificial/synthetic fibre
manpower		staff, workforce, human resources, etc.

6.2.4 Inclusive pronouns

Where 'he' or 'his' appears only once, 'he or she' or 'his or her' can be substituted or the noun repeated. In some cases the sentence may be recast in the plural or reworded to eliminate the pronoun altogether:

> when the author returns his corrected proof

could become

> when the author returns his or her corrected proof
> when authors return their corrected proofs
> when the author returns the corrected proof

In certain contexts 'we', or 'you' can be substituted:

> If a diner is dissatisfied with the service in a restaurant, he should
> complain to the manager.

could become

> If we are [*or* you are, one is] dissatisfied with the service in a restaurant,
> we [*or* you, one] should complain to the manager.

or

> A diner who is dissatisfied with the service in a restaurant should
> complain to the manager.

When one is talking about the interaction of two individuals, for example a parent and a child or a copy-editor and an author, rewording can be more difficult; each case must be looked at individually.

Robert Burchfield has pointed out:

> The pronouns they, them, and themselves have been employed since the
> 15th century (by Caxton, Shakespeare, Fielding, Chesterfield, Charlotte
> Yonge, Bernard Shaw, and others), as the OED expresses it, 'in reference
> to a singular noun made universal by *every, any, no*, etc., or applicable to
> one of either sex (= "he or she")'.
>
> It produces an unavoidable clash of number . . . but one that has the
> support of some of our greatest writers.
> (*Sunday Times*, 5 November 1989)

An example where 'they' provides the simplest, clearest solution is:

> Each author presented an evening of readings from their own work.

However, many authors regard this clash of number as wrong, so do not introduce it without the author's approval.

Most people regard it as an inelegant and unacceptable solution to use 's/he', 'he or she' (repeatedly), or 'he' and 'she' in alternate chapters.

One should remember too that in certain historical, cultural or social contexts 'he' or 'she' is in fact the only correct pronoun: before a certain date (which differs according to the country) a voter was always 'he'; and in a society described by an anthropologist all the marriage brokers may be women.

6.2.5 **Parochialisms**

For simplicity, this section is written purely from a British standpoint, but of course the same principles apply, whichever country one is in.

When you are copy-editing information books, think of readers in other countries. Alter 'this country' to 'Britain', 'our' (where appropriate) to 'British', 'the Great War' to 'the First World War', 'the [last] war' to 'the Second World War', 'in the last few years' or 'recently' to 'the early 1990s' or whatever is appropriate. For the correct use of 'Britain', 'UK', etc., see 'Specific forms' on p. 149.

Spell proper names correctly, e.g. Pearl Harbor, Lincoln Center, Australian Labor Party.

If textbooks, particularly school books, contain many references to cricket, petrol, British money, radio and television programmes, etc., consider whether they should be changed to make the book more suitable for use overseas; educational authorities, naturally enough, prefer books that are related to the children's everyday life. Similarly references in prefaces to sixth forms, GCSE, etc., may need to be amplified to show that the book will fit into other educational systems, and how it will do so.

In other books American or British terms may be kept unless they are likely to cause confusion. Watch out for words that have different meanings in the two languages, as, for example:

	American	*British*
to protest	to protest against	to protest that something is true, e.g. to protest one's innocence
to slate	to put on a list, e.g. for promotion	to criticize severely
to table	to set aside a motion, rather than discuss it	to put a motion down for discussion

One guide to differences in terminology is Norman Schur, *British English, A to Zed* (Oxford, Facts on File, 1987).

Leave American or British turns of phrase, provided the sense is clear. One particularly confusing usage is 'every other', so change

> This should be done every other week.

to

> This should be done every second week.

'Quite' can be ambiguous too, as – particularly in British English – it can mean 'moderately' as well as 'wholly'; make sure the sense is clear.

Avoid abbreviations or slang which may be meaningless outside the United Kingdom: it is easy to notice unfamiliar or unintelligible terms and abbreviations from other countries, but you will need to think whether such terms as LSE or 'tube' will be clear to overseas readers.

If one is talking about something unaffected by the season, it is better to give a month or say 'early in 1987' rather than use a phrase like 'in the spring of 1987', as spring in the Southern Hemisphere is at a different time of year.

6.3

CAPITALIZATION

Many authors have strong feelings about capitalization, so follow their system if they have a sensible one. If their usage is inconsistent or unhelpful, suggest an alternative system, giving specific examples. If you do introduce a system yourself, it is easy to be led, by the thought of 'consistency', into having too many capitals or too few. For example, if House has to be capitalized, to show that it is the House of Commons, this does not mean that government, prime minister and all other associated words must have an initial capital.

If the system is an unusual one, outline it on your style sheet for the typesetter and proofreader.

Titles and ranks

Titles and ranks are nearly always capitalized when they accompany a personal name, e.g. 'King John'; they may or may not be capitalized when they are used in place of a personal name, e.g. 'the king'; they are rarely capitalized when they refer to the rank and not a particular person, and then only if they are preceded by 'the', e.g. 'all kings', 'a king', but 'the King would be bound by the laws of . . .'

Administrative posts can be tricky, though in context no one is likely to be confused by 'the foreign secretary', 'the first secretary', 'the minister'.

Institutions, movements, denominations, political parties

'Church' is often lower case except when part of a title such as Roman Catholic Church. Similarly 'state' is usually lower case except in books on political theory or in references to federal systems, where state may be the province and State the nation-state.

Parliament is often lower case, but Commons, Lords and House are capitalized to avoid ambiguity.

Protestant, Catholic, etc., are usually capitalized. Radical/radical, Liberal/liberal, Democrat/democrat, etc., can be a problem: if you cannot easily tell which meaning is intended, tell the author that you will ask the typesetter to follow the typescript; this gives the author a nudge to check the usage or to tell you that no distinction was intended.

Periods, events, etc.

The names of geological and historical periods (e.g. Carboniferous Period, Iron Age, Dark Ages) and wars are usually capitalized.

Genera and species

Generic names have an initial capital, but species epithets do not, e.g. *Viola tricolor*. (See also section 13.5.1.)

Geographical names

North, south, etc., are capitalized if they are part of the title of an area or a political division, e.g. South West Africa, Western Australia, the West, but not if they are descriptions in general terms, e.g. southern Scotland, the south of Scotland.

Astronomical names
In science books sun, moon and earth may be capitalized (see section 13.4.4).

Trade names
Makes of car and other products are capitalized, e.g. a Jaguar. Even though some trade names are now used as common nouns, proprietors insist on a capital for their product, e.g. Xerox, Kleenex, Thermos. Common proprietary names are identified in dictionaries, and it may be better to substitute another term, e.g. photocopy for Xerox, (paper) tissue for Kleenex, vacuum flask for Thermos. Watch out for proprietary names of drugs. It is not necessary to put any of these names in quotes.

Book, journal and article titles
See pp. 234–7.

Cross-references
Be consistent in your use of capital or lower case for chapter, table, figure, etc., when referring to them by number ('see chapter 7').

6.3.1 **Use of small capitals**

Small capitals are often used for AD, BC, except with lining figures, where small capitals would look too small: AD 1990. In the USA they are used for a.m. and p.m. Small capitals are also used for quoted words originally in capitals and for most capitalized roman numbers, e.g. vol. XII, though full capitals are always used in titles such as Henry VII and for LXX (Septuagint). Some authors type lower-case roman numbers to indicate small capitals rather than full capitals; ask the author if you are not sure what is required.

Full capitals should be used for musical keys, for example Suite in F minor.

Ask the designer whether small capitals should be marked within italic, bold and sans serif, as true small capitals may not be available, and the designer may consider the simulated version (e.g. sloped roman small capitals or a smaller size of full italic capitals) unsatisfactory.

Although subscript capitals are small in size, they should be marked as full capitals and not small capitals.

6.4

CROSS-REFERENCES

'Figure' and 'plate' are often abbreviated in references in parentheses and footnotes, but spelt out in the text; 'chapter' and 'appendix' are usually abbreviated only in footnotes; 'section' may be replaced by a section mark (§) and equations may be referred to either in full or as '(6.3.3)', the parentheses distinguishing it from a section number; 'table' is never abbreviated. Be consistent in using a lower case (or capital) initial for *all* these words.

Use pp., ff., not p., f., if more than one page is referred to (see section 6.1.1). Where there are also references to pages of other books, it may be clearer for the reader if internal cross-references are followed by 'above' or 'below'.

Unless the cross-reference is to a whole section, a page number is more useful to the reader than a section number. However, the page number would have to be inserted at proof stage, which is expensive; if the book contains a large number of cross-references, warn the production department and see that the insertion of the cross-references is allowed for in the original estimate and not charged against the author's correction allowance. It may save a little money if you can leave space for approximately the right number of digits, changing 'pp. 000' to 'pp. 000–00'. If the relevant folio numbers are used in the cross-references, change the digits to zeros or bullets, to remind the author to fill in the page numbers on the proof; write the folio numbers in the margin, to help locate the passage later.

Try to check that the author uses 'see' and 'cf.' (compare) correctly; many people use 'cf.' when they really mean 'see'.

Footnotes
If there are many cross-references to notes, it is best to number the notes by chapter rather than by page; if they are to be numbered by page, change 'see n. 75' to 'see p. 000, n. 0'.

If the typescript contains a great many cross-references to section numbers, the section number should appear in the running head. (See section 9.4.4 for running heads to endnotes.)

6.5

DATES AND TIME

6.5.1 **Dates**

In non-fiction keep dates simple: 1 May, 1 May 1991, May 1991. The American style is May 1, May 1, 1991, and May, 1991, with or without a comma after the year. If you do change the American to the British style, see whether the comma after the year is needed to punctuate the sentence, and leave or delete it accordingly.

If several dates within one month are given, so that it would be clumsy to give the month each time, say 'on the 12th'.

Decades are best expressed as 1960s (not 1960's or '60s) or thirties (not 'thirties). Century numbers are usually spelt out: the fourteenth century (adjective fourteenth-century). Some authors prefer to hyphenate 'mid-fourteenth' in the noun 'mid fourteenth century', even though there is no such century; others prefer to omit the first hyphen in the adjective 'early-fourteenth-century'.

Pairs of dates are usually elided to the shortest pronounceable form – 1971–4, 1970–5 (or 1970–75), but 1914–18, 1798–1810 – with the following exceptions. BC dates cannot usually be elided, because 25–1 BC means something different from 25–21 BC, though a year of office may be given in the form 49/8 BC. Pairs of dates are usually left in full in the book title (the titles of other books should not be altered, of course), so as to provide a balanced title page; and the same may apply to chapter and other headings. If an author consistently elides to the last two digits (1974–76) you may decide to retain that system.

Depending on the readership of the book, it may be sensible to give pairs of days in full: 24–8 May has been read to mean 24 (April) until 8 May.

Where a single year, such as a financial year, comprises parts of two calendar years, an oblique stroke is used (1971/2 or 1971/72). This leaves the en rule to indicate a period covering more than one year: 'the years 1945/6–1968/9'.

When talking of a stretch of time between two years, say 'from 1924 to 1928' or '1924–8', not 'from 1924–8'; similarly say 'between 1914 and 1918', not 'between 1914–18'. 'To' may also be better than an en rule if each date contains more than one element:

18 September to 19 January	*rather than*	18 September–19 January
c. 1215 to *c*. 1260		*c*. 1215–*c*. 1260

or a spaced rule may be used if there are no parenthetical dashes nearby with which it could be confused.

One should try to avoid starting a sentence with a figure, especially if it is a non-lining figure and so resembles a lower-case letter; one may have to turn the sentence round, for example changing '1971 was an important year' to 'The year 1971 was [an] important [one].'

Names of months may be abbreviated in tables and footnotes, but use names rather than numbers because 5.4.75 means 5 April in Britain, 4 May in the USA. The International Organization for Standardization lays down that if numbers only are used, they should be in the order: year, month, day, for example 12 January 1991 would be written 1991–01–12, with hyphens or en rules between the numbers.

AD and BC need be used only where there is any likelihood of confusion. AD and AH (*anno Hegirae*, used in Islamic dates; see appendix 11) precede the year number, though when used loosely, as in 'fifth century AD', they follow the date. BC, BP (before the present, taken to be 1950) and CE (Christian era or common era) follow the date. (For the use of small capitals see pp. 121–2.) Lower-case bp, bc or ad is used to indicate a radiocarbon date that has not been recalibrated. Though there are usually no commas in dates, BP dates do have a comma or space when they consist of five or more digits, e.g. 13,500 BP. (For geological dates see section 13.8.)

In England until 1752 the legal year began on 25 March, so the year 1673 comprised what we would now call 25 March 1673 to 24 March 1674. The dates between 1 January and 24 March are therefore often given in the form 23 March 1673/4. If the author gives only one year number it should be made clear in the preliminary pages whether the contemporary system or the modern one is being followed.

The Gregorian calendar was introduced in 1582, but the Julian calendar remained in use in England until 1752. The Gregorian (New Style) calendar was ten days ahead of the Julian (Old Style) calendar from 1582 to 1600, eleven days ahead from 1601 to 1699 and twelve days ahead from 1700 to 1752. The author should say in a note whether New Style or Old Style dates are being used, or should identify them 'NS' or 'OS', or give both, e.g. 11/21 October 1599, 25 October/6 November 1709. In Russia the Gregorian calendar did not come into use until 1918 (1 February 1918, Old Style, became 14 February, New Style).

In books dealing with Islam consider whether the book should give Islamic as well as Christian dates, and which should be given first; the two dates usually have an oblique stroke between them. Similarly with books on Judaism.

Change vague references that will soon become misleading: 'in the last ten years', 'recently', and so on should be changed to 'in the 1980s', 'since 1990' or whatever is appropriate.

6.5.2 Time

Time is treated in the same way as other quantities: words are used for periods of time such as 'it took him six months', figures for exact measurements and for series of numbers. Use figures in 8.0 a.m., words in eight o'clock, no hyphen in half past eight. With the 24-hour clock use 19.45 to avoid confusion with years. Remember that 12.0 noon is neither a.m. nor p.m., as these mean 'before noon' and 'after noon'.

A hyphen is usual in 'a five-minute start', an apostrophe in 'five minutes' start'. Apostrophes of this kind are often omitted from proper names such as Hundred Years War, but they should be retained elsewhere.

For astronomy see section 13.4.3.

6.6

FOREIGN LANGUAGES

Hart's Rules are a good guide on difficult points, and *The Chicago Manual of Style* also has a useful chapter on foreign languages. This section merely warns you of some common pitfalls.

Foreign-language material falls into three categories:

1 Texts for people who know or are learning the language. Such material will be in the original characters, or, if transliterated, will usually contain all diacritical marks. Foreign conventions such as *guillemets* (« ») are likely to be retained except in elementary books.

2 Foreign proper names and technical terms in a book to be read by people who may not know the language. Words from non-Roman alphabets will usually be transliterated; and some or all diacritical marks may be omitted from European languages other than French, German and Italian. Foreign words in an English sentence should be in the nominative form:

> he was Director of the Institut für angewandte Sozialwissenschaft

unless a different case is necessitated by a word within the foreign phrase:

> to form the ARD (Arbeitsgemeinschaft der öffentlichrechtlichen Rundfunkanstalten Deutschlands)

In German words, ü etc. are preferred to ue etc. where appropriate, and German nouns should retain their initial capital if they are italicized. For the use of italic, and of English plural forms, see section 6.7.1.

3 Tables, figures, maps, etc., borrowed by an author from books or journal articles in another language. Not only should the wording be translated, but such conventions as *guillemets* and decimal commas should be anglicized.

Alphabetical order. See section 8.2.2.

Marking the typescript. All the desired accents and ligatures must be shown in the typescript and listed for the designer so that the appropriate typesetter can be chosen.

When the Scandinavian ø or the Polish ł are required, make it clear that these are letters with strokes across them and are not deleted.

Arabic

In transliterated Arabic the author may represent both ʿ*ain* and *hamza* by a typewritten single quote, but they must be clearly distinguished for the typesetter. Some authors type a raised c for an ʿ*ain*, leaving the vertical quote for the *hamza*. There are special sorts, but the ʿ*ain* is often represented by an opening quote or a Greek rough breathing, the *hamza* by a closing quote or smooth breathing. Because of this use of single quotes, double quotes should be used for quotations in books containing much transliterated Arabic.

Chinese

Many westerners have now adopted the Pinyin system of romanization in place of the Wade–Giles system; but the old spelling of some familiar names is often retained, particularly where the Pinyin version gives a very different pronunciation, e.g. Beijing for Peking. Ask the commissioning editor whether Chinese words are, or should be, romanized according to the Pinyin system.

French

Accents may be omitted from capitals and small capitals, provided the author approves and the book is consistent. Some typesetters prefer not to accent capital A even if other capitals have accents.

A French government working party has recommended that circumflexes should be omitted from many words, but retained when they may help to distinguish, say, *mûr* from *mur*. Opinion is divided, so consult the author and your publisher before deleting them yourself.

Accents and ligatures were not always used in medieval texts, so do not add them without asking the author; but any ligatures that are wanted must be marked for the typesetter.

For capitalization of book titles see p. 242 below.

In surnames and place names 'Saint' and 'Sainte' are normally spelt out and followed by a hyphen.

German

All nouns have capitals, and words are sometimes letterspaced for emphasis. If the author wishes ß (called *Eszett*) to be used for ss, every occurrence must be marked, because not every ss becomes ß. In capitals or small capitals ß always becomes SS. For ligatures see *Hart's Rules* (39th edn, pp. 104, 108).

In pre-1900 works one may meet ue, oe, Th (for T) and variations in capitalization.

There are various ways of indicating quotations. If *guillemets* are used, they usually point inwards (» «).

Greek
See section 14.1.

Latin
See section 14.1.

Russian
The Russian alphabet can be found in appendix 5. Consult the author as to whether any sloping Cyrillic is to be used; if so, see that it is clearly marked on the typescript.

Turkish
Note that Turkish employs an undotted i as well as a dotted one.

6.7

ITALIC

Italic is used for:

- titles of published books, except for the Bible, the Koran and books of the Bible, which are roman without quotes. Titles of chapters, articles, short stories and unpublished theses are roman in quotes. Preface etc. are roman without quotes
- titles of periodicals; but article titles are roman and usually in quotes except in the author–date system (see p. 257). For use of roman 'the' or italic '*The*' in periodical titles see p. 236
- titles of long poems which are virtually books in themselves, e.g. *Paradise Lost*; but titles of short poems are roman in quotes. (See also p. 235)
- titles of plays and films, radio and television programmes
- titles of major musical works such as operas, oratorios, ballets and song cycles given descriptive titles by the composer; but roman in quotes for nicknames given by other people, e.g. Beethoven's 'Pastoral' Symphony, and for the titles of songs. Roman without quotes for titles such as Symphony No. 5 in C minor
- titles of paintings and sculptures
- names of ships, apart from such prefixes as HMS (HMS *Repulse*);

but types of ship, aircraft and car are roman (a Spitfire, a Rolls-Royce)

- genera, species and varieties; but genera mentioned in the plural (e.g. staphylococci) or in a general way (e.g. 'illness caused by a staphylococcus') are roman and lower case. Orders, families, etc., are roman
- mathematical variables (including geometrical 'points' and generalized constants such as constants of integration); but operators and chemical elements are roman
- foreign phrases, not yet naturalized, in an English sentence; but roman for proper names such as institutions and streets, and roman in quotes for foreign quotations
- names of parties in legal cases (see section 14.2.4), but v. between them is roman
- directions to the reader, e.g. *see also* in an index, or *above* in a caption; also stage directions in plays
- identification of letters or words referred to, e.g. 'the letter *h*'; alternatively roman, with or without quotes, may be used
- emphasis, but it should be used sparingly. Authors of textbooks may italicize a phrase near the beginning of a paragraph, as a kind of subheading. Or they may italicize technical terms when they are first used; if so, they should not use italic for other kinds of emphasis as well

Italic should not be used for the names of Acts of Parliament, for hotels, theatres, pubs, etc., or for possessive s following an italic word (unless the italic is being used for emphasis), e.g. 'the *Discovery*'s home port', 'it was *the butler's* fingerprint'.

6.7.1 Foreign words and phrases

In general books keep italic to a minimum; in novels, for example, it can look very self-conscious, and any foreign words used are probably proper names or anglicized words, which would not be italic anyway.

In more specialized books italic may be used for foreign words (except the names of persons, institutions, places, etc.) in an English sentence, but not usually for foreign quotations. Some authors italicize foreign words only the first time they occur; this is an acceptable system, provided there are no foreign words that may be momentarily mistaken for English ones, e.g. *place* (French 'square') or *Land* (German 'region'). Of course, if the author is using italic for another purpose, say to indicate words of linguistic interest, other foreign words should not be italicized.

It is sometimes difficult to know where to draw the line between italic and roman: for example, if *louis d'or* is italic and franc is not (because it is now part of the English language) the author may complain of inconsistency. Most authors follow the general usage in their subject; some follow the *Concise Oxford Dictionary*. I think *The Oxford Dictionary for Writers and Editors* (now also published as the *Oxford Writers' Dictionary*) is a better guide.

If a foreign word is italicized, it should have the correct accents; it should be in the masculine or feminine form, as appropriate:

her *protégée* looked *distraite*

The word should probably be in the nominative:

his parents received a *blaue Brief,* a warning letter written in blue

unless it is within quotes. If it is roman it does not matter whether the word has an accent or not (or whether it agrees in gender), provided the author is consistent. It is usual to include the accents where they help to show the pronunciation, as in the third syllable of protégé; but if one accent is included, all must be: protégé not protege.

Roman is used for i.e. and e.g., and sometimes for ibid. and op. cit.

Plurals

Look at the author's use of native or English plurals for foreign words used in an English sentence: the plural form in some languages looks like a different word from the singular, and in such cases it would be better to use the English plural ending. Plural s is usually italic even if it is not strictly the plural form of the foreign word, e.g. *qanats*.

Explanation of foreign words

If the author uses a lot of foreign words, for example Indian terms for castes, ceremonies, etc., a glossary may be needed.

6.7.2 **In headings**

Where headings or running heads are in small capitals or italic, foreign words and titles of books etc. – which would normally be in italic – are sometimes put in quotes. This tends to give foreign words a self-conscious look; and it may be better to omit the quotes even though the word is italic in the text. In some books, words that are italicized in the text are set roman within italic headings.

6.7.3 **Italic punctuation**

Italic punctuation should be used only within an italic phrase, not before or after it:

In *Camilla: or a Picture of Youth*, Fanny Burney portrays . . .
The best-known case, *Smith* v. *Jones*, raises an interesting point of law

Where an italic subheading ends with a colon, the colon is regarded as part of the heading.

6.8

MEASUREMENTS

In science and mathematics books SI (Système International d'Unités) units are now normally used (see section 13.3). The basic SI units are:

Physical quantity	Name of SI unit	Symbol
length	metre	m
mass	kilogram	kg
time	second	s
electric current	ampere	A
thermodynamic temperature	kelvin	K
luminous intensity	candela	cd
amount of substance	mole	mol

In historical works it may be best to leave the imperial measurements and provide a conversion table in the preliminary pages.

In other books metric measurements should be added to or substituted for imperial ones. It may be necessary to ask the author how accurate the measurements are: for example, must 100 yards have an exact equivalent or an approximate round number?

Remember that abbreviated units of measurement, whether metric or imperial, have no full point and take no s in the plural: 52 kg, for example.

MONEY

If whole pounds or dollars appear in the same context as fractional amounts, they should be treated in a similar way, e.g. '£6.00, £5.25 and £0.25', not '£6, £5.25 and 25p'. Do not use £ and p or $ and ¢ in the same expression. You may need to distinguish between currencies that have the same denomination, for example US$ and A$.

Pre-decimal British money should be in the form:

£6 *or* £6 os od	£6 5s *or* £6 5s od
5s *or* 5s od	£6 5s 4d
4d	5s 4d

In the past s and d were italic with points, but now they are more often in the same style as p (roman with no point); if you do include points, do not include one after the £ digit. Except in quotations, substitute 5s for 5/-, 5s 6d for 5/6. Where sums are grouped in the text, treat them consistently, but note that £0 is never used and os is used only if there is a £ digit; so £6 os od, 6s od and 6d are consistent.

In historical works where terms such as guinea are used throughout, an explanatory note may be needed in the prelims; but if such terms are used only once or twice, it may be best to explain them where they occur.

Indian rupees can be given either in millions (Rs. 1,000,000) or in lakhs (Rs. 100,000, written Rs. 1,00,000) or crores (Rs. 10,000,000, written Rs. 1,00,00,000). If the editor wishes to retain lakhs or crores, see that the notation is explained in the preliminary pages; and warn the typesetter and proofreader on your style sheet.

Where sums of money are tabulated, it is best to put the units in the column heading rather than beside each item (see fig. 9.2, p. 218).

6.10

NUMBERS

For science and mathematics books see chapter 13.

'Numeral' and 'figure'
To some typesetters 'numeral' means a roman numeral; they use 'figure' to mean an arabic numeral. To avoid possible misunderstanding, it is best not to use 'numeral' on its own where you are referring to a number to be set in arabic.

6.10.1 Old style (non-lining) and lining figures

Old style or non-lining figures have ascenders and descenders and look right with small capitals:

0 1 2 3 4 5 6 7 8 9

They are easier to read in large groups (for example in tables); but they have the disadvantage that the 'one' in most typefaces looks like a small-capital roman 'one'. This can be confusing in bibliographical references, where arabic eleven (11) and roman two (II) may be confused. Another complication is that most mathematical superscripts and subscripts are lining, and authors of books that contain them feel that it is a bad thing to use two 'ones' that look so different. Also non-lining figures next to full capitals can look at first glance like subscripts: $3T_3$.

Lining figures are usually the same height as full capitals and so align well with them.

0 1 2 3 4 5 6 7 8 9

Only one kind of figure is used in a book, with a few exceptions: as I have just mentioned, superscripts and subscripts in mathematics are nearly always lining figures; also the designer will ask for lining figures to be used in headings set in full capitals, and for non-lining figures to be used in headings set in small capitals. Point out any headings and running heads that contain arabic figures, and any other potential problems.

6.10.2 **Ambiguous numbers**

Distinguish capital O and zero, l and 1, roman and arabic one. Avoid the abbreviation ll. (lines) if lining figures are to be used. See that any handwritten figures are legible and unambiguous; for example the Continental 1 can be read as a 7, and some American 4s can be read as 7s. The word 'billion' should be avoided or clarified: in Britain it used to mean a million million; in the USA, and increasingly in British and Australian usage, it means a thousand million. Ask the author, if it is not clear.

6.10.3 **Words or figures**

Most publishers use words for small numbers (usually those below 10, 12 or 100), except for exact measurements, cross-references and series of quantities; where numbers in the same paragraph fall below and above the chosen limit, use figures for both: 'between the ages of 10 and 15', not 'ten and 15'. Round numbers above the chosen figure may be expressed in words when they are not part of a series. Where there is a series of round millions 2m or 2m. is often used; with a pound or dollar sign, 2 million may also be used. In financial reports one finds 25k for 25,000.

Where two series of quantities are being discussed, e.g. numbers of wards and numbers of beds, it may be clearer if words are used for one series of quantities: 'ten wards held 16 beds each, but fifteen others contained as many as 40'.

Spelt-out numbers such as twenty-one are hyphenated. Use figures to avoid a hyphen in an already hyphenated compound: '62-year-old man', not 'sixty-two-year-old man'.

One should try to avoid starting a sentence with figures, especially if they are non-lining and so resemble lower-case letters. If the number cannot be spelt out one may have to turn the sentence round.

Figures must be used before abbreviations: 5 kg, 6%.

6.10.4 **Commas in thousands**

In science and mathematics books there is usually no comma in thousands. Numbers with five or more digits either side of the decimal point have a space: 8478 but 84 782, 782.689 52. However, in a table containing both four-figure and five-figure numbers, the four-figure numbers must be spaced too, in order to align.

Authors of general books usually include a comma in numbers with four or more (or five or more) digits. If four-figure numbers have no comma in the text, you will need to add one in tables where four-digit numbers must align with five-digit ones.

Commas and spaces are not used in dates (except for BP dates), in line numbers or in many reference numbers, where one should follow the usage of the issuing authority.

6.10.5 **Decimal points**

Say whether decimal points should be low (on the line) or medial (raised). The low point is usually used in science and mathematics books. Where the author has borrowed, say, a French or German table or diagram, change the decimal commas to points.

The decimal point should normally be preceded by a digit; add a zero where the author has no digit before the point, except in quantities that never reach 1 (such as levels of probability) and ballistics. Do not add zeros after a decimal point to give a consistent number of digits.

6.10.6 **Percentages**

Percentages are usually given in figures, whether per cent or % is used; but if the percentages are not exact ones they may be spelt out if followed by per cent. In some cases per cent is used in the main text, and % in tables and footnotes (or in tables only). Although per cent is an abbreviation, it takes no full point; it should be roman, not italic; and for Americans it is one word.

Make sure that percentages are distinguished from actual numbers in tables. Do not worry if percentages do not add up to exactly 100; the individual percentages are usually rounded up or down, and the total should fall between 99 and 101, though given as 100.

6.10.7   **Elision of pairs of numbers**

Page numbers. In Britain, page numbers are elided as far as possible except for 11 to 19 in each hundred, which retain the 'tens' digit: 21–4, 130–5, but 211–15. Some publishers prefer to repeat the 'tens' if the first number ends in zero: 130–35.

In the USA page numbers are often elided to the last two digits, unless the tens digit is a zero; e.g. 61–78, 121–24, 1121–24, but 100–108, 106–8. If the author's system is consistent and easy to follow, it is probably not worth changing.

Measurements, such as length, temperature, wavelength, latitude and longitude, percentages, should not be elided, because it is possible to use a descending scale as well as an ascending one: 21–2 might mean 21 to 22 or 21 to 2. Where an author consistently elides such pairs of numbers it will probably not be worth changing them unless elision really does lead to ambiguity.

Dates. See section 6.5.1.

Figures interspersed with letters cannot be elided, for example folio numbers which are followed by 'verso' or 'recto' (fos. 22v–24r) or numbers preceded by '*circa*' (*c.* 1215 to *c.* 1260).

Roman numbers should not be elided.

Other numbers, such as population, amounts of money, etc., are probably best treated according to the author's system. See that the author does not say 2–3,000 to mean 2,000–3,000 if there is any chance of ambiguity.

6.10.8   **En rule between numbers**

See section 6.12.1

6.10.9   **Roman numbers**

Full capitals are used for titles such as Henry VII and for LXX (Septuagint); such numbers should not be followed by a full point (except, of course, at the end of a sentence). Small capitals (if available) are used for most other capitalized roman numbers, for example volume numbers, unless these occur in combination with lining figures. Lower case is used for preliminary page numbers and such things as scene numbers in drama references which contain two roman numbers that need to be distinguished. Some authors type lower-case roman numbers to indicate small capitals rather than full capitals; ask the author if you are not sure what is required.

6.10.10 Numbered items within paragraphs

Within a paragraph a number with just a closing parenthesis can be ambiguous:

> This should contain 1) author's initials or forename, followed by 2) author's surname, 3) title of article

It is better to use the form (1), etc.

6.10.11 Numbers and letters

Combinations of figures and letters (except units of measurement) are often unspaced: 2a, 17ff., 8n. See table 6.1 on p. 124.

6.11

PROPER NAMES

The names of foreign persons, places, institutions, etc., should not be italicized (except in italic headings).

Consistent forms – native or anglicized
If foreign names appear in the text or as places of publication, check that the author consistently uses either the anglicized form (if any) or the native form of each. It is easy to miss forenames that are inconsistently anglicized.

In books intended for readers who do not know the original language, some or all diacritical marks may be omitted from native forms if there is no anglicized form. As French, German and Italian are widely known, accents are usually retained; for books about other countries, ask the author to add accents to proper names if necessary.

There may be more than one correct form of a place name, e.g. Basle, Basel. *The Oxford Dictionary for Writers and Editors* gives preferred forms of a number of these; but if an author consistently uses one of the other forms, ask before changing the spelling.

Rees, *Rules of Printed English*, 256, gives a list of geographical names showing their forms in various languages.

Specific forms

Use United States rather than America(n), wherever there is any possibility of ambiguity. Similarly England, Great Britain (England, Scotland and Wales), the United Kingdom (Great Britain and Northern Ireland), the British Isles (United Kingdom plus the Irish Republic) should be used accurately.

Note that Holland is, strictly speaking, only the name of two provinces of the Netherlands: Noord-Holland and Zuid-Holland.

Up-to-date forms

Watch for out-of-date names, particularly for newly independent countries, though of course one should normally use contemporary rather than modern names in historical works, for example St Petersburg in a book about nineteenth-century Russia, but Leningrad in one about the Second World War.

If, say, African place names have to be brought up to date, ask the author to do it, for it is not only the names of countries that have been changed; some towns and natural features have different names as well, and it is more difficult to find out the up-to-date forms.

Some common mistakes

Use Habsburg	*not* Hapsburg
Hong Kong	Hongkong
Cape Town	Capetown
Nuremberg	Nuremburg
The Johns Hopkins University	John Hopkins University
Western Australia	West Australia

See Rees, *Rules of Printed English*, 303, for some personal titles which differ slightly in spelling from place names.

Don't be misled by the stressed syllable into misspelling

Apennines Caribbean Philippines

Prefixes such as de, von, van
Except in anglicized names such prefixes are usually lower case (except, of course, at the beginning of a sentence).

French names
Do not abbreviate Saint and Sainte in surnames and place names. They should be hyphenated to the following element: Sainte-Beuve.

Dutch names
's (abbreviated from 'des') and 't (abbreviated from 'het') should usually be preceded and followed by a space, though in names of towns such as 's-Gravenhage there is a hyphen; ij is treated as a compound letter and so both elements should be capitalized at the beginning of a proper noun.

Names of companies
Retain the ampersand, provided the author uses it consistently. Stet it so that the typesetter knows that it is not to be spelt out.

Inverted forms for bibliographies etc.
If you are inverting names to bring the surname to the beginning of the entry, there are one or two pitfalls. For example, unwesternized Japanese and Chinese names already have the surname first, and in Spanish and Portuguese names it may be the penultimate element that should come first, e.g. Federico Gutiérrez Granier should be under Gutiérrez, not Granier. An invaluable guide is *Names of Persons: National Usages for Entry in Catalogues* (3rd edn, London, International Federation of Library Associations, 1977).

6.12

_____

PUNCTUATION

Follow the author's system; if there is no system, use the minimum punctuation necessary to clarify what would otherwise be ambiguous or misleading. This section does not deal with general rules of punctuation (for those consult Carey, _Mind the Stop_). It attempts to cover points which may cause difficulty for new copy-editors; and as en rules cause most difficulty, it deals with those first.

6.12.1 **En rules**

An en rule is longer than a hyphen, and can be used either as a parenthetical dash or to convey a distinction in sense. Write 'N' or 'en' (ringed) above it, and make clear whether it is to be spaced or closed up: en rules for parenthetical dashes are always spaced, en rules for sense are usually closed up.

To convey a distinction in sense
En rules are used when the first part of a compound does not modify the meaning of the second part. They can usually be thought of as standing for 'and' or 'to'.
　En rules are used to mean 'and' in such phrases:

Bruno–Tyson fight
Labour–Liberal alliance
oil–water interface
gas–liquid chromatography
theocratic–military site
Urdu–Hindi issue
red–green colourblind (but hyphen in blue-green if it means bluish green)

Distinguish between 'the Bruce-Partington plans' (one person) and 'the Bruce–Partington plans' (two people).
　Although 'Sino-Japanese' and 'Chinese–Japanese' mean the same thing, it is usual to have a hyphen in the first (i.e. where the first part of the word is a prefix that cannot stand on its own) and an en rule in the

second. Hyphens are also used in such compounds as 1-chloro-3, 6-dimethylnaphthalene. Some people prefer an oblique stroke (solidus) in terms such as 'oil/water interface' or where one or more elements consist of more than one word, e.g. Bedford/Milton Keynes boundary.

The en rule should not replace 'and' if the word 'between' is used: say 'the period between 1920 and 1930', not 'the period between 1920–30'.

En rules are used to mean 'to' in such phrases as:

1914–18 war
pp. 1–20
London–Glasgow railway
input–output ratio

The en rule should not replace 'to' if the word 'from' is used: say 'from 1970 to 1976' not 'from 1970–6'.

It may be better to substitute 'to' for the rule if there are also hyphens in the compound: one could have '5–10 day interval', but if one wanted to hyphenate '10-day' it would be better to have '5- to 10-day interval'; similarly '10- to 14-year-olds' is better than '10–14-year-olds'.

En rules meaning 'to' and 'and' are usually unspaced: theocratic–military, chapters 8–9, 101–50. However, spaced en rules may be used between groups of numbers and words to avoid implying a closer relationship between the words or numbers next to the en rule than between each of these and the rest of its group:

6. 6–8	*but*	6. 6 – 7. 8
September–January		18 September – 19 January
1215–1260		*c.* 1215 – *c.* 1260

But these spaced en rules should be used cautiously, especially if there are also parenthetical dashes, as the reader may not be able to tell one from the other; and it may be better to substitute 'to' in such cases.

Parenthetical dashes

Spaced en rules are now most often used. If the dashes are unspaced in the typescript, put a space sign either side of each one (see p. 53). Unless the parenthetical phrase is at the end of a sentence, check that there is a pair of dashes – not one or three – and that the second one is correctly placed.

Other uses

An en rule with a space before it can be used to indicate that a speech breaks off abruptly (an ellipsis in such cases suggests a pause, rather than an interruption).

Use a hyphen rather than an en rule when the author is talking about parts of words, as in 'the prefixes pre- and post-'. Opinion is divided as to whether an en rule or a hyphen is a better way of symbolizing a missing letter in a word (if the author uses dashes rather than points).

6.12.2 **Em rules**

Unspaced em rules were commonly used for parenthetical dashes; but a spaced en rule is now usually employed (see above).

Em rules are sometimes used to introduce lines of dialogue, for example in James Joyce's stories and in some foreign texts; in such a system there is no sign to show where the speech ends, and it may be sensible to substitute quotation marks in a foreign-language reader for schools, to help the pupil.

Em rules may be used to indicate the omission of a word or part of a word:

> She was said to have had an affair with   that season.
> Would Mr T— consider taking responsibility?

If these have been typed low (with the key used for underlining), tell the typesetter they should be raised ('Centre on x height').

In indexes and bibliographies em rules may stand for a repeated entry heading or author's name (two rules being used for entry heading plus subentry heading, or for joint authors' names respectively), though many publishers prefer to use indention. If you use rules in an index, see that it will be clear to the reader exactly how much is represented by the rule.

Em rules are also used in tables (see p. 220).

6.12.3 **Hyphens**

Some subjects have a conventional usage, and some authors have strong views, so ask before imposing your own system. Introduce hyphens only to avoid ambiguity:

best known example	best-known example
deep blue sea	deep-blue sea
four year-old children	four-year-old children
little frequented place	little-frequented place

and do not feel that similar words must be treated 'consistently', e.g. lifebelt, life-jacket. *Hart's Rules* give lists that you may find helpful. American authors tend to use fewer hyphens than the British do. They may also write hyphens as double dashes like equals signs; warn the typesetter if you think there is likely to be confusion.

Look at any hyphens at the ends of lines in the typescript, and stet those that are to be retained if the lines are broken in different places.

Floating hyphens, as in 'sixteenth- and seventeenth-century architecture', 'pre- and postwar', may be avoided by rewording. If rewriting would lead to a clumsier sentence, see how many hyphens are in fact necessary. Sometimes the sense will be clear if the first hyphen is omitted; but in 'phosphorus- or sulphur-containing compounds' the sense would change. Sometimes a hyphen will have to be added to the second compound: 'pre- and postwar' is clear, but does 'nitro-' in 'nitro- or chlorophenylnaphthalene' mean nitrophenylnaphthalene or nitronaphthalene?

If you can, avoid ex- (former) qualifying more than one word, as in 'ex-public schoolboy'.

6.12.4 **Brackets**

To a typesetter the word 'brackets' signifies square brackets; round brackets are called 'parentheses' or 'parens'. The curly brackets that group items in a table are called 'braces'. For the conventional order of brackets in mathematics see p. 310.

Square brackets

Square brackets should be used to indicate words interpolated by the present author in quotations; the material within the square brackets does not affect the punctuation of the outer sentence. In editions of texts both square and angle brackets may be used (see section 11.5.8).

Square brackets may be used in bibliographies to enclose an author's name, publication place or date that does not appear in the publication cited. In such a case the entry may be punctuated as though the square brackets were not there:

> Geddes, D. *St Michael's Church, Amberley*. Arundel, Blathwayt Press, [1871]

For legal references see section 14.2.

If square brackets are used for interpolations, it could be misleading to use them also to replace parentheses within parentheses. In British style use parentheses within parentheses; but in American style use square brackets within parentheses.

6.12.5 Apostrophes

Possessives

The inclusion or omission of the possessive s should be decided on the grounds of euphony; this means that some possessives will have an s and some will not, but systems differ. *Hart's Rules* (39th edn, p. 31) recommend that in English names 's should be used in all monosyllables and disyllables, in longer words accented on the penultimate syllable, and in other longer words where it sounds right; however, the s is usually omitted when the last syllable of the name is pronounced *iz*: Bridges', Moses', but James's, Thomas's.

Delete any apostrophe that has crept into its, yours, ours, theirs, hers.

Where possible, reword to avoid the combination of a possessive with quotes or a parenthetical phrase:

> *not* 'L'Allegro's' significance in Milton's work
> it was James, his brother's, camera
> it was John (my host's) car
>
> *but* the significance of 'L'Allegro' in Milton's work
> it was his brother James's camera
> the car belonged to John, my host

Plurals

Apostrophes should not usually be used to indicate plurals:

the Joneses	*not*	the Jones's
1960s		1960's
NCOs		NCO's

However, some people prefer to use apostrophes after lower-case letters:

dotting the *is*   *or*   dotting the *i*'s

Omissions

An apostrophe is not needed in commonly used abbreviations such as:

thirties (= 1930s)	flu
bus	phone

6.12.6 **Commas**

As you know, the inclusion or omission of a comma can change the sense. Some authors do not realize that this happens with 'because' and 'in order to'.

> She said Auckland was attractive because he lived there [it was attractive because he lived there]
> She said Auckland was attractive, because he lived there [she said it because he lived there]
> He claimed that he had attended church, in order to avoid the penalties of the law [he claimed this in order to avoid the penalties]
> He claimed that he had attended church in order to avoid the penalties of the law [he said this was why he had attended church]

A common fault is the omission of commas round 'however'; at the beginning of a sentence this can be misleading:

> However we tried, we could not do it
> However, we tried as hard as we could

A comma should be consistently omitted or included before the final 'and' or 'or' in lists of three or more items:

red, white and blue   red, white, and blue

If the author's usual style is to omit the comma, an exception should of course be made if the sentence is a complex one:

red, white and blue, and green banners fluttered in the wind

In American style the comma is more often included.

6.12.7 **Common faults of punctuation**

There are some mechanical things that authors' typists very often forget.

1 There should not be a comma before an opening parenthesis, except in an index where subentries are in parentheses.

2 A full point should come before the closing parenthesis if the whole sentence is in parentheses; otherwise after the closing parenthesis:

He wore a hat. (The sun was very strong.)
He wore a hat (the sun was very strong).

3 At the end of a sentence there is no need to add a full point after an abbreviation that ends in a point or after a punctuation mark finishing a quotation or a book or article title:

The article was called 'Ruins in Malmesbury, Wilts.'
He was editor of *Which?*
She was awarded a Ph.D.

The most usual exception is if the abbreviation or question mark or exclamation mark is within parentheses inside the sentence:

He edited a magazine (*Which?*).

If the main sentence is a question or exclamation, and a quoted question or exclamation ends at the same point, two sets of punctuation will be needed:

'Which of you shouted "Fire!"?'

4 Parenthetical dashes stand on their own, without commas. If an author feels that a comma is needed in a particular case:

the family consists of Mohammad Musa – my 31-year-old host, – his mother, his 17-year-old wife . . .

it would be better to substitute parentheses for the dashes:

> Mohammad Musa (my 31-year-old host), his mother, his 17-year-old wife

5 There should be no full point at the end of items in a list of plates, figures, etc., or at the end of broken-off headings.

6 Commas should be consistently included or omitted after 'that is' or 'i.e.'

7 'For example' and 'e.g.' are used in two ways. If they form the whole of a parenthetical phrase, they should be between commas:

> it was, for example, his habit to . . .

If they introduce an example or list of examples, they should be preceded by a comma or other mark of punctuation; but I think it is clearer if no comma follows:

> superstitions, for example the belief . . .

8 A colon introducing a list or other displayed material should not be followed by a dash.

9 Semicolons or full points, *not* commas, should be used to separate main clauses that have different subjects and are not introduced by a conjunction.

6.13

SAFETY

Safety is extremely important: if you are copy-editing a cookery book, chemistry textbook, car maintenance handbook or any other set of practical instructions, ask the author to confirm that the materials are correctly named, that the quantities are correct, that diagrams (such as wiring diagrams) are accurate and that any safety measures such as protective clothing or adequate ventilation are mentioned early enough. For example, in cookery books translated from French, bay leaves (*laurier*) have been translated as laurel leaves, which are poisonous; and in a chemistry textbook an extra zero made a mixture in a recommended experiment dangerously explosive.

In illustrations, people should be shown wearing any necessary protective clothing and taking any other appropriate precautions.

See also section 3.1.4 on negligent misstatement.

6.14

SPELLING

The spelling of any book and article titles cited should not be made consistent with the rest of the book; and the spelling of quoted material is usually left unchanged (see sections 11.1, 11.5). Otherwise follow your house style or the author's system. Watch out for words with alternative spellings: the fact that both spellings are in common use makes it easy to miss inconsistencies:

acknowledgement	acknowledgment
ageing	aging
appendixes	appendices
biased	biassed
by-law	bye-law
centring	centering
connection	connexion
disk (computers)	disc (recordings)
dispatch	despatch
encyclopedia	encyclopaedia
focused	focussed
gipsy	gypsy
gram	gramme
guerrilla	guerilla
inflection	inflexion (use 'inflexion' in maths)
inquiry	enquiry
-ise	-ize (but see below for words that must be spelt -ise)
judgement	judgment (use 'judgment' in legal works)
medieval	mediaeval
movable (but 'moveable' in legal works)	
premiss	premise
programme, *but* computer program ('programmer' has two *m*s in both cases)	
reflection	reflexion
storey	story
wagon	waggon

Even if the author is using the -ize spelling, the following words must be spelt -ise:

advertise	disfranchise	misprise
advise	disguise	mortise
affranchise	emprise	practise
apprise (inform)	enfranchise	precise
arise	enterprise	premise
braise	excise	prise (open)
chastise	exercise	reprise
circumcise	expertise	revise
comprise	franchise	seise (legal term)
compromise	guise	supervise
concise	improvise	surmise
demise	incise	surprise
despise	merchandise	televise
devise	misadvise	treatise

The following should be spelt -yse, not -yze (except in American spelling):

analyse	dialyse	hydrolyse
catalyse	electrolyse	paralyse

Watch out, too, for the inclusion or omission of accents on such words as 'elite', 'regime', 'role', and for the spelling of proper names; and also, of course, for hyphens.

Distinguish between:

dependant (noun)	*and*	dependent (adj.)
forbear (abstain)		forebear (ancestor)
forgo (do without)		forego (precede)
principal (chief)		principle (rule)
prophecy (noun)		prophesy (verb)

Note the following differences in spelling:

siege	*but*	seize
unmistakable		unshakeable

Watch out for the following words, which are often misspelt:

accommodate	minuscule
analogous	pavilion
battalion	sacrilegious
desiccation	stratagem
embarrass	superseded
gauge	trade union (*but* Trades Union Congress)
harass	vermilion
idiosyncrasies	weird
millennium	

Ligatures

Ligatures (combinations of two or more letters) are not used for ae, oe in anglicized words such as manoeuvre, Oedipus; but they are used in Old English and usually in modern French. Ring them or put a 'close up' mark above them, and mention them on your style sheet. You don't need to mark the ligatures which typesetters use for roman and italic ff, fi, fl, ffi, ffl, etc.

6.14.1 American (US) spelling

If you are retaining American spelling, keep an American dictionary, such as the *Random House Dictionary of the American Language* or *Webster's New World Dictionary: Third College Edition*, beside you. A list of some common differences is given below, but Americans may use the 'British' spelling of some of these words, as they are alternatives. Also the changes listed do not apply to all words: for example en- is not always replaced by in-.

-am (not -amme), e.g. gram, program
-ay (not -ey), e.g. gray
-ck- (not -que-), e.g. check, checkered
-ce (not -se), e.g. practice (verb as well as noun)
-e- (not -ae-), e.g. anemia, archeology, esthetic
-e- (not -oe-), e.g. fetal (also used in British spelling)
-er (not -re), e.g. caliber, center, liter, somber, theater
-et (not -ette), e.g. buret
-eu- (not -oeu-), e.g. maneuver
f- (for ph-), e.g. sulfur

im-, in- (for em-, en-), e.g. imbed, inclose, insure (= ensure)
-ing (not -eing), e.g. aging, eying
judgment
-l- (not -ll-), e.g. marvelous, woolen
-ler, -led (not -ll-), e.g. traveler, traveled, *but* controller, controlled
-ll- (not -l-), e.g. fulfill, installment, skillful, willful
-og (not -ogue), e.g. catalog
-ol- (not -oul-), e.g. mold, smolder
-or (not -our), e.g. honor, labor
-ow (not -ough), e.g. plow
-per, -ped (not -pp-), e.g. worshiper, worshiped, *but* shipper, shipped
-se (not -ce), e.g. defense, license (noun as well as verb), offense, pretense
sk- (not sc-), e.g. skeptical
tire (noun), not tyre
toward, as well as towards
un- (not in-), e.g. undefinable
-z- (not -s-), e.g. analyze, cozy, paralyze

6.15

MISCELLANEOUS POINTS

This section contains a few extra points of style and syntax that tend to cause trouble. We should aim at clarity, simplicity and consistency, rather than pedantry; but we should retain useful distinctions in meaning, by discouraging authors from using words incorrectly. The following are common solecisms: 'infer' to mean 'imply', 'disinterested' to mean 'uninterested', 'protagonist' to mean someone who supports a theory.

There is a risk that an essential distinction in meaning may be lost, now that journalists and others seem reluctant to use the word 'might'. A news item about an earthquake said:

> But no action was taken to reinforce the columns, action that
> independent experts believe may have saved motorists on Tuesday.

The use of 'may' implies that some motorists were saved, and that the 'action' is possibly the reason why they were; but what the writer actually meant was:

action that independent experts believe might have saved motorists

If the action had been taken, it is possible that motorists would have been saved.

I, we, the present writer
'I think' is preferable to 'in the present writer's opinion' or 'we think', though an impersonal form may be necessary in a multi-author work.

A or an
Some authors still write 'an historical', 'an hotel'; try to persuade them to let you change this.

With abbreviations it is sometimes difficult to know whether to use 'a' or 'an'; abbreviations can be pronounced as though they were spelt out (a Mr Brown), or as a word (a NATO base), or as separate letters (an MP): and there are borderline cases.

It or she
Countries, ships, etc., should be described as it rather than she.

Singular or plural verb
See that the author treats each group noun such as 'government' as consistently singular or plural. It is very easy to be inconsistent about this, according to the context: 'The Labour Government was forced into a corner; after some weeks of tension they agreed among themselves ...'

'None' may be followed by a plural verb, but 'neither' as an adjective or pronoun should be followed by a singular verb.

'A number of ... are/is'. I suggest you use 'the number is ...' and 'a number ... are'.

'Data', 'errata', 'media', 'strata' and 'criteria' (singular 'criterion') are plural nouns and should normally be treated as such; but in data-processing 'data' is now treated as a singular collective noun.

Position of 'neither' and 'both'
See that these are correctly placed, e.g. 'which neither suits him nor me' should be 'which suits neither him nor me'; 'which both suited him

and me' should be 'which suited both him and me'. Watch out for
'neither . . . *or*': authors slip up, especially where there is a long
clause between 'neither' and 'nor'.

Position of 'only'
If there is any possibility of ambiguity, 'only' must be placed in the cor-
rect position; otherwise place it in the most natural-sounding position.
For example,

> Carpets only cleaned on Saturdays

could mean

> Only carpets are cleaned on Saturdays
> Carpets are cleaned, but not dyed, on Saturdays
> Carpets are cleaned on Saturdays only

'Owing to' and 'due to'
At the beginning of a sentence it is better to use 'owing to' or 'because
of' than 'due to':

> The accident was due to poor visibility
> Owing to [*not* due to] poor visibility, the car hit a stationary lorry

'That' and 'which'
Strictly, 'that' should be used for defining clauses and 'which' for non-
defining. Defining clauses have no punctuation, while non-defining
clauses must be between commas:

> He stopped the second car that was driven by a woman
> He stopped the second car, which was driven by a woman

The punctuation distinction is the crucial one; 'which' can be used
in a defining clause, without loss of clarity, and can be clearer if there is
another 'that' in the sentence:

> the process which produces that particular effect.

Position of descriptive phrase
Such a phrase at the beginning of a sentence continues in force until
the subject changes or is restated. In the sentence: 'In 1672 he went to

Mantua and married a dressmaker in 1678', the date 1672 applies to both verbs, and the sentence should be turned round to read 'He went to Mantua in 1672 and . . .' Or one could say 'In 1672 he went to Mantua, and he married . . .'

Dangling participles
Watch out for these, and reword them. For example, avoid:

> Having pitched the tents, the horses were fed and watered
> Shot in a factory, Eisenstein moves his camera so that the machinery
> seems to come alive

Split infinitives
Avoid them if you can do so without distorting the sentence; but sometimes a split infinitive is the lesser of two evils:

> A few verbs appear to marginally permit pronominal indirect objects
> He chose to publicly explain dearth solely in terms of bad husbandry

In the following quotation the author or copy-editor has avoided splitting infinitives:

> Very honourable exceptions were Italian restaurants, said positively to
> like children, and Chinese ones, said positively to love them

but the sense would have been clearer if the sentence had been:

> Very honourable exceptions were Italian restaurants, said to positively
> like children, and Chinese ones, said to positively love them

Subjunctive
If the author uses the subjunctive, see that it is used correctly; do not introduce it yourself except to clarify the meaning.

Adjectival nouns
To avoid headline language, keep adjectival nouns to a minimum, preferably not more than two in a row, e.g. *not* 'Water resources development plan board meeting'.

Ditto marks

Ditto marks, 'ditto' and 'do' should be avoided in printed matter, except in a quotation. Sometimes it is possible to tabulate the material so that no repetition is necessary; otherwise the word or phrase should be repeated.

7 Preliminary pages

The preliminary pages may consist of any or all of the following items:

*half-title	recto
*list of series editors	half-title or verso
*list of other books in the same series or by the same author	verso of half-title
*frontispiece	verso, facing title page
*title page	recto
*publication date, publisher's and printer's names and addresses, copyright notice, ISBN, CIP data, etc.	verso of title page
*dedication or epigraph	recto if possible
contents list	recto
list of plates, figures, maps and tables (usually in that order)	fresh page for each
list of contributors	fresh page
foreword, preface	rectos if possible
acknowledgements	fresh page
note on the text/transliteration, etc.	fresh page
conversion tables for imperial measures, currency, etc.	fresh page
list of abbreviations	if only 1 page, facing
general map(s) relevant to the whole book	first page of text, if this will not entail a blank recto

The items are usually in this order, though the epigraph may be placed just before the text. The contents list should precede any preface or foreword, so that the reader can turn to it easily.

Preliminary pages in complex books are usually numbered in lower-case roman, so that extra material can, if necessary, be added at proof stage or for a new edition. The numbering starts with the half-title, but no number will be printed on the pages that contain the asterisked items in the list above, or on any blank pages, so the first page number to be printed will probably be v or vii. The arabic page numbering should always start at 1.

One should look for ways of keeping the number of preliminary pages to a minimum, but there are certain conventions. The verso of the half-title is used only for certain things (see below). The contents list, the foreword or preface, and anything of more than one page usually starts on a right-hand page; anything shorter may be on a left-hand page; and a short acknowledgements list or note on the text may even be fitted on to the last page of the contents list or preface. A dedication or epigraph is usually on a right-hand page, with a blank verso; but if you are short of space the dedication could face the title page, if there is room there, and an epigraph could be placed on the last verso of the prelims, facing page 1.

Provide all the wording for the preliminary pages; the typesetter may not be familiar with things that seem obvious to you, such as your publisher's address. The sheets of typescript should be lettered or numbered; it may be best to letter them, to allow for the addition of material not provided by the author. For example, the author will provide the title page, contents list and any preface, and will call these fos. 1–3, with the text starting on fo. 4. You need to add a half-title, the copy for the verso of the title page, and perhaps a series list to face the title page. So it is simplest to letter the prelims A–F and to say on the last folio, 'Text starts fo. 4' or 'Fo. 4 follows.'

7.1

HALF-TITLE

Prepare a sheet for the half-title showing the wording, which is usually just the book title, series title, the names of the series editors and the volume number, but may also include a blurb or information about the author or series. The subtitle is usually omitted from the half-title; but include it if you think the main title is not sufficiently meaningful on its own. (If it is not, perhaps you should suggest a better main title to the commissioning editor, because the main title is all that will appear in many bibliographies.)

If the preliminary pages are complicated, and contain items (such as a dedication or epigraph) that are not mentioned in the contents list, the typesetter will find it helpful if you list the preliminary material on the half-title, giving the printed page numbers, where possible, and making it clear what should start a fresh page or a right-hand page. If some material is not yet available, include it in the list, followed by 'to come' and the number of printed pages it is expected to occupy; and put a folio in the preliminary material headed, for example, 'Preface: copy to follow, approx. 2 pp.' However, there is no need to include blank folios in the typescript to represent blank pages. Say, both on the half-title and on the appropriate folio, where the arabic pagination is to begin. In the following example I have given the folio letters in square brackets, but they need not be included in the list.

[A]	p. i	half-title
—	ii	blank
[B]	iii	title page
[C]	iv	imprints
[D]	v	dedication
—	vi	blank
[E–I]	vii	contents list
[J]	recto	preface – to come, approx. 2 pp.

Arabic pagination starts at fo. 4

Even if you do not list the items, it helps the typesetter if you say, for example:

Prelims fos. A–F
Text fos. 2–479

so that it is easy to see whether anything is missing.

The main text of a book should normally start on a right-hand page, but there are exceptions: for example, in a book of musical pieces, each of which occupies two pages, it is essential that each piece starts on a left-hand page. In that case it is probably better to number the preliminary pages in arabic, especially if the preliminary matter ends on a right-hand page. If you are left with a blank right-hand page before the first page of text, try to put something on it; if there is nothing else, you can repeat the book title as a kind of part title.

7.2

VERSO OF HALF-TITLE

This page may be used for a list of other books in the series or by the same author, for a list of series editors (or editorial board) if this will occupy too much space for the half-title, for a frontispiece printed on text paper, or, if necessary, for a dedication (see below). If the list of books includes some published by another firm, give the publishers' names, so that your sales department does not receive orders for them.

7.3

FRONTISPIECE

A frontispiece should not be turned on the page. It may be possible to print a landscape-shaped photograph upright on the page if the sides are masked; or the author may agree to switch the frontispiece and one of the other illustrations.

7.4

TITLE PAGE

Prepare a sheet with the complete wording. See that here, and on the half-title, the title, style for volume number (usually arabic), form of author's name and affiliation (details such as degrees, honours, position held) are the same as on any brief for the jacket designer. If you are at all doubtful about any of these points, check them now, as changes at a later stage are a nuisance to the sales and publicity departments as well as being expensive.

Label the subtitle. There is no need for a colon after the main title, as the subtitle will be on a separate line and probably set in smaller type. If the main title contains a colon, say 'All one title; do not break at colon.' It is usual to omit punctuation at the end of displayed lines on the title page, unless this would be misleading.

The number of the edition (if not the first) should be given (see section 15.3.2). The form of authors' names should be in accordance with their own preference; the inclusion of their qualifications or position will depend on the proposed market for the book. If the author dies before the book is published, some publishers put 'the late' on the title page; in any case any degrees or personal honours will be omitted; the author's academic position, if any, may be retained as still being relevant, though it should be preceded by 'formerly' or 'sometime'. A 'publisher's note' may be necessary in the preliminary pages to explain that someone else prepared the typescript for publication or saw the book through the press.

The name of the translator, artist or person who wrote the foreword may also need to be given on the title page.

The publisher's name or device should appear. Some publishers give the place and date of publication as well.

7.5

VERSO OF TITLE PAGE

It is useful to have duplicated sheets giving the standard wording, with spaces for the information that is different for each book.

The following should be included (for reprints and new editions see section 15.3.3):

- publisher's full name and address(es)
- publication date (unless this has been given on the title page)
- copyright notice
- possibly a general notice on copyright. In a book of plays or music there may be a note about performing rights
- International Standard Book Number
- Cataloguing in Publication data (see section 7.5.6)
- printer's name and address
- some publishers also give the name of the copy-editor, designer, etc., and information about the typeface

7.5.1 Publisher's name and address

Watch for circumstances that will entail some variation from the usual wording. For example, the address of an American branch will be omitted if your firm does not have the American rights for a book, or decides, on the grounds of cost, not to obtain American rights for items in an anthology.

7.5.2 **Copyright notice**

The familiar © copyright notice was introduced internationally by the Universal Copyright Convention (the UCC). Signatories to the UCC (and they include the UK (1957), the USA (1955), Australia (1969) and the USSR (1973)) give each other copyright protection within their individual countries provided that 'from the time of first publication' all copies 'bear the symbol © accompanied by the name of the copyright proprietor and the year of first publication'. Many countries belong to a much older copyright union, which is usually referred to simply as 'Berne' (where it was first formed, in 1886). Berne does not require a particular copyright notice of its members; nor, with the major exception of the USA (where need for the © copyright notice is a part of internal legislation), does the law of most countries absolutely require it. It is simply needed to acquire UCC protection, and since most countries are members of UCC it follows that it is sensible (wherever possible) to include a proper © notice in all publications.

Nowadays there are only two circumstances where it is impossible to include a © notice.

The first is a reprint of a work which was originally published before the country in question became a signatory to the UCC. Thus, in the UK, no work in its original form first published by a UK publisher before 27 September 1957 is entitled to a © notice. If the work has a new introduction, then we may have only

Introduction © [copyright proprietor] 199–

A © notice for the text will be possible only if it appears, post-1957, in a significantly different form: a new edition of a Shakespeare play, for example, is entitled to a © notice if it is significantly different – in punctuation, spelling, or whatever – from any version which is known to have been published before.

The second case where a © notice should not be added is where the work, when first published, did not contain a notice because of the conditions of the manufacturing provisions of the old US Copyright

Act. Briefly, before the new US Copyright Act of 1976 it was necessary, except under certain special circumstances, to omit a © notice altogether in the case of a US-authored work manufactured outside the USA but intended for import into the USA. Since 1 January 1978, this prohibition no longer exists, and a © notice can be included in all works entering the USA but must not be applied retrospectively to works that have already entered the USA without a © notice in deference to the old Act.

Under the Universal Copyright Convention the copyright notice should appear 'in such location as to give reasonable notice of claim of copyright' (by US law on the 'title page or page immediately following'). The correct form is:

© copyright proprietor, year of first publication

The copyright symbol, name of proprietor, and date should follow each other closely, ideally in a single line; the contract should tell you who the copyright holder is. Watch out for circumstances that may entail a different copyright line.

In a British edition of a book first published in the USA, the copyright date will be the date appearing in the US edition. As well as the date of first publication, there may be an earlier date if the author registered an earlier version of the work, such as a performing version of a play, at the Library of Congress. There may also be a later date, the date of renewal of copyright.

Translations. There may be two copyright notices, one for the original work (if it is still in copyright) and one for the translation. The one for the translation would probably be:

English translation © [copyright proprietor] 199–

An edition of a text would have a copyright notice for the text (if it was still in copyright) and another for the editorial material, which might read:

Introduction and notes © [copyright proprietor] 199–

An anthology would need acknowledgements for the individual items (see section 3.7.2); and the acknowledgements for some US items would include copyright dates. The copyright notice for the book should be qualified, and might read:

Introduction, selection and notes © [copyright proprietor] 199–

Reprints and new editions. See section 15.3.3.

General notice on copyright
Some publishers, either as a matter of course or in some of their publications, include a general warning about photocopying, information storage, and so on. The decision on whether this is a sensible precaution, and on the exact wording, must be left to each publisher, but it should be remembered that the law does in fact allow some use of copyright material without permission and that due allowance, in such a notice, may have to be given to the existence of a blanket licence scheme which may allow photocopying by readers without specific permission.

7.5.3 **Publication date**

The date of first publication should be given, plus the date of first publication by your firm (if this is different) and the dates of all your reprints and new editions (see section 15.3.3). Some publishers do not give the original publication data if they are not the original publisher, but say, for example,

First published in Great Britain 1991

Other publishers give not only the original publication date but also the original publisher.

If the title, content, etc., have changed, this should be made clear:

First published as *Four Metaphysical Poets* 1934
Second edition, with a new chapter on Marvell, published as *Five Metaphysical Poets* 1964

If the book is a translation of a published work, the title in the original language should be given, together with the original publication date and the name and address of the original publisher. (See also section 11.6.)

7.5.4 **The International Standard Book Number (ISBN)**

The ISBN is always ten digits, and is divided into four parts separated by spaces or hyphens: a group identifier, publisher prefix, title number and check digit, which together make up ten digits, of which the last one may be x (ten). Large publishers have short publisher prefixes, to allow for a large number of titles. If you are interested in the details, here they are:

- group identifier (of one to five digits), identifies the language or geographical area in which the book was published. The group identifiers 0 (zero) and 1 include the UK, USA, Australia, Canada (English-speaking part), Eire, South Africa, New Zealand and Zimbabwe
- publisher prefix, identifying the publisher, may be of two to seven digits, depending on the size of the publisher
- title number, identifying the particular edition and binding of a particular book, may consist of one to six digits, depending on the length of the group identifier and publisher prefix

(These three parts – group identifier, publisher prefix and title number – always total nine digits.)

- check digit, to pick up errors in transcribing the other nine digits, is always one digit: 1 to 9 or x (ten). When an ISBN is fed into a computer the first digit is multiplied by 10, the second by 9 and so on. For example, a book published by Cambridge University Press might have the following number:

group identifier	publisher prefix	title number	check digit
0	521	05875	9

- The computer would carry out the following calculation:

$$
\begin{array}{ccccccccccc}
 & 0 & 5 & 2 & 1 & 0 & 5 & 8 & 7 & 5 & 9 \\
\times\ 10 & 9 & 8 & 7 & 6 & 5 & 4 & 3 & 2 & 1 \\
\hline
\end{array}
$$

0 + 45 + 16 + 7 + 0 + 25 + 32 + 21 + 10 + 9 = 165

If the total can be divided by 11, the number is a valid one.

When an ISBN is included in a bar code, the check digit is different:

it is calculated on a different basis, and it includes the prefix 978 as well as the ISBN.

There is a different ISBN not only for each book but for each edition and binding (e.g. hardback, paperback, limp), so that a bookseller can simply use one number to order the paperback of Hazel, *Cotton Trade* (3rd edn):

ISBN 0 521 05875 9 hardback
ISBN 0 521 05876 7 paperback

Where two or more books are sold as a set, there is a number for each volume and also one for the set, and all these numbers should appear and be identified in each volume:

ISBN 0 521 05875 9 vol. 1
ISBN 0 521 05876 7 vol. 2
ISBN 0 521 05874 0 set of two vols.

The relevant ISBN should also appear at the base of the back cover if there is no jacket, or at the base of the back of the jacket if there is one.

For full information about ISBNs, see *International Standard Book Numbering* published by the Standard Book Numbering Agency Ltd, 12 Dyott Street, London WC1A 1DF.

7.5.5 International Standard Serial Number (ISSN)

The ISSN identifies a serial publication such as a journal or a monographic series that will be published indefinitely. The ISSN remains the same for every issue, provided the title does not change. A few publications will carry both an ISBN and an ISSN: an annual publication will need a different ISBN for each issue, while the ISSN remains the same, provided that the title does not change. Note, however, that different editions of serials must have different ISSNs.

The ISSN does not contain a publisher identifier. It is an arbitrary number made up of seven digits plus a check digit which may be x (ten). A hyphen is printed between the fourth and fifth digits:

ISSN 0000-0000

The ISSN should preferably be printed on the top right-hand corner of the front cover; otherwise it may appear in some other prominent place, for example with other bibliographical information such as the name of the publisher.

7.5.6 Cataloguing in Publication (CIP) data

Some publishers include CIP data, which are provided by national libraries, such as the British Library and the Library of Congress, from preliminary pages sent to them. The data should not be altered in any way without asking the Library first.

Publishers who do not include the block of data will probably include the following:

> A catalogue record for this book is available from the British Library

7.5.7 Printer's address

Books must carry the name of the country in which they were printed. Books printed in the United Kingdom must also include the printer's name and address. If the type is set in one country and printed in another, only the second country (and printer if necessary) need be identified, but publishers often give more than the minimum information.

7.6

DEDICATION AND EPIGRAPH

For the best position for these see p. 168.

Epigraph. It is usually sufficient to give the author of the quotation and the title of the work from which it is taken, without page or line number.

7.7

CONTENTS LIST

All non-fiction works should have one comprehensive contents list, not one per part or a separate one at the beginning of an appendix of tables: it is easier for the reader to have only one place to look. There will be rare exceptions to this rule; but be sure that an exception is justified.

The heading should be 'Contents' not 'Contents list', 'List of contents' or 'Table of contents'.

The list should contain all the preliminary material except the half-title, any lists on p. ii, title page and verso, dedication or epigraph. Lists of illustrations etc. are called 'List of. . .' in the contents list, though their own headings are just 'Illustrations' etc. As the foreword has been written by someone other than the author, the writer's name should appear in the contents list (and in some cases on the title page too) as well as at the beginning or end of the foreword. The contents list should also contain all endmatter such as endnotes (called 'Notes' or 'Notes to the text'), bibliography, glossary and index; if there is more than one index, the title of each one should be given.

It is difficult for a reader to find a particular item if the contents list is too detailed. Look critically at any list containing more than one grade of subheading: detailed contents lists are useful in reference books; but in other books a reader seeking a specific point is likely to use the index. Second-grade subheadings may be run on as a paragraph instead of occupying separate lines; but this makes each item and its page number more difficult to find.

See that all parts and chapters (and subheadings, where appropriate) appear in the list, and that they tally in wording, numbering (preferably arabic), spelling, hyphenation and capitalization of special words, both between text and list, and also with each other. The word 'Part' is usually retained in the part title; but the word 'Chapter' occupies more space and can anyway be taken for granted, so it is usually deleted. 'Appendix' may be deleted before each appendix number if there are many of them, provided you add 'Appendixes' above the first one. Chapters should normally be numbered in one sequence even if the book is divided into parts. There is no need for a point between the number and the title. The authors of individual chapters should be given; their academic positions may be included here if this will not clutter the list too much, or otherwise in a separate list of contributors or at the beginning of the relevant chapter. In a book of reprinted essays the details of original publication may be given in the contents list if they are not complicated, or otherwise in a list of acknowledgements.

If the title of the book appears at the top of the page, cross it out. Add 'o' after the first item, so that the typesetter does not forget to leave room for the page numbers. Ring any folio numbers that may be given for the various items, so that they are not typeset; if the typesetter did set them, it is conceivable that no one would check them and they would appear in the finished book.

If, after your checking and the consequent alterations, the list is rather untidy, it should be retyped. Contents lists are best typed in upper and lower case, with initial capitals only for the first word of each item and any proper names: typographical treatment should be left to the designer. If the layout is complicated, consult the designer before the list is retyped.

7.8

OTHER LISTS

As I have already mentioned, lists of illustrations, abbreviations, contributors and so on, are called 'List of. . .' in the contents list and in their running heads; but the words 'List of' are omitted from the heading above the list. There should be no full point after the item number or at the end of any item; 'facing p. oo' is used only for illustrations which are not in the text pagination, for example separately printed halftones or fold-outs. Check that all lists tally in spelling, capitalization and hyphenation with the captions etc. to which they refer, though the items may be given in a shorter form.

There may be no list of illustrations if the reader is unlikely to want to refer to them separately from the relevant text. If the frontispiece is the only halftone, it may appear as the first item in the contents list: title on the left, 'frontispiece' above the page numbers. The source can be given in a separate note, say at the end of the contents list.

Similarly, one or two general maps may be placed in the prelims and included in the contents list.

If there is no list of illustrations, and the halftones are bound in separately, it will help both the reader and the binder if their position is printed after the end of the contents. For example:

The plates will be found between pages 128 and 129

If not, each leaf that is tipped in, and the first and last page of any group or wrap-round, should have 'facing p. 000' printed at the foot of the page, so that the binder knows where to place them.

7.9

LIST OF ILLUSTRATIONS

If halftones and line illustrations are numbered in one sequence, the list will probably be called 'Illustrations'. If they are numbered separately the individual lists will be headed 'Plates', 'Figures', 'Maps', so that each item can begin with just a number.

For text illustrations add 'oo' at the end of the first item. If the halftones are to be grouped, add 'Between pp. oo and oo' below the heading 'Plates' or above each group. If they are not to be grouped, add 'facing p. oo' after the first item.

It is not necessary to include the whole of the caption in the list; one needs only enough to identify the illustration. If each has a different source it may be most helpful to put the source at the end of each item; but if all the plates come from two or three sources, it is less repetitive to acknowledge them in a separate note at the end of the list or in a separate list of acknowledgements. In some cases the copyright holder will ask for the acknowledgement to be given immediately below the illustration.

7.10

LIST OF TABLES

A list is necessary only if the tables are likely to be consulted independently of the text; but if there is a list in the typescript, consult the author before omitting it.

7.11

PREFACE, FOREWORD, INTRODUCTION

An introduction that is an essential part of the main book should be in the arabic pagination, and not in the prelims; but it need not be called chapter 1. Mathematicians may call it chapter 0; others may leave it unnumbered.

A purely personal note by the author should be called 'Preface' and included in the preliminary pages. It often has the author's initials and a date at the end. If the date has no particular significance, try to persuade the author to omit it, as it may make the book look out of date. However, if the book is on a subject that dates quickly, the author may wish to give the date when the typescript was completed (to make it clear that the book takes no account of new discoveries after that time); in other cases an author will acknowledge help with proofs or index, and any dates should take account of that fact. Try to persuade the author to use the latest possible date, if one must be included.

If the preface is by someone other than the author, it should probably be renamed 'Foreword' or 'Editorial preface', and the writer's name should appear either under the heading or at the end. If the same preface or 'note to the reader' is used in each book in a series, make sure it applies fully to the present one.

7.12

ACKNOWLEDGEMENTS

General acknowledgements of help are best included in the preface, but acknowledgements of sources of copyright material are best listed separately, unless each acknowledgement immediately follows the relevant quotation or illustration (see section 3.7.2).

7.13

LIST OF ABBREVIATIONS

This is usually placed as near as possible to the beginning of the text, preferably on a left-hand page, so that the reader can refer back to it easily. See that all the necessary abbreviations are included and that they agree with the author's usage in the text and footnotes. Check the alphabetical order.

7.14

OTHER ITEMS

These may include a list of contributors, a conversion table, 'How to use this book', a note on sources or editorial conventions, or a list of notation. If there is such a note, see that its title indicates its content correctly, and that the content tallies, so far as you can tell, with what the author has actually done in the text. If you think an explanatory note is needed, suggest this to the author.

8   Indexes

For general background to this chapter I suggest you read M. D. Anderson's *Book Indexing* (Cambridge Authors' and Publishers' Guides). There is also a British Standard, BS 3700: *Preparing Indexes to Books, Periodicals and Other Documents.*

I should explain some of the terms I shall use. A simple entry comprises a *heading* or *headword* and one or more *page references*:

> earthquakes, 24, 96

A complex entry consists of a heading (which may or may not be followed by page references) plus *subentries*, each consisting of a *subheading* followed by page references:

> limestone, 2, 55
>   crinoidal, 128
>   fossils in, 110, 114
>   magnesian, 130

Subentries may start on a fresh line (as in the last example) or they may run on between semicolons:

> limestone, 2, 55; crinoidal,
>   128; fossils in, 110, 114;
>   magnesian, 130

If there are *sub-subentries*, the subentries are likely to be broken off and the sub-subentries run on between semicolons:

> Cambridge University, 114–18
>   architecture, 160
>   colleges: Corpus Christi,
>   227; Jesus, 150
>   rivalry with Oxford, 114

If an entry or subentry is too long to fit on to one line, the continuation lines or *turnover lines* (such as the second line of the subentry 'colleges' in the last example) have to be indented more than the start of a subentry, so that the two cannot be confused.

Most books have a single index; but, in more complex books,

different kinds of information may be separated. An obvious example is a verse anthology, which may have an index of authors, an index of first lines and possibly an index of poem titles. If there is a general index and one or more specialized ones, the general index usually comes last.

8.1

WHAT NEEDS TO BE DONE

The publisher must be satisfied that the coverage, length and general organization of the index are satisfactory. Although a professional indexer will do a competent job, the author may well know more about the subject or the needs of the likely readers and should see a copy of the index before it is sent for setting.

An indexer works from an uncorrected proof while the author is checking his or her proof. If you receive the author's corrected proof before the index is due, look through it straight away, to make sure there are no changes that will affect the index, and particularly changes that will affect the pagination. If there are, telephone the indexer and send photocopies of the affected pages, so that the indexer can take the new pagination into account; otherwise you will have to go through the index typescript looking for references to the affected pages and alter them as appropriate yourself.

Any alterations to proper names etc. must also be incorporated in the index, so make a note of these as you go through the marked proof.

Here is a summary of the routine copy-editing of an index:

1 See that the index is the expected length.
2 If the folios are already numbered, check that the sequence is correct and complete; if they are not, number them.
3 Check the alphabetical order of main headings (see 8.2.2); while doing that, one can size up some of the problems:
   - is the typescript legible?
   - are spellings, capitalization and accents correct? Checking the doubtful ones against the text constitutes at the same time a spot check of the accuracy of the page references
   - headings (see 8.2.1): is the choice sensible and consistent? Are there synonyms?

- coverage: are there obvious gaps; is it over-full? If there is an unlikely gap in the alphabetical order, perhaps a folio is missing
- are there long strings of page numbers that should be grouped under subheadings, or many subheadings that have only one page reference?
- mark space between letter blocks

If there are problems with these points, discuss them with the commissioning editor: putting them right may be beyond the scope of normal copy-editing.

4 Check the order of subentries (see 8.2.3). Should they be run on or broken off? Punctuate them accordingly and mark the indention if it is not clear in the typescript.

5 Read through each entry, looking at consistency of optional spellings, capitals and hyphenation with the rest of the book, and also punctuation and the sequence of numbers (see 8.3)
- are there one or two entries with no page references?
- are there initials or forenames missing?
- are the numbers in the right sequence? If they are not, do not just transpose them; there is probably a typing error in one of the numbers. Are there nonsense numbers such as 11415 (for 114 15)?
- is elision of number spans consistent? Mark the first few with en rules if necessary and give a general instruction
- are numbers indicating main references, illustrations, etc. consistently distinguished (see 8.3)? Should there be a note at the beginning of the index to explain the system?
- are the cross-references correct (see 8.2.4)?

Before passing the typescript on, write the author's name and the abbreviated book title at the top of the first folio, and give the number of the printed page on which the index is to start: 'To start on p. . . . .' The first index may start on a right-hand page if length is not a problem. The second (if there is one) usually starts on a fresh page but may run on from the end of the first. If you did not include the index(es) in your list of running heads, or if their titles have changed since then, put a note on the first folio: 'running head to be . . .' The running head should give the name of the individual index, not just 'Indexes'.

Make sure that the typesetter knows how much to indent turnover lines and broken-off subentries, and where to insert 'continued' lines (see 8.3.8 and 8.3.9).

8.2

GENERAL ORGANIZATION

8.2.1 Choice of heading

The choice of the first word of the heading is very important, because this will decide the position of the entry in the index. Are items indexed under the right word? Are page references split between two synonyms that should be combined? Are there some entries that no reader of this kind of book would look up?

Are the items consistently grouped? For example, an index typescript might include:

farming	France
England	farming
France	mining
Germany	trade

All references to farming should be either under 'farming' or under the country, with cross-references where necessary. If the whole index is organized in a consistent way, the reader soon knows where to look. Make sure the entry includes all the page references: the indexer may have put some in one place and some in the other.

Main headings should normally be nouns (qualified or unqualified) rather than adjectives or verbs on their own. Some authors do use adjectives, and this can work satisfactorily in a few cases; but the heading should not be used as both noun and adjective in the same entry (see below).

The index should, of course, use the same spellings and accents as the text, but if old-fashioned or idiosyncratic terminology or spellings appear in quotations, the correct modern form should be used in the index, with a cross-reference from the other form where necessary.

An index of first lines is the only one in which 'a', 'an' and 'the' start an entry (but see 'Proper names' below). In other indexes the article is usually omitted; if it forms part of a book title or is necessary to make the sense clear, it may be placed at the end of the entry heading.

(a) **When to combine entries**

If a word is used in both singular and plural forms in the text, only one form should be used in the index:

not bishop, duties of	*but* bishops	*or* bishop(s)
bishops, income of	duties	duties
	income	income

This rule does not apply, of course, if the two forms have different meanings, e.g. damage, damages.

When a word has more than one meaning, there should be a separate entry for each meaning, with an explanatory phrase to show which meaning is intended:

Bath (Avon)
bath, zinc

For the order in which to place words with identical spelling, see 8.2.2.

Proper names which merely share the same first word should not be grouped in one entry; for their order see pp. 190–1.

London, 81–4, 91	*not* London, 81–4, 91
London, a poem, 81	*a poem*, 81
London, Jack, 184	Jack, 184
London School of Economics, 83	School of Economics, 83

Booth, John Wilkes	*not* Booth
Booth, William	John Wilkes
	William

Watch out for the indexer who uses the heading as noun and adjective in the same entry:

wall
   cavity   (wall cavity or cavity wall?)
   coverings
   damp
   painting   (wall painting or painting a wall?)

(b) **Proper names**

References to a peer should be collected under the title or the family name, whichever is the more familiar to the reader; if both forms are used in the book, or the peerage is a recent one, provide a cross-reference from the other form. The same principle should be followed when indexing married women. Names such as Russia and USSR, Ceylon and Sri Lanka, may be indexed separately if the distinction is necessary; but, if so, there should be a cross-reference. If the author uses in the text a name which is likely to be unfamiliar to some readers – perhaps a real name instead of a well-known pseudonym such as Mark Twain – add a cross-reference from the familiar name.

Saints, kings and popes are indexed under their forenames: places, institutions, Acts of Parliament, book titles, etc., are placed under the first word after the definite article (if any):

William IV, king of England	*but*	King William Street
		King Lear
Thérèse of Lisieux, St	*but*	St Louis, Missouri
Lewis, John	*but*	John Lewis Partnership

Also indexed under the forename are early names in which the second part is a place name rather than a surname, e.g. Philippe de Mézières under Philippe, John of Salisbury under John, Giraldus Cambrensis under Giraldus.

Compound personal names, whether hyphenated or not, should be indexed under the first element of the surname:

Maugham, W. Somerset
Vaughan Williams, Ralph

Compound place names such as Upper Slaughter, Lower Slaughter, Great Yarmouth, North Shields, South Shields, should be indexed under the first element; but do not change the author's system without consultation.

Names of natural features such as rivers, lakes, seas and mountains should be indexed under the second element:

Everest, Mt
Seine, R.

There are two exceptions to this rule. (1) If the word for mountain etc. is in another language, e.g. Ben Nevis, Eilean Donan, the name is indexed under the first element. 'Loch' is sometimes treated as 'Lake', sometimes placed first. This different treatment of words from another language applies also to the definite article, which stays at the beginning of such names:

> La Paz
> Las Vegas
> Los Angeles

(2) If the name of a geographical feature is used as the name of an area or town, it is not inverted, e.g. Mount Vernon.

Foreign personal names
Helpful information can be found in Anderson, *Book Indexing* and *The Chicago Manual of Style*. Do not forget that the family name is the first element in unwesternized Chinese and Japanese names, so they should not be inverted; and watch out for honorific terms as in U Thant. Spanish names often include two surnames. If you want fuller information about proper names, consult *Names of Persons: National Usages for Entry in Catalogues* (3rd edn, London, International Federation of Library Associations, 1977).

In a book for English-speaking readers, familiar foreign names may follow the pattern of anglicized names: De Gaulle, De Quincey.

8.2.2 Alphabetical order

Alphabetical order can be either word by word (as the index to this book) or letter by letter (as the glossary), in each case counting only as far as the first comma or other mark of punctuation (except a hyphen), and then starting again. See that the same system is used throughout the index.

In the word-by-word method, short words precede longer words beginning with the same letters, and hyphenated words are sometimes counted as two words unless part is a prefix or suffix which cannot stand alone. Words with apostrophes are treated as single words, as are sets of initials such as BBC.

Word-by-word	*Letter-by-letter*
part-time employees	partitioned schoolrooms
partitioned schoolrooms	part-time employees
PLA, *see* Port of London Authority	PLA, *see* Port of London Authority
Port, William	Port, William
Port of London Authority	Portinscale (Cumb.)
Port Sunlight (Ches.)	Port of London Authority
Portinscale (Cumb.)	Port Sunlight (Ches.)

In word-by-word indexes, subentries may be in order of the first significant word (see below).

Abbreviations

The British Standard says: 'In names, Mac and its contractions should be filed as given unless the nature, purpose or tradition of a list requires arrangement as if the contractions were spelt in full. Other abbreviations, including St and related contractions, should be arranged as given, not as if spelt out in the fullest form' (BS 3700, section 6.2.1.5). You may feel, as the compilers of the telephone directory do, that the index user is best served if Mc is treated as if it were spelt Mac, since the reader may not be certain whether a name is spelt Macaulay or McAulay.

If chemical formulae are to be arranged in alphabetical order, each element is treated as a separate word, and subscript numerals are ignored except in otherwise identical formulae:

CO
CO_2
CS_2
$CaCO_3$

Headings consisting of the same words

These should be in the order:

people
places
subjects
titles of books, etc.

Forenames (and other names with titles or appellations only) should precede surnames with inverted forenames or initials and other appellations:

> John, king of England
> John XXI, pope
> John, Anthony

Kings of each dynasty or country should be in numerical order, the dynasties or countries being in alphabetical order.

In personal names with transposed forenames, it is the first forename, not any preceding title, which governs the order:

> Dixon, Sir Andrew
> Dixon, Dr Bruce
> Dixon, Charles

However, where both surname and forename are the same in successive entries, an entry without a title comes first, and the rest are in order of title:

> Dixon, Thomas
> Dixon, Dr Thomas
> Dixon, Sir Thomas

Foreign words

The British Standard on alphabetical arrangement says: 'Modified, additional and combined Roman alphabet letters used in languages other than English should be filed as the nearest equivalents of the English alphabet' (BS 1749, section 4.1); for example German ö and Danish ø should be treated as o and Polish ł as l. This is of course to enable English-speaking readers to find the name easily. Tell the author if you propose to alter the order, as some authors are anxious to show that they know the difference between, say, ø and o; if the index does not follow English alphabetical order, an explanatory note should be added at the beginning.

Foreign-language indexes

In languages with Roman alphabets, the letters treated differently are usually those with accents; but note that in Spanish ll and ch are sometimes treated as separate letters following the l and c entries respectively. In languages transliterated into the Roman alphabet, the order may bear no resemblance to English alphabetical order.

Numbers
Numbers may be grouped (in numerical order) before the main alphabetical sequence, but in most cases it is more helpful to include them in the main sequence, alphabetizing them as though they were spelt out. In chemical prefixes (see below) they are ignored.

Greek letters
These are alphabetized as though they were spelt out, except in chemical prefixes (see below).

Chemical prefixes
Most such prefixes, for example m, r and t in front of RNA, are ignored or spelt out in full. *Cis-*, *trans-* and *cyclo-* may or may not be taken into account; roman prefixes such as iso- are taken into account.

8.2.3 Subentries and sub-subentries

If an entry contains more than six page references, or a reference spans more than nine consecutive pages, it should usually be broken down into subentries. On the other hand there should not be a subentry for every page number. Passing mentions should not normally be indexed; if they are, they are best grouped at the end of the entry:

285; mentioned, 51, 182, 217, 288

Broken off or run on?
There is little point in breaking off subentries which are in chronological or numerical order. Otherwise the decision depends on the space available, the complexity of the index and the type of reader it is intended for: for example one might break off subentries in a school book, for extra clarity, if it would not add much to the length.

If subentries are to be broken off, some indexers run the first one on; but I think it is clearer to break the first one off too, even if there are

no general page references following the heading; in that case no punctuation is needed after the heading. If, however, there are no general
page references and only one subentry, the subentry should be run on:

coal   *but*   coal, industrial uses, 72, 76
 domestic use, 15, 45
 industrial uses, 72, 76

Sub-subentries are usually run on between semicolons if the subentries are broken off, between commas if the subentries are run on
between semicolons. It is extravagant to break off sub-subentries: not
only do they occupy more lines, but also the extra indention for
turnover lines leaves a very narrow measure. If sub-subentries must be
broken off, but they occur in only two or three entries, it may be better
to indent turnover lines differently in those entries.

Order
Check the order, which can be:

- alphabetical, for categories. The alphabetical order may be 'order of
  first significant word', that is, it may disregard such words as 'and',
  'at', 'in', 'of', so that the subentry headings need not be inverted to
  bring the significant word to the beginning
- chronological, for events
- numerical, that is, order of first page reference

I myself find numerical order unhelpful.

 Alphabetical and chronological order can be used in the same index:
for example a history of Newfoundland might include some biographical entries, with subentries arranged chronologically, and also an entry
for fisheries, divided alphabetically by kinds of fish. The two kinds of
order can be used in the same entry. A group of biographical subentries
in chronological order may be followed by an alphabetical group of the
subject's writings or the topics on which he or she expressed views: 'on
slavery, 156; on war, 134'.

 If the subentries are broken off and the order requires so much correction that it cannot be marked clearly with arrows, you may indicate
the final order by ringed numbers; but if the entry is split between two
folios, and there is not a complete sequence of numbers on one folio,

transfer all the subentries to a separate folio so that the keyboard operator can see all the numbers at the same time.

If the subentries are run on and the order is wrong, the whole entry should be retyped.

8.2.4 **Cross-references**

Check that the cross-references refer to existing entries, are correctly worded and make it clear what the entry heading is: for example '*see* social alienation' is no good if the heading is in the form 'alienation, social'; '*see* Brontë' is not enough if there are entries for more than one Brontë.

If the reference is to one entry which contains only a few references, it is better to have all the page references in both places than to make the reader go from one entry to the other. What one must not have is half the page references in one place and half in the other.

It may be helpful to have a cross-reference from a common abbreviation to its full form (or vice versa), especially if the book contains no list of abbreviations; and also a cross-reference from a synonym or an alternative form of a proper name to the form used in the book.

Wording
If the entry is purely a cross-reference, the heading is followed by a comma and '*see*' in italic. If the cross-reference is only part of the entry, '*see also*' is more appropriate than '*see*'. In cross-references to italic headings 'see' and 'see also' are often roman.

The items within a cross-reference should usually be in alphabetical order. The items may be separated by commas if none of them contains a comma. However, if it is necessary to cite the whole of an inverted heading such as 'alienation, social', or if the author cites both heading and subheading ('coal, as a domestic fuel'), a semicolon will be needed between all cross-references in the index. It is not necessary to refer to the subheading if it will be clear which one is intended; it will be enough to say '*see also under*' followed by the heading(s). Where a cross-reference includes a general description, rather than the actual names, of the entries, this description should be in italic: for example an entry on trade might end '*see also individual commodities*'.

Position

If the cross-reference helps to show the limitations of the entry in which it appears, some authors prefer to place it immediately after the heading and before the general page references. For example:

alphabetization (*see also* proper names), 18, 19

shows that the page references for alphabetization do not cover the order of proper names (which is a matter of which part of the name should come first rather than of alphabetical order).

If the cross-reference is a final subentry, it should be treated like the others; if there is a cross-reference from a subentry, it should be treated like a sub-subentry:

religion, 10–11, 107–11, 274	religion, 10–11, 107–11, 274
and myths, 11, 19, 29–31	and myths, 11, 19,
and ritual, 8–11, 29, 129	29–31; *see also* gods
see also gods, priests	and ritual, 8–11, 29,
	129; *see also* priests

8.3

STYLE WITHIN THE ENTRY

8.3.1 Capitalization

Lower case is normally used for headings that do not have capitals in the text. However, it may not be worth changing to this system if nearly all the headings are proper names or if a large number of words are capitalized in the text and you would have to spend a good deal of time checking headings against the text.

Subentry headings should always be lower case (except, of course, for proper names).

8.3.2 Wording

Keep wording and punctuation to a minimum, provided the sense is clear: in the following subentry neither the 'of' nor the comma is necessary:

Napoleonic wars
    effect of, on Norwegian agriculture

In an exceptionally involved index it may save wordiness if an abbreviated form of the main heading (usually the initial letter and a full point) is included in some subentries:

bird
    angel in form of b.
    b. mother makes human mother ashamed
    choice between b.s as best messenger

Although one should avoid wordiness, the entry must be full enough to be self-explanatory. The author of an introductory textbook provided an index with entries such as:

post-neonatal
projection
quasi-stable
quota system
rhythm method
separation
supply

8.3.3 Punctuation

It is usual to put a comma after the heading if it is followed by page references, though one may decide to have a fixed space instead, provided that headings do not end in a number, for example 'Minuet, K103'; dates in that position are often enclosed in parentheses. If there are no general references and the subentries run on, put a colon between the heading and the first subheading, so that there is no confusion as to what the second subheading is a subheading of:

Canterbury: archbishop of, 1, 71; disturbance in, 250

If the subentries are broken off, there is no punctuation at the end of the main entry, whether or not there are any general page references.

Page references are usually separated by commas, but it is acceptable to omit all commas before page numbers, though retaining semicolons and commas between run-on subentries and sub-subentries. In that case the space between page references is standardized and the columns are unjustified, and there is usually no point after 'n' (note).

> limestone 2 55; crinoidal
> 128; fossils in 110n 114;
> magnesian 130

There should be no punctuation at the end of an entry, or at the end of a broken-off subentry or sub-subentry.

8.3.4 Page numbers

If two entries or subentries cover similar ground, see that no page references are obviously missing from either. One is quite likely to find:

> fossils in limestone, 54, 110n., 126
> *and* limestone
>
> . . .
>
> fossils in, 110n., 114

Pairs of numbers, except teens, are usually elided (see section 6.10.7). General page references should be placed before subentries, not interspersed among them, even if the subentries are in chronological order.

Exact references such as '101–6' are preferable to '101ff.'; but you may not have time to check the vague references against the text in order to change them. '*Passim*' references should also be avoided as far as possible. If the index contains a reference 'chap. 6 *passim*', it is more helpful to the reader if the page numbers of chapter 6 are given instead of (or as well as) the chapter number.

The index should distinguish between 65–6 (a continuous discussion of the topic) and 65, 66 (two separate mentions). The reader usually identifies the author's fullest treatment of the topic by the number of pages of continuous discussion (that is by a reference such as 65–9). If the author wants to distinguish the most important references in some other way, bold or italic could be used. Some authors like to put the important references first; such a system should perhaps be explained in a note at the beginning of the index, though the use of italic or bold for this purpose is common enough not to need explanation.

Bold or italic may be used for other things, for example to distinguish pages on which illustrations appear; such a use should be explained in a note.

Index covering two or more volumes
The volume number should be given before the first page reference to each volume in each entry and subentry, because, even if the volumes are paginated consecutively, and therefore there is only one page 705, the user will not know which pages are in which volume.

Author index
If there is a list of references at the end of each paper, the author index will usually distinguish the pages on which those lists appear from references to the authors in the text of each paper (perhaps by the use of italic figures), so that the reader can see at a glance where to find the details of the papers cited.

Combined reference list and author index
The page references to the publication being indexed usually run on from the bibliographical reference and are set within square brackets and/or in italic to distinguish them from the page numbers which are part of the bibliographical reference:

> Werner, E. E., Bierman, J. M. & French, F. E. (1971). *The Children of Kauai.* Honolulu, University of Hawaii Press. [*148*]
> Widdowson, E. M. (1968). The harmony of growth. *Lancet*, **1**, 901–5. [*196*]

with cross-references from co-authors to the main author:

> Bierman, J. M., *see* Werner, Bierman & French (1971)

Index of passages cited
Subentries are usually broken off and the page references ranged right; or the reference to the original work may be in parentheses:

> Homer, *Iliad* (2.4) 44–8, 60–1

For classical books see also section 14.1.

8.3.5 **References to numbers other than page numbers**

If a book is divided into numbered items, the index will probably refer to the item numbers rather than page numbers. Such an index can be set at the same time as the text. Except in bibliographies, where the system is common, there should be a note at the beginning of the index saying that references are to item numbers.

If any pages of introductory material or endmatter are also to be indexed, the index copy will have to wait until page proofs of those sections are available, and the page numbers will have to be distinguished from the item numbers. A short introduction may be paginated in roman; or the page numbers may be italicized.

8.3.6 **References to notes**

Notes should be indexed only if they give additional information about a topic or person.

In any case a footnote need not be indexed if there is already a reference to that page: '16 and n.' is unnecessarily full, because anyone looking at the relevant text on page 16 will find the reference to the footnote; however, some authors insist on retaining this kind of reference. References to footnotes also cause difficulty when a subject is discussed over two or more pages: '27n.–28n.' (meaning pages 27–8 and notes on both pages) looks odd, and so does '27–9n'. And what about any notes on the intervening pages?

References to footnotes should be in the form '169n.' (or '169n') or, if there are several notes on the page (and the author gives the note number in the index typescript), '169 n. 3' (or '169 n3', '169n3').

Endnotes should be indexed under the page on which they appear, not the page on which they are referred to in the text. The note number should be given.

8.3.7 **References to illustrations**

Illustrations should be indexed if they are likely to be consulted independently of the relevant text; page references for text illustrations may be distinguished by being underlined for italic or being followed by '(fig.)'. In the former case there should be an explanatory note at the beginning of the index. Page references to illustrations should not be combined with spans of text references: 121–4, *124* is clearer than 121–*124*, and one cannot elide to 121–*4*.

8.3.8 Indention

If subentries are run on, all turnover lines are usually indented 1 em. If subentries are broken off and any sub-subentries are run on, subentries are indented 1 em and all turnover lines 2 ems. If both subentries and sub-subentries are broken off, subentries are indented 1 em, sub-subentries 2 ems, and all turnover lines – in that entry, at least – are indented 3 ems. If there are only one or two entries in a long index that are complicated and important enough to need broken-off sub-subentries, the 3-em indention needed for turnovers in those entries need not be used throughout the index.

If only the subentries are broken off, and the typescript shows the system of indention correctly, you need only mark the indention of the first subentry and the first few turnover lines, and add a general note: 'subentries indented 1 em, all turnovers 2 ems'.

8.3.9 Layout

You should decide whether the subentries and sub-subentries need to be broken off or should run on. You may also mark indention and the spacing of such things as '16n.' Otherwise layout is usually the designer's responsibility. If the author asks for unusual typographical conventions or layout, discuss them with the designer.

Indexes are usually set unjustified, in order to avoid the great variations in word spacing that occur when an index contains long words that are difficult to break, such as proper names.

Number of columns per page
Most indexes have two columns, but an index of passages cited or an author index may have three columns, and an index of first lines or combined list of references and author index is likely to have one column. An index with a great many long entries may be set in one column.

When an entry runs from one page to the next
The typesetter should repeat the entry heading, and if necessary the subentry heading, followed by (*cont.*), at the top of the left-hand column:

cattle (*cont.*)
634; fattening, 43, 60 2

Although this repetition is really only necessary on a verso, having it at the beginning of every page means that it will be possible to move the index back or forward a page at proof stage if this turns out to be desirable.

⑨ Other parts of a book

9.1

PAGE NUMBERS

There is no need for you to give instructions about page numbers, apart from saying where the arabic pagination is to begin (see section 7.1). However, you may find it useful to have some general background information.

Typesetters use the word 'folio' to mean a printed page number as well as a sheet of typescript (and also a format rarely used for books). It is used for printed page numbers in general, as in the phrase 'folios are at the foot of the page', rather than the number of a particular page: one does not say 'fo. 236' to mean p. 236 of a printed book; 'fo. 236' always refers to sheet 236 of the typescript.

Page numbers may be placed at the foot of the page or in the same line as the running head. They are usually in the running head if the book contains mathematics, because a page number at the foot might be confused with displayed mathematics; but if each chapter starts a fresh page, and therefore that page has no running head, the page number will be moved to the foot of the page, and enclosed in square brackets if necessary to avoid confusion with mathematics.

Page numbers are omitted from all blank pages and from the half-title and its verso, the title page and its verso, the dedication or epigraph page and any part-title leaves; also from the last page of the book if page numbers are at the foot.

The number is also omitted where there is a turned table or figure, or where a table or figure occupies more than the usual depth, provided that this will not mean more than two pages without numbers.

Although no number is printed on these pages, they are, of course, included in the page numbering; and one must make sure that a ringed number appears on the proof, so that there is no doubt where each page belongs. However, any halftones printed on different paper from the text are not usually included in the page numbering.

9.2
_____

RUNNING HEADS

Running heads are unnecessary unless they help the reader to find a particular part of the book. If the chapters have no titles, only the book title can be used for running heads, and their only function would be to help to fill the page. Most non-fiction books do have running heads, but it is worth asking yourself in each case whether they are necessary. Running heads are usually omitted if illustrations are to be extended into the top margin, or if as much text as possible must be fitted on to each page of a fairly simple book.

If the exact form of each running head cannot be decided until the book is paged, and so the running heads cannot be keyed with the rest of the book, they are more expensive. Such running heads should be avoided where possible, but they are needed in dictionaries and catalogues to show what is included on each page or pair of facing pages.

9.2.1   What should be used for running heads

Running heads should help the reader to find a particular part of the book; choose whatever you think will be most useful. The title of the larger section appears on the left, that of the smaller on the right:

Left (or _verso_)	_Right_ (or _recto_)
part title	chapter title
chapter title	main section title

though in a multi-author book one would probably have:

contributor's name	title of article

In journals, running heads may be the same both sides and consist of author(s) and abbreviated article title.

In dictionaries, running heads usually consist of the first and last items on the page; in catalogues there may be a section title and the names or numbers of the first and last items on the page – or the first item on the left-hand page and the last item on the right-hand.

If chapter and/or section numbers are used for many cross-references, they should be included in the running head, unless sections are numbered by chapter (e.g. 2.1, 2.2) and are less than two pages long, in which case the section headings in the text will be sufficient guide. If there are endnotes, *either* the chapter number must appear in the text running heads, in which case the running head to the notes will be 'Notes to chapter 6', *or* the relevant page numbers of the text must appear in running heads to the notes: 'Notes to pages 86–9'. The second alternative is more helpful to the reader, though it does mean that the running heads cannot be completed until the book has been paged. The running heads should give the numbers of the relevant pages only, not the page numbers for the whole of the relevant chapter.

Where the running heads are chapter title (left) and section title (right), and the first section title does not come at the beginning of the chapter, give the chapter title as the right-hand running head in that chapter until the section titles begin. Where a new section starts at the top of a right-hand page, there may be a problem if the running head and subheading are very similar in typeface and position (e.g. both centred small capitals); if so, the chapter title or an abbreviated form of the section title should be used for the running head, to avoid having identical headings one above the other. Where a new section starts below the top of a right-hand page, the title of the new section should be used as the running head. Where more than one new section starts on the page, the first or last new heading may be used as the running head, but the same rule must be used throughout.

Preliminary pages
The running heads are usually the same, left and right, for example 'Preface'. Running heads for lists of plates and so on are in the form 'List of plates' rather than 'Plates'.

Appendixes
The running heads are usually 'Appendix 1' on the left and the appendix title on the right.

Bibliography and indexes
The running heads are usually the same, left and right. Give each index its own running head, for example 'Index of passages cited'.

So in a book such as this one the running heads would include the following:

Left (or *verso*)	*Right* (or *recto*)
Contents	Contents
. . .	
1 Introduction	What copy-editing is 1.1
	Typescripts: hard, electronic, camera-ready 1.2
2 Estimates and specimen pages	Briefing the designer 2.1
	Marking the typescript for an estimate 2.2
. . .	
Appendix 1	Checklist of copy-editing
. . .	
Glossary	Glossary
Select bibliography	Select bibliography
Index	Index

Pages that should have no running head
Running heads are omitted above headings that intentionally start new pages (e.g. chapter or part headings); above all turned illustrations and tables; above text illustrations and tables that extend beyond the type area (except at the foot) and are not turned. Running heads are included above headings that accidentally occur at the heads of pages (including chapter headings in a book with run-on chapters); above text illustrations and tables that fall within the type area and are not turned.

9.2.2 Length

Long chapter titles are not usually split between the left-hand and right-hand page, because one may be left with a nonsense running head if the chapter begins or ends on a left-hand page or there is no running head on a page containing an illustration or table. If you cannot easily shorten the titles to fit on to one page, ask the author to provide shortened forms. Say how many letters and spaces are available; you can work this out from running heads in the pattern volume or from the design specification. If you provide short forms yourself, send the author a list: a change in the running heads at proof stage can be very expensive.

If page numbers are set beside the running head, there should be a space between the two. Allow for this when calculating the length.

9.2.3 **Style**

Running heads are often set in spaced small capitals or upper- and lower-case italic. In some typefaces there are no true italic small capitals, and some designers prefer not to have roman words in an italic running head, so the titles of literary works, or foreign words that are italic in the text, may be distinguished by being enclosed in quotation marks. As quotes tend to give words a self-conscious look, it is probably better not to distinguish foreign words if the roman/italic distinction cannot be retained. If such a distinction is important, ask the designer to retain it if possible. If necessary, warn the author that quotes will be used for book titles, etc.

In upper- and lower-case running heads, initial capitals are normally used only for the first word and proper names; tell the typesetter this if you are not sending a list. Say whether accents should be used on French capitals.

9.2.4 **Copy for the typesetter**

Provide the typesetter with a list if shortened titles are to be used, unless the running heads will differ from page to page and the typesetter knows the exact form they should take. The list should be headed with the author's name and short book title, and should cover the preliminary pages and indexes as well as the text, endnotes and bibliography; and it should give the exact wording and capitalization (and accents and quotation marks where appropriate). Check the list after it is typed: a mistake in a chapter title can be very expensive if the chapter is long; and a mistake in the book title would be even worse. If a chapter or section title – or the book title – is changed at typescript stage, make sure that the new form is included in the list of running heads as well as in the contents list.

9.3

HEADINGS

Unless your publisher has a system of coding all headings, the headings in the preliminary pages and endmatter do not need to be identified in any way: the designer may wish the contents list and index to have a less prominent style than the chapter headings.

For headings to parts, see section 3.5.3.

9.3.1 Chapter headings

The word 'chapter' is often omitted from the chapter heading. If the chapter titles are abnormally long you may want to persuade the author to shorten them: long headings can be off-putting and they are difficult to design effectively. Another problem for designers is a great variation in length, with some one- or two-word titles and others much longer.

9.3.2 Subheadings

Try to confine subheadings to a maximum of three grades in each size of type, except in reference books. In running text a reader finds a great variety of headings confusing rather than helpful; and it is difficult for the designer to specify more than three kinds of heading that will be sufficiently distinct from one another and from table headings, running heads, etc.

Whether the major grades of subheading should be numbered depends on the kind of book. Numbered headings are useful in reference books and textbooks, where they can provide a convenient form of cross-reference. In science books, subheadings are usually numbered, often decimally by chapter:

section 6.1 (first section in chapter 6)
subsection 6.1.3 (third subsection in section 6.1)

A decimal system can make the hierarchy of subheadings clear without having to use a different typographical style for each grade.

However, one should not retain numbers just because they appear in the typescript: in a book about literature, for example, the numbers may merely be the remains of the outline on which the author constructed the book, and they may make the book look like a textbook. If you think it would be better to add or delete section numbers, discuss this with the author. The same grade of subheading should normally be treated in the same way throughout the book.

It can happen that an author combines two short chapters under a general title, and uses for their own titles a major grade of subheading not used elsewhere; if so point this out to the designer.

Some authors number introductory sections with a zero, so that the introductory section in chapter 6 would be 6.0. If sections are introduced by a centred number, some authors omit 1 if it occurs immediately below the chapter title, to give the page a neater appearance; so the first section number to appear is 2. I suggest you do not introduce such a system yourself.

Marginal notes and headings entail wider margins; unless the margins are very wide there will be space for only a word or two, so a long heading may straggle a long way and be difficult to read. If the author wants marginal headings, tell the designer the average and largest number of characters and ask whether such headings would be feasible.

9.3.3 Coding the subheadings

The designer, working from your coding of the typescript, will specify the typographical style for the headings, and say whether those on a separate line are to be centred, full out left or indented. It is for you to see that the hierarchy is logical and clearly marked in the typescript, and to decide whether the lowest-grade heading can be run on at the beginning of a paragraph instead of occupying a separate line: in general these run-on headings should not be used to introduce sections of more than a page or two.

The subheadings should be coded in the margin, by a ringed letter or number, according to their place in the hierarchy. Subheadings in sections to be set in smaller type (e.g. appendixes, bibliography, theorems) should be coded differently from those in text type, because the designer specifies the type size as well as the style for each code letter. If you code the headings before the designer has decided whether the displayed material in the text will be set in the same size as the bibliography and any appendixes, a complicated book might need several codes:

chapter headings: ch. hd or CH
subheadings in text type: A, B, C
subheadings in displayed material: X, Y, Z
subheadings in endnotes or appendixes: 1, 2, 3
subheadings in bibliography: i, ii, iii

Make sure that the coding in the designer's specification and any specimen pages corresponds with the coding in the typescript.

9.3.4 Style

Warn the designer about any factors that may affect the style of the subheadings: for example if they are very long or very short, or contain Greek, arabic figures, lower-case symbols, etc., or if any chapter does not contain the first or an intermediate grade. If subheadings are set in small capitals or italic, one has the same problem as in running heads, that of distinguishing titles of literary works or foreign words that are italic in the text (see section 9.2.3). If the roman/italic distinction is important, tell the designer.

Sometimes there is a problem in marking the end of a short, headed section, where a line of space might break up the text too much. For example, a heading might introduce only one or two paragraphs out of the many that follow. In textbooks there may be examples, or theorems followed by proofs, that are too long to set in italic, and the author may be very anxious that they should not be set in small type, for fear that they should be regarded as less important than the main text. To put space before and after them may break the book up too much; conversely in a book already broken up by much displayed mathematics, such a break may not show up. It may be best to begin them with a run-on heading and to indent them or indicate the end by a symbol; the designer will be able to suggest a suitable device. Make sure that the end is clearly indicated in the typescript.

You should do any editorial marking necessary. For instance, headings occupying a separate line should not be followed by a full point, whereas those which are to run on may have one or may be followed by a fixed em space. In upper- and lower-case headings it is normal to have an initial capital for only the first word and proper names; see that the capitalization will be clear to the typesetter, for example if the heading has been typed in capitals. Add any quotation marks or symbols necessary to make the distinctions mentioned in the two preceding paragraphs. Make clear whether the first line after a heading that occupies a separate line should be indented or not, if this will not be covered by your coding and the designer's specification.

9.4

FOOTNOTES AND ENDNOTES

Publishers ask their authors to present their notes in one batch, double-spaced and numbered in one sequence through each chapter. Authors who present them single-spaced at the foot of the relevant text folio, in a misguided attempt to simulate the final appearance of the book, should, where possible, be asked to provide new copy.

9.4.1 Endnotes or footnotes?

Whether the notes are to be endnotes or footnotes will depend on the readership, the kind of note, the economic factors and the author's view. Endnotes cannot be consulted so easily, but they leave the text uncluttered. They are often cheaper than footnotes: they do not have to be fitted on the text page; and unlike footnotes numbered by page, they do not have to be renumbered by the typesetter. However, there are now computerized page make-up systems that can number footnotes by page.

A book may have both footnotes and endnotes: if it will appeal to general readers as well as scholars, one may relegate to endnotes the sources which few readers will want to follow up, but retain as footnotes the additional pieces of information which the general reader may enjoy but which cannot easily be fitted into the text. In an edition of a text, the editorial notes may be printed as endnotes, to distinguish them from the original footnotes; or the original notes may be printed as endnotes if they are thought to be less useful to the reader; or there may be two sets of footnotes (see below). Where there are both endnotes and footnotes, the endnotes are keyed by number and the footnotes by symbol, usually in the sequence * † ‡ § ‖ ¶, repeated in duplicate if necessary.

9.4.2 **Footnotes**

Very long footnotes should, if the author agrees, be taken into the text or made into appendixes. Very short notes, such as cross-references or short sources of quotations, may be taken into the text too. Try to move into the text any complex mathematical setting, as this would become more difficult to read in footnote-size type.

Footnotes may sometimes be shortened by omitting information already given in the text: for example, if the author, title and page number are mentioned in the text, the footnote need give only publisher, place and date. In fact there is a movement towards omitting publication details from footnotes unless they are of particular significance, provided there is a full bibliography; this is another way of cutting down the number of footnotes, but it should ideally be done before the typescript reaches the copy-editor.

Style
All footnotes should end in a full point. Some publishers start footnotes with a lower-case letter if they begin with one of the following abbreviations: *c.*, e.g., i.e., l., ll., p., pp. and possibly cf., *ibid.*, *op. cit.*, *loc. cit.* If you decide to retain the lower-case forms, and the typesetter is not familiar with this style in your books, explain the system on a style sheet.

If the footnote copy is at the end of each chapter rather than in one batch at the end of the book, give the folio number for the relevant notes on the first folio of each chapter (e.g. 'Footnote copy on fos. 28–9').

Text indicators
In order to avoid having an indicator in a heading, a general note to a chapter may appear without an indicator at the foot of the first page. It should be clearly identified for the typesetter.

Check that all other notes have text indicators and that no notes are missing. It is very important that this should be got right at the type-script stage: a typesetter who notices that a note is missing may delay paging the book until you can say how much space should be left for the note. A missing footnote indicator would mean guessing which page the note refers to, and this could lead to repaging at proof stage and possibly alterations to the index.

It is not enough to see that there are no gaps or repeated numbers in the sequence of notes and of indicators: the two sequences must tally. Authors sometimes delete or add a note, renumber the notes accordingly but forget to change the indicators, in which case all the indicators from that point to the end of the chapter would have to be corrected, and the notes moved, at proof stage. One can usually pick up this kind of discrepancy by checking that note and indicator sequences are both complete and end at the same number; but it is better to see that each note tallies in subject matter with the text preceding the indicator. If a spot check shows that something is wrong, ask the author to check the notes thoroughly.

In science and mathematics books footnotes are relatively rare, and the copy-editor may be instructed to move them into the text (in parentheses) wherever possible. Where footnotes remain, symbols are used as text indicators, to avoid any confusion with superscript figures in the text; the series starts with a dagger if an asterisk is used in the text.

In other books footnotes are usually keyed by superscript figures.

In some computer-aided systems it is as cheap to number the foot-notes from 1 on each page (and this is clearly preferable); but in general it is much cheaper to number the footnotes in one sequence through-out each chapter, so that the numbering need not be changed.

Indicators in the text are less distracting to the reader if they are moved to the end of the sentence or to a break in the sense; but if the author is discussing specific words, it would mislead the reader if the reference was moved. Also one should, if possible, avoid placing two indicators at the same point. Ask the author if you are in doubt. For aesthetic reasons, text indicators are placed after punctuation (except dashes), unless the reference is to a single word at the end of a sentence or of a parenthetical phrase.

9.4.3 **Books containing more than one set of footnotes**

There may be two or more sets of footnotes in an edition of a text. If some are original and some editorial, the editorial ones should be distinguished: they could be keyed differently (perhaps the editor's by number, the author's by symbol), or enclosed in square brackets or followed by '[Ed.]'. It is sufficient to use one of these devices; but if one of the first two is used, it should be explained in the preliminary pages.

There will often be more than one kind of editorial note, for example one textual, one about content; sometimes there are three kinds. Textual notes often start with a line number and so do not need to be keyed into the text; but line numbering is expensive, and the line numbers for prose passages are not known until the text has been typeset, because typesetters do not follow the original line for line as they do with verse. In such cases the text may be typeset before the rest of the book, so that the line numbers can be added to the typescript of the notes.

If the text has a prose translation facing it, the two will probably differ in length, and the notes may be so arranged as to compensate for this, because one kind of note is likely to occupy more space than another. If the notes apply to both text and translation (i.e. are about subject matter rather than textual points) they cannot be keyed by line number, because the two versions cannot easily be set line for line.

9.4.4 **Endnotes**

Endnotes are usually numbered in one sequence throughout each chapter. See that all the notes have text indicators and vice versa, and that the numbering contains no gaps or added numbers such as 15a. For the placing of text indicators at a break in sense and in relation to punctuation, see under footnotes above.

See that essential information is provided both in the text and in the endnotes. For example, if a phrase is quoted in the text, the reader should not have to look at the endnote to discover its author. Similarly, if *op. cit.* is being used, the first reference in the notes must include the author as well as the title; otherwise the reader will look back in vain for Hazel, *op. cit.*

There are two opposing schools of thought as to the best position for endnotes. If there are to be offprints, the notes will be at the end of the relevant chapter; otherwise I myself think they are easier to find if they are in one batch just before the bibliography.

They should be headed 'Notes' or 'Notes to the text'; and if all the endnotes are together, the chapter number and title should appear as a subheading above the notes for each chapter. Authors often provide subheadings such as 'Notes to chapter 3'; this should be changed to '3 The use of prepositions', or whatever the title is.

If the chapter number is included in the running heads for the text, the running heads for the notes could be 'Notes to chapter 0'; but it is more helpful to the reader if the relevant page numbers of the text are given in the running heads for the notes (e.g. 'Notes to pages 85–9').

9.4.5 **Notes to letters and documents**

Notes are sometimes placed at the end of the relevant letter or document, sometimes at the foot of the page, sometimes at the end of the book. If the document is long, notes at the end of it may be difficult to find: if the book contains many long documents it may be sensible to combine two systems and to place the notes either at the foot of the page or at the end of the document, whichever comes first; for example, if a document runs from p. 63 to the middle of p. 69, the notes for pp. 63–8 would be at the foot of the relevant page, and those for p. 69 immediately after the end of the document. By using this system one can number the notes throughout each document without any ambiguity if two short documents, and therefore two notes numbered 1, appear on the same page.

9.4.6 **Notes to tables**

Notes should be placed immediately below the table and should use a different system of indicators from the footnotes or endnotes. See section 9.5.1.

9.4.7 **Marginal notes**

If an author wants to retain marginal notes, consult the designer or production department; marginal notes entail wider margins and are not usually necessary.

9.4.8 **Superscript numbers referring to a bibliography**

See section 10.3.

9.5

TABLES

If the book is to be typeset conventionally, it is not usually necessary to separate the tables from the rest of the text. If the author provides some tables on separate sheets, include them in the folio numbering and mark the best position in the margin of the text: 'Table 6 near here from fo. 115.'

You may need to mark the exact extent of tables that are not on separate sheets, because it is sometimes difficult for a typesetter to distinguish between a general note that is part of the table and a comment that happens to follow in the text (see fig. 9.1). If the typesetter could be certain of placing the table exactly where it is in the typescript, the distinction would not matter, but there might not be space for the table at the foot of the relevant page, in which case the table and its notes would have to be moved to the next page and the intervening space filled with text. A pencil line in the margin may be used to show the extent of the table and its notes; some publishers also code the individual parts of the table and indicate which rules should be included. (For large tables see section 9.5.3.)

As some authors expect tables to be placed exactly where they occur in the typescript, they may use such phrases as 'the trade figures are as follows', or 'the trade figures in the table' even if there are several tables in the chapter. Even authors who number their tables may expect each one to be in exactly the relevant place. Warn the author that the typesetter could find it difficult or impossible to place tables of more than four or five lines exactly where they appear in the typescript, unless

Lendon boys' school may be taken as an example of a school
which was run efficiently and secured good, if not enthusiastic,
reports. With Trinity it was among the earliest to introduce
pupil-teachers.

<u>Hyson Green boys' school, 1854</u>

Present 55

Reading	Letters and monosyllables	25 boys
	Easy narrative	14 "
	General information	0 "
Writing	On slates from copy	7 "
	On paper	27 "
	(15 were not writing)	
Arithmetic	Four rules and below	12 "
	No advanced work	
Extra subjects	History	15 "

This was a poor school which earned a series of bad reports
at this time. It will be seen that the curriculum was in
effect confined to reading and writing.

In 1873 the local Inspector, Mr Capel Sewell wrote a
letter to the chairman of the School Board, which gives some
information about the condition of the elementary schools at
the time when the School Board took over.

Fig. 9.1 Why one should mark the extent of a table. 'This', in the sentence following the table, refers to the school in the table and not to the efficiently run school in the immediately preceding text. If the table cannot be placed exactly where it is in the typescript, the sentence will have to be turned into a note to the table, so that it remains with it.

they may be split between two pages; and perhaps your publisher asks its typesetters to place tables at the head or foot of the page. The author may prefer tables to be split (if necessary) rather than moved, or may feel that if they cannot be placed in the exactly relevant position they would be better grouped at the end of the chapter or in an appendix. If the author insists that the tables must be placed as in the typescript (and says that they may be split), say so in the margin beside each one. If they may be split only in certain places, give the necessary instructions.

Because they are likely to be moved, tables of more than four or five lines should be numbered, and references to them changed from 'as follows' to 'in table 6', or to 'in table 2.3' if they are numbered by chapter. If a table is in the middle of a paragraph in the typescript, and is followed by a new sentence, mark the text to run on.

If two tables share a number, persuade the author to let you renumber them as two separate tables; otherwise their structure may become very complicated. If two tables should appear in the same opening, so that they can be compared, note this in the margin.

If some numbered tables have titles and others do not, you might suggest to the author that the tables will look more consistent and be more useful to the reader if all of them do have titles.

While you are looking at the tables for consistency with one another, see whether those containing similar material are laid out in the same way, so that they can be compared: for example that what are column headings in one table are not side headings in another, and that, as far as possible, similar wording and units are used. If one table shows areas in acres and another in hectares, this probably follows the sources the author consulted; in a specialized book one might want to show exactly what the sources said, but in a more general one it is the area, rather than the way it was measured, that is important, and the author may just not have thought it worth the trouble to convert them. By converting round numbers of acres to round numbers of hectares, one is moving further away from the accuracy of the original measurements; so you should discuss the matter with the author.

The author should use the same terms in similar tables, but only, of course, where similar terms apply: for example census figures may cover slightly different areas in different years, because of a change in boundaries.

Does each table make its point clearly? Is the information in the column and side headings adequate and concise? Are the units, date and source given? Is the information consistent with the text? Authors may obtain more recent data and include them in the table, but fail to alter the text accordingly.

Some authors provide a table and then repeat the same information in the text, rather than just commenting on significant points.

9.5.1 **The parts of a table** (see fig. 9.2)

See that the structure of the table is clear: for example whether two or three columns should be grouped under one heading; this grouping may be shown by a horizontal line (sometimes called a spanner rule) or a brace (bracket) below the shared heading.

Vertical rules are almost always unnecessary, so publishers avoid them. If the author has included vertical rules in a complex table, ask whether any of these must be retained; any essential ones must be

Table 8. *The pattern of peasant labourers' wealth*

Stub	Percentage of wealth invested in domestic goods		Average value of domestic goods	
	1560–1600	1610–40	1560–1600	1610–40
			£ s d	£ s d
Northern lowlands	18	29	10 0	1 9 4
Northern fells	34	—	1 6 8	—
Midland fielden areas[a]	35	46	2 16 6	3 12 8
Midland forest areas[a]	44	39	2 9 6	4 10 0
Hertfordshire	59	69	4 3 9	7 9 10
Eastern counties	—	48	—	3 18 4
Somerset	—	65	—	5 17 0
All England	40	50	2 5 3	4 9 6

Spanner rules →

Based on probate inventories; for the basis of selection of inventories (in some degree affecting the reliability of the 'average value of domestic goods'), see p. 413, n. 2.
[a]Including a few inventories of the 1660s for Northants.

Fig. 9.2 Parts of a table.

identified in the typescript. Some tables have a diagonal rule in the top left-hand corner; if this rule is essential, point these tables out to the designer.

If the table is complex and is not very well laid out, have it retyped. Leave the exact spacing to the designer or typesetter, but indicate where extra space is needed; if a table contains a large number of long rows it may be sensible to ask for extra space after every four or five, to help the reader's eye to follow the correct line along.

Mark capitalization and punctuation; headings and items should have no full point. Ditto marks should be eliminated by using sub-headings or by repeating the relevant words.

Table heading

See that headings are consistent in content and style, and keep capital letters to a minimum. The title, usually preceded by 'Table 1' or 'Table 1.1', should be as short as possible, though without the use of unnecessary abbreviations. The reader wants to be able to see at a glance what the subject of the table is, and any general information may be given in a note below the table. If the same unit applies throughout the table, for example '00,000', it is usually given in parentheses after the title and need not be used in the table columns.

Column headings

Column headings are usually in roman, but a rule used by the author to separate the headings from the columns may look like underlining for italic; clarify this if necessary. See that the headings are consistent in content and style, and contain the minimum necessary information. All units and percentages must be identified, and multiples of units must be expressed unambiguously: '10^3 kg' is better than 'kg $(\times 10^3)$'. It is better to put the unit or % in the column heading than beside each number. Long headings to columns should be avoided, if necessary by using numbers or letters with a key below the table. The headings should have an initial capital for the first word and proper names only.

Stub

The stub is the left-hand column, which identifies the rows in the same way as the column headings identify the columns. Mark up any subheadings and see that they are correctly placed; authors often place the first one as though it were the heading to the whole column. If the author uses spans such as 1–10, 10–20, 20–30, ask whether they should be 11–20, 21–30 and so on, so that the spans do not overlap. The typesetter should be told whether the setting should be unjustified and whether turnover lines should start full out left or indented (and, if indented, how much). If there are indented subentries, it is probably better not to indent turnovers.

Totals
The word 'Total' may be indented or set in small capitals, and there may be extra space or a rule above the total.

Numbers etc.
If the decimals in any column have different numbers of digits after the decimal point, it should be to indicate the accuracy of the result; but some authors are lax about this, and you may want to query it. See that the decimal point is preceded by a digit (a zero if necessary), except in quantities that never reach 1 (e.g. levels of probability) and ballistics. Say whether the decimal point should be medial (raised) or low (on the line), and alter decimal commas to points. Mark decimal points to align vertically if the rows contain similar units, and especially if the column has a total. Even if four-digit numbers are treated differently from five-digit ones in the text – 2438 as against 24,380 or 24 380 – they must be in the same style as five-digit numbers in tables, so as to align with them. If the columns contain words rather than numbers, say how the items and any turnover lines should be aligned.

Check totals, whether stated or (in the case of percentages) implied; but do not worry if percentages come to 99 or 101: the individual figures may have been rounded up or down.

Em rules do not mean the same thing as zero, so do not try to make them 'consistent'; but if the tables contain em rules, spaces, unexplained letter symbols such as *x*, leaders (two or three points), NDA and NA, ask the author what the distinction is and make the meaning clear in the notes to the table. If some tables contain minus quantities, em rules should not be used to indicate a lack of data.

Notes

Notes are placed immediately below the table, though some publishers place any general note immediately below the table title. There are four kinds – general notes, sources, notes on specific parts of the table, and notes on levels of probability – and the same order should be used throughout the book. See that the notes are consistent in style, that any sources are adequately acknowledged and that the author has obtained any permission necessary for the use of any tables taken from other publications.

A general note needs no indicator, but if it does not have one it should precede any other notes. Notes to specific parts of a table should be keyed differently from notes to the text: symbols or superscript lower-case letters may be used, or superscript figures if these are not used for text footnotes or elsewhere in the table.

Levels of probability are indicated by *, **, etc., so do not change the double asterisk to a dagger. The sequence of note indicators should read along the rows: an indicator in the first line of the second column precedes an indicator in the second line of the first column. If a table occupies more than one page or opening, it may be necessary to repeat the relevant notes in each opening.

9.5.2 Tables that include artwork

Watch out for genealogical or similar tables for which artwork will be needed. If there is also a heading or footnote that is not to be included in the artwork, send the typesetter a photocopy of the folio, with the artwork area ringed; it is easy to forget to do this, and to realize only at proof stage that the heading or note is missing; and of course it may then be difficult to find the copy for the relevant heading or note, and equally difficult to find space to fit it in.

9.5.3 Large tables

Authors may tailor the amount of data in a table to the size of the sheet of paper that they normally work on, rather than the number of characters that will fit across a page of the book (either upright or turned). Authors who work with complicated data may use A3 paper; but it may be possible for them to divide the data and make two or more equally useful but smaller tables.

The number of characters that can be fitted on to a printed page depends on the type size chosen and the amount of space that must be left between the columns. Ask the designer for a brief which you can pass on to the author.

It may be easier to fit a table on to a page if the axis is changed, that is if the column headings become side headings and vice versa (see fig. 9.3); but do not do this if it means that tables which the reader may want to compare are orientated differently.

	Heading A	Heading B	Heading C	Heading D	Heading E
Item 1	xxxxxxxxx	xxxxxxxxx	xxxxxxxxx	xxxxxxxxx	xxxxxxxxx
Item 2	xxxxxxxxx	xxxxxxxxx	xxxxxxxxx	xxxxxxxxx	xxxxxxxxx

would fit better as

	Item 1	Item 2
Heading A	xxxxxxxxxx	xxxxxxxxxx
Heading B	xxxxxxxxxx	xxxxxxxxxx
Heading C	xxxxxxxxxx	xxxxxxxxxx
Heading D	xxxxxxxxxx	xxxxxxxxxx
Heading E	xxxxxxxxxx	xxxxxxxxxx

Fig. 9.3 A table with many columns and few items in each column may fit on to a page more easily if column headings become side headings and vice versa.

Say how a table occupying more than one folio runs on from one folio to the next (fig. 9.4) and where it may be split. Give this information on the first folio of each table, either in diagrammatic form as in fig. 9.4(*b*) or in a note such as: 'Table 2.2 is divided into "a" and "b". Both parts, i.e. fos. 41–2 and 43–4, run on horizontally and may be divided at any vertical line in the typescript.' If you are not sure where a table may be split, ask the author. If the whole of certain tables must be visible at the same time, this may mean a fold-out, which is expensive.

It helps the typesetter if you ring, on the second and subsequent folios, the headings which are to be repeated only at the start of each fresh page (or left-hand page). In the example given above, the headings to be ringed would be the items in the stub, because the table runs on horizontally. If the table ran on from the foot of each column, the column headings should be ringed.

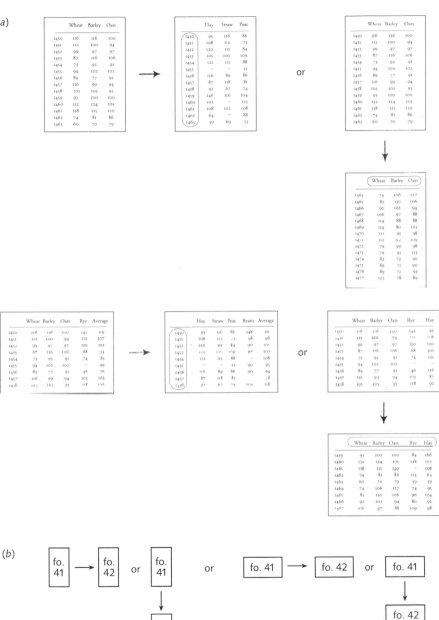

Fig. 9.4 If a table occupies more than one folio, make it clear to the typesetter how the folios relate (a). The instruction may be in diagrammatic form (b). On the tables themselves, ring the headings that are to be repeated only at the start of each page or left-hand page

The table number is usually repeated at the top of each page: 'Table 6 *cont.*' Consider whether a shortened form of the title should also be given. If the table is turned on the page and runs across an opening, the table number, and probably the column headings, would be given only once. Give the typesetter the necessary instructions. Say whether the notes should appear on the first page only, on the last page only, or on every opening.

Tables that are to be compared with one another should be printed the same way up, if possible, so that the reader does not have to keep turning the book. Point these out to the designer if some, but not all, are likely to be turned on the page.

If a large table runs across two folios, see that the line spacing on the folios is the same: a difference of half a line in the spacing of all the items would mean that the lines would get out of step and the typesetter would not be able to tell which line ran on to which.

9.6

APPENDIXES

Appendixes are usually in smaller type than the text, as they are less important; but they may be set in text type if they contain complicated mathematics, long quotations or other displayed material.

Appendixes usually precede any endnotes and bibliography. Tell the typesetter whether each appendix, or only the first, is to start a fresh page: this depends partly on length and partly on whether the appendixes are closely related in subject matter; tell the author if you are planning to run them on. If the book is divided into parts, each preceded by a title leaf, there should be a title leaf before the first appendix too.

The running heads are usually 'Appendix 1' on the left and the appendix title on the right.

Appendixes to individual chapters usually run on from the end of the chapter. In a book that has a list of references at the end of each paper, the appendix precedes the references. If the appendix is long enough to need running heads, these should probably be 'Appendix to chapter 5' on the left and the appendix title on the right.

9.7

GLOSSARIES

If a book contains technical terms that may not be familiar to some readers, the terms should be explained at their first occurrence in the text; but if they are used more than once they should also be listed in a glossary, which is usually placed immediately before the bibliography and index (if any) so that it can be found easily. If the glossary is only one or two pages, it may be placed at the end of the prelims.

Check the coverage of any glossary in the typescript; see whether the author has omitted some difficult words and included some that are unnecessary. See that spelling, accents and ligatures tally with the text. Check also the alphabetical order, the use of italic and the punctuation; avoid (or explain) the use of a foreign alphabetical order.

Glossaries can be difficult to lay out clearly, because they may contain various kinds of information in a very short form: for example, an entry might consist of a French headword, part of speech, meaning of headword, and discussion which might include other French words or phrases. One could perhaps italicize all the French and put all meanings within single quotes; the decision would vary according to the material involved, and it would be sensible to consult the designer if the material was complicated. However, most glossaries are simpler than this, and you should avoid the use of quotation marks if you can. If the glossary is set in a single column, turnover lines are indented, so that the headwords stand out; if headwords and definitions are in separate columns, the turnover lines of the definitions need not be indented.

⑩ Bibliographical references

It is not necessary to back every piece of information by a reference, for example to a dictionary or general encyclopedia. However, the sources of quotations, the grounds for controversial statements, and acknowledgements of other people's work should be given.

Most publishers now give their authors examples of how to word bibliographical references, and this can save the copy-editor a great deal of trouble. Some publishers have a preferred style but are prepared to accept a different one, provided it is complete and consistent; this saves the time and effort otherwise required to put the entries into house style.

There are three relevant British Standards: BS 1629: *References to Published Materials*; BS 4148: *Abbreviation of Title Words and Titles of Publications*; and BS 5605: *Citing and Referencing Published Material.* Other standard reference works, such as *The Chicago Manual of Style*, can also be helpful.

The four usual methods of referring to sources may be called the short-title system (see section 10.1), the author–date system (see 10.2), reference by number only (see 10.3) and the author–number system (see 10.4). The first of these is used in most general books, the second mainly in science and social science books; the third and fourth are used less frequently. For comments on lists of further reading, see section 10.5.

This chapter does not cover what could be called the *op.cit.* system. *Op. cit.* in such references as

> Brock, *op. cit.*

adds no useful information; and if the full reference is not in the bibliography, or there are two books by the same author, the reader will have to search back through the text or notes to find the full citation – and may not be sure that it is the right one. Some publishers include a short title:

> Brock, *Family Relations, op. cit.*

Some add a cross-reference to the full citation after each *op. cit.,* but this could involve inserting a page number at proof stage, and also making it absolutely clear that it *is* a cross-reference and not a reference to a page or note in the work cited. Authors who use *op. cit.* may be asked for a revised version of the notes, substituting fuller references.

The exact punctuation within references does not matter, provided all the necessary information is given clearly and consistently. If the material in the typescript is unsatisfactory, tell the commissioning editor what needs to be done to improve the presentation, as it is probably better to ask the author to do the necessary work. Similarly, if more than one system is used in a multi-author book, discuss with the commissioning editor whether the material should be returned to the contributors or whether it is worth your introducing a consistent system; if a great deal of work would be involved, it may not be, but it will depend on the level and kind of book (see section 12.1.5).

Whatever the system, you should see that every reference in the text and notes tallies (form and spelling of author's name; date; wording, spelling and capitalization of title; publication place; and page numbers, where relevant) with the bibliography or list of references. If there are discrepancies, send the author a list or an annotated photocopy.

You should also check, and if necessary mark, the spacing of the various elements. For example, are authors' initials and groups of numbers such as '18: 2' consistently spaced or closed up?

Punctuation of references in the notes does differ from the punctuation in a bibliography, because the reference may form part of a sentence in the note. For example:

1 See the discussion in J. A. Hazel, *The Growth of the Cotton Trade in Lancashire,* 3rd edn (4 vols., London, Textile Press, 1987–8), vol. 3, p. 2.
2 Colin Haselgrove disputes this in 'The archaeology of British potin coinage' (*Archaeological Journal,* 145 (1988), 99–122); he suggests that it was a special purpose money.

In the bibliography these might become:

Haselgrove, C. C. 'The archaeology of British potin coinage', *Archaeological Journal,* 145 (1988), 99–122
Hazel, J. A. *The Growth of the Cotton Trade in Lancashire,* 3rd edn, 4 vols., London, Textile Press, 1987–8

Titles are treated like quotations and should not be made to conform in spelling and hyphenation to the style used in the rest of the book. If the references appear to have been standardized, for example with British spelling even for US journals, ask the author to check them.

For capitalization see pp. 234–5.

It is sometimes difficult to see what certain elements are, particularly if the reference is to a foreign source; if you are at all doubtful as to how things should be treated, ask the author.

A list called 'References' or 'Works cited' should include all the works cited in the text and no others. A 'Bibliography' may contain either more or less than the author has cited: if there are only a few omissions, it is worth asking the author whether these omissions are intentional; if there are many omissions it should probably be called 'Select bibliography'.

An alternative to a formal bibliography is a discursive note on sources, either for each chapter or for the whole book, explaining which authorities the author has used and discussing their relevance and merits.

10.1

SHORT-TITLE SYSTEM

10.1.1 Form of reference in notes

The most usual form of the short-title system provides a full reference only at the first mention in the book, though it may be better to give a full reference at the first mention in each chapter if there are a great many notes and (a) the book in question is not included in the select bibliography, or (b) there is no bibliography, or (c) the bibliography is much subdivided or is a list of further reading that is not arranged alphabetically. *Hart's Rules* allow for short titles to be used throughout, which is all right if all the works can easily be found in the bibliography.

(a) **Published books**

The numbers in parentheses in the following description refer to the examples given below. For further details about the various parts of a reference, see section 10.1.2.

First reference

author's name	initials or forename precede surname
book title, plus subtitle if this is necessary to clarify the main title (1)	underlined for italic; the title of another work included in the title should be in single quotes (2). (Note that the title of an unpublished thesis should be roman in quotes; see p. 238)
editor, compiler, translator or reviser, if any (3, 7, 8)	if there is no author, the editor or compiler will precede the title (4)
series, if any, plus number within series (6)	series name should not usually be underlined for italic; but a work in more than one volume will have italic for both main title and volume title (if any) (4)
edition, if not the first (5)	
number of volumes, publication place, publisher and date	all in parentheses; place may be omitted where it also forms part of the publisher's name (1)
volume (if more than one) and page number	'vol.' and 'p.' can be omitted if there is no ambiguity. If only the relevant volume is mentioned in the reference, the volume number should precede the place (6)

Examples

1 Mary Hamer, *Writing by Numbers: Trollope's Serial Fiction* (Cambridge University Press, 1987), p. 25.
2 P. W. K. Stone, *The Textual History of 'King Lear'* (London, Scolar Press, 1980), p. 40.

3 Fanny Burney, *Camilla: or A Picture of Youth*, ed. Edward A. Bloom and Lillian D. Bloom (London, Oxford University Press, 1972), p. 112.

4 E. Martin Browne (ed.), *Religious Drama* 2: *Twenty-one Medieval Mystery and Morality Plays* (New York, Meridian, 1958), p. 5.

5 J. A. Hazel, *The Growth of the Cotton Trade in Lancashire*, 3rd edn (4 vols., London, Textile Press, 1987–8), vol. 3, p. 2.

6 P. Carter, *Frognal to Englands Lane*, London Street Names Series, no. 4 (London, Textile Press, 1990), p. 45.

7 Lara-Vinca Masini, *Art Nouveau*, tr. Linda Fairbairn (London, Thames & Hudson, 1984).

8 H.W. Fowler, *A Dictionary of Modern English Usage*, 2nd edn, revised by Sir Ernest Gowers (Oxford, Clarendon Press, 1965).

For translations the original title, language and publication date may also be given.

Sometimes the 'author' will be a government department or other organization:

Central Advisory Council for Education (England), *Children and their Primary Schools* [Plowden Report] (2 vols., London, HMSO, 1967)

Where the report has a familiar title, there will probably be a cross-reference from this to the full citation:

Plowden Report, *see under* Central Advisory Council for Education

If the organization is also the publisher, it may be best to treat the work as anonymous and list it under its title:

Book Production Practice, 2nd edn (London, British Printing Industries Federation and Publishers Association, 1984)

If there is a full bibliography in a single alphabetical sequence, the first reference in the notes may consist merely of author, title, volume and page number, with the date of publication if this is relevant to the argument. If the author's name and the book title are given in the text, the author's initials or forename and the publication date (if either of these is needed) could be given in the text as well, thus saving a note.

Subsequent reference

Very short references, for example to a play or the Bible, are usually given in the text rather than a note. It depends on whether the reader will find it useful or distracting to have the information there.

In a note the information given will usually be:

author's surname	omit initials/forename, unless another author with same surname
short title	may be omitted if there is only one entry under that surname in the bibliography
volume and page number	

e.g. Hazel, *Cotton Trade*, vol. 4, p. 102

For the use of *ibid.* and *loc. cit.* see pp. 243–4.

(b) **Articles in books**

First reference

author's name	initials or forename precede surname
title of article	not underlined, usually in single quotation marks and with a capital only for first word and any proper names. Italic words in title remain italic; words in quotes take double quotes
'in'	
editor's name followed by (ed.)	or (eds.) if more than one editor
book title	underlined for italic
series, if any, plus number within series	series name not usually underlined
edition, if not the first	
number of volumes, publication place, publisher and date	all in parentheses
volume (if more than one) and page number	'vol.' and 'p.' may be omitted if there is no ambiguity

> R. J. Cramp, 'Monastic sites' in D. Wilson (ed.), *The Archaeology of Anglo-Saxon England* (London, Methuen, 1976), pp. 201–52

or the editor's name, preceded by 'ed.' (edited by), may follow the book title and 'in' may be replaced by a comma:

> R. J. Cramp, 'Monastic sites', *The Archaeology of Anglo-Saxon England*, ed. D. Wilson (London, Methuen, 1976), pp. 201–52

Subsequent reference
If the book is listed under its editor in the bibliography the subsequent reference will be:

> Cramp, 'Monastic sites' in Wilson, *Archaeology of Anglo-Saxon England*, p. 64

or the short title of the article and/or the book may be omitted if there will be no confusion with another publication:

> Cramp in Wilson, p. 211

If the book is listed in the bibliography under the author of the article, subsequent references will probably be:

> Cramp, 'Monastic sites', p. 211

(c)   **Articles in journals**

First reference

author's name	initials or forename precede surname
title of article	not underlined, usually in single quotation marks and with a capital only for first word and any proper names. Italic words in the title remain italic; words in quotes take double quotes
name of journal	underlined; main words usually capitalized; may be abbreviated if abbreviation is well known, self-explanatory or listed in the prelims or bibliography

place (if there is more than one journal with the same name)	(see p. 246)
volume number in arabic or roman (see p. 247)	'vol.' not needed; preceded by series number or NS (new series) if appropriate
issue number if volume is not paginated continuously	preceded by a colon; if the issue is designated by a month or a season, it is often with the year, in parentheses: (May 1989)
year	in parentheses
page number(s)	'p.', 'pp.' not needed. Some authors give the first and last pages of the article, followed by the page relevant to that note

See that the volume, year, and page numbers are consistently spaced or closed up.

> Mathew Winston, '"Craft against Vice": morality play elements in *Measure for Measure*', *Shakespeare Studies*, 14 (1981), 229–48
> J. Truman, 'The initiation and growth of high alloy (stainless) steel production', *Historical Metallurgy*, 19:1 (1985), pp. 116–25, esp. p. 119

After a journal abbreviation ending in a full point, the comma may be omitted to avoid double punctuation:

> Tom Williamson and Roy Loveday, 'Rabbits or ritual? Artificial warrens and the Neolithic long mound tradition', *Archaeol. J.* 145 (1988), 219–313

Subsequent reference

| author's surname | omit initials/forename, unless another author with same surname |
| journal title, volume, date and page number, *or* shortened form of article title | |

> Williamson and Loveday, *Archaeol. J.* 145 (1988), 225
> Williamson and Loveday, 'Rabbits or ritual?', p. 225

(d) **Newspapers and magazines**

For a news item, the reference may just give the name of the newspaper (see p. 236) and the date of issue. For a signed or unsigned article, the author (if known), the title and perhaps the page number will be given too:

> Graham Rose, 'New clones mean less guesswork', *Sunday Times*, 13 August 1989
> 'Botha's legacy', *Daily Telegraph*, 16 August 1989, p. 12
> David Honigmann, 'Wars and rumours of wars', review of *The View from the Ground* by Martha Gellhorn, *Listener*, 26 October 1989, p. 31

For references to manuscripts and other specialized material, see pp. 238–40.

10.1.2 **Parts of the reference**

(a) **Author's name**

Authors' names should not be inverted in footnotes or endnotes, unless, of course, the name is an unwesternized Chinese or Japanese name, e.g.

> Lu Gwei-Djen and Joseph Needham, *Celestial Lancets: A history and rationale of acupuncture and moxa* (Cambridge University Press, 1980)

where Lu is the first author's surname.

(b) **Title**

Capitalization
Minimum capitalization – capitals for the first word and proper names only – is often used for article titles; but it is still usual to capitalize the first and all significant words in English book and journal titles. Some authors capitalize all significant words in the main title, but only the first word of the subtitle, as in the example in (a) above; in any case, watch out for inconsistent capitalization of the first word of a subtitle.

Follow the author's system if it is sensible and consistent; but if an author says that inconsistent capitalization follows the title pages of the books concerned, and even words such as 'of' and 'the' are sometimes capitalized, press for standardization on the grounds that readers are likely to think the author (or copy-editor) has been careless rather than scrupulous, and that adherence to this kind of bibliographical detail is not necessary.

In running text, initial capitals help to distinguish titles that are set in roman in quotes (such as those of journal articles or short poems) from other simple quotations; similarly, fully capitalized book titles are more easily distinguished from other italic phrases. If only the first word has an initial capital, article titles must be in quotes in text and footnotes, though this is not necessary in the bibliography.

Many publishers use the same capitalization in the notes and bibliography. However, one or two recommend capitalization of all major words in the notes, but minimum capitalization in the bibliography.

Minimum capitalization can make long lists of titles easier to read. However, to implement a system of minimum capitalization might involve you in numerous decisions as to whether particular words (for example government, Puritan, non-conformist, labour) should be counted as proper names.

See p. 241 for the capitalization of foreign titles.

Poems

Poem titles may be italic or roman in quotes. Italic should be used for long poems that are virtually books in themselves, and for any other poems divided into books or cantos. Roman in quotes is used for poems which form part of a larger volume or other whole. Such systems may look inconsistent even if they have been applied consistently, and you may find it difficult to check them if you do not know all the poems; ask the author if you are in doubt. It is acceptable to treat all poem titles in the same way, provided that one does not need to make a distinction between the titles of individual poems and the title of the collection of which they are a part (e.g. *Lyrical Ballads* or *Songs of Innocence*). In a book where many poems are mentioned, it may be best to use italic for all poem titles, to distinguish them from quoted phrases.

Where a poem is referred to by its first line rather than a title, the capitalization should follow the poem, not the author's system for capitalizing titles.

In references to line numbers, avoid the abbreviation ll. for 'lines' if lining figures are used. If you decide to retain the abbreviation, see that the typescript makes it clear that ll. and not 11 is wanted. References to poems divided into stanzas and lines, or into books, cantos and lines, are usually in the form IV. 8 or II. ix. 16; or all the numbers may be arabic. All such groups of numbers divided by points may be spaced or closed up; but of course this must be done consistently.

Plays

Titles should be italic. References to act and scene numbers are usually in the form Act 3 Scene 4, or, if line numbers are given, 3. 4. 235 or III. iv. 235 (3. 235 or III. 235 if there are not both acts and scenes); they must be consistently spaced or closed up. If all the numbers are arabic, and 'Act' and 'Scene' are not used, points must be used to separate the parts of the reference. If roman act numbers are used with lining figures, they must of course be full capitals.

Essay and article titles

Such titles are usually roman in quotes, though the quotes are not essential in a bibliography. Italic may be used for essay titles in a book discussing the essays, if the journals or collections in which they appeared are not mentioned and so the distinction between roman in quotes and italic is not needed.

It is usual to capitalize only the first word and proper names if the titles are roman in quotes, unless they are likely to be confused with quotations.

Journal and newspaper titles

These should be italic. They may be abbreviated if the abbreviations are explained or self-explanatory. Note that *ELH* and *PMLA* (without points) are actual titles.

It is usual to capitalize the first and chief words, whatever style is used for other titles; there is then less discrepancy between journal abbreviations such as *JPE* and other unabbreviated titles.

The is usually omitted from all journal and newspaper titles in bibliographical references; and *Hart's Rules* recommend that in a sentence the definite article should be lower case roman except for *The Times* and *The Economist*. Even there the article should be lower-case roman if it does not refer to the newspaper (e.g. 'the *Times* correspondent').

236

Editions of texts

It is probably best to cite editions under the author's name, e.g.

> John Locke, *An Essay concerning Human Understanding*, ed.
> J. W. Yolton

However, if the emphasis of the book is on the editor's work, it may be better to use the form:

> J. W. Yolton (ed.), John Locke, *An Essay concerning Human Understanding*

If an edition is very frequently cited a concise short title should be used.

Translations

The amount of detail included will depend on the kind of book you are copy-editing. The simplest would be:

> Lara-Vinca Masini, *Art Nouveau*, tr. Linda Fairbairn (London, Thames & Hudson, 1984)

but the author might think it proper to include the original title and language:

> Hans Kienle, *Modern Astronomy* [Einführung in die Astronomie], translated from German by Alex Helm (London, Faber & Faber, 1968)

and possibly the original publication date and place:

> Roland Barthes, 'Le Discours de l'histoire', *Social Science Information*, 6:4 (1967), 72–5; trans. Peter Wexler as 'Historical discourse' in Michael Lane (ed.), *Structuralism: A Reader* (London, Cape, 1970), pp. 152–5

> Fernand Braudel, *La Méditerranée et le monde méditerranéen à l'époque de Philippe II* (Paris, 1949; 2nd edn 1966); trans. Siân Reynolds as *The Mediterranean and the Mediterranean World in the Age of Philip II* (London, Collins, 1973)

Record sleeves, films, etc.

Where there is an author, that name is given first:

> Bill Evans, sleeve note to *Kind of Blue*, sound disc, Columbia, 1959 CBS
>   (E) SBPG 62066

Films, radio programmes, and so on, are regarded as joint enterprises, and the title comes first:

> *Macbeth*, film, directed by Orson Welles. USA: Republic Pictures, 1948
> *The Archers*, BBC radio programme [plus relevant date]

MSS and other unpublished documents

The titles of unpublished theses or dissertations and other unpublished books and articles are usually roman in quotes; theses should be labelled as such, and the name of the university given:

> Robert J. Fusillo, 'The staging of battle scenes on the Shakespearian
>   stage' (Ph.D. dissertation, University of Birmingham, 1966), p. 74

A paper delivered at a conference will be treated like an article in a book, if the proceedings were published; if they were not, the name of the organizing body, the title of the conference and the date should be given:

> Thomas Cocke, 'Monastic sites: an eighteenth century view', paper
>   presented at Cambridge Antiquarian Society conference on Monastic
>   Houses in Cambridgeshire, Ely, 12 March 1988

The titles of manuscript collections should be roman without quotes, and such citations should contain the name of the depository and a full reference following the usage of the depository concerned, e.g. British Library, Additional MS 2787, though parts of the reference may be abbreviated, provided that the abbreviation is explained or self-explanatory, e.g. ULC Add. 3963. 28. The titles of individual manuscripts should be enclosed in quotes, unless they are merely descriptions such as Account Book:

> E. Topsell, 'The Fowles of Heauen', *c.* 1614. Huntington Library,
>   Ellesmere MS 1142

Some manuscript material will have neither author nor title, and the full reference will be:

British Library, Cotton MSS, Claudius C xi, fol. 5
Bibliothèque Nationale, Paris, fonds français, 1124
Gonville and Caius College, Cambridge, MS 489/485, fol. 3

with later references:

BL, Cott. Claud. C xi, fol. 5
BN, f. fr. 1124
Gonville and Caius, 489/485, fol. 3

Do not try to make references to one source consistent with those to another, but if the author appears to refer inconsistently to a single source, query it.

In references to folios it is better to use fo. and fos. or fol. and fols. rather than f. and ff. Avoid the use of superscripts for v (verso) and r (recto). If manuscript references contain roman numbers followed by v or r, mark a thin space before the letter; if it is followed by ff., mark a thin space after it: fols. xii v ff.

Technical reports, patents, etc.
These range from reports published in the normal sense, e.g.

British Standards Institution, *References to Published Materials* (London, BSI, 1989; BS 1629)

to more specialized reports. All carry an indication of their source and a reference number:

B. Ellis and A.K. Walton, *A Bibliography on Optical Modulators*, 1971. RAE-TR-71009
Philip Morris Inc. *Optical Perforating Apparatus and System*, European patent application 0021165 A1. 1981–01–07
Winget Ltd, *Detachable Bulldozer Attachment for Dumper Vehicles*. Inventor: Reginald John England. 8 Mar. 1967. 4 pp. (incl. 1 fig.). Appl. 10 June 1963. Int. Cl. E02F 3/76. GB Cl: E1F 12. GB Patent Specification 1060631

Government and other official papers
Follow the author's system as far as you can, and beware of the following pitfalls. In references to Command Papers follow the author's use of C, Cd, Cmd, Cmnd and Cm, as these refer to different series:

1–4222	1833–69
C 1–9550	1870–99
Cd 1–9239	1900–1918
Cmd 1–9889	1919–56
Cmnd 1–9927	1956–86
Cm 1 –	1986–

Some documents, such as *Hansard* (official name *Parliamentary Debates* since 1892), are numbered by column rather than by page, so do not add p. before all arabic numbers.

In scholarly books it is not necessary to spell out or explain standard abbreviations such as Cal. S.P. Dom. Follow the author's use of roman or italic, provided it seems to be consistent.

The Chicago Manual of Style has a section on the citation of US documents.

Statutes
See section 14.2.1.

Law reports
See section 14.2.5.

Classical references
See section 14.1.10.

Biblical references
Books of the Bible should be roman, not italic. If chapter numbers are arabic, a point or colon must be used between chapter and verse number: Genesis 8.7 or 8:7. Roman lower-case chapter numbers may be followed by a point, comma or space (viii. 7; viii, 7; viii 7); but the abbreviations v. and vv. (verse, verses) should be spelt out to avoid confusion with chapter numbers. See that references are consistently spaced or closed up.

A series of verses within one chapter is separated by commas (2 Corinthians 8.7, 10, 13). A series of references in different chapters is best separated by semicolons, to avoid confusion in mixed references such as 6:4, 5; 8:9.

A long passage within one chapter has an unspaced en rule between the verse numbers (6.4–12). A passage continuing into another chapter may have a spaced en rule if the parts of each reference are spaced (6. 8 – 7. 2), provided that there can be no confusion with parenthetical dashes: but 'to' may be better (6. 8 to 7. 2). If the en rule *is* to be spaced, make this clear in the typescript. References to a passage continuing into another chapter should consist of chapter numbers both sides of the en rule (chapters 6–8) or chapter and verse numbers both sides of the rule (6.2–8.35), but not chapter and verse one side and chapter only the other, e.g. 6.6–8 must not be used to mean chapter 6 verse 6 to the end of chapter 8.

Roman Catholic translations of the Bible deal differently with the books which the Authorized Version gathers under the title of 'Apocrypha'. Also those Roman Catholic translations that have been made from the Latin Vulgate often differ from the Authorized Version in their names for certain books of the Bible and in their numbering of the Psalms. The Ten Commandments are not itemized as such in the Bible, and the official Roman Catholic numbering differs from that found in Anglican prayer books.

Foreign works
In all modern European languages except English and French, and in Latin and transliterated Slavonic languages, capitalization in the titles of books, essays, poems, etc., follows the rules of capitalization in normal prose. That is: the first word and all proper nouns (in German all nouns) take an initial capital, and all other words take a lower-case initial.

Translations of the titles (where necessary) are usually roman in square brackets following the original titles. If Greek or Cyrillic type is used only in notes and bibliography, the author should perhaps be asked to substitute transliterated titles.

In general, publication details should be in English. When citing German, Spanish and French works, for example, B(and), t(omo) and t(ome) should be replaced by vol(ume).

Similarly it is clearer to give the publication place in English throughout; the author ought in any case to follow some consistent system. If the place names are not to be anglicized, consider whether the less familiar names should be followed by the anglicized forms in square brackets.

French references. Authors may capitalize only the first word and any proper nouns, or they may follow the practice given in *Hart's Rules* (39th edn, p. 93) for book and play titles, which is that if the first word of the title is the definite article or an adjective, the first noun and any preceding adjectives take an initial capital, e.g. *Les Femmes savantes, La Folle Journée, Second Discours,* but *A la recherche du temps perdu.* If all significant words are capitalized in English journal names, the same system may be used for French journals, particularly where there are also abbreviated titles such as *Annales ESC.* Some French bibliographical abbreviations are given in appendix 7.

German references. All nouns in titles should be capitalized. If ß is used only in the notes and bibliography, ask the author whether 'ss' may be substituted. If he or she thinks the distinction important, tell the typesetter to follow copy. Some German bibliographical abbreviations are given in appendix 7.

Russian references. Use a capital for the first word and proper nouns only, in titles of literary works, newspapers and journals. Unless sloping Cyrillic type is to be used, titles of books and journals may be set in upright Cyrillic; within a passage of Russian they would be enclosed in *guillemets* (« »); in a list of references or in passages of English the *guillemets* would be omitted.

Short title

A short title given in the text or a note should lead one unerringly to the right entry in the bibliography. An author's surname is not enough if there is more than one book by the same author, or if there are two authors with the same surname; and easily distinguishable short titles should be used for books with similar names. Abbreviations should be self-explanatory, though a frequently cited source may be abbreviated further, provided the abbreviation is given in a list preceding the text (if there are footnotes) or at the beginning of the endnotes or the bibliography; to give such an abbreviation only immediately following the first full reference in a note is not as helpful, because the reader may not remember where the first full reference occurred or may not be reading the whole book. Abbreviations should be italic if the full form would be italic. Consult the author before abbreviating titles of books not listed in a select bibliography.

The short title should not normally include an ellipsis; however, authors of books containing a number of titles in less familiar languages such as Polish or Russian may use short titles consisting of the first few words of the title plus an ellipsis. Do not initiate such a system yourself without consulting the author.

I think the easiest way to ensure a consistent system of short titles is to mark up a spare copy of the bibliography. If one ticks each item there when it is first cited in a note, and indicates the short title used in the second citation by ringing it or deleting the other words of the title in the bibliography, one knows at a glance whether a book has already been cited and what its short title should be. I myself note the folio number of every occurrence in the margin of this spare copy, in case I need to refer back or alter an earlier short title.

Ibid.

Ibid. can refer only to the immediately preceding reference, or part of it, e.g. '*Letters*, p. 515' may be followed by '*Ibid.*' (– exactly the same reference) or '*Ibid.* p. 518'. Do not, however, use *ibid.* if there are two references in the preceding note; and if an author uses *ibid.* only for an identical reference, do not extend its use to those which are not identical. If *ibid.* contains an implicit volume number and you are putting p. before page numbers only where there is no volume number (see p. 247), it is better to be inconsistent and include p. after *ibid.*

Ibid. – like *idem, eadem, op. cit.* and *loc. cit.* – may be roman or italic, provided all are treated in the same way throughout the book. Some publishers omit the comma after them, to avoid double punctuation.

Idem, eadem, loc. cit., op. cit.

Publishers ask authors not to use these Latin terms, which do not help the reader. If an author insists on keeping them, their use should be restricted as follows. *Idem* or *id.* may be used instead of repeating a male author's name in successive references; the female form is *eadem*. There seems no advantage in using these forms, since they will be unfamiliar to many readers and are only slightly shorter than a normal surname. *Op. cit.* may be used with the author's name to denote the same book as cited in a recent reference, but it should be avoided if two books by that author are cited within, say, twenty pages of each other. *Art. cit.* may be used in a similar way, to refer to an article. *Loc. cit.* may be used with the author's name to indicate the same work and page as in a recent reference.

(c) **Series**

The series name should not be underlined if there is a volume title; but some historical society volumes may contain two or three works and have no volume title, in which case the individual works are roman in quotes and the series name is italicized. If there is only one work in such a volume, the name of the work will be italic and the series name roman.

> H. E. Salter, *Cartulary of Oseney Abbey*, VI, Oxford Hist. Soc., 101 (1936), 208
> D. Sylvester, 'The open fields of Cheshire', *Hist. Soc. Lancs & Cheshire*, 108 (1956), 12–15

Some series of volumes are not true 'series' (open-ended groups of individual volumes) but multi-volume works, in which case the title of the whole work is used in place of, or precedes, the volume title and is italic, e.g. *New Cambridge Modern History*, vol. VIII. If the volume title is given, it should be in italic also.

There is no need to expand NS (= new series), but it should be underlined for small capitals (if available) when non-lining figures are used.

(d) **Edition number**

The author should cite the edition used, even if it is not the latest one. Hardback editions should usually be cited, though it may be useful, in a book for schools, undergraduates or the general reader, to mention a paperback edition.

Some authors indicate the edition by a superscript number after the title, e.g. *Usage and Abusage*^{2}, or a subscript number before the publication date, e.g. $_2$1989. This is acceptable except in the author–date system; but as it may be an unfamiliar convention to some readers, the more conventional style of '2nd edn' before the parentheses could be substituted. Be consistent in your use of 'second edition' or '2nd edn'. The edition number is sometimes included in the parentheses with place, date and number of volumes.

(c) Publication place and publisher of books

Authors are usually asked to give both place and publisher; but some may give only the place or only the publisher, and you may decide to follow this system. If an author gives only the place in some references and only the publisher in others, it is easier to opt for place in all of them, as finding the publisher may entail much research. A list of the addresses of British publishers may be found in *Whitaker's Books in Print* (London, Whitaker); American addresses are in *Books in Print* (New York, Bowker) and Australian ones in *Australian Books in Print* (Melbourne, Thorpe). A more accessible source for the best-known publishers is *Writers' and Artists' Yearbook* (London, Black).

An author who usually gives only the place may add the publisher of books and pamphlets published by societies or individuals; this information may be helpful and should be retained.

Usually only one publisher and place are given, either the primary one or the one most relevant for readers, for example a British publisher of a book first published in the United States.

You may find different forms of a publisher's name, or different publication places; this probably means that the publisher has changed hands or moved, and that the author has followed the title page. Check that the same details are given for the same book.

Place. Some authors omit the publication place if it is London (or Moscow, or whatever is the most usual place); there should be a note at the beginning of the bibliography to explain such a system.

Give enough details to prevent confusion between two places with the same name. For example add Mass. (or MA; see appendix 3) after the Massachusetts Cambridge if Harvard University Press is not mentioned. Include the name of the state if the town may be unfamiliar to many readers, for example Englewood Cliffs, N. J. (or NJ). Note that Dover is usually Dover Publications, not Dover, Kent.

If both place and publisher are given, it is all right to omit the place if it is implicit in the publisher's name, for example Cambridge University Press.

If the place of publication is not known, n.p. (no place) is used instead. If the place is ascertainable but does not appear in the book cited, it is enclosed in square brackets. It is best to reserve square brackets for data omitted from the publication, and not to use them to avoid having two sets of round brackets, one inside the other.

Publisher. Publishers' names may be shortened if this is done consistently and short forms are unambiguous, e.g. EUP could be Edinburgh University Press or English Universities Press, ULP could be University of London Press or University of Liverpool Press, Arnold could be Edward Arnold or E. J. Arnold. Be consistent about the use of 'and' or '&' in publishers' names.

(f) **Publication place of journals**

If a journal might be confused with another with a similar title, or is not widely known, the name of the place or institution where it is published may be given in parentheses after the title.

(g) **Publication date**

The date should be of the edition consulted. If the work referred to has no date in it, and its date of publication is not known, n.d. (no date) takes its place; if the date is ascertainable but does not appear in the book, it should be enclosed in square brackets.

Multi-volume works. If the publication date applies only to the volume cited, this is made clear by placing the volume number before the publication details:

> John Smith, *Collected Works*, vol. 1 (Newnham University Press, 1960),
>   p. 63

If the date or date span applies to the whole work, the number of volumes will be given and the relevant volume number will follow the parentheses.

> John Smith, *Collected Works* (21 volumes, Newnham University Press,
>   1960–89), vol. 1, p. 63

If publication is not yet complete, it is usual to put a space after the en rule, e.g. 1960– .

Journal references. The date is usually in parentheses between volume and page number, e.g. 2 (1957), 63–6.

(h) **Volume and page number**

Order of volume number, date and page numbers. As mentioned above, the volume number should precede the publication date for a book if not all the volumes were published in that year. If the typescript appears to be inconsistent, ask the author whether this is the system being followed.

Arabic or roman for volume numbers. Follow the author's system if it is sensible and consistent; some authors use arabic for journal volume numbers and roman for book volume numbers. See that it will be clear to the typesetter whether an arabic or roman figure one is wanted: some typists type II for 11 (eleven), others type lll for 111 (roman three).

Roman volume numbers should be marked for small capitals (if available) unless lining figures are being used.

Vol. and p. in references to books, poetry and documents. Follow the author's system if it is consistent and sensible. One system is to include vol. and p. only where there is any possibility of ambiguity, that is where both volume and page numbers are arabic, or where there is an arabic or roman number on its own and it may not be clear whether the number refers to a volume or a page: a small capital roman 'one' can look like a non lining arabic 'one', and a small capital roman v or x could be mistaken for a lower case roman number. There should be no ambiguity if all unidentified numbers are page numbers, that is if volume numbers are preceded by vol. when they appear on their own and if arabic volume numbers (and roman ones if they also occur in the book) are separated from the page number by a colon when they appear together. If there are also references to lines of poetry, it may be as well to include p. for the page references.

If p. is used for some page references it should be used consistently, but do not add p. indiscriminately before arabic numbers: some documents are referred to by column, paragraph or folio. Ask the author if you are not sure.

Remember to use pp., not p., if more than one page is cited. This includes references such as pp. 21f., pp. 36ff. Remember that f. and ff. should be consistently spaced or closed up to the preceding number. Page numbers are usually elided (see section 6.10.7).

Do not use v. as an abbreviation for 'volume'.

Vol. and p. in journal references. There are devices that will usually distinguish volume and page numbers without the use of vol. and p.

In books using the author–date system the volume number may be bold (**4**, 5) or followed by a colon (4:5 or 4: 5), or the page number may be preceded by p. or pp. If an issue number is also needed it can be in parentheses after the volume number: 4(1): 125.

With the short-title system, the year separates volume and page: 4 (1990), 5. If an issue number is needed, the style may be 4:2 (1990), 5. If the volume number is roman, a comma may be used without ambiguity: IV, 2 (1990), 5.

See section 14.2 for the order within journal references in legal works.

Some authors give the first and last page numbers of a journal article, immediately followed by the page relevant at this point, e.g.

> *Camb. J. Pub.* 5 (1990), 121–32, esp. p. 128
> or *Camb. J. Pub.* 5 (1990), 121–32 (p. 128)

Where particular pages of an article are referred to, check that these fall within the span of page numbers given for the whole article.

10.1.3 Bibliography

Scholarly monographs with bibliographical references in the text or notes should have a bibliography or list of works cited. Consult the author if there is no bibliography in the typescript, and say that you will not easily be able to check consistency of content in references to the same work. If the bibliography omits a few of the works cited, ask the author about the omissions, as they may be unintentional; if it omits many, call it 'Select bibliography'.

Textbooks and more general books may contain lists of 'Further reading' (see section 10.5). These may omit some or all of the works cited in text and notes, and will probably include some not cited.

See that the list is correctly named. Check the order of the entries, and see that they are consistent in the amount of information they contain, the order in which it is given, and the punctuation.

Position

The bibliography is usually placed before the index. This is a better place than before the endnotes, because it is easier to find.

Even if there is a separate bibliography for each chapter, they are best grouped at the end of the book for ease of reference, unless there are to be offprints. Lists of further reading in school books, however, *are* usually at the end of each chapter, because each forms part of the individual teaching unit.

List of abbreviations

Some authors include a list of abbreviations at the beginning of the bibliography; but if the abbreviations are also used in the footnotes the list is better placed in the preliminary pages. If they apply only to the endnotes and bibliography, such a list should come at the beginning of the endnote section. Italic abbreviations should normally be used for italic titles; but do not make all abbreviations italic; some, such as LSJ, are abbreviations of authors' names and should be left roman.

Subdivisions

The author should be dissuaded from subdividing the bibliography too much, as this may make it difficult for the reader to find a specific reference. Documents and manuscripts are best listed separately because they do not fit into a list arranged alphabetically under author; documents are probably best grouped by country and department, manuscripts by depository and collection. News items from newspapers are not listed individually; the names of newspapers cited are often listed in a separate section of the bibliography.

Works by a person who is the subject of a book are best separated from books *about* that person, and may be listed chronologically or alphabetically.

Order of entries

In an alphabetical list, the order is by authors' surnames; government documents or anonymous works are listed under the first word, not counting the definite or indefinite article. (For points about names and alphabetical order see sections 8.2.1, 8.2.2.)

More than one work by the same author. Except in the author–date system, original works usually precede works edited by the same writer. Each group should be arranged alphabetically or in date order; or articles may follow books; but the same system should be used throughout the bibliography. Works by a single author precede works by that author in collaboration with others.

Editions should be entered as they are cited in footnote references (under author or editor). If they are cited under the editor, there should be a cross-reference from the author's name.

Form of entry

If the references are embedded in discussion they should be in the same form as in the notes (see above); but in an alphabetical list the author's surname should precede the initials or forenames, and in all lists the punctuation is usually simplified.

> Carr, J. L. 'Uncertainty and monetary theory', *Economics*, 2 (1956), 82–9
> Chomsky, Noam. 'Explanatory models in linguistics' in J. A. Fodor and J. J. Katz (eds.), *The Structure of Language*, Englewood Cliffs, N.J., Prentice-Hall, 1964, pp. 50–118
> Hazel, J. A. *The Growth of the Cotton Trade in Lancashire*, 3rd edn, 4 vols., London, Textile Press, 1987–8

Where the title is the first item, a definite or indefinite article at the beginning is usually omitted:

> *Chicago Manual of Style*, 13th edn, University of Chicago Press, 1982

Authors' names are normally upper and lower case; if they are typed in capitals, mark any letters that might confuse the typesetter, for example the L in MacLehose.

Where the authorship remains exactly the same, this may be indicated by indenting subsequent publications 1 em, with 2 ems for turnovers. However, all the names must be given when the authorship changes in any way.

> Bloggs, A. J. First publication. Turnovers
>   indented 2 ems
>   Second publication, indented 1 em
> Bloggs, A. J., and X. Y. Jones. First publication
>   Second publication

Note that, although the name of the first author should be inverted, the names of second and subsequent authors need not; it does not matter, provided a consistent system is used.

If the author particularly wants rules to represent a repeated author's name, one does not need to repeat the name when the co-authors change:

Bloggs, A. J. First publication
— and X. Y. Jones. First publication

Two rules may be used to indicate that the first two authors remain the same, and so on. If you think rules should be retained, tell the designer; but do not introduce them unless it is your house style.

If the names of the second and subsequent authors are inverted, it is quite common to omit the comma before 'and', to avoid double punctuation:

Brown, H. W., Forbes, A. S. and Smith, S. D.

However, if the following name is not inverted, a comma removes any chance of ambiguity:

Forbes, A. S., and S. D. Smith

If the author's name does not appear in the work cited, it should be enclosed in square brackets.

Articles. Encourage the author to give the first and last (or at least the first) page number(s) of an article. If the author cannot trace them all, it is better to include those that are available than to omit them all for the sake of consistency.

Comments. If each item is followed by a comment, consult the designer about a suitable way of distinguishing the comment from the reference.

10.2

AUTHOR–DATE SYSTEM

This system, known in one of its typographical variants as the Harvard system, gives author and year of publication in the text and the full reference in a list of references or a bibliography.

If the list is called 'References', check that all published works referred to in the text are included in the list, and vice versa: a wrong date can be altered fairly easily at proof stage, but the addition of a reference or the name of a second author in the text would be expensive. Personal communications and other unpublished works, such as theses, may be excluded from the list, in which case a full reference should be given in the text, for example '(S. C. Champney, personal communication 1990)'; for theses see p. 238.

An author may use the author–date system for modern or secondary sources, but the short-title system for earlier or literary sources; for example, in a chapter on elms the author might cite '(Richens, 1983, p. 119)' but '(Shakespeare, *2 Henry IV*, 2.4.331)'.

It is sensible to run your eye down the reference list before going through the text, to make sure that the items are in the right order (so that you can find them easily), that authors' names are spelt consistently, and that there are no dates that obviously need altering, for example two 1988 under one author, or possibly 1988 followed by 1988a (see section 10.2.1). You might not notice this when checking individual entries against text references. In looking down the list, you may notice different dates given for papers published in the same collected volume, or a date that does not seem to tally with other dates given for the same volume number of a particular journal, for example 1980 in a reference to volume 19, where the other references to volume 19 are dated 1990.

When going through the text, put a small pencil tick by each reference in the text and in the list, as you check it. The ticks in the text enable you to see at a glance any reference you have missed; and the tick in the reference list shows that that reference has been cited in the text. The author should be asked about any unticked items in a reference list.

You may need to go back and alter a text reference. To make it easier to find them, some copy-editors put the folio number of each text reference by the item in the reference list. Other copy-editors find this too time-consuming, but put a tick for each text reference so that they know how many they have to find.

10.2.1 **Form of text reference**

The author's name, date of publication and page reference (if one is needed) are given in parentheses: 'the synthesis of amino acids (D'Arcy, 1920, pp. 131–8) amazed . . .' The reference may be simplified still further, by omitting the first comma and substituting a colon for the second and pp.: '(D'Arcy 1920: 131–8)'. If the author's name forms part of the sentence, it is not repeated in the reference: 'the synthesis of amino acids by D'Arcy (1920, pp. 131–8) amazed . . .'

If the author published two or more works in one year, these are labelled 1990a etc. (with the letter closed up to the preceding date), or 1990a, b if more than one is cited in a single text reference. Some authors use 1990 and 1990a rather than 1990a, 1990b, and it may not be worth changing this.

When citing a new edition of an older work, the original date should be included, as well as the date of the new edition, to which the page numbers refer:

(Burney [1776] 1968, p. xxiii)

It can sometimes avoid ambiguity if '&' is used instead of 'and' between the names of joint authors: e.g. ' in the work of both Smith & Brown and Jones & Robinson'; but if the author has used 'and' throughout it is not worth changing. The same system should be used throughout, though '&' can be used in the parentheses and 'and' in running text.

Et al. should be used consistently; for example references to works by three authors may give all three names at every occurrence or may give them in full the first time and then the first author plus *et al.* With three to five authors, the decision whether to use *et al.* may depend on whether there is another group with the same first author and the same date, which could be confused; for example Smith, Jones and Robinson 1990 and Smith, Taylor and Champney 1990 would both become Smith *et al.* 1990. However, now that *et al.* references have become much more common, ambiguity is sometimes avoided, not by giving all the names, but by labelling those with the same year 1990a etc., even though the second and later authors are not the same: e.g. Jones, Norman, Hazel and Robinson 1990 would become 'Jones *et al.*

1990a' and Jones, Smith and Robinson 1990 'Jones *et al.* 1990b'. If a and b are used in this way, it is best to order the list of references according to system 3 on p. 255.

The person's initials should be included in two kinds of text reference: where there are articles or books by two authors with the same surname, and where the reference is to a personal communication not included in the list of references, e.g. '(N. C. Brock, personal communication 1990)'.

Where several references are cited together in the text they may be placed in chronological or alphabetical order, or in order of importance, but one system should be used consistently throughout. Consult the author if you are not sure what the system is.

See that the following are consistent: the inclusion or omission of a comma between the author's name and the date, the use of '&' or 'and' for joint authors, and the use of *et al.* Where a colon is used between year and page reference, see that it is consistently spaced or closed up:

(Smith 1988: 22–4)   *or*   (Smith 1988:22–4)

Check the punctuation in groups of references. Publications by the same author(s) are usually separated by commas:

(Smith, 1988, 1990)   *or*   (Smith 1988, 1990)

but, where page numbers are given, the references are separated by semicolons and the author's name may be repeated:

(Smith 1988: 12–14; Smith 1990: 21)

Publications by different authors are usually separated by semicolons:

(Smith, 1988; Taylor, 1987)

though they may be separated by commas if these are not used elsewhere in the reference:

(Smith 1988, Taylor 1987)

10.2.2 **List of references or bibliography**

Published works should be in one alphabetical list, or one list for each chapter. If there are also references to manuscript sources etc., these may be listed separately.

Position
In multi-author books, the list should be placed at the end of the individual paper, especially if there are to be offprints. In other books it should probably be before the index, where it will be easier to find than at the end of a chapter.

Order of entries
For alphabetical order of authors' names see sections 8.2.1 and 8.2.2. Each author's publications are listed chronologically within the following groups.

Works by a single author are listed before those written in collaboration with others.

The *joint works* may be grouped in any of the following ways:

1 alphabetically by co-author (irrespective of the number of authors), so that the order would be Jones 1985, 1989; Jones & Abrams 1988; Jones, Abrams & Smith 1986; Jones, Norman, Hazel & Robinson 1982; Jones & Smith 1985

2 author with one other, in alphabetical order of second author; author with two others; and so on. The order would be Jones 1985, 1989; Jones & Abrams 1988; Jones & Smith 1985; Jones, Abrams & Smith 1986; Jones, Norman, Hazel & Robinson 1982

3 if there are many *et al.* references in the text, they will be easier to find if works by two authors are grouped as in 2 and those cited as *et al.* are listed chronologically, whatever the name of the second author. The order would be Jones 1985, 1989; Jones & Abrams 1988; Jones & Smith 1985; Jones, Norman, Hazel & Robinson 1982; Jones, Abrams & Smith 1986. If the author is differentiating those published in the same year by labelling them a and b, the a, b etc. will of course have to appear in the list: Jones, Norman, Hazel & Robinson 1982a; Jones, Smith & Robinson 1982b

If you plan to use system 3, make sure the author understands and approves of it; and perhaps add an explanatory note at the beginning of the list of references.

Follow the author's system if it is clear and consistent.

All the co-authors should appear in the reference list, unless there are more than six authors, in which case it is now common practice to list only the first three, followed by *et al.*

Form of entry

See that the entries are consistent in the amount of information that they contain, the order in which it is given, and the punctuation. If the author divides the list of references by chapter, see that adequate information is given at the second or subsequent mention: 'Bloggs (1989), see above' could involve the reader in looking through the lists for all previous chapters to find the full citation. It is best to give the citation in full each time.

Authors' names are usually set in upper and lower case, and if so should be marked accordingly.

Indention can be used in place of the authors' names before subsequent items with exactly the same authorship; but all the names must be given when the authorship changes in any way.

> Bloggs, A. J. 1989. First publication. Turnovers
>   indented 2 ems
>   1990. Second publication, indented 1 em
> Bloggs, A. J., & Jones, X. Y. 1985. First publication
>   1988. Second publication

Note that, although the name of the first author should be inverted, the names of second and subsequent authors need not; it does not matter, provided a consistent system is used.

If the author particularly wants rules to represent a repeated author's name, one does not need to repeat the name when the co-authors change. Two rules may be used to indicate that the first two authors remain the same, and so on. If you think rules should be retained, tell the designer, but do not introduce them unless it is your house style.

If the names of the second and subsequent authors are inverted, it is quite common to omit the comma before '&' or 'and', to avoid double punctuation:

Brown, H. W., Forbes, A. S. & Smith, S. D.

However, if the following name is not inverted, a comma removes any chance of ambiguity:

Forbes, A. S., & S. D. Smith

See that the use of '&' or 'and' is consistent.

The date (followed by 'a' etc. if necessary) immediately follows the name of the author(s), so that the reader can easily find 'D'Arcy 1920a'. The date is often within parentheses.

Article titles, if given, should have a capital only for the first word (plus proper names and German nouns) and need not be in quotation marks.

Journal and book titles should be underlined for italic. In unabbreviated journal titles and in book titles, initial capitals are commonly used for all significant words, though book titles may have minimum capitalization.

Journal titles may be given in full; or standard abbreviations may be used either for all journals or for the most familiar ones. Because of confusion caused by abbreviation there has been a trend, especially in medicine, towards giving journal titles in full. Follow the author's system, and consult the commissioning editor or volume editor if you are in doubt as to which system to use in a multi-author book. Lists of abbreviations may be found in publications such as the following:

Chemical Abstracts
Index Medicus
Journal of Physiology: Suggestions to Authors
World List of Scientific Periodicals

There is a British Standard: BS 4148, *Abbreviation of Title Words and Titles of Publications*.

Edition number. See p. 244 above.

Place and publisher. See pp. 245–6 above. In science books, both place and publisher are usually given for books, often with a colon between them.

The complete reference would read something like the following:

Walker, E. P. 1975. *Mammals of the World*, 3rd edn. Baltimore, Md:
  Johns Hopkins University Press
Washburn, S. L. 1981. Longevity in primates. In *Aging: Biology and
  Behavior*, ed. J. L. McGaugh & S. B. Kiesler, pp. 11–29. New York:
  Academic Press
Watts, E. S. & Gavan, J. A. 1982. Postnatal growth of nonhuman
  primates: the problem of adolescent spurt. *Human Biology*, **54**, 53–70

No comma is needed after the journal title, though one is normally
included except after an abbreviated title ending in a full point. If volume numbers are to be bold, this needs to be marked; alternatively
there may be a colon between volume and page number, or the author
may include vol. and p. (e.g. 12: 145–9 or vol. 12, pp. 145–9).

10.2.3   Combined list of references and author index

If the reference list is to double as an author index, return the list to the
author when you have edited it. The author should fill in the page
numbers from the page proof and return the list with the subject index.
The page numbers should be entered at the end of each reference in
square brackets or underlined for italic, to distinguish them from the
page numbers in the reference (see p. 198). There are usually cross-
references from second and subsequent joint authors to the main
author.

Tell the typesetter it will follow at page proof stage.

10.3

REFERENCE BY NUMBER ONLY

10.3.1   Form of text reference

In this system each publication or group of publications is numbered
in the order in which it is referred to in the text; the text reference is just
the relevant number. There is usually a separate numbering sequence,
and list of references, for each chapter.

In the Vancouver style, now used by many biomedical journals, references are numbered consecutively by arabic numbers in parentheses.

References cited only in tables or captions are placed in the sequence according to the first reference in the text to that table or illustration.

Where other numbers appear in the text, the reference numbers may be italic within parentheses or square brackets, to distinguish them; or they may be superscripts perhaps within parentheses or square brackets, though this can make them very bulky, and some authors object to their following the punctuation as note indicators do:

Smith, [146] Jones, [147]

In a variation of the number system there is a consolidated reference list for the whole book, with a separate numerical sequence for each letter: that is, one for all (first) authors beginning with A, and so on, but not in alphabetical order within each letter, so that Allen 1985 might be A1 and Abelard 1982 might be A2. The text references are in the form: 'noted by Gurney (G11)'.

10.3.2 **List of references**

Position
As I have already said, there is usually a list of references for each chapter or paper. In multi-author books, the list should be placed at the end of the individual paper, especially if there are to be offprints. In other cases the lists should probably be grouped before the index, where they will be easier to find than at the ends of chapters.

Form of entry
In this kind of list of references there is no need to invert the author's name or to place the date immediately after it. Some authors run-on all the references that share one number; but it is probably clearer for the reader if each publication is set out on a separate line. The number may be in parentheses (as in section 13.10), or may be followed by a point or just a space (as below).

Some authors, repeating a reference cited in an earlier chapter, may give just a cross-reference:

18. See chapter 6, no. 10

It is more useful to the reader if the full reference is given at each occurrence.

Otherwise the general style should follow that of either the short-title system (see section 10.1) or the author–date system (see section 10.2).

In the Vancouver style, authors are asked to present references in the following form, for the journal or book publisher to style further if they wish:

> Nicolaides KH, Bilardo CM, Scothill PW, Campbell S. Absence of end diastolic frequencies in the umbilical artery: a sign of fetal hypoxia and acidosis. Br Med J 1988; 297: 1026–7
>
> Eisen HN. Immunology: an introduction to molecular and cellular principles of the immune response. 5th ed. New York: Harper and Row, 1974:406

Journal titles are abbreviated in accordance with the style used in *Index Medicus.*

10.4

AUTHOR–NUMBER SYSTEM

10.4.1 Form of text reference

This system is similar to the author–date system except that each author's publications are numbered and the reference in text or notes is 'Jackson (14)'.

10.4.2 List of references

Position
There is usually one list, before the index.

Form of entry
Authors' names are inverted and immediately followed by the number; authors' names need not be repeated before items with exactly the same authorship, but they should be repeated (and a new sequence of numbering started) when the authorship changes in any way:

Bloggs, A. J. (1) First publication. Turnovers
        indented 2 ems
    (2) Second publication, indented 1 em
Bloggs, A. J., and Jones, X. Y. (1) First publication
    (2) Second publication

10.5

LISTS OF FURTHER READING

Lists of further reading may be divided by chapter or by subject, and often contain comments. They may omit some or all of the books cited in the text and any notes, and will probably contain some not cited.

Position
If each chapter is a completely separate unit, the lists may be best placed at the end of the relevant chapter; otherwise a list subdivided by subject may be placed before the index.

Form of entry
Each section of the list may be in alphabetical order, in which case the authors' names should be inverted; but the date need not follow the author's name. Alternatively, the books may be listed in order of importance, subject matter, date, etc., or may be embedded in paragraphs of discussion. See that the author has used a consistent and helpful order.

The general style should follow that of either the short-title system (see section 10.1) or the author–date system (see section 10.2).

Literary material

QUOTATIONS

Identify any quotations that are to be displayed (set in smaller type than the text and/or indented, for example), if they are not clearly distinguished in the typescript. Make sure that it will be immediately obvious to the typesetter where such a passage is to begin and end, if the quotation starts or finishes in the middle of a line in the typescript. See that sources are sensibly placed.

Tell the author about any changes you propose to make in the treatment of quotations, because this is something about which some authors feel strongly.

11.1.1 Layout

Prose
Has the author a sensible system for deciding which quotations should be displayed? It is usual to display prose quotations of more than, say, sixty words, but one may use other criteria:

- One may run-on those that form an integral part of the sequence of the argument, and display examples on which the author is commenting.
- One may display small quotations when they are of exactly the same kind as those over sixty words, or where long and short ones are grouped.
- One may display all the quotations that the author has displayed in the typescript.

In order to give the beginning of the passage a neater appearance, some publishers do not indent the first line of a displayed prose quotation, even if it was originally the beginning of a paragraph. However, if a quotation contains short lines of dialogue and the first speech is only one line, it looks better to indent the first line:

'Really?'
'I thought you knew that!'
'How could I?'
'John said he'd told you the whole story when you were staying with them last Christmas.'

Verse

It is usual to display verse if there is at least one complete line. If the author runs some verse on in the text, consider whether it should be displayed or, if not, whether line breaks should be indicated by capital letters (if the original had them) and/or spaced oblique or upright strokes; strokes are the only completely clear way. If a displayed verse quotation starts with a broken line, the first word should be indented to approximately its true position in the complete line.

If it may not be clear to the typesetter whether a quotation is verse or prose – for example a Latin verse quotation with no capitals at the beginnings of the lines, or German prose which happens to have a capitalized noun at the beginning of each line – label each one and say 'set line for line' in the margin, where appropriate. If you are not sure yourself, ask the author.

If one or two verse quotations include the poem title, point this out to the designer, who might otherwise not notice them.

Plays

If there are quotations from different plays, it is probably sensible to standardize the layout and typographical style used for speech prefixes (speakers' names) and stage directions, unless the differences have some significance.

Quotations in footnotes

These cannot be set in a smaller size of type, and prose quotations may be better run on in the text of the note than indented. Verse quotations are usually displayed, though they may be run on with spaced oblique or upright strokes to indicate line breaks.

11.1.2 **Quotation marks** (also called 'quotes' or 'inverted commas')

When to use them
Displayed quotations have no quotation marks at the beginning and end, unless there is any possible ambiguity. If quotations are distinguished only by the use of quotation marks, and more than one paragraph is quoted, an opening quote should appear at the beginning of each paragraph. If you run-on a quotation displayed in the typescript, remember to add quotation marks.

Dialogue from novels retains its own quotation marks even when displayed; but displayed quotations from plays never need quotation marks, provided at least one speech prefix is included in the quotation.

Single or double quotes
In British style, single quotes are normally used, except for quotations within quotations: 'he described the scheme as "totally unworkable"'. Where two sets of quotation marks occur together, they should be separated by a thin space, and you may need to mark this for the typesetter.

Since displayed quotations have no quotes at the beginning and end, quotations within them will have single quotes:

he described the scheme as 'totally unworkable'

In books containing transliterated Arabic, it is sensible to use double quotes to avoid any confusion with the '*ain* and *hamza*, which are indicated in the standard system of transliteration by a single opening and closing quote respectively.

Some authors have their own system of quotation marks, which they are anxious to retain: for example double quotes for speech and single for thoughts, or double quotes for quotations and single quotes for words or phrases used in a special sense. If you retain an unusual system, warn the typesetter not to 'correct' it.

In more complex books, quotation marks may be used to convey two or more of the following:

1 mentioning the word:
'John' is a four-letter word

2 giving the meaning of a word:
   'John' means 'God is gracious'
3 quoting what someone else has said:
   'John,' he said
4 'sneer' quotes:
   'John' Smith, alias Ebenezer Crumpet Smith

Philosophers, logicians or linguists may want to distinguish 1 from 2; 3 and 4 hardly ever cause problems, because it is usually clear when quotes are being used in these ways. One can use single quotes for 1, 3 and 4, and double for 2; or double for 1, 3 and 4, and single for 2; or single for 1 and double for all the others. Ask the author what system is being used; and if you cannot check the subtle distinctions in usage, say so. Warn the typesetter to follow copy. If long quotations are to be displayed, ask the author whether they should be enclosed within the appropriate quotation marks. If a phrase is quoted within a quotation, ask whether the phrase should be within single or double quotes; the usual rule of single first, then double within single, will, of course, not apply.

Punctuation and closing quotes

Where a quotation forms part of a longer sentence, the usual rule in Britain is that the closing quote precedes all punctuation except an exclamation mark, question mark, dash or parenthesis belonging only to the quotation. The position of the full point depends in theory on whether the quoted sentence is a complete one; as it is impossible to be certain about that without checking the original source, many publishers follow a rule of thumb that the full point precedes the closing quote if the quotation contains a grammatically complete sentence starting with a capital letter:

   I have often heard you say 'It cannot be done.'

though the British Standard BS 5261 recommends that in such a case the full point should follow the closing quote:

   I have often heard you say 'It cannot be done'.

Authors who are textual scholars may place the full point according to whether it is part of the quotation; so do not make their system consistent without consulting them. American authors place the closing quotes *after* commas and full points, so explain the British rule to them if you propose to use it.

When a quotation is broken by words of the main sentence, and then resumed, the punctuation before the break should follow the closing quote unless it forms part of the quotation. However, in fiction the usual convention for placing commas before and after 'he said' is that the first comma precedes the closing quote and the following one precedes the opening quote:

> 'Father,' he said, 'is looking well today.'

Typesetters are so used to this system that some tend to follow it even if the punctuation is placed in the typescript according to whether it forms part of the speech and would remain if 'he said' were omitted, as in the following examples:

> 'Father', he said, 'is looking well today.'
> 'Father,' he said, 'you're looking well today.'

Unless the author has punctuated according to the sense, it may be better to stick to the conventional system, to save a lot of proof correction.

11.1.3 Style within quotations

Follow copy for capitalization, italic and punctuation, and normally for spelling (unless the quotation is the author's own translation). However, it is usual to normalize typographical conventions such as the use of single quotes, en or em rules for parenthetical dashes, italic/roman punctuation and the position of punctuation with closing quotes. Tell authors what you plan to do, and try to dissuade them from retaining unnecessary distinctions. If they insist, tell the typesetter to follow copy.

Some authors think they should retain the original punctuation at the end of displayed quotations even if it looks odd within the sentence: for example, a quotation at the end of a sentence may end with a comma, or a quotation in the middle of a sentence may end with a full point. In my experience, authors who have insisted on retaining this system at typescript stage have changed their mind at proof stage; so try to persuade them to change the system before the book is sent for setting.

If some words are omitted from a quotation, indicate the omission by an ellipsis of three points. This may be preceded or followed by a full point or other mark of punctuation; but, as full points are differently spaced from the points of an ellipsis, the typesetter must be able to see at a glance whether the first or last of a group of four points is to be a full point. Some publishers nowadays use a standard ellipsis of three points, not preceded or followed by a full point, because many authors type anything from two to five full points and it is impossible to tell, without checking the source, whether the sentence preceding the ellipsis has been quoted in its entirety. If the author wants to retain full points, make sure it is clear which they are, and warn the typesetter to follow copy. If the author wants to distinguish the omission of one or more paragraphs (or several lines of verse) from the omission of a few words, a row of points on a separate line may be used.

It is usual to omit ellipses at the beginning and end of quotations, unless they are necessary for the sense. It is, after all, clear that the quotation is only an extract from the original work and is not complete in itself. However, if authors want to show that a passage, quoted out of its original context for reasons of space, slightly misrepresents the original author's views, they may include an ellipsis to indicate this; to give an improbably short example, an author might write 'Lütterfelds admired the English enormously . . .' because the original passage continued 'but he found their class snobbery distasteful'. When citing only the relevant part of a regulation, an author may be anxious to make clear that this is not the whole regulation.

Unless the preceding sentence ends in a full point, a quotation can start lower case without an ellipsis. If the sentence does end in a full point, change this to a colon, if you can; otherwise keep or add an ellipsis at the beginning of the quotation, or change the first letter to a capital within square brackets. Another place where an author may feel it necessary to substitute a capital within square brackets is where a quotation resumes in mid-sentence after an ellipsis.

In transcriptions of inscriptions etc., a point, hyphen or en rule may be used to indicate each missing letter, and the number of points or rules must be followed exactly.

Other conventions may not be worth preserving, for example full points after 'Mr' and 'Mrs' in characters' names which appear frequently both in quotations and in surrounding commentary. Discuss the conventions with the author, and tell the typesetter and proofreader about anything that might look like an unintentional inconsistency. For the retention of old or idiosyncratic spellings, and the use of '[*sic*]', see section 11.5.

Make sure that square brackets are used for anything added within quotations by someone other than the original author. If you think some of the parentheses should in fact be square brackets, ask the author. It is not usual to place ellipses in square brackets, unless the quoted author also used ellipses. For the use of parentheses in translations see p. 284.

An author who italicizes part of the quotation for emphasis should say 'my italic' (not 'author's italic', which would be ambiguous) after the quotation:

> . . . the significance of his phrase, 'living as I did in an *underworld*' (p. 115; my italic).

Square brackets should be used if the remark comes at the end of a displayed quotation or within a quotation.

11.1.4 Accuracy

Ask the author about possible transcription errors, for example misspellings, unlikely punctuation and passages that do not make sense. Look out also for the occasional British spelling when a British author quotes a US source, and vice versa.

Spot-check easily accessible quotations, to see how accurate they are; try to use the edition the author used, because different editions of a poet's work may differ in punctuation etc. If you find discrepancies, you may need to return the typescript to the author to check thoroughly. Check against each other all quotations that appear more than once, for example words and phrases quoted in discussion of a longer quoted passage.

11.1.5 **Translations**

In a book on literature in another language, where quotations are accompanied by translations into English, the translations of longer, displayed passages may be displayed below them or given in footnotes, but translations of short passages should be in parentheses in the text.

11.1.6 **Copyright**

As you go through the typescript, look for quotations that will need copyright clearance (see section 3.7.1). Check that permission has been obtained where necessary.

11.1.7 **Sources**

The source should include the author and work, if these are not obvious from the context; in scholarly books one should also give the page number or line number. Spot-check references for accuracy if you can, for example that the page cited in an article falls within the page numbers given for that article in the bibliography, or that four lines of verse are not called lines 44–8. See that the sources are concise, clear and consistent. If it is clear from the text that a series of quotations are from the same source, the source need be given only once, with just a page or line number for each subsequent quotation.

Sources for displayed quotations may be set in parentheses, full out right on the following line (or the last line if there is room); or those for prose quotations may run on. If the sources are short they may be placed just before the colon introducing the quotation. It is more expensive and less helpful to the reader to put short sources in footnotes; but if there is a special reason for placing sources there, the note indicator is best placed at the end of the quotation rather than in the phrase introducing the quotation.

Even with quotations that are not displayed, it may be better to give the source in the text rather than in a footnote. See whether this would break up the author's argument too much, and whether it would mean having parts of the text retyped after you had inserted the sources. It probably depends on how frequent and how long the sources are: a large number of page references to a single book would probably be better in the text. The source is usually in parentheses between the closing quote and the following punctuation. For style within the sources see chapter 10.

11.1.8   **Before and after displayed quotations**

Look at the punctuation introducing the quotation. In some cases no punctuation is needed, for example where there would be no punctuation if the whole sentence were written by the same person:

> The golden head of the image in Nebuchadnezzar's dream symbolizes
> A worthi world, a noble, a riche . . .

or

> When Quarles says
> O what a crocodilian world is this . . .

Where punctuation is needed, follow the author's system if it is satisfactory; if it is not, a colon (*not* a colon and a dash) may be better.

If the author interpolates a phrase such as 'said X' after the first phrase of a long quotation:

> 'I came into this kingdom', said Queen Mary, 'under promise of assistance . . .'

there are three ways of dealing with it.

1 The whole quotation can be displayed, with 'said X' in square brackets:

> I came into this kingdom [said Queen Mary] under promise of assistance . . .

2 The first part of the quotation can be in text type, in quotation marks, only the part after 'said X' being displayed:

> 'I came into this kingdom', said Queen Mary,
> under promise of assistance . . .

3 The interpolated phrase can be reworded (if necessary) and moved

to precede the quotation, all of which can be displayed:

> Queen Mary said:
> I came into this kingdom under promise of assistance . . .

The third way is the clearest for the reader, but ask the author before making the change.

If two or three displayed quotations appear together in the typescript, the author may not space them out, because the use of quotation marks makes it clear that they are separate. Mark space to be inserted between them if you are not retaining the quotation marks.

Make sure it is clear to the typesetter whether the line following the quotation is a new paragraph or should start full out.

11.2

POETRY

As I have already mentioned, poetry should be identified as such in the typescript if it is not obvious at a glance whether a displayed quotation is prose or verse.

11.2.1 Layout

Poetry may be set in text type if this will not mean a large number of turnover lines, and if small type is not used for prose quotations. It may be visually centred; but it is cheaper to align it all (apart from indented lines and turnovers, of course) either full out or indented.

Displayed verse does not need quotation marks unless these were part of the original.

See that the author's system of indention is sensible and will be clear to the typesetter; mark the indention of individual lines if necessary. You should in any case distinguish turnover lines in the original by using a 'run on' mark, and ask the designer to specify the indention for any turnover lines in your own edition. In 'concrete' poetry, warn the typesetter to follow the layout of the lines exactly.

Where a line of verse is split to indicate a caesura, make clear to the typesetter that the space must be retained.

At the foot of each folio where this is not absolutely clear, indicate whether a space should be inserted after the last line on that folio, or whether the verse should run straight on to the next folio.

If long stanzas must not be split between recto and verso or verso and recto, tell the typesetter and warn the author that pages will have to be left short. If stanzas may be split, ask the typesetter to try to avoid separating rhyming lines.

Warn the designer if some poems in the book do not have titles, unless the first line may be used as a title if the poem has no name. Otherwise the design may rely on the title to give prominence to the beginning of each poem.

11.2.2   **Accents to indicate scansion**

Use -èd rather than a mixture of -èd and -éd, unless the author wants to retain the individual poets' usage; but do not add an accent without the author's approval. Elided syllables may or may not be indicated, e.g. 'riven', 'riv'n' or 'rivn'.

11.2.3   **Indexes**

Books of poems usually have an index of first lines, plus an index of authors if there are many and they are not arranged alphabetically in the book. Indexes of titles are more unusual.

11.3

PLAYS

11.3.1   **List of characters**

The list should be on a left-hand page facing the beginning of the play, so it will often be preceded by a half-title, to avoid a blank right-hand page. See that all the characters are included in the list and are spelt the same way as in the play itself.

11.3.2 **Stage directions**

Stage directions are usually set in italic, often with the names of speaking characters distinguished by being set in roman, either small capitals or upper and lower case; single sentences often do not end in a full point.

There are various conventions: two hypothetical ones are listed below, to show you what to look out for when you brief the designer. Authors and editors of plays usually have strong views on layout and the style for stage directions.

Convention A, for, say, a Shakespearian play with very few stage directions. In this convention all entrances are centred, all exits full out right.	*Convention B*, for a modern play with discursive stage directions. In this convention all broken-off stage directions may be indented, say 2 ems.

1 *Description of scene*
   centred   full measure

2 *Entrance or other action between description of scene and first speech*
   centred   either full measure, as continua-
                                              tion of 1, or broken off in square
                                              brackets

3 *Phrase between speech prefix and first word of speech*
   in square brackets, with no   in square brackets, with no
   initial capital and no full point   initial capital and no full point
   at end; often precedes colon or   at end; often precedes colon or
   point   point

4 *Similar phrase in middle of speech*
   in square brackets, with initial   in square brackets with initial
   capital but no full point at end   capital but no full point at end

5 *Full sentence in middle of speech*
   centred on a separate line, with
   capital at beginning and full
   point at end, but no square
   brackets

if applies to speaker, run on in speech; if applies to someone else, probably broken off. In both cases in square brackets, with capital at beginning and full point at end

6 *Full sentence between speeches*
   as 5

broken off within square brackets

7 *Exits*
   full out right, often preceded by
   opening square bracket. If refers
   to speaker, 'Exit' is placed at end
   of last line of the speech, if there
   is room. If 'Exeunt', on a line by
   itself

if brief, perhaps full out right, preceded by opening square bracket. If long, probably broken off in square brackets

While copy-editing, make sure that all the actors who take part in a scene 'enter' or 'exit', if appropriate.

11.3.3 Speech prefixes

Characters' names are usually abbreviated and set in small capitals, though italic upper and lower case may be used if long names are given in full; the disadvantage of italic is that it may not be clearly distinguishable from stage directions or any italic in the first line of the speech. See that abbreviated forms are consistent and unambiguous. In old-spelling texts, the speech prefixes are often made consistent, even though the original, inconsistent spellings are retained in the dialogue.

The speech prefix is usually set at the beginning of the first line of a speech, followed by a colon, full point or space, the remaining lines of the speech being indented. Editors of French plays may want to follow the French convention of centring the character's name above the speech, but this is extravagant of space, so ask whether it is really necessary to retain the convention.

11.3.4 **Broken lines in verse plays**

If a line of verse is split between two or three speakers, the beginning of the second (and third) speech aligns with the end of the preceding one.

> To wrong such a perfection.
> LEANTIO   How?
> MOTHER   Such a creature
> To draw her from her fortune, which no doubt

11.3.5 **Act and scene numbers**

Act and scene numbers that did not appear in the original edition (for example in a Shakespeare play) may be set full out right rather than in the outer margin, to save work at proof stage. Points are usual between act, scene and line number, though commas may be used if different kinds of figures are used for acts, scenes and lines. The usual convention nowadays is to use arabic figures for all three; a more traditional system is to use capital roman numerals for act numbers, lower-case roman for scene numbers, and arabic figures for line numbers.

11.3.6 **Running heads**

The act and scene number should appear in the running head. It may be set in a short form (for example 5.3) at the inner edge of each page; or in a fuller form it could be used as the right-hand running head or 'Act 5' left and 'Scene 3' right.

11.3.7 **Performing rights**

If the play is in copyright there may need to be a notice in the preliminary pages about performances.

11.4

ANTHOLOGIES AND COLLECTIONS OF ESSAYS

With an anthology of modern poems the greatest problem for the copy-editor is likely to be the wording and placing of acknowledgements to suit both British and American copyright holders (see section 3.7.2). A full source and acknowledgement may be given at the end of each piece; or only the author's name and the title of the piece may be given in the text, all the acknowledgements being listed in the preliminary pages. In a volume of reprinted papers, the source may be given immediately below the heading of each paper, in a footnote on the first page of each paper, or in the contents list or editor's preface.

In an anthology of poems and prose pieces, should the author's name or the title of the piece be given the greater prominence? A child's interest is more likely to be caught by an intriguing title, but the author's name may be more important for older readers. One needs to consider also the best position for any notes on individual authors, pieces or textual points: should one make the anthology look more inviting by printing some or all of the notes at the end of the book, or should one keep them with the text, where they are more easily referred to? If the latter, should a note on the individual author precede the piece(s) by him or her, and should notes on specific textual points be at the foot of the relevant page; or should all the notes follow the pieces by that author? The answer will depend on the kind of reader for whom the book is intended, and on the degree of economy that must be achieved. For information about editorial apparatus, see section 11.5.

The running heads may need some thought: if there may be two or more items in an opening, it will not be satisfactory to have the author on the left and the title of the piece on the right.

Some problems of consistency arise: for example, should all the items be given titles if some have them; should spelling be made consistent? Again it depends on the level of audience and kind of material; but one should not depart from the original style without good reason.

If essays are being reprinted photographically, one cannot attempt to impose any consistency other than of 'chapter' headings and running heads. If the essays are being reset, capitalization and spelling in the text should be made consistent, and a consistent system of bibliographical references should be imposed if this will not cause a disproportionate amount of work. Authors sometimes edit their essays for republication, perhaps to make them less out of date; see that it is made clear how much the essays have been altered. If the essays have already been published in a book, there may be cross-references that will have to be expanded or omitted; also the bibliographical references may be incomplete because a full form was provided in a list at the end of the original publication.

11.5

SCHOLARLY EDITIONS

In what follows, 'volume editor' is used to mean the editor of the particular book or text, as against the commissioning editor.

11.5.1 How closely to follow the style of the original

Very occasionally a document may be reproduced facsimile; more often it will be edited and reset. The volume editor and commissioning editor must decide how closely the edition should follow the original; and the decision will depend on whether they want to make available what the author said, or the way in which he or she said it. Old-style spelling or lavish capitalization may act as a barrier between the modern reader and the argument; marginal notes and superscripts may make the book more expensive. Some volume editors are so scrupulous about following the text exactly that they lose all sense of proportion and retain things that have no significance, for example the non-indention of certain paragraphs in handwritten letters. Some useful guidance will be found in *Art and Error: Modern Textual Editing*, edited by Ronald Gottesman and Scott Bennett (London, Methuen, 1970).

Obtain the volume editor's agreement to any changes you propose to make from the style in the typescript, and see that the preface or textual note makes clear how closely the text has been followed.

Converting handwritten material into type

Once one converts manuscript (via typescript) into type, one is not producing a facsimile edition, and there is no point in retaining features which belong to manuscript: for example single underlining usually becomes italic, double underlining small capitals. Ampersands are normally spelt out, because they look very obtrusive when set in type.

Typographical conventions

It is usual to normalize typographical conventions such as the use of single quotes, en or em rules for parenthetical dashes, italic/roman punctuation and the position of punctuation with closing quotes. Some volume editors want the original printer's house style retained, including such practices as renewing the quotation marks at the beginning of every line. Try to dissuade the volume editor from retaining unnecessary distinctions; but if you are unsuccessful, warn the typesetter to follow copy for the things you list. It is not enough to say just 'follow copy', because the typesetter will not know how far this applies, for example whether the material must be set line for line, whether the original must be followed for italic/roman punctuation, and so on.

Layout and headings

It is usual to standardize the layout, unless this would mislead the reader, as it might in transcribed inscriptions. If inscriptions must be transcribed line for line, say so; for prose it is more usual to show line breaks in the original by a single vertical or oblique line. Such strokes are usually spaced if they occur between words, closed up if they occur within words. Page divisions in the original may be indicated, if necessary, by double vertical or oblique strokes, with the original page or folio number between the strokes or in square brackets after them.

Marginal headings may be taken into the text as subheadings, used as running heads, printed as footnotes or omitted; consult the designer. If they are retained, they may appear in the outer (usually wider) margin, rather than in the left-hand margin as they may have done in the original manuscript. Warn the volume editor about this.

In editions of correspondence, the address of the sender and/or addressee may be omitted unless it has any particular significance; but there should be a sensible system. If the date is part of the heading to each letter, it may be omitted from the letter itself. If the address and date are included, it is usual to follow the original as to whether they are placed at the beginning or end of the letter, but not for the exact position; the line divisions in the parts of the valediction may be followed, but not the exact position of each part or of the signature. Signatures may be set in small capitals.

Spelling, superscripts, capitals, italic and punctuation
In textual studies and definitive editions of pre-nineteenth-century works, modern diaries, notebooks and letters, old or idiosyncratic spelling is often retained, with the exception of i/j, u/v and long s. Some founts today have no long s, but if long s is to be retained, f is not an adequate substitute: a roman f has a complete crossbar, where a long s (ſ) has only a tiny stroke at the left-hand side; similarly an italic long s (*ſ*) is like an italic f but without any crossbar.

Superscript letters and tildes in contractions are normalized to modern usage unless there are good reasons to the contrary.

Spelling errors are rarely worth preserving; where they are, '[*sic*]' should be inserted only where the mistake changes the sense, for example 'he' for 'she'.

In making seventeenth- and eighteenth-century works available for their subject matter rather than for textual study, the volume editor may capitalize and italicize according to the more moderate modern practice, and may also repunctuate in the modern style. In editions of correspondence it is usual to provide a missing capital letter at the beginning of a sentence, and a missing full point at the end of one.

11.5.2 Editorial changes to the text

Author's alterations, additions and deletions
A published edition usually provides the final or 'best' version of the text if more than one version exists. The 'best' version may include words from various versions, plus the volume editor's own conjectural readings; and volume editors should make clear in the preface, or in notes at the relevant points, exactly what they have done. They will normally annotate only the variants that change the sense, or additions or alterations in the manuscript that indicate a significant change of

mind on the author's part; but if they are discussing the author's alterations to a draft of a poem, the only clear way may be to publish the text with crossed-out words and alterations immediately above them.

If some material deleted by the author is of particular interest, it may be printed in a footnote, or it may be printed in the text and suitably annotated.

Editorial omissions and additions

Unless they are covered by a general note in the preliminary pages, all omissions and additions should be clearly identified. Omissions within a paragraph are usually indicated by an ellipsis of three points; if full points are to be retained, the volume editor must include them in the copy and make clear whether they precede or follow the ellipsis. Omissions of one or more lines of verse or one or more paragraphs of prose are usually distinguished from smaller omissions. If one or more numbered sections are omitted, write, say, 'No section 8' (ringed) in the margin, to reassure the typesetter that no copy is missing.

Editorial additions should be within square brackets. If you think some of the parentheses in the typescript should be square brackets, ask the volume editor.

11.5.3 **Copy for the typesetter**

If the edition is to be reset from a nineteenth- or twentieth-century edition, and the volume editor has made very few changes, the edition itself or clear black photocopies of it are probably the best copy. See section 3.4.2 for how to mark photocopies. Photocopies of earlier printed versions are often much more difficult to read, and should be replaced by double-spaced typescript. If volume editors refuse to have the text typed, because of the risk of introducing errors, they should mark up the photocopies as clearly and simply as possible, with a minimum of marginal marks; they should provide one or two sample pages before preparing the rest, so that the publisher can see whether they will be sufficiently clear for the typesetter.

11.5.4 **Preliminary pages**

The copyright notice will probably have to be qualified, because the text itself may not be in copyright; or there may need to be two notices, one for the text and one for the editorial material. If the text has already been published, the date of first publication should usually be given on the verso of the title page, in addition to the date of your own edition.

If the author wrote a preface or introduction to the text, the volume editor's introduction will have to be called 'Editorial introduction' or something similar.

Although one may feel that the arabic pagination should start with the text itself, remember that the editorial introduction will be indexed and that large numbers can be clumsy in roman numerals.

11.5.5 **Notes**

If the volume contains a number of separate texts, such as letters or inscriptions, each text may have an introductory headnote. The other notes may be placed at the end of the relevant text, or at the foot of the page, or at the end of the book (see section 9.4.5).

A volume of correspondence may have biographical notes. If there are a large number of people who appear only spasmodically, it is probably best to have all the biographical notes in a separate section preceding the index, so that the reader can find the relevant note easily. If the biographical material is included in the notes to the document, it may be as well to proof the book in galley first: minor characters may be identified at a late stage, or the editors may realize that someone identified in a note on p. 52 also appears on p. 26; if the biographical note cannot be found by looking at the first page number given for that person in the index, the relevant references should be distinguished typographically.

11.5.6 **Glosses**

If verse has short lines and the glosses are also short, each gloss may be placed beside the relevant line; the glossed words need not be identified if there is no chance of confusion. Alternatively the glosses may be placed at the foot of the page or the end of the poem or extract, each gloss being preceded by the line number (if any) and the word it explains. If the glossed or annotated words must be identified in the text, each of them may be followed or preceded by an asterisk.

With prose passages, line numbers cannot be known until the text is typeset; and the publisher may decide to delay typesetting of the glosses or textual notes until the line numbers have been inserted.

Very short glosses look better if run on; but this cannot be done satisfactorily if they are set before it is known which part of the text will appear on each page.

Longer textual notes may be placed at the end of the book. If the relevant words are identified in the text by an asterisk and repeated at the beginning of the note, it may be enough to give the page number in the endnotes; the notes can be set to a narrower measure, allowing space for the text page number to be inserted at proof stage beside the first note for that page.

Check that any catchwords and line numbers are correct; the catchword may be in bold or italic, with the gloss in roman, or the gloss may be in italic if the text editor wants the catchword to appear exactly as in the text.

11.5.7 **Line numbers**

Consider whether line numbers are really necessary. The line numbers for prose passages or for passages that contain both prose and verse (for example some scenes in Shakespeare's plays) cannot be known until the text has been typeset, because the prose will not be set line for line; so the line numbers cannot be inserted in the notes until the text is set.

Lines are usually numbered in fives or tens, and the numbers are placed at the right, within the text measure. They are on the same side of the page on both left-hand and right-hand pages, so that they can be typeset with the text before the page division is known. The right-hand side is more suitable for verse, because there is more space there.

In notes and sources avoid the abbreviation 'll.' for 'lines' if lining figures are to be used. If you retain the abbreviation, ensure that the typescript makes it clear that 'll.' and not '11' is wanted.

Check that line numbers in notes and glosses are correct.

Plays

A line of verse split between two or three speakers counts as one line, and stage directions are ignored in the numbering; if they are referred to in a textual note the line number may be given in the form '139.1' (line 139 plus 1).

Parallel texts

If the text has a facing prose translation, only the lines of the original text will be numbered, because no prose translation can be exactly line for line.

11.5.8 **Illegible or missing letters in the original**

Where a known number of letters in an inscription are totally illegible, it is usual to indicate each illegible letter by a point, hyphen or en rule, and so one must keep the same number as in the typescript. Where the letters are almost illegible but may be guessed at, the conjectural letters may be placed within angle brackets. It does not really matter what conventions the volume editor employs, provided that they are easy to typeset, consistently used, and easy for the reader to follow. They should be explained in the preliminary pages.

The following is a typical set of conventions for a book on inscriptions:

[ ]   enclose letters supposed to have been originally in the text but now totally illegible or lost

( )   enclose letters added to complete a word abbreviated in the text

⟨ ⟩   enclose letters either omitted or wrong in the text

{ }   enclose letters which are superfluous in the text

[[ ]]   enclose letters thought to have been present but later erased. Underlining is sometimes used instead of double square brackets

vacat   indicates a vacant space in the text

| marks the beginning of a line

|| marks the beginning of every fifth line

. . . .   represent lost or illegible letters equal in number to the number of dots

——   represents an uncertain number of lost or illegible letters

You will find other sets of conventions explained in published editions of correspondence etc.

11.5.9 **Parallel texts**

A foreign text may have a translation on the facing page; or two versions of the same text may be printed on facing pages for comparison. Discuss with the volume editor which version should be on the left-hand page and which on the right-hand. A translation should probably follow the original and so be on the right-hand page.

Consider whether the typesetter will be able to understand a foreign text sufficiently to be able to keep the two versions in step (to the nearest line) when paging the book. If not, you will have to arrange the paging yourself when galley proofs are available.

11.6

TRANSLATIONS

There is a British Standard on the presentation of translations: BS 4755.

The translation, not being the original text, may usually be made consistent with your house style. Find out whether the author, translator or volume editor is to answer any queries you may have, and confirm that the translation has been approved by the author and/or series editor; later changes could be very expensive.

Abbreviations and acronyms, such as those of names of organizations, should be translated into their English equivalent (if any), or spelt out – and if necessary translated – at their first occurrence.

Passages from the text that are quoted in the introduction may have been translated in slightly different words from those used in the text. Check this if you can do so fairly easily, as it could mislead or irritate the reader if the two versions do not tally.

If the volume editor wants occasionally to cite the original foreign word or phrase in the translation, parentheses may be used for this word or phrase and square brackets for editorial interpolations.

Where a foreign author translated quotations from an English source into his or her own language, or used a published translation, see that these quotations are not translated back into English but are taken direct from the original source, and that the appropriate page references are given. Similarly where, say, a French author has quoted a German author in translation, the German source should, if possible, be translated direct, or an existing English translation used (and acknowledged).

For diagrams, tables, etc., where there is little wording to be translated, translators often provide photocopies from the foreign edition, with the wording translated; see that everything has been translated, including decimal commas to decimal points.

Preliminary pages

The translator's name should be given, either on the title page or in the preface. If the text has been published in the original language, the original title and the date of publication should be given on the verso of the title page; if the translation was made from a second or later edition, the number and date of the relevant edition should be given. There should be a copyright notice for the translation, and also for the original edition if that is still in copyright. The British Standard says that the following should also be given:

the place or country of the original publication
the name and address of the original publisher
the name of the language from which the translation was made
    (which may not be the original language).

For example:

> Originally published in Japanese as *Chikyu-shi* by Iwanami Shoten, Tokyo, 1979 and © Minoru Ozima 1979
> First published in English by Cambridge University Press 1981 as *The Earth: Its Birth and Growth*
> English edition © Cambridge University Press 1981

Translator's notes

Observations by the translator (whether in brackets in the text or in a footnote) should of course be distinguished from the translated material; the British Standard recommends that they should be preceded by the words 'Translator's note'.

Bibliography
If the bibliography is reprinted from the original, it may be necessary to transliterate titles given in other alphabets, to add information about English editions of works cited and to anglicize bibliographical terms and places of publication.

⑫ Multi-author and multi-volume works

12.1

BOOKS WITH MORE THAN ONE AUTHOR

This section is primarily concerned with contributory works such as symposia, where each paper or chapter is written by a different person, but of course the same kinds of problem are found in books written jointly by two or three authors: the typescript is likely to be more inconsistent, and one needs to know which author to consult about queries and whether the other(s) should receive copies of all letters.

In what follows, 'volume editor' is used to mean the editor of the particular book, as against the commissioning editor.

12.1.1 What volume editors can be asked to do

All the contributions should pass through the volume editor's hands before they reach the publisher; but the extent and quality of the work that volume editors do depends very much on their experience and efficiency, and also on the time at their disposal. They may receive contributions over a period of weeks, months or even years, and they may forget what they did to the first contributions by the time they receive the later ones. They will almost certainly have to hurry over the last contributions, which may reach them late or incomplete.

The commissioning editor and volume editor should draw up some instructions for contributors as early as possible. The commissioning editor can explain why certain faults in typescripts can delay a book, and emphasize that, if the volume editor and contributors are careful about these points, the publisher and typesetter will be able to deal with the typescript more quickly.

The volume editor must be responsible for the quality of the book and for obtaining the contributors' agreement to any changes made before the typescript reaches the publisher. It must be agreed who will answer the copy-editor's questions: it is always better to send queries about content (missing or unintelligible material) and references to the contributor; but some volume editors prefer to answer all copy-editing queries themselves.

If the book is to be published quickly, the volume editor should send each paper for copy-editing immediately after completing work on it, especially if there are illustrations to be redrawn.

If the contents list could not be finalized at an early stage, the volume editor should send the final list as soon as possible, showing the order in which the contributions are to be printed; also a list of contributors, with their affiliations (academic positions held, degrees or honours), if the volume is to contain one, so that the copy-editor can check names and affiliations against the information given at the beginning of individual papers.

The volume editor should also send an up-to-date list of addresses for contributors, to be used both for any queries and for the dispatch of proofs.

12.1.2 **Text**

The volume editor should see that:

1 the text is well written
2 there are no incongruities in conference papers, arising from the fact that the words were first spoken: for example, discussions may have been typed from a tape recording full of unfinished sentences; or a paper may start 'I had intended to talk to you today about . . .' Also some contributors revise their papers in the light of questions asked during the discussion, and the typescript of the discussion may include questions already answered in the preceding text
3 consistent conventions are used for such things as abbreviations, capitalization, nomenclature or short titles for works referred to by more than one contributor; that a list of the preferred forms is provided for the copy-editor; and that abbreviations are explained where necessary
4 handwritten additions are legible
5 subheadings are of not more than three grades (or whatever number has been agreed) and they are coded A, B or C in the margin
6 references to papers and books are in the agreed style and tally with the list of references or bibliography

7 a list of running heads is provided if the titles of the papers are long

8 bold, italic, Greek and other symbols are clearly identified

9 cross-references between contributions are added, where appropriate

12.1.3 **Illustrations**

The volume editor should see that:

10 adequate originals are provided for halftones and line drawings and these are numbered in separate sequences (where appropriate) and clearly identified by the contributor's name

11 separate typewritten lists of captions are provided

12 the position of all text illustrations is marked in the margin of the typescript

13 all conventions, such as abbreviations, are consistent in all figures and with the text, and all lettering is in English

14 the top of a photograph is marked on the back if necessary, and those parts of photographs which must or may be omitted are indicated

15 any grids to be retained in graphs are indicated

The commissioning editor may also ask the volume editor to see that contributors obtain permission to use all copyright material.

12.1.4 **The arrival of an urgent typescript**

If time is short, the typescript will arrive in batches. Even if the first batch of papers arrives well before the due date, it is worth looking at them as soon as possible to see whether the volume editor is doing the right things, so that one can, if necessary, ask for additional work to be done on the later papers.

Check the contents list and ask the volume editor whether it shows the correct printing order: provisional lists are often revised, as some papers may never arrive.

Ideally, the typescript should not be sent for setting until it is complete, but you may not receive all the contributions by the due date. The production department will be able to tell you whether the typesetter can deal most conveniently and quickly with two or three large batches or with a number of smaller ones.

The typesetter may be asked to provide paged proofs; but if some of the papers to appear at the beginning of the book are not available, it will not be possible to assign page numbers to page proofs of the others. The index cannot, of course, be made until the page numbers are known.

12.1.5 How much to do to the typescript

If the volume editor has not dealt fully with the numbered points above, you will have to do as much as you can within the time available. Any style sheet for the typesetter or proofreader should make clear whether or not (or how far) the chapters or papers are consistent with one another; each one must, of course, be consistent within itself. If the contributions are not consistent when they reach you, your decision as to how far to make them consistent will depend on the kind of book it is.

(a) If it is not a collection of papers but a book with a beginning, a middle and an end, designed to be read right through – the sort of book that does not give the contributor's (or co-author's) name below the chapter title – the book should be treated as a single unit and a consistent system of capitalization, spelling and italic should be imposed throughout.

(b) Conference papers have to be published quickly. The contributors may be inexperienced, but you will have time to rewrite only those pieces which are really ambiguous, misleading or obscure. These volumes usually have a consistent style for subheadings, bibliographical references, abbreviations, spelling, spelling-out of numbers, etc.

(c) For festschrifts and other volumes with eminent contributors, the commissioning editor and volume editor may decide that there is no need for complete consistency between contributions, and that contributors may retain, for example, American spelling and their own system of nomenclature and bibliographical references.

(d) If collections of already-published papers are to be reprinted photographically, it is not possible to impose any consistency other than of 'chapter' headings and running heads. If the papers are to be reset, capitalization and spelling in the text should be made consistent, and a consistent system of bibliographical references may be imposed. See that the papers are complete in themselves: that any cross-references are clear and that bibliographical references are complete.

12.1.6 Paging

If there are to be offprints, each paper will probably start on a right-hand page; the list of references or bibliography will usually run on from the end of the paper, as will any discussion of that paper; but discussion covering more than one paper will start on a right-hand page.

12.1.7 Notes

If there are to be offprints, endnotes will be placed at the end of each paper, preceding the list of references. Otherwise they will probably be at the end of the book, just before the bibliography.

12.1.8 References and bibliographies

If there are to be offprints, the list of references or bibliography will usually run on from the end of the paper; a list of references may do so even if there are not to be offprints.

In science books the author–date system (see section 10.2) is often used; if some contributors have failed to include the titles of journal articles, and there is not time to obtain them, it is probably better to retain those that have been provided, even though this leaves the volume inconsistent. The list provided by the contributor may not contain all the references in the text; if you cannot obtain the missing references from the contributor in time, add the author's name to the list and ask the typesetter to leave space so that the rest of each reference can be added at proof stage. If some contributors have numbered their references, it may not be worth changing these to the author–date system.

If the reference lists or bibliographies are to be at the end of the book, consult the volume editor as to whether they would be more useful if amalgamated. If they are amalgamated they must be made consistent.

Also two contributors may refer to different 'Smith 1990'; these would have to be distinguished in the list and the text references by calling them 1990a and 1990b.

Publishers do not always attempt to achieve complete consistency between separate lists if time is short, though obviously one must make sure that a book or article is shown with the same author, title and date in each list in which it appears.

12.1.9 Abstracts or summaries

If abstracts or summaries are supplied, discuss with the volume editor whether there is any real need to include them. If they replace a missing paper they should be treated as if they were a paper; if not, they should probably be omitted or could form the first section of the paper.

12.1.10 Running heads

In categories (b) to (d) in section 12.1.5, the running heads are likely to be the contributor's name on the left and the paper title on the right. If the volume editor has not provided a list of shortened titles, ask for one or send your own for approval.

12.1.11 Copyright

Where contributors, or the institutions for which they work, retain copyright in their papers and ask for a copyright notice to be included, see that the necessary copyright line is inserted at the foot of the first page of the paper. There will also be a copyright notice for the whole book on the verso of the title page.

12.1.12 Contributors' names and affiliations

In collections of papers, contributors' names usually appear below the paper titles; their affiliations and/or addresses may appear there or in the contents list or in a separate list of contributors in the preliminary pages.

If the author of a scientific paper has moved from the institution at which the research was carried out, there will probably be a note to that effect at the beginning or end of the paper.

For books in category (a) in section 12.1.5, the contributors' names are likely to appear in the contents list. If there are only two or three authors, and no volume editor, the authors' names will appear on the title page, and the special responsibility of each for certain parts of the book will probably be explained in the preface rather than in the contents list.

12.1.13 **Illustrations**

In a collection of independent papers, illustration and table numbering will start afresh in each paper; it helps the typesetter if you give the number of each on the first folio of the paper. If illustrations in different papers should be related in size, scale or conventions, tell the artist.

In books in category (a), illustrations and tables are each numbered in one sequence through the book or decimally by chapter.

See also points 10–15 in section 12.1.3.

If the book has to be produced quickly, only really bad drawings can be redrawn, and the contributor's own lettering will be used if possible. The volume editor or copy-editor will check any corrections to drawings. If there is a little more time and several figures have been redrawn, it is better that the individual contributors should check them, because their originals may have contained errors or ambiguities. Discuss this with the production department.

12.1.14 **Offprints**

If some papers have more than one author, the production department must be told whether there are to be, say, twenty-five offprints per paper or twenty-five per contributor. If there are introductions, discussions or separately printed halftones, are there to be offprints of those too, and, if so, who should receive them? In general, halftones or pages of text that belong to different offprints are not backed up; but this will depend on the cost. Each offprint must carry the following information on the first page or a cover: book title, editor's name, copyright owner and date, publisher's name and 'Printed in [country]'.

Reprinted from J. Butcher (ed.), *Copy-editing Indexes*
(Copy-editing Symposium 26)
© Society of Freelance Editors and Proofreaders 1991
Newnham University Press
Printed in Great Britain

12.1.15 **Proofs**

Give the production department an up-to-date list of the contributors' addresses, making it quite clear which part of the text and which separately printed halftones, if any, are to go to whom. If the contributor's name appears at the beginning of the paper, there will be no problem, but if it appears only in the preliminary pages, write the chapter number beside each contributor's name on the list.

Make clear who is to receive the marked proof and the typescript. The revised proof will go to the volume editor only, but the practice with first proofs varies. As contributors do not always deal with proofs quickly, the marked proof may be sent to the volume editor; the contributor in any case receives a copy of the proof and should be asked by the publisher to send any corrections to the volume editor within a certain time. The volume editor is asked to collate the corrections – or to correct the proof on behalf of the contributor if the latter does not send corrections by the due date – and to send the marked proof to the publisher. Things become more complicated, of course, if there are two volume editors, or if the marked proof is to go to the contributor and some papers have two authors.

12.2

WORKS IN MORE THAN ONE VOLUME

There are four main kinds of work in more than one volume:

1 works that are an integral whole – in effect one book – and published at one time, but which are too long to be fitted into one volume
2 works such as biographies, collected letters or essays, which can be described as a single work but are so long that they are planned as two or more volumes, to be divided chronologically or by subject so

that each volume is fairly self-contained and has its own title. These
may be published at one time or volume by volume

3 books which consist of two parts published simultaneously, of
which one is likely to have a larger sale than the other: some people
buy the complete book, others only the more general volume

4 series. As series are published over a long period and are likely to be
consulted singly, they will be similar in general appearance (style of
subheadings etc.), but may differ in such conventions as spelling.
This section is not concerned with books in this fourth category

The commissioning editor and marketing department decide
whether books in categories 1–3 should be sold separately or only as a
set. In general, those in category 1 will be available only as a set, and
those in 2 and 3 will be available separately, though if those in 2 are published simultaneously they may be sold only as a set. Those sold separately should, of course, be complete in themselves. For those sold as
a set, the copy-editor should do what seems most helpful for the reader.

Books sold only as a set
These may be paginated consecutively, but this is not necessarily more
useful to the reader, who will not remember exactly where the volumes
divide, so cross-references may still need a volume number. If the
volumes are paginated consecutively, the arabic pagination in volume 2
will start with the next odd number after the last page number of
volume 1; the prelims will be paginated separately, starting with i in
each volume.

The book will almost certainly have only one index, but here again
the reader will need some reminder as to where the volumes divide,
either in a note at the beginning of the index or by the inclusion of the
volume number before the first page reference for each volume, e.g. 1.8,
159, 354; 2.396. Parts, chapters, illustrations and tables will often be
numbered in one sequence even if the volumes are paginated separately.

Although it is more useful to the book-buyer to have only one
bibliography and one index to consult, the library-user will probably
find it helpful to have the complete contents, showing the division into
volumes, in each volume, or at any rate in volume 1. A list of abbreviations and a glossary may also be needed in each volume.

Volumes sold separately
The contents lists will cover only the relevant volume, and each volume will have its own list of abbreviations. The note on editorial conventions may or may not be repeated in each volume; if it is, see that it contains all the conventions relevant to that volume, and that, if it contains a large number that are not, it is clear to the reader that the list contains the conventions for the complete work and not just that volume.

Each volume may have a complete index, perhaps consolidated into a final index volume; or a partial index with a complete index in the final volume; or no index until the final volume.

12.2.1 Numbering of volumes

The volumes should normally be numbered in arabic; if there is a special reason for roman numbering, tell the designer.

12.2.2 Preliminary pages

Half-title and title page
See that the volume number and volume title are included.

Verso of title page
If the volumes are to be sold as a set, each volume should give the ISBNs for all the individual volumes and also one for the set (see section 7.5.4).

Contents list
If the volumes are to be printed simultaneously and sold only as a set, should each volume contain the complete contents list showing the division into volumes? If the volumes are not to be printed simultaneously, it will, of course, be impossible to include page numbers for later volumes, so one would normally include only the contents of the current volume.

Preface

Whether the preface should appear in each volume will depend on its usefulness to the reader. In general it will appear only in the first volume of books in category 1. Those in categories 2 and 3 may have a different preface in each volume.

Lists of illustrations and tables

There is no need to include the complete list in each volume, unless the illustrations are relevant to the whole work. If the contents list covers all the volumes, and the list of illustrations only one volume, the latter should probably be headed 'Illustrations in volume 1' to make the distinction clear.

List of abbreviations

This should be printed in each volume: it is not worth the trouble of pruning such lists in order to include only the relevant entries in volumes 2 etc. of books that will be sold as a set. Even if one does so, there should probably be a complete list in volume 1.

Acknowledgements (see section 3.7.2)

Even if the book is to be sold only as a set, each volume should contain its own list of acknowledgements (where appropriate), so that they are available to the person reading that volume.

12.2.3 **Cross-references**

The volume number must be included in references that will fall in one of the other volumes, if the volumes are to be paginated separately; it may be helpful even if they are to be paginated in one sequence.

12.2.4 **Consistency**

The volumes should be consistent in spelling, capitalization, etc. If the volumes will be published over a number of years, keep a full note of the conventions, and try to make sure that the volume editor has a copy when he or she starts work on the next volume. However, one may decide not to follow earlier volumes for minor conventions that are no longer house style. Consult the author or volume editor if you wish to change the style.

If the same editorial note is included in each volume, see whether it should be modified for the current volume.

12.2.5 **Illustrations**

If a map is relevant to more than one volume, it should be repeated; in which case it may be less confusing to number the maps in a separate sequence in each volume, even if the book is to be sold only as a set. The map would then be included in the relevant place in the numbering for each volume.

If the volumes are not all to be published at once, or if there are many illustrations, it is better to number them separately in each volume. Otherwise the numbering may become very cumbersome; and without a volume number it may be difficult to tell which volume contains the illustration.

12.2.6 **Sending the book for setting**

The typesetter and printer will probably treat each volume as a separate unit, because each represents a book to be printed and bound. So send the first volume for setting before the rest, if it is completely ready, and return it for press before the rest if you have been able to complete the contents list etc.

⑬ Science and mathematics books

The complicated notations used by scientists and mathematicians pose special problems and so require more than usually detailed marking up by the copy-editor, even for those typesetters who specialize in this kind of setting. This chapter attempts to give some working principles for the choice of nomenclature and its clarification for the typesetter. The books listed in section 13.10 are all valuable for reference. For the physical sciences at least, the summary of standard notation in reference (1) is very useful and pp. 23–49 of (2) will be helpful in the biological sciences and medicine. A list of the more common mathematical symbols and their descriptions is given in appendix 8. Many journals issue instructions or recommendations to authors, which can be a source of information for specialized books.

13.0.1 Nomenclature

For all nomenclature follow where possible the conventions of the Royal Society set out in (1): the Royal Society's recommendations for units of measurement follow the Système International (SI). If authors use conventions that differ from those of the Royal Society, consult them before making changes.

13.0.2 Capitals and hyphens

Scientists and mathematicians often use terms that have not yet become absorbed into general scientific language and may be unconventionally hyphenated and capitalized. The use of the minimum possible hyphenation and capitalization will make decisions easier: it will usually be obvious whether to make compound terms into two distinct words or one: and if a lower-case l is used in Ohm's law it will not be necessary to worry about the t in Cauchy's theorem or the e in Maclaurin's expansion. Proper names used adjectivally (such as newtonian, gaussian, cartesian) are usually lower case.

Watch out for systems that are not immediately obvious: there is, for example, one which says that where a prefix to a word starting with a vowel ends in one itself there should be a hyphen only if the vowels are the same: tetra-acetate and tri-iodide, but tetraiodide and triacetate. See also section 6.12.3.

Single-letter prefixes are sometimes joined to the words they qualify (e.g. z-axis, X-ray, t-test) and sometimes not (e.g. B cells, S wave, T lymphocyte). As with all hyphenation, it is advisable to send the author a list for approval showing what hyphenation you would like to impose.

When two or more hyphenated terms are condensed in the same phrase the hyphens should be left hanging (α-, β- and γ-rays) and identified as hyphens if the typesetter could confuse them with, say, minus signs.

13.0.3 **Abbreviations**

With a very few exceptions, all abbreviations should be spelt out or explained when they first occur. The exceptions will, of course, depend on the subject and level of the book (e.g. DNA and RNA in postgraduate biology). Capitalized abbreviations are usually set in full capitals without points (except where small capitals are by convention always used; see section 13.6.4); lower-case abbreviations are usually set with points (although this convention seems to be declining). See also section 13.3 on units.

Useful lists of abbreviations and contractions are contained in (1) p. 43, (2) pp. 23–49, (3) pp. 42, 83 and 109–13 and (4) pp. 16–21.

13.1
_____

GENERAL POINTS

13.1.1 **Headings and running heads**

If mathematics containing superscripts, fractions or bold, for example, occurs in headings and running heads it may restrict their typography. Point this out to the designer before the book is designed or estimated.

Mathematics in headings, table headings and running heads should be marked up exactly as in the text. Whether the heading is italic or roman, this should not affect the mathematics, e.g.

    3.2 The sinusoidal spiral $r^n = a^n \cos n\theta$

and

    3.2 The sinusoidal spiral $r^n = a^n \cos n\theta$.

If the heading is bold, it is acceptable for the mathematics to be bold provided this does not cause confusion, e.g.

    3.2 The sinusoidal spiral $r^n = a^n \cos n\theta$

is visually acceptable, but

    5.9 Traction $t(n, x, t)$

should be rendered as

    5.9 Traction $t(n, x, t)$.

See also p. 320.

13.1.2   **Footnotes**

The more complicated the content of the book, the more reason there is to persuade the author to eliminate footnotes. If footnotes are added to a page already fragmented by small type, displayed equations and formulae, the effect can be very messy. It should also be remembered that mathematical setting of any complexity becomes more difficult to read in a footnote size of type: unavoidable mathematics and structural chemical formulae in footnotes should be pointed out to the designer at the earliest possible stage.

Choose indicators carefully to avoid confusion with scientific or mathematical nomenclature. symbols are usually best, but it may be necessary to dispense with the asterisk and start with a dagger. In tables having several notes, superscript roman or italic lower-case letters can usually be used without ambiguity. Use different indicators for notes to text and notes to tables.

See also sections 9.4.1 and 9.4.2.

13.1.3   **References**

Science books most commonly use either the author–date system or, to a lesser extent, the number system: see sections 10.2 and 10.3.

13.1.4 **Equations**

If mathematical and chemical equations are numbered in separate sequences, the numbers should be differentiated typographically. Mathematical equation numbers should be in normal type, ranged right in parentheses, whereas chemical equation numbers may be either normal or bold type in square brackets, or bold in parentheses (again ranged right). No leader dots are needed.

Check that each numbering sequence is consecutive (whether the author numbers every equation or only those that are referred to). If more than one equation is allocated to an equation number, the number should be centred vertically and the equations may be linked on the right side by a large brace. If an equation occupies more than one line, the number should be on the last line.

It is preferable to punctuate equations in the same way as any other written statement. The alternative system of using no punctuation at all after displayed material is acceptable if consistent; as it is not always possible to predict just what the typesetter will display, give a general instruction.

An equation will be displayed if it has been displayed in the typescript, or if it has been run on but the typesetter cannot squeeze it into the remainder of a line without breaking it at an unsuitable place. Keep an eye open for potentially inconsistent sequences or cases of inconsistent displaying/running-on by the author. It is generally preferable to mark for display any run-on equations that may produce inconsistency. Equations that are more than one line deep should only be run on if they can easily be changed to one line (see pp. 310–11).

Guidance should be given on where to break long equations if they may be too long for the line. This is best done by marking suitable breaks with a pencil line and adding a marginal note to the typesetter (such as 'Break here if necessary'). Equations should, if possible, be broken before an operational sign and not within brackets:

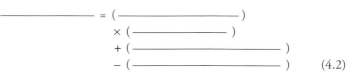

$$(4.2)$$

Another possible solution is to set the equation in a smaller type size.

Where displayed equations are part of a sentence, any linking words (such as and, therefore, thus) are part of the text and should not be displayed. However, modifying statements such as 'for $x \leq 1$' or 'where $n = 2q/w$' are often presented as part of a displayed equation, on the same line. In this case they should be separated by an em space. Whether or not space has been left on the typescript, mark it as follows:

$$\left| g(\underline{x}) - g(\underline{y}) \right| < \underline{n} \ \square \ \text{for} \ \left| \underline{x} - \underline{y} \right| \leqslant \underline{m}$$

13.1.5 Illustrations

See chapter 4. The following points are of special importance in science books.

Transfer as much peripheral matter as sensible to the caption (see p. 86), but tell the author that you are doing this.

Scale bars on photomicrographs etc. are better than magnifications; not only are they more graphic, but they avoid the need to recalculate magnifications when photographs are reduced. If magnifications are given in the captions, remember to check the proofs against the artwork and make any adjustments, if the author has not done so.

Stereo illustrations must not be relabelled except for part letters ((*a*), (*b*). . .) and spacing between them should not be altered.

Graphs
The grid and the top and right-hand edges of the 'box' are unnecessary and may be deleted from a graph, except in the rather unusual case where the reader is to take measurements from it. Suggest such deletions to the author.

Check that axes have been labelled in a consistent style and that arrows on the ends of unnumbered axes are used consistently.

13.2

NOMENCLATURE

See also sections 13.3–13.6 on units, astronomy, biology and chemistry. The Royal Society's *Quantities, Units and Symbols* (1) is recommended as a working guide. Points on mathematics are well summarized in (5) pp. 7–41.

A great deal of typographical subtlety is required in the setting of scientific and mathematical matter, and it is very important to ensure that the typesetter can see clearly how each symbol should be rendered. The Roman and Greek alphabets in various styles, arabic figures, and a vast range of special symbols are all used. A list of frequently used mathematical symbols and their names is given in appendix 8.

Variables (including geometrical 'points' and algebraic 'constants' such as constants of integration) are usually set in italic (sloping) type; operators such as differential d, representations of pure numbers such as exponential e and imaginary i are usually set in roman (upright) type; chemical symbols and symbols for units of measurement are always in roman type. Vectors are usually set in bold (either roman or italic), but italic with an arrow over is acceptable. The upright/sloping distinction is carried through to Greek symbols, and bold Greek faces are available. Multiple letters used to stand for functions or operators are set in roman (e.g. log, ln, Re, Im, det, ker, lim, max, min, sup, sin, tan, cos). The use of shell capitals $\mathbb{R}$ (real numbers), $\mathbb{C}$ (complex numbers), $\mathbb{Q}$ (rational numbers) and $\mathbb{Z}$ (integers) is now an accepted convention. Standard symbols for variables are given in (1) pp. 12–20, (2) pp. 23–49.

Unless there are ambiguities, the spacing of mathematical symbols is best left to the typesetter. Space should be marked before unit symbols if they have been typed closed up; see pp. 313–14.

Lining figures (0, 1, 2, 3, 4, . . .) are, in general, to be preferred to non-lining figures (0, 1, 2, 3, 4, . . .) in which it is difficult to distinguish zero from lower-case o and one from small capital ɪ, and which cause problems with fractions and subscripts and superscripts. However, non-lining figures are more readable in bulk and so are usually used in books of tables (e.g. log tables).

13.2.1 The marking of italic

Where batches of typed material are predominantly of the same kind (e.g. mainly mathematics or mainly chemistry) some typesetters can be relied upon to realize this and to set them appropriately without any marking by the publisher; in that case the *exceptions* need to be pointed out. However, for this system to be safe one needs to know one's typesetter: if in doubt *all* italic everywhere should be marked and, in mathematics, the first occurrences of any roman. For the marking of subscripts and superscripts see section 13.2.3.

13.2.2 **The marking of bold**

Vectors and tensors are traditionally distinguished from their scalar equivalents by the use of bold type. The typescript may be presented with the required characters already bold, or identified by means of a typed underline or arrow over. In all cases it is worth asking the author (a) how the vectors or tensors should be set and (b) whether *all* of them have been identified. If the answer to the latter is no, then you may need to return the typescript, as it takes an expert eye to tell whether scalar or vector quantities are being used. Alternatively, if the bold occurs infrequently, you could ask the author to provide a list. If you are familiar with the rules of vector multiplication, it is worth checking the balance of bold symbols in equations. Remember that vector multiplication of two vectors is indicated by a $\times$ or $\wedge$ and results in a vector ($a \times b = c$) whereas scalar multiplication of two vectors is indicated by a multiplication point and results in a scalar ($e \cdot f = g$).

The Royal Society recommends the use of bold italic rather than bold roman, because this more neatly ties up each vector with its corresponding scalar value; however, in a typeface that has a rather light bold, the extra distinction afforded by roman could be helpful.

If second-order tensors are to be distinguished from other vectors they are set in bold sans serif – again italic, if bold italic is being used for vectors.

13.2.3 **Superscripts and subscripts**

A list of recommended symbols is given in (1) pp. 11–12.

Italicization of superscripts and subscripts follows the same rules as for other symbols: italic should be used only if the sub/superscript is itself a variable, hence '$X_n = Y$ for $n = 1, 2, 3$', but roman should be used if the sub/superscript acts as a label, hence '. . . where P_e is the output per editor and P_c the output per copy-editor'. Capitalized subscripts should be full capitals (i.e. *not* marked as 'small capitals'). They need to be fully marked: if all are italic or all roman a blanket instruction will suffice for many typesetters, but if mixed then the italic ones should always be underlined. Some authors are accustomed to having their subscripts italic regardless of their meaning, so it is advisable to explain the system.

Where superscripts and subscripts occur together, three distinct renderings are possible: $X_a{}^2$, X_a^2 and $X^2{}_a$. The second ('aligned') has the same meaning as the first ('staggered') and is neater. In some (but not all) cases the third possibility ($X^2{}_a$) should have its distinction made unambiguous by the use of parentheses: $(X^2)_a$. Check which rendering your author requires, and give an instruction to the typesetter.

Certain symbols such as the asterisk and the prime are related to the variable in a way that necessitates their being set adjacent to the letter (e.g. X'_n not X_n').

If it is not clear that superscripts or subscripts are such, they should be marked by a V-shape in pencil. Double superscripts or subscripts should be marked by a double-V.

Awkward expressions may be dealt with in the following way:

$$x^a, \quad \text{where} \quad a = z^{4\pi r^2}$$

The legibility decreases with the size of type, and complicated mathematics of any kind should be avoided in footnotes.

13.2.4 Ambiguous symbols and their clarification

Make sure that all badly written or typed symbols and misleading spacing are elucidated. Watch out for symbols that were not on the author's word processor and have had to be adapted (e.g. A for Å, u for μ, ι for ɩ, – > for →).

Complicated expressions are often clearer to the typesetter when neatly handwritten than when typewritten, as some word processors have no subtleties of spacing or sizes of characters, though in hand writing one has to be more careful to avoid possible capital/lower-case ambiguities.

It may in some cases be clearer to underline or ring letters from different alphabets (such as script or German) in colour. This must be done totally (i.e. marking even unambiguous letters) and the meaning of each colour explained in the margin at the beginning of each batch.

Ambiguous mathematical signs or letters should be identified by their names or, if no further confusion is possible, just by the indication 'sign' or 'letter'. The following list summarizes the most common sources of ambiguity.

$a, \alpha, \propto$ (proportional)

$A, \Lambda, \wedge$ (vector product)

B, β

$c, C, \subset$ (contained in), ((parenthesis)

d, δ, ∂ (partial differential). Differential operator d preferably set roman, not italic

$e, \varepsilon, \xi, F, \mathscr{E}, \in$ (element of). Exponential e preferably set roman, not italic; e represents an electron as a particle, e its charge

g (grams), g (acceleration due to free fall). When the latter has vectorial significance it may be set bold roman or bold italic, **g** or *g*

h (hours), h (possible mathematical variable). Planck's constant, h, may have a stroke, $\hbar$ (where $\hbar = h/2\pi$)

i, ι. i is preferably set roman when it denotes $\sqrt{(-1)}$

j is preferably set roman when it denotes $\sqrt{(-1)}$

k, K, κ, k (kilo-)

$l, \ell, I, 1, | |$ (modulus), l (litre)

$L, \angle$ (angle)

m (metre), m (variable, e.g. for mass)

$n, \eta, \cap$ and $\cap$ (intersection)

o, O (these may be used to denote 'order of magnitude' as in $o(1)$ and $O(1)$), 0, Greek $o, \sigma, \theta, \Theta$, sign $\circ$. Note especially the need to indicate a zero when superscript or subscript

p, P, ρ, p (pence)

r, τ, Γ

$s, S, \int$ (integral), s (seconds), ς (terminal sigma)

t, *T*, *τ*, *Γ*, *r*, + (plus)
u, *U*, *μ*, *v*, ∪ and ∪ (union)
v, *V*, *υ*, √
w, *W*, *ω*
x, *X*, *ψ*, *χ*, × (multiplication)
y, *Y*, *γ*, *Y*
z, *Z*, 2

Δ, *Λ*, *A*, Δ (sign), ∧ (vector product)
θ, *ϑ* (alternatives which may or may not have a distinction
    intended), *Θ*, ⊖ (sign)
π, *Π*, Π as a product sign
Σ, Σ as a summation sign
ξ, *ζ*
φ, *φ* (alternatives which may or may not have a distinction
    intended), *Φ*, ∅ (empty set), zero in computer printout,
    Scandinavian ø, Ø
ψ, *Ψ*
ω, *ϖ* (curly pi)
superscript 1, ′ (prime or minutes)
superscript 0, O, o, ° (degree)
decimal point, multiplication point; either may be medial or low
    (see below)
= (equals), C=C (double bond)
– (minus), - (hyphen), – (en rule), — (em rule), C—C (single
    bond)
|, /, \ (signs)
‖ (parallel), ‖ ‖ (norm)
∠ (angle), < > (signs), ⟨ ⟩ (angle brackets), ≺ ≻ (signs)
∤ (does not divide)
≂, ≃, ~, ≈, ≅, ≤, ≥, ≦, ≧, ≠, ≢ (various approximation and
    inequality signs). Check that any differences in usage are
    intended.

Ambiguous sorts in mathematical setting
In some typefaces (e.g. Times) italic lower-case vee (*v*) is almost identical with Greek nu (*ν*). There is, however, an alternative italic vee (*v*)

which avoids confusion: ask the typesetter to use this if necessary. In sans serif faces capital I (I) and lower-case el (l) look the same and this may necessitate changing the notation or spelling out litres.

13.2.5 **Miscellany**

Decimal point
This should be preceded by a figure, if necessary a zero (although some authors prefer to omit the zero in quantities such as probability that never exceed unity). The point is now usually on the line (see next paragraph).

Multiplication point
This is an en point (see glossary), and the Royal Society now recommends a medial point only. It should be possible to avoid any confusion over the significance of a point: multiplication between numerals should be denoted by a cross ($\times$); and usually no sign of multiplication is needed between letter symbols (except between vectors). The important thing is to ensure that, wherever the point *is* used, there can be no ambiguity. Medial multiplication point/low decimal point (or vice versa) should be specified as an instruction to the typesetter, and any ambiguous ones in the typescript marked individually.

A medial point may be used to represent missing symbols (e.g. $f(\cdot)$, $|\cdot|$); this should be a bold en point.

High plus and minus signs
These (as opposed to the usual medial ones) are used occasionally (usually in school books) when the sign is a property of the number rather than an operator. Hence: $^{-}2 + {}^{+}3 = {}^{+}1$. The signs are larger than the usual superscript plus and minus.

Large numbers
It is usual to have a thin space (say a ninth of an em) rather than a comma in numbers of 10 000 and above. Similar spaces should be inserted to the right of the decimal point at intervals of three digits if there are more than four. This should be marked, a light stroke sufficing after the first in each batch.

Colons

If it is not obvious that a colon is indicating a ratio, it should be clarified. The spaces each side of the colon in a ratio should look the same, and may be indicated by space before as well as after the colon, using vertical lines. The colon is *not* equally spaced in the representation of a set, $\{x: x \geq 0\}$, or a function, $f: A \rightarrow B$.

Brackets

Where several brackets have to be used in a mathematical expression the sequence should be $[\langle\{[(. . .)]\}\rangle]$ but it is unlikely to be worth changing a consistent system so long as it is one of different kinds of brackets. The correct size of bracket must be used for a given depth of mathematical expression; displayed two-line expressions and those involving summations or integrals require larger brackets than single-line expressions. Watch out for wrong use of small brackets when the enclosed expression is mainly single-line but includes a two-line fraction, summation or integral somewhere in the middle.

Some brackets have a precise significance and should not be changed. Check with the author before imposing a sequence. Note that it is possible to have asymmetrical brackets such as $(0, 1]$, $[2, 9)$.

Square roots

$x^{1/2}$ and $\sqrt{x}$ are both acceptable for single letters (or figures), but should be used consistently. For larger terms, if the author has used overbars (vincula) it is better to replace them, as the bars may interfere with the characters in the line above.

$$\sqrt{1 + x} \quad \text{becomes} \quad (1 + x)^{1/2} \quad (\text{or } \sqrt{(1 + x)})$$
$$1/\sqrt{1 + x} \quad \text{becomes} \quad 1/(1 + x)^{1/2} \quad (\text{or } (1 + x)^{-1/2}).$$

Consult the author if many such changes will be needed.

Fractions

Purely numerical fractions can be set within a line's height. Fractions containing letters or other symbols must either occupy two lines or be presented on one line by using a solidus ($2/n$). For economy of composition (and the look of the page) the latter alternative should always be used in running text; in displayed equations the two styles should not be mixed in a single equation or group of equations. When changing fractions to the solidus form, insert sufficient parentheses to avoid ambiguity or alteration of meaning, e.g. change $\frac{1}{x+1}$ to $1/(x+1)$ not $1/x + 1$. Even simple numerical fractions such as $\frac{1}{2}$ are often best set using a solidus when occurring as superscripts: superscript two-line fractions are very small. More examples of rearrangements of mathematics are given in (5) pp. 14–16.

Two-line fractions can be marked for conversion to one-line by sloping marks at the ends of the rule: $\frac{x}{y}$, one-line to two-line similarly: x/y. A marginal note to the typesetter explaining your marking at the first occurrence is a wise precaution.

Exponential
Because the invariable use of e for exponential may commit one to very complicated expressions set entirely in superscript, exp (. . .) may be substituted for anything containing complicated superscripts or subscripts to the superscript expression. This should be used consistently through a sequence of expressions, but not necessarily throughout the whole book. Explain the system to the author.

Limits
Symbols with limits above/below (such as summation signs, product signs, integral signs, lim and sup) take up more than one line depth. This is no problem in displayed maths, but if printed in running text would introduce uneven line spacing. To avoid this, limits in running text should be set after the symbol, as in Σ_0^n. An overall instruction to use, for example, Σ_0^n in running text and $\sum_0^n$ in display should be sufficient (see appendix 8).

Matrices and determinants
Check that the correct nomenclature has been used by the author, and that it is unambiguous. Matrices have large parentheses or square brackets to left and right (note that these must be large enough to enclose properly all the terms inside); determinants have straight vertical rules to left and right (in manuscript, confusion between very large square brackets and rules is easy). Note also that a determinant must be a square (i.e. have the same number of rows as columns) whereas a

matrix need not be. Elision of missing terms is represented by *three* dots (horizontally, vertically or diagonally as appropriate); terms may be grouped within a matrix or determinant by dashed lines. Check that the alignment of different-size expressions on the same line is consistent. It may be worth reminding the typesetter that the matrix $\begin{pmatrix} 3 \\ 2 \end{pmatrix}$ is not supposed to be a fraction.

Elision

Elision of any kind should always be by *three* dots. Any commas or operational signs should come after each term and after the ellipsis if a final term is included, e.g. $x_1, x_2, \ldots, x_n$ and $x_1 + x_2 + \ldots + x_n$ but $x = 0$, $1, 2, \ldots$.

Theorems

Theorems, corollaries and lemmas are often difficult to separate off adequately from the text. The use of a line space at the end is not always obvious when there is much displayed mathematics. This is often solved by making theorem statements italic, and putting a symbol such as $\square$ at the end of the proof. Even so, the end of every theorem, lemma, example, etc., that is not followed by a heading should be marked on the typescript and a general note added at the first occurrence asking the typesetter to leave extra space.

When theorem statements are to be set in italic, note that a blanket underline throughout is not usually acceptable: mathematical expressions should be set exactly as elsewhere, with correct use of roman/ italic symbols, and brackets, numbers, colons, signs, etc., all upright as usual; references to numbered theorems and equations may, however, be italicized. Thus: *Let $x(t)$ be a solution of equation (3.2), defined on $[0, a')$, $a' \leq a \ldots$. Then, for $x \in \ker A \ldots$*

13.3

UNITS

SI units should nowadays be used for all scientific and technological books (see (1) pp. 22–9). The SI base units are the metre, kilogram, second, ampere (no accent), kelvin, candela and mole. There are, however, a few units widely used in particular fields which are likely to be retained for a considerable time – for example the ångström unit (Å), the bar, kcal (although this is gradually being replaced by J), mmHg, and the wave-number (v in cm^{-1}). Some imperial units are still used in the USA.

The names of the units are given in lower case, even when they are derived from a proper name. Symbols (i.e. abbreviations of units) are set in roman, without points, and do use initial capitals when derived from a proper name. Plural forms of full names (but not of symbols) may be used. Hence: 1 watt, 3 W, 3 watts. Abbreviations such as amp and amps should be discouraged: the correct forms are 4 amperes and 4 A.

If authors quote another worker's results the units may be inconsistent with their own; this is especially likely to happen in tables and figures. Other things being equal, units should be made consistent with the style of the book, but possible exceptions are that the matter is being quoted essentially for its historical interest or that the conversion would imply a different order of accuracy and it could appear odd if readings were 'taken at intervals of 0.3048 m' rather than every foot. Decide individual cases on their merits.

Multiplication by powers of ten in table column heads and on graph axes can easily be ambiguous: it should always be clear how the factor is related to the units, and the information is best incorporated in the statement of the units, although some authors prefer to keep the factor in the body of the table.

13.3.1 Symbols

For the division of units the index is better than the solidus, but the use of the solidus for simple cases only, e.g. m/s but $J g^{-1} K^{-1} s^{-1}$, may be adopted. The Royal Society recommends that where a solidus *is* used, it should occur only once: J/(g K s) and not J/g/K/s. There is a case for keeping the solidus in school books: 'per' can sometimes be used in place of a second solidus (e.g. kg/ha per day).

Figures should always be used with symbols: 5 kg, never five kg, for example. The space between the figure and the units symbol (5 K) is usually (though this varies between typesetters) a quarter of an em, as is that between multiplied units symbols (m s^{-1}); space should be indicated if none has been left by the typist.

Per cent or % should be used consistently throughout the text, but the former does not preclude the use of the sign in tables or illustrations and in matter quoting large numbers of percentages in succession. The sign % on its own should be used only as an axis label on a graph or *solitary* column heading. If it is used to introduce a phrase (e.g. % workers) it should be replaced by percentage. 'A few per cent' is incorrect and should be replaced by 'a small percentage'. Percent is used only in US books.

13.3.2 **Temperatures**

The Royal Society recommends that the symbol K be used for both absolute temperature and temperature interval. Note that °C refers to actual temperature only. In the context of measurements in Celsius the unit used for temperature interval is commonly deg. In scientific work it is not necessary to add C after deg. The ° is part of the unit and should be closed up to the C, the standard space coming between figures and °: this should be marked by the copy-editor (and a marginal note made to the typesetter at the first occurrence). Unattached ° signs are wrong and should be avoided, the alternatives being '2, 3 and 4 °C', and '2 °C, 3 °C and 4 °C'.

13.3.3 **Magnifications**

Use × 300 in preference to 300 ×. The multiplication sign may need to be identified. In illustrations scale bars are preferable to magnifications in the caption.

13.4

ASTRONOMY

There is no absolute authority on style, although the International Astronomical Union (IAU) has from time to time made recommendations (6). Various styles and conventions can be found in modern astronomy books. As with other subjects, there has been a change over time in the conventions most commonly used, reflecting the changes in typesetting methods and a decline in the use of capital letters and full points in abbreviations.

The main objective should be to make the meaning clear and this is best done by adopting one of the accepted conventions for each context.

13.4.1 **Abbreviations used in astronomy** (acceptable alternative in brackets)

right ascension	RA
declination	dec. (Dec.)
position angle	p.a. (PA)
magnitude	mag
Universal Time	UT
light year	l.y.
astronomical unit	AU (a.u.)
parsec	pc

13.4.2 **Positional coordinates, time periods and angles**

Right ascension coordinates are in units of time. Formerly, the common style was

$$12^h\ 13^m\ 30^s \text{ or } 12^h\ 13^m.5$$

which is still acceptable. This is being superseded by the style

12h 13m 30s or 12h 13.5m

because the superscripted style is not convenient for typing. As single-letter abbreviations are needed in this context for periods of time, the following are acceptable in astronomy where there is no possibility of confusion:

second	s
minute	m
hour	h
day	d
year	y

Where superscripted units are used, the unit is conventionally placed to the left of any decimal point. This applies to coordinates in angular measure, for example:

21° 7′ 30″ or 21° 7′.5 or 21°.125.

Declination is measured in degrees. Northern declinations are written as positive and the plus sign should always be retained (e.g. dec. + 25° 3′.7). Southern declinations are written as negative.

For small angular sizes, use arcsec or arcmin and not ′ or ″.

13.4.3 **Time**

For time intervals, use, for example, 2d 3h 5m 6s or 2.085 d (with units spaced as shown). Many different types of time are used in astronomy, so a time will typically specify the system being used by means of following initials, such as UT for Universal Time. Times written either with or without a point between hours and minutes are acceptable, e.g. either 1430 UT or 14.30 UT.

13.4.4 **Use of initial capitals**

For the sake of consistency, use a capital letter for Earth, Moon and Sun in a context where the name of any other planet, moon, etc., would be given an initial capital. (Written without an initial capital, the word moon means natural satellite.)

There is no need to give initial capitals to adjectives such as solar, lunar, martian, jovian, etc., or to solar systems or universe. Titles of theories, laws and effects may have initial capitals when they are proper names but otherwise are probably best left without, e.g. Hubble law, Doppler effect, but general relativity, big-bang theory, steady-state theory.

'Galaxy' is conventionally written with an initial capital when it refers to *the* Galaxy, i.e. the one in which the solar system lies, sometimes referred to as the Milky Way Galaxy. The adjective 'galactic' is best without a capital if inconsistency is to be avoided.

13.4.5 **Magnitude**

Magnitude may be used loosely as part of a descriptive adjective (e.g. 'a 5th-magnitude star') or as a precise unit (e.g. 'the star dimmed by 1.25

mag'). It should be noted that the smaller the magnitude the brighter the object and that magnitudes of very bright objects may be negative. The abbreviation 'mag' is not followed by a point.

13.4.6 Names of stars and other astronomical objects

A commonly used class of star names is formed from a Greek letter followed by the genitive case of the Latin constellation name (e.g. α Orionis). There is a standard, official three-letter abbreviation for each constellation which may be used in star names (e.g. α Ori). The Greek letter may be written out in full either with or without an initial capital (e.g. alpha or Alpha Orionis). This is favoured in books for the American market since readers are thought to be unfamiliar with the Greek alphabet. All three forms are equally acceptable. Watch out for the incorrect use of the nominative case of the constellation in star names (e.g. α Orion).

Many galaxies, nebulae and star clusters are referred to by their numbers in one or other of two catalogues, that compiled by Messier, and the New General Catalogue plus its sequels, the Index Catalogues. The conventional form is M1, M2, etc., *without* a space, but NGC 2045 and IC 145, *with* spaces.

The forms of designation of some objects may be based on position coordinates and include plus or minus signs or a degree sign.

13.4.7 Special symbols

Astronomical texts sometimes use the astrological symbols for the Sun, Moon and planets as a convenient shorthand. The symbols for the Sun ($\odot$) and Earth ($\oplus$) are those most commonly seen, usually as subscripts, e.g. $M_\odot$ for the mass of the Sun or $R_\oplus$ for the radius of the Earth.

The symbol for the constellation Aries, Υ, is used to represent the vernal equinox or 'the first point of Aries'.

13.4.8 Miscellaneous

Words of foreign origin, such as the word for lunar seas, 'maria', are not italicized.

The abbreviations for the spectral types of stars are written without spaces, e.g. the Sun is a G2V star.

In the conventional notation to distinguish neutral and ionized forms of an element, there is a thin space between the symbol for the element and the following roman numerals, e.g. H I and H II for neutral and ionized hydrogen regions. The forms H^0 and H^+ are also used.

Radio astronomy, radio galaxy and radio telescope are all still normally written as two words although they are occasionally seen as one word. Infrared and ultraviolet are single unhyphenated words. Redshift is now normally written as one word in astronomy.

13.5

BIOLOGY

Biology books make particularly extensive use of Latin and Greek names (or words derived therefrom) for species, the taxa (or groups) into which they fall, aspects of their structure, the way they function and the kind of environment in which they live.

13.5.1 Biological classification and nomenclature

Main groups
The basic nomenclatural groups or taxa, in descending order, are: phylum or division, class, order, family, genus and species. All group names from family upwards are Latin names with plural endings. They should be set in roman with an initial capital (e.g. Coleoptera, Ericales). Genus and species names are always set in italic and have singular endings. The generic name has an initial capital but the specific epithet does not, thus *Lophophora williamsii*. These two names constitute the scientific name of a species and are together known as the binomen (zoology), binomial (botany) or the binary combination (bacteriology). 'Binomen' is used below to cover all three.

The binomen should be given in full at the first mention; thereafter the genus may be abbreviated to its initial letter (hence *L. williamsii*). This abbreviation may be preserved through changes of the specific name so long as there is no ambiguity. Hence *Bacillus subtilis . . . B. subtilis . . . B. megaterium*. Partial abbreviations should, in general, be avoided but in cases of ambiguity such as '*S. aureus* and *S. faecalis . . .*' it is permissible to use '*Staph. aureus* and *Strep. faecalis . . .*'.

While generic names may be referred to separately (e.g. *Homo*), the specific epithet must normally be accompanied by the generic name (i.e. *Homo sapiens,* not *sapiens* alone). A specific epithet may, however, stand alone if it occurs in a key or a section covering only a single genus in which the specific names are used repeatedly. A species within a genus may be referred to in general terms by the roman abbreviation sp. (plural spp.) after the generic name (e.g. 'some *Spirorbis* spp.').

Useful tables giving the plant and animal kingdoms down as far as orders are to be found in the appendix of (7). Comprehensive lists of bacteria and fungi can be found in (8) and (9).

Authorities

The name of the worker who originally classified the species will some-times follow the binomen in roman, especially if there is some contro-versy about the classification. Many biologists recommend that the authority appears at the first mention of each species, even in works not concerned with taxonomy. The best-known authority is Linnaeus, whose name may be abbreviated to L. (e.g. *Parage aegeria* L.), and others may be partially abbreviated (e.g. Lamarck to Lam.). If the authority is written in parentheses this is a significant distinction, denoting that the species has been moved to a genus different from that given by the original authority. Botanists and microbiologists then follow this with the new authority (not in parentheses), for example *Shigella dysenteriae* (Shiga) Castellani & Chalmers. Zoologists do not do this. In some books it may be necessary to include the date of classification after the authority.

Subdivision of species

In zoology the subspecific name (also lower-case italic) may be added to the binomen. In cases where the specific and subspecific names are identical the former may be abbreviated to the first letter, for example *Lagopus s. scoticus*. Botanists set out the subspecies as *Veronica serpylli-folia* L. subsp. *humifusa* (Dickson) Syme. Note that subspecies should be abbreviated to subsp. not ssp. The plural form is subspp.

The botanical code of nomenclature recognizes such subordinate taxa as subspecies, varietas (abbreviated to var. or v.), subvarietas (subvar. or subv.), forma and subforma. These are treated like the subspecies above.

Names of cultivated varieties of plants (cultivars) are printed in roman type and positioned after the binomial, for example *Pisum sativum* L. Marrow fat. The abbreviation cv. may be inserted before the cultivar name. The provenance is often indicated with plants thus: *Picea sitchensis* (Bong.) Carr. provenance Queen Charlotte Islands.

Headings
Italicized biological names may become roman or remain italic when they occur in italic headings or running heads. One system should be applied consistently.

13.5.2 **Common and other names**

Non-scientific names of plants and animals and anglicized versions of Latin names used in a general sense should be lower-case roman (e.g. aphid, petunia, crustacean, staphylococcal infection, oligochaete). English species names sometimes have an initial capital either for each word or for the first word only, to avoid ambiguity (e.g. 'the Common Toad is now very rare in . . .').

If a common name has two parts, one being a 'group name', the latter will be a separate word only when used in a sense which is systematically correct, i.e. house fly but butterfly, silkworm: the house fly is a true fly, but the butterfly is not, nor is the silkworm a worm.

Lower-case roman is used for names of anatomical structures (e.g. gluteus maximus muscle, foramen ovale), diseases (e.g. systemic lupus erythematosus, lichen planus) and viruses (e.g. parvovirus, herpes zoster).

A proper name in an eponymic term has an initial capital, but when used in an adjectival form generally does not: hence Petri dish and Gram stain but müllerian duct.

See also section 13.9.4 (medicine).

13.5.3 **Other biological nomenclature**

Bacterial strains
Bacterial and viral species are often subdivided into strains. They are usually denoted by roman capital letters, which may have a number or subscript number, for example, the *Escherichia coli* bacteriophage T4 or T_4. (See also section 6.10.1.)

There are specific nomenclature and abbreviation lists for such subjects as respiratory physiology and immunology in (10) and various handbooks; but conventions in specialized fields change, so consult the author or follow the existing system if consistent.

Genetic terms
Genes and chromosomes are denoted by letters and numbers. Bacterial and bacteriophage genes are always italic but authors vary in their usage of italic for genes from higher animals. These are frequently roman – e.g. hsp (heatshock protein), tRNA genes. There seems to be very little consensus or unifying authority. However, a common style is emerging for genes and their products: e.g. aspartyl transcarbamylase would be from the *atc* gene and the product could be referred to either as ATCase or Atc.

Oncogenes are denoted as: c-*myc*, c-*ras* etc. Plasmid names are roman and start with a lower-case p.

Endonucleases should take the form *Eco*RI, *Sau*3A etc. The first three letters come from the name of the bacterium from which the enzyme was extracted (in the case of *Eco*RI, it is *Escherichia coli*) and the numbers at the end are usually roman. A few, such as *Sau*3A, take an arabic number after the first three letters.

Chromosomes are denoted by roman capitals (the best-known being the sex chromosomes, X (female) and Y (male)). Generations are referred to also by lettered symbols in roman capitals: the parental (P), the first generation (F_1 or F1), the second generation (F_2 or F2) and so on. The letter *n* used to denote the chromosome complement of a cell may be (consistently) roman or italic, and may be preceded by an arabic figure.

Blood groups

The groups (A, B, O, etc.) are set in roman capitals, and so are the antigens after which the groups are named. The genes that determine the antigens may be denoted by the corresponding italic letters (*A* gene produces A antigen and A blood group). Rhesus is abbreviated to Rh (without a full point).

13.5.4 **Biochemical terminology**

Biochemical abbreviations

Organic compounds with long names frequently have their names abbreviated to initial capitals without full points. With a few exceptions (which will depend on the level of the book), they should be spelt out in full at the first mention, followed by the abbreviation in parentheses. The following may be so well known as to require no explanation in specialist texts.

ADP, adenosine diphosphate; also CDP, GDP, TDP, etc.
AMP, adenosine monophosphate; also CMP, GMP, TMP, etc.
ATP, adenosine triphosphate; also CTP, GTP, TTP, etc.
cAMP, cyclic AMP
CoA, coenzyme A
DNA, deoxyribonucleic acid
EDTA, ethylenediamine tetra-acetic acid
NAD (NAD/NADH), nicotinamide-adenine dinucleotide (in its
    oxidized and reduced forms)
NADP (NADP/NADPH), nicotinamide-adenine dinucleotide
    phosphate (in its oxidized and reduced forms)
RNA, ribonucleic acid

Messenger, transfer and ribosomal RNA are denoted by lower-case roman m, t, r (e.g. mRNA). RNAase is used for the ribonuclease enzyme (similarly DNAase). American RNase/DNase is also acceptable. The abbreviations for amino acids are all three letters with an initial capital (e.g. Ala for alanine). A known sequence of amino acids in a polypeptide is represented by a hyphenated string of these abbreviations (Asp-Cys-Glu-Ser). The single-letter code may also be used. Nucleotides are abbreviated to their initial letters (A, T, C, G, U) and sequences are given as, for example, ATTAGG (hyphens between letters are optional).

Molecular weight

This is often confused with molecular mass. The former is a relative quantity with no units and its symbol is M_r. Molecular mass is expressed in daltons.

Biochemical nomenclature

Authors should be encouraged to follow the Recommendations of the Nomenclature Committee of the IUBMB and the IUPAC–IUBMB Joint Commission on Biochemical Nomenclature. A very useful digest, and source of references, for these is the *Instructions to Authors* (4) of the *Biochemical Journal* (revised yearly). Much fuller information can be found in the second edition of the IUBMB *Biochemical Nomenclature and Related Documents* (3).

The *Merck Index* (11) is a useful reference book for checking the names of chemicals, biological substances and drugs. Note, though, that it is an American publication and various chemical names may have different spellings, or even different forms. For example, American has estrogen for oestrogen, epinephrine (or the trade name Adrenalin) for adrenaline and furosemide for frusemide. In international symposium typescripts, particularly, both may appear and it is worth asking the symposium editor to check consistency of usage. Cross-references may be needed in the index.

13.6

CHEMISTRY

13.6.1 **Nomenclature**

For all chemical terminology the recommendations of the International Union of Pure and Applied Chemistry (IUPAC) should be followed. These may be found in the *Compendium of Chemical Terminology: IUPAC Recommendations* (12).

The symbols for the elements are set in roman type. This will be understood by the typesetter, but any italic characters occurring should be marked. Generalized radicals, metals, etc. (R, M, etc.), may be italicized if the author insists, but the preferred style is now roman.

Superscripts and subscripts are deployed as follows: $_a^m X_n^c$ where $m =$ mass number, $a =$ atomic number, $c =$ electrical charge, and $n =$ number of atoms per molecule, and X is the element symbol (not the element name). This should be adhered to as closely as possible, and in particular the common mistake of X^m for isotopes avoided.

Chemical names should be spelt out wherever practicable, unless the symbolic formula is graphically useful; hence ions are generally preferable as symbols: Cu^{2+} rather than cupric ion (use Cu^{2+} and not Cu^{++}, to avoid Mn^{++++} or worse).

13.6.2 Prefixes

Many prefixes are used in chemical names and a good deal of variation is possible. If an author has a consistent system, follow it gratefully. One system is: *italic* to be used for prefixes which define *positions* of named substituents or which are used only to define stereoisomers, but not for other prefixes; *hyphens* to be used with italicized (but not with roman) prefixes of more than one letter and with *all* single-letter prefixes, figures and symbols. Hence *ortho*-xylene, *o*-xylene, *cis*-isomer, *N*-methyl, which denote substitution at particular atoms; but isobutane, pentamethyl, cyclobutane. (Note that the abbreviations *o*-, *m*-, *p*- are preferable to *ortho*- etc., and that t- is preferable to tert.)

In general, the order of names in an alphabetical list should be determined by the roman part of the word – the italic ignored – but authors may have reasonable alternative systems of their own.

13.6.3 Structural formulae

In all cases, but especially where they occur in running text, complex formulae should be simplified as much as possible. It is often unnecessary to portray single or double bonds: where they are retained and any ambiguity is possible, identify them for the printer as 'bond' (see section 13.6.4). Structural formulae could be changed to $CH_3.CO.OCl$ or $CH_3C(=O)OCl$ for example. Grouping points should be consistently medial or (preferably) low. Hexagons could be replaced by Ph or Ar. But consult the author before making significant changes.

The larger a structural formula is, the less likely it is to appear just where required on the page, and if there are many of them in the book it will probably be worth using a numbering system, and altering text references appropriately: make sure that the altered sentences are still grammatically complete. If a formula is in the middle of a paragraph in the typescript, link the ends of text with a loopy line or write 'run on' at the side.

Any sensible numbering system of the author's may be used: the most common one is still roman numerals in one sequence throughout the whole book, even though this can result in some inconveniently long numbers; when using this system the numbers should be small capitals within parentheses, and the number dealt with as part of the illustration rather than as a caption. Arabic numbering, typographically distinguished from equations by, for example, square brackets or bold type, is less cumbersome: this should be decimally by chapter if other numbering systems are.

The number of structural formulae that will have to be drawn will depend on the typesetter: consult the production department, giving a list of folios on which formulae occur if there are not a great many, or pointing out some examples to illustrate the range to be covered if they occur frequently.

13.6.4 **Miscellany**

Isotopes. These should be written as ^{14}C or carbon-14 as appropriate. Square brackets, closed up against the name, are used to indicate isotopic labelling: [^{14}C]glucose, [γ-^{32}P]ATP. If the label is not in the name immediately following, then a hyphen (and no brackets) should be used (e.g. ^{32}P-inositol phosphate or ^{32}P-labelled inositol phosphate but, for the abbreviation, [^{32}P]InsP).

Molarity is indicated by a small capital M. It is sometimes confused with number of moles – which should be abbreviated to mol.

Concentration. Watch out for mistakes such as 10 mg/ml protein which should read 10 mg protein/ml.

Oxidation states are indicated by small capital or superscript capital roman numbers, thus: manganese(IV) or Mn^{IV}. Note that in the former case the parentheses are closed up against the name.

Conventions. pH (negative log of hydrogen ion concentration); pK (negative log of dissociation constant); plurals are pH values and pK values.

Steroids. Small capital A, B, etc., are used for labelling the rings of steroids.

Stereoisomers. d, l and *dl* are now no longer used, and should be replaced by (+), (–) and (±) respectively. Absolute configuration is denoted by small capital D, L and DL.

Identification of carbon atoms. The best way of referring to carbon atoms in a molecule is by C-1, C-2, etc., using a roman C and a hyphen. An alternative system is $C_{(13)}$ etc. (the parentheses are necessary to avoid ambiguity); this is useful if bonds are given (e.g. $C_{(13)}$—$C_{(14)}$). See also (4).

Arrows rather than equals signs should be used in chemical equations. (These will normally be 2 ems long.)

Orbitals. The Royal Society recommends that the quantum symbols s, p, d, etc., be set in roman.

Bonds in molecules should always be marked for the typesetter. Some typesetters use em rules, but a special sort is available and it is best to mark 'bond' against every one (or the first of each batch if many). In the phrase 'C—CH$_3$ group' mark the line as a 'bond' since the expression is a graphical representation; but in 'C–C bond' it could be marked as an en rule, since it is equivalent to 'carbon–carbon bond'. On the same basis, 'carbon–carbon double bond' could be represented by 'C–C double bond' (using an en rule), but it may be felt more desirable to use the double bond sign, 'C=C bond'. An inconsistency in appearance should be avoided.

13.7

COMPUTING

Texts on computing have two special characteristics.

The first characteristic relates to the text. Computing is a relatively new subject and is expanding very rapidly. This has the result that new words and phrases are being introduced all the time. Often these, having originated in the United States, are slightly different from the British forms. For example, a new area of computing which developed in the late 1980s is called object-oriented, rather than 'orientated'. Of course, the most common example is program, rather than the British 'programme'. This plethora of unusual spelling means that copy-editing the text should be avoided in all but the most glaring examples. It is usually the case, however, that anglicization of common words ('colour' for 'color', 'centre' for 'center') presents no problem.

The second characteristic is that these texts frequently contain sections, and sometimes complete examples, of computer programs. These programs are set in a special way (often dependent on the program itself) and the text must be marked up in a way which describes that setting faithfully. During the mark-up care must be exercised in two areas. The first is the general text and the second is a section of a computer program which may appear within the general text, may be presented as a figure or may constitute a whole appendix.

Within the general text, most of the references to variables etc. can be treated the same way as in mathematics. In some cases, however, there are items in the text which are the same as items within some computer program and both occurrences must use the same typeface.

The typeface for a computer program depends on the kind of computer language used for that program. From the point of view of typesetting, there are five different types of computer programming languages. These are fixed-format languages (FORTRAN, COBOL, CODASYL, . . .), free-format languages (Algol, Pascal, Coral, Ada, . . .), logic programming languages (Prolog, LISP, . . .), formal specification languages (VDM, etc.) and functional languages (ML, Miranda, etc.). The first two types are often referred to as procedural languages, the last three generically as functional languages.

13.7.1 **Fixed-format languages** (see fig. 13.1)

The most common fixed-format languages are FORTRAN and COBOL, although there are other aspects of programming languages such as CODASYL database languages which are COBOL-related and which should preferably be set in a fixed-width type. In these cases the position of each character on a line is significant, which is why a fixed-

```
         DIMENSION IROT(N),IV(N),V(N),IEIG(N),EIG(N),A(N,N),P(N,N),Q(N,N)
C
C        TOL IS A SMALL REAL NUMBER USED TO CHECK FOR EQUALITY.
         DATA TOL/1.0E-20/
         IER=0
         IF (N .GT. 1) GO TO 10
         IER=-1
         RETURN
C
C        SET IEIG AND IV.
C        IEIG IS AN ARRAY OF INTEGER SUCH THAT IEIG(K) STORES THE VALUE OF
C        I(K) FOR ALL K .LT. ISTEP.  FOR K .GE. ISTEP, IEIG(K) POINTS TO
C        THE (K-ISTEP+1)-TH SMALLEST VALUE OF A(L,L) WHERE L IS IN
C        S(ISTEP).  IV IS AN ARRAY OF POINTER SUCH THAT IV(K) POINTS TO THE
C        KTH SMALLEST VALUE OF V.
      10 DO 11 I=1,N
         IV(I)=I
      11 IEIG(I)=I
         DO 14 I=2,N
         K=IV(I)
         T3=V(K)
         J=I-1
      12 KN=IV(J)
         IF (T3 .GE. V(KN)) GO TO 13
         IV(J+1)=KN
         J=J-1
         IF (J .GT. 0) GO TO 12
      13 IV(J+1)=K
      14 CONTINUE
```

Fig. 13.1 Example of FORTRAN, a fixed-format language. (From *The Computer Journal*, **26** (2), 1983, 185.)

width typeface is used (e.g. Courier typewriter fount). It is essential that lines are not broken. Normally the author can be asked to submit a clean typewritten copy which can be photo-reduced (if necessary) and pasted in. This method cannot be used, however, if there are variables or subprograms from the program segment referred to within the text. Here the typewriter fount must be used. Because lines cannot, in general, be broken, the program segments which do not naturally fit within the measure must be either made into figures or photo-reduced. The one exception where lines may be broken is within comment. Here a second line can be used but the comment character (C for FORTRAN, * for COBOL) must appear on every line and the appropriate indention must be preserved.

13.7.2 **Free-format languages** (see fig. 13.2)

The first standard free-format language was Algol 60, although this is little used now and has been replaced by Pascal or Ada. There are two features of free-format languages. The first is that some words are used for special purposes and are called 'reserved words'. The second is that the structure of a program is represented by indenting inner parts of the program. These parts usually start with the word 'begin' and finish with the word 'end', but this is not always the case.

Where sections of free-format program are typeset it is customary for the reserved words to be set in bold and for the remainder of the program to be set in italic, except that 'comments' (which, in some cases, begin with the word 'comment' and end with a semicolon, in others are marked by /* at the beginning and */ at the end of each line of comment, and in others are enclosed in { and } brackets on each line) are normally set in roman. The indentions are usually one em.

Where the sections of program are set in a fixed-width fount it is customary for the reserved words to be set in capitals and the rest of the program in lower case. The indentions are then two or three spaces.

Free-format languages still present some problems when the measure is insufficient to accommodate the layout determined by the author. In free-format languages lines may be broken but only in a limited way. The best place to break a line is at a semicolon (which ends the line) or at a reserved word (which starts the next line) or, if neither of the above

```
events(Interrupt.event):=
begin
  let hiding := false
  let save = image X.dim(screen) by Y.dim(screen) of off

  proc( )                          !My interrupt routine
  if hiding then hiding := false else
  begin
    let the.time= time( )
    copy screen onto save
    xor screen onto screen
    hiding := true               !← A
    while hiding do
    begin
      let x = random( ) rem X.dim(screen)
      let y = random( ) rem Y.dim(screen)
      print the.time at x,y       !Display
      for i = 1 to 100 do { }     !Delay
      print the.time at x,y using xor !Erase
    end
    copy save onto screen
  end
end
```

Fig. 13.2 Example of a free-format language typeset. (From *The Computer Journal*, **33** (2), 1990, 115.)

is possible, at an operator (which ends the line). In some cases where a line is broken at a reserved word the whole text up to the next partner word should be indented. When a line is broken the next line is usually given a further indention of one em (or two or three spaces). Comments may be word-wrapped across the full measure, subject to any indent, but if the /* and */ (or { and }) notation is used these delimiters must appear on every line.

13.7.3 Logic programming languages (see fig. 13.3)

The two logic programming languages which dominate are Prolog (dominant in Europe) and LISP (dominant in the USA). Both may be either in a fixed-width typeface or typeset. A common practice is to use a sans serif fount which, although not fixed width, still stands out from the normal text. Both languages avoid reserved words, but in both, some lines can be very long and must be broken. It is not possible to give a complete answer to where to break a line but, in general, aim to break it just after an operator (:=, +, −, ∧ , ∨, ||), and indent the second part of the broken line by a further one em. If there is a choice of operators then select the one which is at the highest level (see section 13.7.4). Comments are treated as for free-format languages.

```
high_season(europe,[june,
    july,august]).
high_season(africa,[december,
    january,february]).

low_season(europe,[january:
    60,february:
    55,...,december:75]).
low_season                  %a week in June in Africa
    (africa,[june:65,...])      %is 65% of the high-
                                %season cost

trip(Town,Accommodation,Price,Travel) :-
    travel(Town,Travel),stay(Town,Accommodation,
    Price).
```

Fig. 13.3 Example of Prolog, a logic programming language. (After *The Computer Journal*, **30** (5), 1987, 397.)

13.7.4 **Formal specification languages** (see fig. 13.4)

From the point of view of typesetting, formal specification languages can be treated in the same way as logic programming languages. Authors are inventing new formal languages as quickly as they are writing texts, but these usually conform to a general pattern. They could be set in Times (italic for the program), typewriter fount or sans serif. They may include reserved words (though not frequently), in which case they are treated in the same way as in free-format languages.

$McBinop(x, y: MCN, f2: Binop) r: \text{set of } MCN$
ext rd $V: \mathbb{B}$
pre *true*
post if $BinOpResultInterval(x, y, f2) \subseteq Interval(MN)$
  then $r = \{z \mid BinOpResultInterval(x, y, f2)\} \cap MCN$
  else if V
    then ($exception$ (Floating point overflow) $\vee$
    $r \in BinOpResultInterval(x, y, f2)$)
    else *true*

Fig. 13.4 Example of VDM, a formal specification language. (From *The Computer Journal*, **32** (5), 1989, 434.)

Authors frequently invent their own operators but these can be spotted as they are represented by a new symbol. Where line breaks are necessary they are handled in the same way as in logic programming languages. For example:

post structure (res) = structure (rel 1) $\wedge$ hierarchy (res) = hierarchy (rel 1) $\wedge$ state (res) = state (rel 1) – state (rel 2).

can become

post structure (res) = structure (rel 1) $\wedge$
hierarchy (res) = hierarchy (rel 1) $\wedge$
state (res) = state (rel 1) – state (rel 2).

Again comments are treated in the same way as in free-format languages.

13.7.5 **Functional languages** (see fig. 13.5)

Functional languages display all the same characteristics as formal specification languages.

$reduce(f, n, a) < =$

    if $a = nil$ **then** n

    else $reduce(f, f(first(a), n), rest(a))$

$multiple\_reduce(f\_list, n\_list, a) < =$

    if $a = nil$ **then** n_list

    else $multiple\_reduce(f\_list, funmap(f\_list, n\_list,$ $first(a)), rest(a))$

        where $funmap(f\_list, n\_list, x) < =$

        if $f\_list = nil$ **then** nil

        else $eager\_cons((first(f\_list))(x, first(n\_list)),$

        $funmap(rest(f\_list), rest(n\_list), x))$

Fig. 13.5 Example of a functional language. (From *The Computer Journal*, **30** (5), 1987, 440.)

Fortunately, in this day of desk-top publishing, most texts on computing have been prepared in typeset form by the author. Although usually one can reproduce the layout faithfully one must remember that authors are rarely entirely consistent and they may not know the house style, so both of these factors must be checked carefully.

It is useful to obtain copies of the International Organization for Standardization (ISO) standard definitions of the languages, where the segments quoted give a clear indication of what layout should be used. These may be obtained through the British Standards Institution.

13.8

GEOLOGY

It is usual to differentiate between units of time (Period, Epoch, Age) and terms describing rocks (System, Series, Stage). Thus an event could have occurred during the Cretaceous Period and the rocks would be of the Cretaceous System. Avoid using terms such as 'Cretaceous' on their own; it is better to refer to the 'Cretaceous Period' rather than the 'Cretaceous'. Distinction should be made between a process (e.g.

folding) and the results of a process (e.g. folds). The noun 'outcrop' is usually replaced by 'crop out' when used as a verb.

Time and rock units may be subdivided into Early, Middle, Late (time) and Lower, Middle, Upper (rocks). Mid- is often used instead of Middle, with or without a hyphen.

Ma is strongly to be preferred to m.y. for million years; an alternative is Myr. Ga is the abbreviation for thousand million years. Quaternary and Recent time is often given as years BP (before present, which is taken as 1950 for calculations), and the comma is normally used in thousands here: 100,000 BP. Another way of expressing Recent time is with ka for thousand years: 100 ka (lower-case k) is the same as 100,000 BP. To avoid confusion, it is better not to use 'a' when there is no prefix. Geological ages that are presented as a range should always have the oldest (i.e largest) number first (e.g. 2.3–1.9 Ga, not 1.9–2.3 Ga).

Capitalization of geological terms can be a problem. Much depends on whether or not an officially defined term is being used. It is probably best to follow whatever system an author is using, unless it appears to be inconsistent. With names of biostratigraphical zones, e.g. *Didymograptus hirundo* Zone, the fossil name is italicized and Zone has a capital Z; names such as this are often shortened to *hirundo* Zone, with the 'h' kept lower case. Fossil names should be treated in the same way as biological species names.

Spelling is another problem area. Does the author use palaeo- or paleo- (both are permissible but the former is the more usual British spelling and the latter American), Cenozoic, Cainozoic or Kainozoic? Although Cainozoic is etymologically correct, the American spelling Cenozoic is usually used and Kainozoic only rarely.

Note that Precambrian is one word (not Pre-Cambrian) and that Holocene and Recent have the same meaning.

In giving the orientation of linear features, it is common to abbreviate the compass points: E–W, SW–NE, NNW–SSE; en rules are to be used here. In quoting the latitude and longitude of localities, remember that the compass point is separated from the degrees, unlike degrees of temperature: 20° 15' 17" N. Mineralogical endmember components are often subscript to the abbreviated mineral name: Fo_{42}; $Ca_{41}Mg_{39}Fe_{20}$.

13.9

MEDICINE

Medical books share some copy-editing problems with biology books (see section 13.5), but in addition present a number of problems of their own.

13.9.1 **Style of writing**

Medical writing is full of jargon. Much of this is perfectly acceptable; rewriting in 'proper English' is not only unnecessary but may well change the author's meaning. The problem for the copy-editor, therefore, is where to draw the line between what is acceptable and what is not. This can only really be resolved by experience, but the following guidelines may be helpful:

- Avoid phrasing that dehumanizes the patient. For example, authors often refer to a case (i.e. an instance of a disease) when they mean a patient (i.e. a person who is ill with the disease). A patient with pneumonia can be examined and admitted to hospital; a case of pneumonia cannot.
- Resist the tendency of authors to create verbs from nouns. For example, 'the patient was endoscoped and lasered' can be reworded as 'the patient underwent endoscopy and laser treatment'.
- Avoid phrases that are inaccurate. Often these are condensations, such as 'a cardiac diet' where 'a diet for cardiac patients' is meant. Sometimes a term is simply used incorrectly. A common example of this is 'dose' being used where 'dosage' is intended, the former being the amount administered at one time, while the latter is the regulation or determination of doses. 'X-ray' is also frequently used incorrectly to mean the image obtained with X-rays; either 'X-ray film' or 'radiograph' can be substituted.

Unlike jargon, slang is never acceptable, and slang phrases such as 'prepped' for 'prepared' should always be rewritten.

13.9.2 **Abbreviations**

There is an understandable tendency on the part of authors to use abbreviations rather than repeat long medical terms. Taken to extremes, though, this makes the text unreadable, and some terms need to remain in full. Journals may restrict the use of abbreviations to an approved list. Where an abbreviation is to be used, follow the accepted practice of giving the term in full at first mention, followed by the abbreviation in parentheses: for example, 'An atrial septal defect (ASD) is found in . . . '.

A useful reference book that lists most of the commonly encountered medical and scientific abbreviations is (13).

13.9.3 **Terminology**

A good medical dictionary is indispensable for checking the spelling of anatomical names, diseases, etc. *Dorland's Illustrated Medical Dictionary* (14) and *Churchill's Illustrated Medical Dictionary* (15) are both good, though both are American. *Churchill's* does cross-reference the English spelling of words such as anaemia and leucocyte to the American spelling, but not vice versa.

Huth's *Medical Style and Format* (16) has a useful chapter on the minefield of specialist terminology used in different branches of medicine such as cardiology, pulmonary medicine and immunology.

13.9.4 **Drug names**

A vital part of most medical books is the information given on drugs and their dosages. The author should have been informed by the publisher that it is his or her responsibility to ensure that the recommended dosages are correct, but the spelling of the drug names should always be checked. *The Merck Index* (11) is about the best single reference book for this, and the *British National Formulary* (17) covers British drugs, though both contain more information about the drugs than will be required. *Pharmaceutical Terminology* (18) is an alphabetical list of drugs, specifically designed for those who require only the correct spelling of the names.

Unless a trial of a particular brand name (trade name) is being described, the generic (non-proprietary) name of the drug should be used throughout. (This will obviously not be possible for those drugs, usually new ones, that do not have a generic name.) If the trade name has been given, put this in parentheses after the generic name at the first mention: for example, 'was treated with vincristine (Oncovin)'. Note that generic names are lower case and trade names have an initial capital.

13.9.5 Units

SI units are generally used in medicine, but there are still areas where they are controversial or unfamiliar. In these instances accepted usage should be followed (e.g. mmHg for blood pressures).

13.9.6 References

In books either an author–date system (see section 10.2) or a number system (section 10.3) of references is acceptable. The Vancouver style (19), which is a variant of the number system, is increasingly being adopted by biomedical journals (see section 10.3).

Abbreviations for journal titles usually follow the style used in *Index Medicus* (20).

13.9.7 Anonymity of patients

If it is necessary in an illustration for any part of a patient to be shown that will allow either outright recognition or recognition by inference, then written permission for publication is necessary from both the patient and the responsible clinician. An obvious example would be a photograph that shows a condition of the face. It needs to be checked that permission has been sought and granted.

Usually, though, it is possible to remove clues to the identity of the patient without compromising the purpose of the illustration. Instructions should be given to mask or crop names and hospital numbers on all radiographs, endoscopic pictures and scans of any sort, and to mask either the entire face or at least the eyes on photographs. You should look out for other identifying clues in the text: in a court case in the United States, someone claimed that they could be identified from a medical case description.

13.10

REFERENCES

(1) The Symbols Committee of the Royal Society. *Quantities, Units and Symbols*, 2nd edn, London, 1975

(2) The Royal Society of Medicine. *Units, Symbols and Abbreviations*, 4th edn, London, 1988

(3) C. Liébecq (ed.) *Biochemical Nomenclature and Related Documents: A Compendium*, 2nd edn, published for the International Union of Biochemistry and Molecular Biology, 1992 (available from Portland Press Ltd, Commerce Way, Colchester CO2 8HP)

(4) *The Biochemical Journal's Instructions to Authors* (revised yearly; available from The Biochemical Society, 59 Portland Place, London W1N 3AJ)

(5) Ellen Swanson. *Mathematics into Type*, revised edn, Providence, R.I., American Mathematical Society, 1982

(6) IAU style manual. In *Transactions of the International Astronomical Union*, vol. XXB, ed. D. McNally, Dordrecht, Kluwer, 1990

(7) *Chambers Science and Technology Dictionary*, Edinburgh, 1988

(8) J. G. Holt & N. R. Krieg (eds.). *Bergey's Manual of Systematic Bacteriology*, 10th edn, Baltimore, Md, Williams & Wilkins, 1984–6

(9) D. L. Hawksworth, B. C. Sutton & G. C. Ainsworth. *Ainsworth and Bisby's Dictionary of the Fungi*, 7th edn, Slough, Commonwealth Agricultural Bureau, 1983

(10) *Council of Biology Editors Style Manual,* 5th edn, Bethesda, Md, 1983

(11) *The Merck Index,* 11th edn, Rahway, N.J., Merck, 1989

(12) V. Gold (ed.). *Compendium of Chemical Terminology: IUPAC Recommendations*, Oxford, Blackwell Scientific, 1987

(13) C. M. Logan & M. K. Rice. *Logan's Medical and Scientific Abbreviations*, Philadelphia, Lippincott, 1987

(14) *Dorland's Illustrated Medical Dictionary,* 27th edn, Philadelphia, W. B. Saunders, 1989

(15) *Churchill's Illustrated Medical Dictionary*, New York, Churchill Livingstone, 1989

(16) E. J. Huth. *Medical Style and Format*, Philadelphia, ISI Press, 1987

(17) *British National Formulary*, London, British Medical Association/ Royal Pharmaceutical Society of Great Britain (revised twice yearly)

(18) B. De Lorenzo. *Pharmaceutical Terminology*, 2nd edn, Thorofare, N.J., Slack, 1988 (available from Slack Inc., 6900 Grove Road, Thorofare, NJ 08086)

(19) International Committee of Medical Journal Editors. Uniform requirements for manuscripts submitted to biomedical journals, 4th edn, *British Medical Journal* (1991) **302**: 338–41 (copies available from British Medical Journal, British Medical Association, Tavistock Square, London WC1H 9JR)

(20) National Library of Medicine. *List of Journals Indexed to Index Medicus*, US Department of Health and Human Services, National Institutes of Health (published annually, and also as part of each January issue of *Index Medicus*; available from the Superintendent of Documents, US Government Printing Office, Washington, DC 20402)

Other special subjects

CLASSICAL BOOKS

Many of the problems of copy-editing and typesetting books containing Latin and Greek arise from the unfamiliarity of the languages and the subject matter; some basic information is listed below. There are also several conventions of style and presentation which require no specialized classical knowledge and which author and copy-editor should be aware of, even if they decide to alter them.

14.1.1 Greek typefaces

There are upright, sloping and sans serif typefaces, with associated bold founts; a sloping fount is normally used for mathematics. Classical texts may be set in either upright or sloping Greek. Emphasized words in Greek are not 'italicized' but letterspaced, underlined or set in bold.

14.1.2 Alphabets

There are twenty-four letters in the classical Greek alphabet, including seven vowels:

A	α	alpha (a)	Ξ	ξ	xi (x)
B	β	beta (b)	O	o	omicron (o)
Γ	γ	gamma (g)	Π	π	pi (p)
Δ	δ	delta (d)	P	ρ	rho (r)
E	ε	epsilon (e)	Σ	σ	(ς final) sigma
Z	ʒ	zeta (z)	C	c	lunate sigma } (s)
H	η	eta (ē)	T	τ	tau (t)
Θ	θ	theta (th)	Y	υ	upsilon (u)
I	ι	iota (i)	Φ	φ	phi (ph)
K	κ	kappa (k)	X	χ	chi (ch)
Λ	λ	lambda (l)	Ψ	ψ	psi (ps)
M	μ	mu (m)	ω	ω	omega (ō) (or Ω)
N	ν	nu (n)			

There are also four obsolete characters: digamma or wau (Ϝ), stigma (Ϛ), koppa (Ϙ or Ϟ), and san or sampi (Ϡ). These occur occasionally in linguistic discussions and were used in classical Greek as numerals (see below). The Mycenaean Linear A and Linear B syllabic scripts are usually reproduced photographically from calligraphy; a complete list of the characters in the syllabaries is given in Ventris and Chadwick, *Documents in Mycenaean Greek*, 2nd edn (Cambridge University Press, 1973), pp. 33, 41.

The upper- and lower-case forms of several letters in the classical alphabet are easily confused, and where the letters are used singly several are also easily confused with similar English letters. This is particularly relevant in some Aristotle references where Greek capitals are used for book numbers. Identify letters as Greek in cases where doubts could arise, and draw attention to occurrences of the less familiar characters.

There are two forms of the conventional lower-case sigma: ς is used only as the final letter of a word, σ only in some other part of a word. This distinction is not observed when C (capital) and c (lower case) are used for sigma.

Notice that there is no dot over the Greek iota (ι).

None of the diphthongs in Greek are printed as ligatures. Long vowels (α, η, ω) may have an iota subscript (ᾳ, ῃ, ῳ) which becomes a separate letter when the word is capitalized (ΑΙ, ΗΙ, ΩΙ). However, the iota is often written as a separate letter (adscript) even in lower case. With this, as with the lunate sigma (c), it is important to check that the author uses the same convention throughout.

Authors sometimes provide photocopies of previously printed texts which use different conventions from their own; so publishers should as early as possible ask authors to incorporate their own conventions throughout, and show them how to do this in the clearest way.

The Latin alphabet is like the English one, except that it has no W or w. I and i are now normally used for J and j (which were in any case later, non-classical forms). The distinction between U, u and V, v is sometimes retained, but V (capital) and u (lower case) are now more often used for both vowel and consonant. C (capital) is sometimes used for G (capital) in abbreviations (e.g. C. and Cn. for Gaius and Gnaeus), and in early inscriptions.

It is rare now to use ligatures for diphthongs such as ae in Latin.

See *Hart's Rules*, 39th edn, pp. 114–15, for the division of Greek and Latin words at the end of a line.

14.1.3 **Breathings**

Greek has a rough breathing (ʽdenoting aspirates) and a smooth breathing (ʼdenoting non-aspirates) on all words that begin with a vowel or a rho (ρ) or where there has been a crasis (fusion of two words, as in τἀγαπά, where the mark is called a *coronis*). Words beginning with diphthongs take the breathing over the second letter. Breathings are not now printed over a double-rho (ρρ) occurring in the middle of a word.

Latin has no breathings.

14.1.4 **Accents**

There are no accents in classical Latin, though occasionally stress marks are used to demonstrate pronunciation (and then they are placed over any scansion marks, as in *amícus*). Draw the typesetter's attention to any such marks or combination of marks. Post-medieval Latin may have accents.

Greek has three accents: grave (ʽ), acute (ʼ), and circumflex (ˆor˜). *Hart's Rules* (pp. 112–13) give some of the basic rules governing their use, but these are extremely complicated and there are many exceptions. When in doubt follow copy. When a grave or acute accent falls on the same letter as a breathing, it follows the breathing; when a circumflex and a breathing coincide, the circumflex is placed over the breathing. These combinations of accent and breathing are sometimes not at all clear if the Greek is handwritten or photocopied, and it may be necessary to clarify them in the typescript.

There is also a diaeresis mark (¨), which indicates that the vowels over which it appears are to be pronounced separately and not as a diphthong. The diaeresis is printed under a grave or acute accent when they fall on the same letter. Some authors include the diaeresis only in cases where they consider there is a real possibility of confusion; for example they may write εὔζωνος, not εὖζωνος, on the grounds that the position of the breathing makes the form sufficiently distinct from εὔζωνος. Try to see that the author uses the mark consistently, i.e. that the same word does not appear both with and without it.

14.1.5 Punctuation

Greek uses ; for ? and · for ; but is otherwise the same as English (! is often used in modern editions). The apostrophe (denoting an elision, as in English) is easily confused with the smooth breathing; it is printed the same but is never printed *over* a vowel. Warn the typesetter to leave a word space after an elided word, rather than closing up the next word.

Problems can arise when Greek words and phrases occur in an English context. The typesetter should be told that punctuation between a Greek word and the following English word is English unless otherwise marked, and that punctuation within a group of Greek words is Greek unless otherwise marked. In the first example below, the commas after the first two Greek words should be labelled as English; and in the second, the ; needs to be marked as Greek:

> the various instruments described, αὐλός, κιθάρα, φόρμιγξ, may be . . .

> the use of τίνες ἐστέ; here is . . .

Latin is printed with the same punctuation marks as English.

In neither Latin nor Greek is the initial word of a sentence invariably capitalized (usually only at the beginning of a quotation or 'paragraph').

14.1.6 Numerals

The Latin notation up to 100 is familiar. Further signs are D (500), M (1,000), X̄ (10,000), C̄ (100,000) and �X̄ (1,000,000). In inscriptions VIIII is often found for IX.

The Greeks had two different notations: the earlier, 'acrophonic' system, found particularly in epigraphic texts, is tabulated by A. G. Woodhead, *The Study of Greek Inscriptions*, 2nd edn (Cambridge University Press, 1981), p. 110. The later, 'alphabetic' system is set out in

Hart's Rules, p. 116; it uses the lower-case letters of the classical Greek alphabet plus the obsolete letters stigma, koppa and sampi (see above), accented to distinguish units, tens, hundreds and thousands (thus $\beta' = 2$, $\beta = 2,000$).

14.1.7 Dates

The Greeks named years by Olympiads (quadrennially from 776 BC) or by archonships.

The Romans named them by consulships or counted them AUC (*ab urbe condita* = from the foundation of Rome, 753 BC).

Use BC or AD where there could be any doubt about which is intended. The correct form is 250–245 BC, AD 245–50; do not elide BC dates except a year of office in the form 449/8 BC.

14.1.8 Symbols

In textual or epigraphic studies there is a system of signs (the Leiden system) used to indicate the state of the original text and the extent and nature of the volume editor's own restorations. (A text in its original form usually does not have word spacing, accents or punctuation, and is written in majuscules (capital letters); if it is an early text it may even be written from right to left, or alternately left to right and right to left.) These conventional signs include double and single upright lines, parentheses, square and angle brackets, braces, dots and dashes: Woodhead (*Greek Inscriptions*, pp. 6–11) gives a useful short explanation of them. The Leiden system is generally accepted, but there are (as always) idiosyncratic usages, and the conventions an editor is using should be explained in the note on 'sigla' which precedes most editions (where the editor also gives the abbreviations that are used for the various MSS and families of MSS).

In lexicographical and etymological works symbols like asterisks and daggers are used very variously and should be explained. Typical usages can be found listed in the larger Latin and Greek dictionaries.

Solidi separating parallels and analogues should be spaced: e.g. *cupiditas / cupido*.

14.1.9 **Abbreviations**

The *Oxford Classical Dictionary* and the larger Greek and Latin diction-aries (H. G. Liddell and J. R. Scott, *Greek–English Lexicon,* ed. H. Stuart Jones; C. T. Lewis and C. Short, *Latin Dictionary* and P. G. W. Glare, *Oxford Latin Dictionary*) give conventional abbreviations of classical authors and their works and also of standard 'modern' textbooks. Soph., Eur., Aesch., etc., are preferable to S., E., A., etc. Authors sometimes forget to italicize the appropriate part of an abbreviation (e.g. Soph. *OC* = Sophocles, *Oedipus Coloneus,* and *SVF* = *Stoicorum Veterum Fragmenta*).

The following miscellaneous abbreviations often occur in classical books:

ap.	*apud,* quoted in
AUC	*ab urbe condita,* from the foundation of Rome
EM	Early Minoan, a historical period; also LM and MM for Late and Middle Minoan
fr.	fragment
h.l.	*hic locus,* this passage
h.v.	*haec verba,* these words
init.	*initio,* at the beginning
schol.	*scholium,* an ancient commentary
str.	strophe, part of a choral ode, often printed alongside the relevant part of a text
s.v.	*sub voce,* under the heading
temp.	*tempore,* in the time of
var. lect.	*varia lectio,* variant reading

See further in the lists of abbreviations of the larger dictionaries, and in sections 14.1.10 and 14.1.11.

14.1.10 **References**

Classical works

Where possible, references should be to the conventional division of the work into books, sections or lines, rather than to the page numbers of a particular edition. Where there is no one standard division or arrangement of the text, the reference should include the name of the relevant edition: thus Aeschylus, fr. 26 Nauck.

There are various acceptable styles for the punctuation of figures in a composite reference. The two commonest are in the form Horace, *Odes* 4.2.3 (the numerals referring to book, poem and line respectively), Virgil, *Aeneid* 2.6 (book and line), and Horace, *Odes* IV.2.3, Virgil, *Aeneid* II.6. Both are preferable to Virgil, *Aeneid* 2,6 where the comma is ambiguous.

It is now usual to refer to books of Homer's works by figures, not Greek letters (thus Homer, *Odyssey* 2.5–9, not *Odyssey* β, 5–9).

References to Plato and Aristotle usually give section, subsection (actually page and column, the column being denoted by an English letter, usually lower case), and line: thus Plato, *Republic* 496a5–7 and Aristotle, *EN* 1107a2–b7.

There is no need to mention the work where an author wrote only one (or where they are all collected under one title): thus Herodotus 1.95 (book, section), Thucydides 7.24 (book, section), Catullus 24.18 (poem, line), Demosthenes 46.24 (speech, section), etc.

See also sections 14.1.11 and 14.1.15.

Contemporary works
A widely used set of abbreviations of classical journals and periodicals is given in *L'Année philologique*. A Greek word or phrase occurring in the title of a book or article is sometimes printed in capitals, but for aesthetic reasons this practice should be discouraged.

14.1.11 **Transliteration**

Classical names may be anglicized, latinized or hellenized (Virgil, Sophocles, Odysseus); but attempts to do one of these things absolutely consistently lead to very odd results, and it is probably best just to use the most familiar form in each case (see, for example, the usage in the *Oxford Classical Dictionary*). There are many borderline cases, and internal consistency is the only rule which can be applied to these. Avoid using one form of a name when it refers to a person and another form when it is part of the title of a book (e.g. Oidipous and *Oedipus*

Coloneus), or latinizing some of an author's works and anglicizing others (e.g. Aristophanes, *Aves* and *Ranae*, but *Clouds* and *Wasps*).

14.1.12 Metrical analysis

The commonest scansion marks are – (long), ◡ (short), × or ◡ (anceps), ◠ (resolved long), x̄ (long anceps), single vertical bar (marking division between feet) and double vertical bar (marking a caesura, the break between periods). But there are various other signs and combinations of signs to which it may be worth drawing attention, since the typesetter is unlikely to hold all sorts. See further A. M. Dale, *Lyric Metres of Greek Drama* (2nd edn, Cambridge University Press, 1968) and the *Oxford Classical Dictionary, s.v.* Metre.

Uprights are preferable to oblique strokes to show line breaks in quotations of Greek and Latin verse that are run on.

14.1.13 Texts and editions

Most editions of prose and verse texts have an apparatus criticus, which is a summary of variant readings and suggested restorations. It is printed beneath the text in smaller type and is keyed in by line numbers which may be printed in bold. Various fixed spaces indicate the subdivisions within each entry.

Editions of Greek plays are usually preceded by 'hypotheses', which are introductions to the plays (sometimes themselves in verse) by other ancient writers. The section of hypotheses normally starts a fresh page, and the text starts another.

The ranging of lines of verse may require particular attention. Hexameters are normally ranged left, while elegiacs have alternate lines indented; but there are many complicated versification schemes, particularly in the choruses of Greek plays, which may require special layout and where it may be important to distinguish turnovers from indented new lines. The volume editor should make this clear.

The running heads to a text normally have author left and title right (in Greek or Latin, as appropriate). There is no real need for running heads except in anthologies.

14.1.11 **Commentaries**

Commentaries normally make a section after the text in smaller type (i.e. as endnotes), but they may exceptionally be printed beneath the text when they are very short or when there is not a full critical apparatus; see, for example, J. Adam, *The Republic of Plato* (2nd edn, Cambridge University Press, 1963).

Commentaries are usually keyed to the text by section and/or line numbers followed by lemmata (catchwords). The lemmata are normally set in bold and followed by a colon (also in bold) with the commentary running straight on. Stretches of commentary are often preceded by a summary (usually with a centred subheading).

The punctuation and accentuation of lemmata can cause problems; the following rules are used in the Cambridge University Press series, Cambridge Greek and Latin Classics:

1 Punctuate lemmata in the following way:

1209 φονᾷ 'is intent on death'.

1211 ὀχήματα: lit. 'containers'.

1213 This line is highly suspect.

1214 πῶς: Jebb takes the view . . .

1219 σοι is an ethic dative.

2 For the purposes of accentuation, lemmata in the commentary should be treated as separate headings, complete in themselves, so that what was a final grave in the text will become an acute in the lemma, and accents will not be absorbed from enclitics which do not themselves appear in the lemma. This rule applies also to entries in indexes, but not to entries in the apparatus criticus. In the 'text' of the commentary the rule should be generally applied to isolated Greek words or phrases, except when the accentuation is itself the subject of the note.

3 In run-on quoted Greek, retain a grave accent on the word preceding an ellipsis; i.e. treat as if a word followed.

4 Where the last Greek word in a lemma is elided in the text, elide it also in the lemma (even though the next word is not reproduced).

5 Where a lemma contains one or more ellipses, use three dots to mark each 'gap'.

6 A lemma should not conclude with an ellipsis. In general retain the beginning and the end of the phrase under discussion as the lemma,

with some of the intervening section as well if it is a long phrase. With long sentences, use 'etc.' or κτλ. in moderation.

7 In a verse commentary, where a lemma contains words from more than one line, mark the line break by a spaced vertical line, *not* an oblique stroke.

Running heads that indicate the lines or sections under commentary are the most informative.

14.1.15 Indexes

There is often an index locorum and an index of Greek and Latin words as well as a general index. In the index locorum it is necessary to use some device to distinguish clearly between the locus and the page references to it.

One system is to separate off part of the locus by parentheses:

> Horace, *Odes* 1 (2.1), 34–7, 46–7; (3.6), 45–8, 67–9, 78–9
> 2 (5.1), 45, 64–7

Here the first number in the line refers to the book, the figures in parentheses refer to the poem and the line, and subsequent figures give the page references.

In a less complicated entry the whole of the locus can be placed in parentheses:

> Euripides, *Alcestis* (112f.), 34–7, 47; (192), 48
> *Medea* (55–9), 11–14

For further examples see the indexes of W. K. C. Guthrie, *A History of Greek Philosophy* (6 vols., Cambridge University Press, 1962–81).

Another system is to range right all the page references so that they are physically separated from the classical references; see, for an example, G. E. R. Lloyd and G. E. L. Owen, *Aristotle on Mind and the Senses* (Cambridge University Press, 1978).

14.2

BOOKS ON LAW

Information about how to refer to US and Australian laws and legal cases will be found in *The Chicago Manual of Style* and the Australian Government Publishing Service *Style Manual for Authors, Editors and Printers*, respectively. There are, for example, differences in the use of italic or roman, and of parentheses or square brackets.

14.2.1 **References to statutes**

Before 1963 titles of statutes were punctuated with a comma between the name and the year (e.g. the Finance Act, 1962), but from 1963 the comma was dropped (Finance Act 1963). In references to statutes, however, the distinction is not copied: the comma should be omitted from all titles, both before and after 1963. Titles should always be set roman, not italic.

Session and chapter references of statutes are often given in tables of statutes (see below) and sometimes in footnotes. Every statute is classified by chapter number within the parliamentary session in which it was passed, and up to 1963 parliamentary sessions were identified by regnal year: thus, for example, the Act of Supremacy 1558, which was the first chapter in the parliamentary session in the first year of Elizabeth I's reign, is numbered 1 Eliz. 1 c. 1 (the monarch's numeral can alternatively be roman). Where a parliamentary session extended from one regnal year to the next, two regnal years are cited, e.g. 12 & 13 Will. 3 c. 2 (the Act of Settlement 1700). In regnal year references the monarch's name should be abbreviated as follows: Edw., Hen., Ph. & M. (Philip and Mary), Eliz., Jac., Car. or Chas., Will., Geo., Vic. or Vict.

From 1963 regnal year references were replaced by calendar years: thus the Finance Act 1962 is numbered 10 & 11 Eliz. 2 c. 44, but the Finance Act 1963 is simply 1963 c. 25.

Statutes are subdivided into sections, subsections, paragraphs and subparagraphs, identified respectively by arabic figures, arabic figures in parentheses, italic lower-case letters in parentheses, and roman lower-case numerals in parentheses: e.g. Representation of the People

Act 1949, s. 63 (1) (*c*) (i). Check that the author uses the correct terminology when referring to subdivisions. Phrases such as 'Subsection 1 of section 63 states . . .' are better rewritten 'Section 63 (1) states . . .'

Rules (such as the Rules of the Supreme Court) are divided into Orders and rules, Articles (e.g. Articles of Association) into clauses and articles. The following abbreviations are used:

	Singular	*Plural*
section	s.	ss.
subsection	subs.	subss.
paragraph	para.	paras.
subparagraph	subpara.	subparas.
Order	Ord.	Ords.
rule	r.	rr.
clause	cl.	clauses
article	art.	arts.

These abbreviations should normally be used in references to specific subdivisions, except at the beginning of a sentence, where they should always be spelt out; and they should be spelt out where the reference is non-specific: thus 'according to s. 63' but 'Section 63 states' and 'according to this section'.

14.2.2 References to statutory instruments

The titles of statutory instruments (delegated legislation such as Orders in Council, Regulations) may be followed by the year and number in parentheses or they may be referred to by year and number alone: thus, 'according to the Town and Country Planning General Development Order 1988 (SI 1988 No. 1813)', or simply 'according to SI 1988 No. 1813'.

14.2.3 References to Command Papers

See pp. 239–40.

14.2.4 **References to cases**

The name of a case is usually given as, for example, *Smith* v. *Anderson*, the names of the plaintiff and the defendant being set in italic and the v. (for versus) roman. Where the plaintiff is the state, the abbreviation R. (not Reg.) is used for both Rex and Regina. The names of companies should be styled consistently 'Co. Ltd' or 'Co., Ltd' (the former is preferred nowadays). The abbreviation for public limited company is plc. Ampersands are frequently used in the names of companies but should not be used to join the names of two parties: thus *Smith & Co. Ltd* but *Smith and Jones* v. *Anderson.*

In general books, cases may well be referred to simply by name followed by the year in parentheses, e.g. *Johnston* v. *Duke of Westminster* (1986). But full references quoting volume and column/page of the law reports or periodical in which the case appears are normally given in specialized books on law. There are three different kinds of reference, arising from the different ways in which report volumes are numbered: (1) where there is one volume per year and the year forms the number of the volume, the year is given in square brackets, e.g. [1986] AC 839; (2) where there are several volumes per year, the year is given in brackets followed by the volume number within that year, e.g. [1986] 2 All ER 613; (3) where the volumes are numbered independently of the year, the year is given in parentheses before the volume number, e.g. (1986) 279 EG 501.

References to English law reports and periodicals should always conform to one of these styles. The rules apply to many non-English reports as well, but some have different styles of references: for example the place or name of the court may be given in addition to the name of the reports, or the order of items in the reference may differ.

References to Scottish cases are styled differently. Cases reported in the Session Cases reports are styled as, for example, *Winston* v. *Patrick* 1980 SC 246; cases in the Justiciary Cases reports as, for example, *MacKenzie* v. *HM Advocate* 1983 JC 13.

Nowadays there is usually no comma between the name and reference of a case. If a comma is used it should be placed *before* dates in square brackets, *after* dates in parentheses. In Scottish case references the comma precedes the date. There should never be a comma between the name of the report or periodical and the column/page number.

However, some authors prefer to cite the first page of the complete case as well as the page or pages specifically referred to; here there should be a comma between the two (sets of) numbers, e.g. *Brown* v. *Sparrow* [1982] 1 WLR 1269, 1274–5.

See section 14.2.6 for examples of the styles of references most commonly used.

14.2.5 **Abbreviations of law reports**

The following are some of the most commonly cited English law reports and periodicals together with their abbreviated form and form of reference.

AC	*Law Reports, Appeal Cases*	[1982] AC 888
All ER	*All England Law Reports*	[1984] 3 All ER 262
Ch	*Law Reports, Chancery Division*	[1985] Ch 190
CLJ	*Cambridge Law Journal*	(1979) 38 CLJ 278
Cr App R	*Criminal Appeal Reports*	(1987) 85 Cr App R 358
Crim LR	*Criminal Law Review*	[1982] Crim LR 743
EG	*Estates Gazette*	(1956) 168 EG 96
ICR	*Industrial Court Reports*	[1981] ICR 660
JP	*Justice of the Peace Law Reports*	(1981) 145 JP 344
KB	*Law Reports, King's Bench Division*	[1952] 1 KB 107
Law Soc Gaz	*Law Society's Gazette*	(1985) 82 Law Soc Gaz 2581
LGR	*Knight's Local Government Reports*	(1980) 79 LGR 38
LJ	*Law Journal*	(1958) 108 LJ 140
LQR	*Law Quarterly Review*	(1983) 99 LQR 536
MLR	*Modern Law Review*	(1984) 47 MLR 481
NLJ	*New Law Journal*	(1981) 131 NLJ 1310
P	*Law Reports, Probate, Divorce & Admiralty Division*	[1967] P 265
QB	*Law Reports, Queen's Bench Division*	(1885) 16 QB 242
		[1963] 2 QB 494
		[1980] QB 137
RTR	*Road Traffic Reports*	[1976] RTR 437
Sol Jo	*Solicitors' Journal*	(1892) 126 Sol Jo 116
TLR	*Times Law Reports*	(1942) 59 TLR 70
		[1952] 2 TLR 194
WLR	*Weekly Law Reports*	[1984] 2 WLR 196

The way reports and periodicals are numbered may have changed over the years: see, for example, *Law Reports, Queen's Bench Division* and *Times Law Reports* above. The titles of some reports and periodicals may be abbreviated in two or three different ways, all of which are acceptable: for example *Solicitors' Journal* may be abbreviated Sol Jo or SJ; *Cambridge Law Journal* may be abbreviated CLJ or Camb LJ. Authors also vary in their punctuation of abbreviations, for example C.L.J. or CLJ; Sol Jo or Sol. Jo. Follow the author's system provided it is consistent. Abbreviations are always roman; if full titles are given for some reports and periodicals they may be set consistently roman or italic according to the author's preference.

14.2.6 **Examples of references to cases**

The following illustrate the styles usually followed:

> *Moorgate Mercantile Co. Ltd* v. *Twitchings* [1975] 3 All ER 314
> *R.* v. *Secretary of State for the Home Department, ex parte Benwell* (1985) 128 Sol Jo 703
> *Re F (wardship: adoption)* (1984) 13 Fam Law 259, CA

However, v. may be roman or italic provided it is consistent, and the point may be omitted.

In the third example above, the name of the court (the Court of Appeal) is included in abbreviated form in the reference.

In American books names of cases are sometimes italic in the text but roman in the notes. This distinction is not followed in English books.

14.2.7 **Quoting from statutes and cases**

Extracts from statutes must be quoted exactly. Authors may even want to retain the typographical conventions of the original, such as em rules after colons and double quotation marks. If possible, extracts should follow the original in layout.

In ordinary books on law in which extracts from cases are introduced as quotations, alterations to such extracts should normally be limited to typographical conventions (as for quotations in general).

But in casebooks where the extracts form the body of the text the author may be willing for you to standardize such things as capitalization, italicization and forms of abbreviation.

14.2.8 Names of judges

In law reports the names of judges are usually set in capitals and small capitals. Extracts from cases quoted in books on law normally follow the same style, though small capitals throughout are preferred to capitals and small capitals nowadays. Some authors prefer to have judges' names set in (small) capitals wherever they occur, in the text as well as in quotations.

The title of a judge is written in abbreviated form after his or her name: thus for example Chief Justice Lord Lane is given as LORD LANE CJ, and Justice Sheen as SHEEN J (plural JJ, as in ROSE and ROCH JJ).

14.2.9 Tables of statutes and cases

Almost all books on law include tables of statutes and cases. These are always set as the last two items in the preliminary pages, and copy for them should be sent to the typesetter at the same time as the index copy.

Statutes are listed by title and chapter number (see above); they are conventionally given in alphabetical within chronological order, though the alternative of chronological within alphabetical is acceptable.

Cases are always listed alphabetically. Here the use of italic and roman is usually the reverse of that in the text; thus for example *Bell* v. *McCubbin* in the text becomes Bell *v.* McCubbin in the table of cases.

Some books on law also include a table of rules and Orders. Here items are listed strictly chronologically, so that, for example, SI 1985 No. 52 comes before SI 1985 No. 61.

14.2.10 Italicization

The *Cambridge Law Journal* suggests that italic should be used for all Latin words and phrases except those in common use such as bona fide, de facto, de jure, (obiter) dicta/dictum, habeas corpus, intra vires, prima facie and ultra vires. Some other candidates for roman rather than italic are: caveat, gratis, mala fide, mandamus, nisi, subpoena. There is no set rule about this, but the appearance of the page is improved if italic is kept to a minimum.

14.2.11 Capitalization

Act is always capitalized even in non-specific references, to avoid ambiguity, but bill can be lower case: thus 'the Act' but 'the bill'. Unless a court is referred to by name, court is normally lower case, as are assizes, bench, judge, sessions, and so on. Titles of statutes always have the first *and* chief words capitalized.

14.2.12 Bibliographical references

The titles of some major textbooks include the name of the original author, e.g. *Williams on Wills.* The name of the editor of such a work need not be given provided the edition is identified by number.

References to journal articles are generally given in the style of case references, e.g. C. Munro, 'Detention after arrest' [1981] Crim LR 802, 806; D. K. Tarullo, 'Beyond normalcy in the regulation of international trade' (1987) 100 Harvard Law Review 546; or even (for first and subsequent references) simply Munro [1981] Crim LR 802, 806; Tarullo (1987) 100 Harvard Law Review 546.

14.3

MUSIC

Sections 14.3.1–5 are concerned mainly with simple school editions, such as song books, though 14.3.1 and 14.3.4 cover general points of style. Section 14.3.6 deals with the text of books about music, 14.3.7 with music examples within the text.

14.3.1 **Style for music**

If there is a melody line only, there is no vertical line at the beginning of the stave (see ex. 1).

Example 1.

Where a group of staves for different instruments or voice-parts make up a musical passage, the staves are joined by a straight bracket (ex. 2).

Example 2.

but the two staves comprising a piano part are joined by a curly bracket (ex. 3).

Example 3.

Dynamics (expression indications such as *diminuendo, f*) usually appear in bold italic lower case; any abbreviations, such as *dim.*, should be consistent, as should the use of full points. Dynamics usually appear between the staves, but may appear above or below the stave to which they refer.

Tempo directions (e.g. fast, allegro) are usually set in bold roman upper and lower case, and above the stave.

Names of instruments and voice-parts (such as violin, alto, chorus) are usually placed either just to the right of the straight bracket (exx. 2 and 4)

Example 4.

or if there is room – to the left of the staves (see ex. 5).

Example 5.

Alternatively the name may appear above the bar where that instrument or part begins (ex. 4).

The names of voice-parts are usually abbreviated after the first mention, and instrument names are often abbreviated from the start. See that the abbreviations are unambiguous; for example, 'tr' could be either trumpet or trombone. The standard abbreviations for voice-parts are:

S	soprano
A	alto
T	tenor
Bar.	baritone
B	bass

There is no commonly accepted set of abbreviations of instruments, but *The New Grove Dictionary of Music and Musicians* uses the following:

Pic	Piccolo
Fl	Flute
Ob	Oboe
Cl	Clarinet
Eng Hn	English Horn (cor anglais)
Bn	Bassoon
Hn	French Horn
Tpt	Trumpet
Trbn	Trombone
Vn	Violin
Va	Viola
Vc	Violoncello (cello)
Db	Double-bass

Optional parts (e.g. descants) are printed as smaller notes. These should be distinguished in the MS by being written smaller or in red, or highlighted. Give the typesetter the necessary instructions (e.g. 'Descant, written in red, to be set smaller').

Guitar chords are indicated by single letters (sometimes capital letters for major chords, lower case for minor) or a letter and a number, e.g. G7.

Bars may be numbered (see ex. 4), or 'rehearsal letters' (or numbers) may appear at intervals, so that a particular bar can be found easily: 'bar 35' or 'the third bar after F'. An incomplete first bar is not included in the numbering. A bar number may be printed every five or ten bars, or at the beginning of each line, though in musical examples it is more helpful to print the number of the bar that the author particularly refers to.

If the author has lines of unequal length in the MS in order to keep certain phrases on one line, tell the typesetter to follow the MS and leave the right-hand edge ragged.

In an edition including only one part (e.g. a chorus edition) which has long periods of silence, it is usual to include cue notes – a bar or so of the most obvious piece of orchestration etc. preceding the entry of the part or chorus – so that the performers do not have to rely entirely on counting many bars' rest in order to know when to come in. The cue notes should be smaller, and labelled with the instrument or voice to which they refer.

14.3.2 **Style for words of songs**

In a song, the words of the first verse (or first two verses) are printed between the staves, the other verses being printed after the music. If the words between the staves are not completely legible, type out the wording separately; but make it clear that this typed version is for clarification and that these verses are not to appear twice.

In the verses between the staves, syllables are hyphenated, so that each one is below the relevant note or notes (see ex. 2). The author should insert these hyphens; but check that the breaks are sensible and that it is clear which syllable belongs to which note. Additional information about syllables can be given throughout the words by the use of an accent or apostrophe, e.g. 'blessèd', 'giv'n'. If accents are used, they should be consistently grave or acute.

Italic should be kept to a minimum; for example it may be used to distinguish instructions (such as 'Repeat verse 1') from the words of a song, or to pick out the words of choruses that are printed only the first time they are sung.

If more than one size of type is to be used, identify the passages to be set in the second size.

Check the indention scheme of songs; authors sometimes have over-elaborate and inconsistent schemes for indenting rhyming lines, refrains and choruses.

14.3.3 **Style for sources etc.**

General notes on performance should appear above the music. Any footnotes to the music are probably most unambiguously keyed in by symbols.

In an anthology the composer's name and the source may appear immediately below the heading of each piece. The author, translator and source of the words usually appear below the words (or as a note at the foot of the first page if all the words are printed between the staves). If author and composer appear above the music, the author should be on the left and the composer (and arranger, where appropriate) on the right.

Acknowledgements for all copyright material should appear in a list in the preliminary pages or at the end of the book, though some may also have to be included on the relevant page, if the copyright holder insists.

If there is a discography, and individual songs on discs are regularly discussed in the text, use roman with inverted commas for song titles, italic for disc titles.

14.3.4 **Copy-editing music and the words of songs**

Examine music copy closely at the earliest possible moment, in case there are a number of things that the author will have to be asked to do. Look out for the following:

- illegibility: words, and also whether notes are clearly positioned on or between the lines of the stave
- discrepancies in wording and punctuation if there is more than one edition
- whether the words are correctly hyphenated and it is clear how the syllables fit the music
- omitted repeat marks. (The position of the repeat in a song may be clear from the words)
- whether there is an indication of speed
- spot-check for discrepancies in music between, say, piano and melody editions (including accidentals, staccato, marks of expression such as *crescendo*, *f*); also discrepancies in accidentals

between different parts in the same bar

- spot-check whether there are enough notes or rests in a bar to complete it. Authors often omit dots after dotted notes or tails from quavers; and sometimes the split bars where the music repeats (which should have, say, three beats before the repeat mark, and the fourth at the beginning of the repeat) do not make up a whole bar
- if two parts are written on the same stave, spot-check whether each part has a complete set of notes; for example when a crotchet is shared between two parts, it should have two stems. Stems rise from the right of the note for the upper part and descend from the left for the lower part
- spot-check whether some staccato dots in a group seem to have been omitted
- check that the piece ends with a double bar

If more work has to be done on the music, the author can also be asked:

- to add slurs (curved lines grouping notes together, used to indicate musical phrases and also in songs to show when one syllable covers two or more notes)
- to see that any use of accents or apostrophes, to show when syllables are pronounced or elided, is consistent
- to see that a time signature and key signature are included at the beginning of each piece, and that the key signature appears at the beginning of each subsequent line of music. (NB: it is possible for the time or key to change in the course of a piece)
- to see that all clefs are included at the beginning of every stave throughout the piece
- to see that quavers are linked, unless each covers only one syllable

If the music must be rewritten, the author can be asked also:

- to use a consistent style for the things mentioned in section 14.3.1
- to use italic sparingly in the words for songs
- to be consistent about capitalizing the first letter of each line of verse to be printed between the staves, in accordance with the style of verses to be printed below

14.3.5 **Paging music editions**

Any piece of music occupying an even number of pages should start on a left-hand page, so that the reader does not have to turn more pages than necessary within that piece. If the pieces vary in length, ask the author whether the order can be varied; if it can, ask the typesetter to suggest the best order from the point of view of make-up.

In a words-only edition, the items can run over from a recto to a verso, but preferably not where there is a chorus which is printed only the first time it is to be sung.

If there is more than one edition
It is sensible to use the same typesetting for both editions as far as possible (preliminary pages, headings, words of songs). Keep variations to a minimum, though the sources and acknowledgements in a words-only edition should cover only the words. See that the relevant notes on performance etc. appear in each edition. If they are to be set separately, check that the words (including punctuation etc.) are identical in both editions, and spot-check the music.

Preliminary pages
Preliminary pages are kept to a minimum, and usually paginated in arabic, partly because they are short and partly because the text may start on a verso.

The title page should contain the name of the edition if there is more than one.

The verso of the title page may include a note on performing rights; and a note on copyright and acknowledgements is often placed there. Check that the copyright notice is correctly worded and suitably qualified if your publisher does not hold the copyright in the music etc.

If the text has to start on a left-hand page, see that it is not preceded by a blank right-hand page. Repeat the book title if necessary.

If the order is to be changed to aid make-up, tell the author, and see that the contents list, item numbers and cross-references are altered accordingly.

14.3.6 **Books about music: text**

A set of conventions for use in the text is given below, but the main thing is that the author's system should be clear and consistent.

Warn the designer if ♯ ♭ ♮ are used in the text ('the F♯ chord') as they are special sorts available only in certain founts; if they occur very rarely it may be best to substitute the word ('the F sharp chord'). Other music symbols in the text will normally have to be produced as artwork and stripped in.

Keys. Use 'F sharp minor' or 'F minor' (not hyphenated), with a capital only for the key itself; note that this should be a full capital, not a small capital. Specify minor always, major where this is needed for clarity.

Pitch names. Check that the author uses a consistent system ('three bars after the d♯³'). The Helmholtz System of pitch names should be familiar to most musicians and writers on music (see ex. 6);

Example 6.

either superscript figures or primes may be used: c¹, c², c³ or c′, c″, c‴. (It is not necessary to italicize these pitch designations.)

Intervals. Spell these out, for example 'a sixth', 'a minor third'.

Chord names should be 'a 6–4 chord', not ⁶₄.

Time signatures too should be written on the line of text and not as fractions: '3/4 time'. Ask authors to avoid using C and ₵ for 'common' and 'alla breve' time signatures mentioned in the text, as these may have to be artwork.

Dynamics, such as *diminuendo, piano,* should be lower-case italic, and spelt out unless the author is quoting from a score that uses abbreviations such as *pp, mf.*

Tempo indications, as in 'this passage must be played presto', should be roman. Tempo indications used as the name for a whole movement (e.g. 'the Andante con brio') are roman, with a capital for the first word only.

British and American authors use different names for some of the basic terms:

British	American
bar	measure
bar line	measure line
breve	two whole notes
semibreve	whole note
minim	half note
crotchet	quarter note
quaver	eighth note
semiquaver	sixteenth note
demisemiquaver	thirty-second note

References to works

Italic should be used for:

- major musical works such as operas, oratorios, ballets, with a title given by the composer, e.g. *Symphonie fantastique*; but not for nicknames given by other people, e.g. the 'Jupiter' Symphony, the 'Emperor' Concerto
- complete song cycles, e.g. *Dichterliebe*; but individual songs within a cycle are roman in quotes, e.g. 'Im wunderschönen Monat Mai'
- specific names, e.g. *Missa Papae Marcelli* and the translation *Pope Marcellus Mass*; but the English name for Beethoven's *Missa solemnis* is a genre title, Mass in D, and is therefore roman (see below)

Roman without quotes should be used for:

- genre titles:

  Tchaikovsky's [*or* Chaikovsky's] Symphony No. 4 in F minor Op. 36
  Beethoven's Fifth Symphony
  Mass in B minor
  Piano Concerto No. 1 in A minor

- title or tempo indication of a whole movement, e.g. Allegro con brio (with a capital for the first word only)

- titles of movements from the Mass: Kyrie, Agnus Dei (with a capital for the first word and God only); but sections within the movement should be roman in quotes: 'Et in terra pax', 'Kyrie eleison'

Watch out for consistency in the following:

- punctuation, e.g. comma/no comma before 'Op.'
- capitalization of 'Op.' and 'No.', which should be treated in the same way
- capitalization of foreign titles; in the examples above, only the first word and proper names (but all nouns in German) are capitalized
- capitalization of 'minor' in the title of works, e.g. Piano Concerto No. 1 in A minor

Not all works have opus numbers. Mozart is given K (Köchel) numbers, e.g.

Eine kleine Nachtmusik, K525
Piano Concerto No. 17 in G, K453

Schubert is given D (Deutsch) numbers:

String Quintet in C, D956

J. S. Bach is given BWV numbers (Bach Werke Verzeichnis):

Triple Concerto in A minor, BWV 1044
Prelude in C major, BWV 870

In references to movements use 'in the first movement of the Symphony No. 5', 'Op. 108, first movement, bar 10', or 'Op. 108, Andante con brio, bar 10'. In short references in notes or on diagrams, roman numerals are used for movements: 'Op. 108, i.10'. 'Bar(s)' and 'measure(s)' may be abbreviated to b., bb. and m., mm.

Roman numerals are also often used for acts of operas and major divisions of oratorios, e.g. Act ii Scene 3, with references in notes shortened to ii.3.

14.3.7 **Music examples in the text**

For general style see section 14.3.1.

Music examples without stave lines (e.g. rhythmic patterns ♩♪♫) can appear within a line of text. Any more complex music examples should be numbered 'Example 1' etc. and referred to by number in the text, because the typesetter may be unable to place them exactly where the author wants them to fall (cf. section 4.2.2). Explain this to the author, who can then say whether a particular example must appear exactly where it is in the typescript. If so, write in the margin 'Ex. 16 must be placed exactly here' and ring the instruction.

Check that the numbering of examples is correct and that none are missing. If examples within the text line are numerous they must be lettered or otherwise labelled for identification during make-up. Make it clear that these letters are not to be typeset.

If you can, check whether the music example matches the explanation in the text. A spot check can reveal whether there are problems and whether the author should be asked to recheck all the examples.

Check also for consistent use of the conventions mentioned in sections 14.3.1 and 14.3.4. Music historians and ethnomusicologists often use arcane or archaic features of notation: the music setter may be unfamiliar with the symbols or conventions, and in such cases the author may be asked to supply a carefully drawn specimen of each difficult symbol or a photocopy of published versions of the conventions used.

Musicologists often use small type for editorial additions (e.g. *musica ficta* accidentals) and may indicate this in their manuscript by writing in red. The convention should be explained to the reader in a preface or footnote. The best ways of instructing the music typesetter about this and other features of a scholarly transcription are dealt with in *Editing Early Music*, cited below.

If a music example ends with an incomplete bar, there should be no final bar line; if it ends with a complete bar there should be a single bar line; only if the example ends at the end of the piece (or an important section) should a double bar be added. Ask the author to check against the score if necessary.

If the music examples are on the same folio as text, photocopy the folio, cross out the text and send this photocopy to the music typesetter, writing by each example its number and the folio number.

It is also sensible to make a list of all the examples, with number and folio number, so that you can check at each stage that none have been overlooked.

Separate typewritten copy must be supplied for any lettering to be set separately and stripped in (e.g. captions for examples; and occasionally the words of vocal music, though these are more often set by the music typesetter, as are tempo and expression marks).

14.3.8 **Useful references**

Caldwell, John. *Editing Early Music,* Oxford University Press, 1985: very useful for scholarly editions

Holoman, D. Kern. *Writing about Music,* Berkeley, University of California Press, 1988: the first published attempt (based on American usage) at a copy-editors' and authors' handbook

New Grove Dictionary of Music and Musicians, London, Macmillan, 1981: the most authoritative source for correct spellings of composers' names, their works, musical terms, etc.

Ross, Ted. *The Art of Music Engraving and Processing,* 2nd edn, Miami Beach, Fla, Hansen House, 1974: a more practical guide for the music engraver and typesetter, which shows the publisher what they can be asked to do

There is also a British Standard, BS 4754: 1982 (1989), *Presentation of Music Scores and Parts.*

⑮ Reprints and new editions

Perhaps I should start with some definitions.

An 'impression' is a number of copies printed at any one time. When a book is reprinted or reproduced from the same setting of type, with only minor alterations, this printing is a 'new impression' or a 'reprint'. The term 'new [or second] edition' should not be used unless the text has been significantly changed. The word 'edition' is also used to distinguish different bindings (for example a paperback edition) or a reset version even if the text remains unchanged; such uses of the word 'edition' should be distinguished from real new editions, in which the text has been changed (see examples on p. 373).

15.1

REPRINTS

Most publishers have a 'corrections file' in which they keep any corrections sent by the author or other people. In addition, authors are usually asked whether they have any small corrections for a reprint. Before writing to them it is sensible to look in the corrections file, to see whether the author has already sent some corrections (and whether these can be made easily); also whether one needs to ask the author about corrections sent in by other people. Some 'errors' are matters of opinion rather than of fact.

One usually marks corrections on photocopies of the relevant pages. Make sure that these are from the latest impression, and that all pages with any alteration are included, even those where there is just a deletion or a change of page number. Write each correction in the margin, as if you were marking a proof. However, if some of the corrections are complicated or affect a line or more, it is easier for the typesetter if those lines are typed and attached to the top or bottom margin and clearly keyed in. Write author and short book title at the top of the first photocopied page, if it is not the title page.

If the corrections are marked in a copy of the book, list on the flyleaf all the pages involved, as a small correction could easily be missed otherwise.

Try to think of any other corrections that follow from those the author has listed: for example, if the spelling of a name is altered, see whether it is mentioned in the index and if so whether it needs to be altered there or on the other pages listed there.

Draw the designer's attention to any illustrations that need alteration, and to anything else relating to design.

Preliminary pages
See section 15.3.

Text
See that the new matter is consistent in style with the rest of the book, and that there is room for it. It is essential that each alteration affects as few lines as possible: substitutions must be the same length, and new material cannot be added unless one can find (or make) room for it. If necessary, a pair of facing pages can become one line longer or shorter than the rest of the book. If you are not sure whether a correction is feasible, ask the production department.

If the book already contains a list of corrigenda or an erratum slip, see whether all the corrections can now be incorporated into the text. If all or some are made, the list of corrigenda should be deleted or modified.

See whether the index will need revision. If possible, revise it now and send marked-up photocopies of the relevant index pages for correction with the rest.

Illustrations
See section 15.4.

Jacket and cover
See that a copy of the jacket or cover for each edition (binding) is corrected. The blurb, author's affiliation and series list should be brought up to date; and you may wish to include extracts from reviews, or to advertise different books on the jacket or back cover. See that the relevant ISBN and bar code appear, and that your publisher's addresses are up to date. If genuine cloth will not be used to bind the book change 'cloth' to 'hardback' or 'hard covers' in such phrases as 'also issued in cloth'; and see that the price is changed if necessary.

Proofs

Proofs are usually checked by the publisher, unless the author has particularly asked to see them. The proofs may consist only of the pieces the typesetter has reset (which may be only a few lines from each corrected page). Check them against the copy and see that the corrections are consistent in style with the rest of the book (e.g. in the use of lining or non-lining figures) and that they do in fact fit into the available space. If they are shown in position on the page, see that they are correctly placed. If you are sent the camera-ready copy, mark any corrections on a photocopy of the relevant page.

See that the index has been revised (if necessary) and that any changes to illustrations have been made.

15.2

NEW EDITIONS

In most firms new editions are treated like new books; but check the corrections file and reviews file, to make sure that all outstanding points have been raised with the author.

If the copy is not a typescript but a corrected copy of the last impression, and it is not clear whether the book will be reset, consult the production department. Let them know if some alterations are to be made only if the book is to be reset, or whether some corrections will be modified if the book is not to be reset, so as to fit them into the available space. A typesetter's estimate will probably be obtained before you complete your marking.

If it is decided that the whole book will not be reset, treat it like a reprint apart from the preliminary pages (see below). If it is to be reset, the whole book should be copy-edited. In either case, see that the old and the new material employ the same conventions; and if chapters, illustrations, etc., are renumbered, change any cross-references to those numbers. If the book is to be reset, or altered so much that the index cannot be revised before the book is sent for setting, return the old index to the author to keep for revision at proof stage.

For illustrations see section 15.4.

15.3

PRELIMINARY PAGES

15.3.1   **Half-title and verso**

Bring the series list, or list of other books by the author, up to date.

15.3.2   **Title page**

Bring the author's affiliation up to date; if the author has retired or died, add 'formerly' before the appointment; and after some years you may decide to delete it. Add '[second] edition', if applicable. You may need to update the publishing imprint.

15.3.3   **Verso of title page**

Bring the publisher's addresses up to date if necessary.

Copyright date (see also section 7.5.2)
The copyright date should never be *altered*, though another date may be added. A reprint or a change in binding does not justify an additional date; but a new edition in which the content is changed should have one. If this is the first copyright notice – that is, if earlier editions were published before September 1957 or were subject to the US 'manufacturing clause' – the notice should read '©. . .' and the new date of publication. If earlier editions were published after September 1957, the dates of those editions should be given:

> © [copyright holder and date of each substantive edition, not paperback edition or reprint, after September 1957]

For example, the copyright notice for a book first published in 1956, with new editions in 1970 and 1993 and reprints in 1974, 1979 and 1985, would read:

> © [copyright holder] 1970, 1993

If copyright in the book has been transferred, say to a widower, since publication of the previous edition, there will be two copyright notices:

First edition © J. Smith 1986
Second edition © E. Smith 1986, 1990

Where the book has been revised by someone other than the author:

© J. Smith 1986
Revisions and additional material © D. Brown 1990

ISBN

In a *reprint* the ISBN is changed only if there is a change in the binding or format; for example a paperback ISBN should be added if the original edition was only in hardback and the reprint is wholly or partly paperback. ISBNs will have to be added to books that were first published before ISBNs were introduced; and the group identifier (see p. 175) will have to be added to early Standard Book Numbers, so that:

Standard Book Number: 521 05875 9
becomes   ISBN 0 521 05875 9

Alter 'clothbound' to 'hardback' or 'hard covers' if appropriate.

A *new edition* has new CIP data and a new ISBN for each binding. The Standard Book Numbering Agency recommends that the ISBNs of preceding editions should also be given. If there is only one preceding edition, the ISBNs could be given in the form:

ISBN 0 521 20304 x 2nd edition
(ISBN 0 521 05679 9 1st edition)

Where there are several, it would be better to add the ISBNs to the printing history:

First published 1975 (0 521 20550 6)
Reprinted 1976, 1978, 1980
Second edition 1981 (0 521 23868 4)
Reprinted 1983, 1986, 1987, 1989
Third edition 1992 (0 521 40074 0)

If CIP data are to be included, new data must be obtained for a new edition.

Printing history
The date of each edition and reprint published by your firm should be included.

First published 19—
Reprinted 19—, 19—
Second edition 19—

or, if appropriate,

Reprinted with corrections
  where there are more alterations than in an ordinary reprint but
  not enough to justify calling it a new edition
Reset
  if the type has been reset for reasons other than extensive changes
  to the text (which would be a new edition)
Paperback edition
  if there is a change in binding but not extensive changes to the text

To avoid any typesetting when reprinting, a publisher may print two series of numbers below the publication information in the first impression:

First published 1990
98 97 96 95 94 93 92 91   10 9 8 7 6 5 4 3 2 1

The first series represents successive years after publication, the other the number of the reprint. When the book is reprinted, numbers are deleted so as to leave the date of the latest reprint as the last number in the first group and the number of the reprint as the last (or anyway lowest) number in the second group. So if the fourth reprint was published in 1996 the two groups would read:

98 97 96   10 9 8 7 6 5 4

Printer's imprint
If the book is being reprinted (but not reset) by a different printer, some publishers alter 'Printed' to 'First printed' and add below it 'Reprinted in Great Britain [or other country] by . . .' In any case the new printer's country, name and town must be given; if you do not know who is reprinting the book, ask the production department. A new edition has a new printer's imprint.

15.3.4 **Contents list**

Add any new material and make any alterations necessary to chapter titles etc., and to page numbers.

15.3.5 **Preface**

In a new edition there should be a preface explaining how this edition differs from the last, so that those who already own the book can decide whether they should buy the new edition. If there is a new preface, alter the title of the old preface to 'Preface to the first edition' above the preface, in the contents list and in the running heads. The preface to the second edition normally precedes the preface to the first edition unless the original preface provides information a new reader will find useful. Change the page numbers on the preliminary pages, where necessary; the pages which have only a change of page number should be sent for correction with the rest.

If you are in any doubt as to whether additional preliminary material can be fitted into a reprint, ask the production department.

15.4

ILLUSTRATIONS

15.4.1 **Placing etc.**

Sometimes reprints are imposed differently from the original impression; sometimes separately printed halftones are grouped instead of being scattered, or are reprinted on text paper without the original pagination being altered, so that there may be, for example, two unnumbered pages (with halftones on one or both) between pages 68 and 69. If the reprint is to be a paperback, separately printed halftones and fold-outs may be omitted, and an endpaper illustration may be moved into the prelims. Alter the contents list and/or list of illustrations and acknowledgements if necessary; also look through the text for references to those illustrations.

If the author wants to add a text illustration in the middle of the book, and you are not resetting, it is best to call it, for example, fig. 56a (even if it is not closely connected with fig. 56) rather than have to renumber all the later figures, check all the cross-references and reset all the affected lines.

If the plate or figure numbering is altered, check all the text references.

15.4.2 **Originals**

If the author wants to use some of the old halftones in a new edition, ask the production department whether the printer has a printing image of them. Line illustrations can be reproduced from a copy of the book, but any alterations will be carried out more easily on the original artwork if this is still available.

15.5

PERMISSIONS

Many copyright owners require an additional fee when a new edition is published, or when more than a certain number of copies of the book have been printed. See that permission has been obtained for continued use, and also for any new material, and add any new acknowledgements. Delete any acknowledgements for material now omitted.

Appendix 1
Checklist of copy-editing

This list is not exhaustive, so read the relevant section of the book: the relevant chapter or section number is given beside each heading or individual item.

An asterisk indicates things that should be done or considered at a planning or estimate stage, a dagger those that may be dealt with by the designer or production department, or covered by general instructions to the typesetter.

GENERAL

Completeness and organization (3.5)

* check that no folios missing. If no fo. 66, make this clear
* number folios in one sequence. If extra folio added after 66, number it 66a; say '66a follows' on 66 and '67 follows' on 66a.
* mark where arabic pagination begins
* mark 'run on', 'fresh page', 'recto', 'verso blank', where appropriate.
  (†A general note saying whether chapters start on fresh pages, rectos, or run on, is also useful)
  if extent has changed since estimate, tell production department; give details if cuts or additions localized
  check all numbering systems: chapters, sections, illustrations, tables, equations, etc.
  ask commissioning editor or author for any missing material
  find out and tell designer and production department the length, position and arrival date of anything that cannot be supplied immediately

Legibility, ambiguous characters, special sorts (2.1.1, 3.4, 13.2)
see all handwriting is legible
identify capital O/zero, l/1, roman one/capital I; minus/em rule/en rule, x/multiplication sign, decimal/multiplication point; Greek letters, etc., where necessary
identify phonetic symbols, e.g. ɑ/a, ɡ/g, ː/: (see appendix 4)
identify superscripts, subscripts where not clear in typescript and diagrams. Say whether they should be aligned or staggered if superscripts and subscripts appear together
mark up bold

* warn production department of any unusual characters that typesetter may not have in stock; see whether something else could be used instead. If not, make it clear exactly what is wanted, and say whether each unusual character is used more than once or twice and if so whether it occurs throughout or only in one or two sections (2.1.1)

Numbered or lettered paragraphs

are cross-references unambiguous? (6.4)

if numbers or letters are necessary, they should be consistently with or without parentheses, and preferably not with closing parenthesis only

similar kinds of paragraph should have similar indention (3.5):

2. xxx	*or*	2. xxxx
xxxxxxx		xxxx

Breaks in text where no subheading (3.5.5)

mark each ⊃—

if spacing between paragraphs is erratic, say 'extra space only where marked'

where large spaces have no significance, draw line across them

Books with offprints (12.1)

each paper should probably start on a right-hand page

if notes and references are to be printed at end of each paper, put copy with individual papers

acknowledgements must be within paper

figure and table numbering usually starts afresh in each paper. Give number of figures and tables on first folio of each paper, and put caption copy with paper

illustrations and caption copy should be identified by contributor's name if numbered separately

if plates are in one group, try to arrange it so that plates from different papers are not printed on the same leaf

provide copy for offprint line

Design specification

copy sent with typescript should be amended in a contrasting colour where necessary and identified as the copy to be followed. Any specimen pages should be amended throughout, if necessary

Copyright (3.7)
check that all sources (quotations, tables, line drawings and halftones) are
acknowledged, and that acknowledgements comply with copyright holder's stipulations about wording, position of acknowledgements, etc.

Author's argument
errors of fact (names, dates etc.)
inconsistencies and contradictions in author's argument
? is level of language appropriate to readership
obscure, misleading or ambiguous sentences
non sequiturs
mixed metaphors
grammar, and punctuation for grammar (see also Punctuation below)
paragraphing
libel (3.1)
bias and parochialisms (6.2; see also below)
safety (3.1.4, 6.13)

HOUSE STYLE (6)

(*not* to be implemented in book, article and journal titles, or in quotations
except author's own translations)
stet first occurrence (in text, notes and prelims) of optional spellings and of
departures from normal style
mark abbreviations (6.1), sources, etc. to be spaced or closed up according to
your house style

Abbreviations (6.1)
? unfamiliar ones explained in list in prelims or at first occurrence
? consistent, e.g. % or per cent
? consistent in use of capitals or small capitals
? consistent in omission or inclusion of points in USA etc.
in British-style books remove points in St and other contractions that
include last letter of singular
consistent inclusion/omission of commas with 'i.e.', 'e.g.', 'etc.'
avoid 'l.' (line) if lining figures used

Bias and parochialisms (6.2)

watch out for bias and stereotypes

change 'this country' etc.; spell out abbreviations likely to be unfamiliar to overseas readers

Capitalization (6.3)

mark all capitals where confusion is possible

mark all small capitals (if available), e.g. for complete words, vol. nos., abbreviations where appropriate (e.g. AD, BC), except where lining figures are used

? capitalization of special terms consistent

Cross-references (6.4)

check chapter, section, table, figure, equation numbers; change roman to arabic where necessary

consistently capital/l.c., abbreviated or not

above, below rather than *supra, infra*

change folio numbers to two or three zeros or bullets so that author and proofreader pick them up at proof stage; rewrite folio numbers in the margin

if footnotes to be numbered by page, change reference to footnote from 'n. 61' to 'p. 000, n. 0'

Dates (6.5.1)

consistent style. Avoid arabic numbers for months, even in footnotes, as 1.4.91 means 1 April in Britain, 4 January in USA

change 'two years ago' to actual year

Italic (6.7)

check that correctly and consistently used

plural 's' italic, possessive 's' roman

Numbers, units, etc. (6.10)

spelling-out, elision (but see section 6.10.7 for quantities that should not be elided)

comma or space to indicate thousands

change decimal comma to point; say whether decimal points are to be low or centred

remove point and plural 's' after abbreviated units

add zero before decimal point if no digit there at present, except in levels of
probability and ballistics

Punctuation (6.12)
hyphenation
stet hyphens at end of typed lines, where appropriate
mark spaced en rules for parenthetical dashes
mark any (unspaced) en rules needed for sense, e.g. 'input–output ratio'
punctuation with closing quote (11.1)
possessives, e.g. Thomas' or Thomas's
comma at end of clause if one at beginning, and vice versa

Spelling (6.14)
correct spelling errors
stet first occurrence (in text, notes and prelims) of optional or US spellings
make use of accents consistent. Tell typesetter if accents needed on French
capitals; no accent on French capital A unless author particularly wants it
mark oe ligatures in French, if required; ae ligatures in Old English. Tell
typesetter if they are needed
check spelling of proper names, especially those which have two accepted
forms. Is author consistent in use of native/anglicized forms?
consistent use of ü/ue etc. where appropriate

PRELIMINARY PAGES (7)

(for reprints and new editions see 15.3; for works in more than one volume
12.2)
see that copy is complete (i.e. *all* wording supplied) and that order of items
is clear. If one item is not available, give approximate length, or exact
length if prelims are to be paginated in arabic with the text
* mark fresh pages and rectos
say where arabic pagination to begin

Half-title (7.1)
list of preliminary matter for typesetter if not all items are in contents list
(e.g. series list, dedication, epigraph)
provide series wording if necessary; are series editors etc. still the same?

Verso of half-title (7.2)

? list of books in series, or author's other books, needed. Provide up-to-date
version

Frontispiece (7.3)

provide illustration and caption

Title page (7.4)

title, author's name and qualifications or affiliation should be as on any brief
for the jacket or cover

Verso of title page (7.5)

check copyright notice: ? right owner and date(s). Should it be qualified or
omitted?
? notice about performing rights
publication history
publisher's and printer's names and addresses
insert CIP data and/or Library of Congress catalogue card number if
required
? is ISBN correct

Dedication and epigraph (7.6)

? which page

All lists

remove 'list of' from heading
put 'o' opposite first item
delete point at end of each item

Contents list (7.7)

? complete (e.g. preliminary matter and index included)
? too full; query if more than first grade of subheading included
? not full enough
check that it tallies in numbering (preferably arabic), wording, spelling, capitalization (where appropriate), hyphenation and order with prelims and
text
† mark up for style

List(s) of illustrations (7.9)
? necessary
? tally with captions, but each contains minimum necessary for its purpose

List of tables (7.10)
? necessary
check against table headings

Preface (7.11)
add initials and date if your house style
if series preface or note to reader, does it apply fully to this volume?

Acknowledgements (7.12)
? available and complete

List of abbreviations (7.13)
? needed
check coverage
check order, and use of italic and points

Other preliminary matter (7.14)
? note on notation, system of transliteration, etc., needed

RUNNING HEADS (9.2)

make sure each running head will fit across page
say whether capital initial for all significant words or only for first word and proper names
say whether typesetter is to use new or old section title if new section starts below top of page; if more than one new section, should first or last be used?
supply list if contents list cannot be followed exactly, e.g. if short forms needed or quotes round words italicized in the text
if first section title does not come at beginning of chapter, give chapter title as first right-hand running head

SUBHEADINGS (9.3)

* ? too many grades
check numbering system; is it helpful?

  * code each grade
    mark capitals in u. and l.c. headings
    no full point if broken off, ? full point if run on
  * take marginal headings into type area
    add quotes to words or phrases usually distinguished by italic, if necessary

FOOTNOTES AND ENDNOTES
(9.4; see also 'References in notes', p. 386)

? are notes full enough/too full
check that all notes have text reference and vice versa
number throughout chapter if endnotes or if footnotes that are not to be
    numbered by page; if already numbered throughout chapter, check that
    complete sequence with no gaps or additional numbers
move text indicators to break in sense, where appropriate

Footnotes

? too long; if so, can they be moved into text?
† tell typesetter whether a footnote that runs over on to another page should
    have a rule or 'continued' line to divide it from the text on the second page
say on half-title where footnote copy can be found

Endnotes

running heads should be 'Notes to pages 000–0'

TABLES (9.5)

? are they useful; would they be better as graphs?
  * indicate extent of table and notes if not clear in typescript
    mark approximate positions in margin, if separate in typescript
    if some have titles, should they all?
    check numbering. Unless there are very few, all tables over 4–5 lines should
      be numbered in case they have to be moved
    in text change 'as follows' to 'as in table 5'
    if table of over 4–5 lines is in middle of paragraph, mark text to run on
    show where horizontal rules should be inserted
    check length of spanner rules
    identify any vertical rules that are essential
    check that table and column headings include *minimum* necessary wording,
      and that units are identified

check totals and any other figures that can be cross-checked; do spans overlap?

add zero before decimal point if no digit there at present, except in levels of
probability and ballistics

change decimal comma to point

comma or space to indicate thousands, including four-digit numbers where
these need to align with five-digit ones

delete full point at end of item

replace ditto marks as appropriate

? are source and date given for data

? has permission been obtained, if necessary

see that table notes are consistent, keyed differently from footnotes or endnotes

† say whether setting may be unjustified in narrow columns

† say whether turnovers flush left or indented (and, if indented, how much)

say how items in column should be aligned: flush left in each column, or
decimal point or units aligned

Large tables (9.5.3)

if it occupies more than one folio, make clear how it runs on (sideways or
downwards)

if too big for a page, where can it be split?

† give instructions about 'continued' lines for table titles and column headings, and about placing of any notes with indicators in the table

NUMBERED OR UNNUMBERED LISTS (3.5)

? are these laid out clearly for the reader and identified for the typesetter

† mark indention scheme

? are any numbering/lettering systems helpful and consistent

? are any cross-references to items unambiguous

OTHER TABULATED MATERIAL

punctuation at the end of broken-off phrases should, within reason, be
consistent (or consistently omitted)

replace ditto marks (6.15)

do not use small type if this would imply that displayed material was quoted
from elsewhere

APPENDIXES (9.6)

* mark fresh page or run on
* mark small type for whole or part of appendix, where applicable

GLOSSARY (9.7)

should one be compiled?
check alphabetical order, use of italic, punctuation. Avoid (or explain) use of foreign alphabetical order
check that essential terms are included

INDEX (8; see also fuller checklist in 8.1)

is coverage satisfactory?
check that entries are concise but informative
check alphabetical order of entries
check order and punctuation of subentries and sub-subentries. Should they be run on or broken off?
check cross-references. Information in one place, with cross-reference in the other (or in both if few page references). Never half in each place
check capitalization and use of italic
elide pairs of numbers
check consistency of references to notes
† say whether and where 'continued' lines should be inserted
† say how much turnover lines and broken-off subentries should be indented

Author index cum list of references (10.2.3, 8.3.4)

? add cross-references from second etc. authors
? have '*et al.*' authors been indexed

JACKET/COVER COPY (3.9)

? accurate and complete: e.g. book title, author and affiliation, series title, blurb, illustration and credit, ISBN, bar code, publisher's name, price

BIBLIOGRAPHICAL REFERENCES (10)

References in text

author–date system (10.2): check names and dates against list of references, make use of &/and consistent, also use of *et al.*, punctuation between name and date, between two references, between date and page number: a in 1960a to be consistently roman or italic

numbered references (10.3, 10.4): check complete sequence of numbers

* should numbers be in parentheses or square brackets to distinguish them from superscripts used in the text?

References in notes

? consistent system for first and subsequent mentions

check wording, spelling, capitalization, date, etc., against bibliography; standardize capitalization system unless good reason for not doing so.

remove *op. cit.*, *loc. cit.* except soon after full citation, substituting short title where necessary

ibid. etc. consistently italic or roman, preferably not followed by comma, to avoid double punctuation

? *ibid.* correctly used

do not try to make Command Paper abbreviations consistent

standardize punctuation, use of vol. and p.; use pp. if referring to more than one page. Close f., ff. up to number

mark roman volume numbers (but not page numbers) to be small capitals (if available), except where lining figures are used

mark space in 'p.33' etc. if none in typescript

mark sources such as IV. ix. 6, 6.4 to be consistently closed up or spaced

standardize use of parentheses

? are abbreviations (e.g. for documents, journals) explained somewhere, if necessary

Bibliography or list of references

? is bibliography easy to use or subdivided too much

check alphabetical order of authors, order of publications by one author, pair of authors, etc.

check convention for titles by same author: usually indention where author(s) exactly the same, repeat names where any change

check completeness, order, punctuation within each item. If text references are 'Smith 1960', date should follow immediately after author's name

mark italic and capitalization

are quotes consistently included/omitted round article titles?

check consistency of abbreviations

mark arabic volume numbers for journals to be bold (where appropriate)

mark roman volume numbers to be small capitals (if available) except with lining figures

are publication places consistently anglicized/not anglicized? Should native names be followed by English name in square brackets?

? too many publication places given

? publishers' names consistent in style, except where name has changed

† mark indention of turnovers

LITERARY MATERIAL (11)

Quotations (11.1)

spot-check for accuracy

check all items that are quoted twice (i.e. phrases from a longer quoted passage) for consistency

double to single quotes

square brackets for editorial interpolations

punctuation to introduce quotation, and position of punctuation with closing quotes

ellipses: ? standardize number of points (usually three) plus full point if required

check that all quotations have sources, and that sources are placed in best position

spot-check sources for accuracy; are right number of lines given (e.g. four lines not called 101–5)?

Displayed quotations

* mark any quotations that are to be distinguished from main text by indention or use of small type

mark following line of main text full out or new paragraph

should first line of displayed quotations start full out or indented?

remove quotes from beginning and end of quotations set in small type. (? Retain quotes if quotations are to be indented text type)

punctuation at the end changed to fit surrounding sentence, e.g. so that sentence does not end with a comma

Poetry (11.2)

mark 'prose' or 'verse' if not obvious, e.g. Latin verse with no capitals for
    new lines, German prose with capitalized nouns starting lines

make sure that stanza breaks are clear

† give instruction about turnover lines

Plays (11.3)

see that stage directions, and names within them, are consistent in style and
    punctuation

make speech prefixes consistent in form of name, punctuation, etc.

? do all characters enter/exit as appropriate

? is alignment of beginning of speech in middle of verse line clear

see that act and scene nos. placed correctly and punctuated consistently

SCIENCE AND MATHEMATICS (13)

identify Greek, script and bold letters. Differentiate between roman and
    italic within maths and chemistry, and mark italic in running text

identify letter l/arabic one, roman one/capital I, capital O/zero, x/multi-
    plication sign, en rule/em rule/minus; clarify confusion between mathe-
    matical signs, letters, etc., e.g. ϕ and $\emptyset$, $\in$ and ϵ. (See fuller list in section
    13.2.4)

identify multiplication points and say whether to be centred or low

identify superscripts, subscripts, where not clear in copy. Say whether they
    should be aligned or staggered if superscripts and subscripts appear
    together

check numbering and punctuation of equations. Move equation numbers
    from left to right, if appropriate

add brace and centre equation number if one is necessary to make clear that
    group of equations shares one number

check correct sequence of brackets

convert units to SI where possible, or give SI equivalent

? system of solidi/indices for units consistent

spacing between number and unit symbol(s)

spaces/commas for thousands

? abbreviations, for both special terms and units, consistent

spelling-out of numbers

two-line fractions in running text changed to one-line where possible. See
    that brackets are inserted where necessary, and that sequence of brackets
    is correct

? change exponential 'e' to 'exp' where appropriate

mark inclusion/omission of vinculum with square roots, adding parentheses where necessary

† say whether limits must be set below and above characters or may be set beside them.

Chemistry (13.6)

? spell out abbreviations for elements and compounds

mark en rules, em rules, bonds etc.

mark small caps. for M (molarity), L and D (laevo, dextro)

? italicization and hyphenation of prefixes in names of chemical compounds consistent

? artwork needed for structural formulae. ? simplification possible

Biology and medicine (13.5, 13.9)

check abbreviation/spelling-out and italicization of generic and specific names, italicization of genes, capitalization for trade names of drugs

? strains of organisms used in experiments always typed in the same form

watch out for capitalization in common names

ILLUSTRATIONS (4)

? are illustrations appropriate to the nature and level of the text

ask author to confirm that safety aspects have been double-checked

? has permission been obtained to reproduce any borrowed illustrations

check that content is consistent with text and captions

separate illustrations from the text

check that originals are complete, and clearly and correctly identified; all illustrations should be numbered for identification, even if numbers not to be printed; folio numbers may be used for unnumbered figures

mark approximate position of text illustrations in margin (provide list of folio numbers if illustrations are few or localized). For a book requiring a paste-up, see that a duplicate of this information is provided if necessary

Captions (4.1.1)

provide separate list of captions

check sources correctly acknowledged

points consistently included or omitted after illustration number and at end of caption

ring illustration number if not to be printed

first page of each group of illustrations that is to be printed separately from the text should be labelled 'facing p. 000' below the caption if there is no list of illustrations in prelims

† say whether each caption is to be the same width as the illustration (if so, give the width of each one) or text measure; also whether turnover lines are to start flush left, to be indented or to be centred

All diagrams (4.2)
ring any figures included in text; make copy for artist when necessary
see that roughs are intelligible
provide notes for artist
see that lettering is consistent with the text
if using author's lettering, will this be legible after reduction?
† if diagrams to be relettered, ask for lettering to match the text, e.g. not sans serif, not upright Greek capitals if sloping ones used in text
provide a list of lettering if complicated and handwritten on rough

Maps (4.3)
see that author has provided typed list of place names with separate columns for towns etc., or compile one yourself; check spelling and coverage against text

Graphs (4.4)
see that axes are adequately and consistently labelled. The labels of vertical axes should read upwards

Halftones (4.5)
see that top is identified, scale provided and masking indicated if necessary

REPRINTS (15)

Text and illustrations
* get corrections from author, corrections file and reviews file. Are all corrections necessary? Will they fit into the available space?
mark corrections, in style consistent with rest of book, on a photocopy of the relevant pages from the latest printing
make consequent changes, e.g. in cross-references, index

Preliminary pages (15.3)
update series list, ? series editors

? update author's/contributors' appointments

update publisher's address(es)

update printing history

check ISBN, ? add one for paperback; change 'cloth' to 'hardback' or 'hard covers' where appropriate

change page numbers if something has been added or material has been squeezed up

add any additional material to contents list and alter page numbers where necessary

Jacket/cover

add review quotes

is ISBN correct and complete?

update information about author

update series list

? new back copy for jacket

if new illustration or design, check that new credit given

change price(s) if necessary

? new bar code needed

NEW EDITIONS (15)

Text and Illustrations

find out whether book is to be reset

* see that all corrections in corrections file are included, provided author agrees with them

see that new and existing material is consistent

obtain permission for (both new and old) copyright material

if numbering of illustrations etc. changed, correct all cross-references

arrange for revision of index

Preliminary pages (15.3)

update series list, ? series editors

update author's/contributors' appointments

add '[Second] edition' to title page

update publisher's address(es)

add new copyright date

add new ISBN (followed by ISBN for previous edition)

add new CIP data, if required

update printing history

see that contents list and other lists are complete and tally with text

should be a preface explaining how new edition differs from old (if this is not self-evident). Alter title of old one to 'Preface to the [first] edition' in heading, running heads and contents list

Jacket/cover

update blurb, add review quotes of earlier edition

see '[Second] edition' is on front and spine

substitute new ISBN, bar code

update information about author

update series list

? new back copy for jacket

new price(s)

PROOF STAGE (5)

(This section does not cover proofreading; for that see 5.1, 5.2.)

? proof complete

? any late material, such as index, foreword or acknowledgements list, now available. If not, chase it

? pages numbered correctly; are ringed page nos. included on pages that will have no printed page numbers?

? running heads correct; have correct page nos. been inserted in running heads such as 'Notes to pages 000–0'?

collate author's proof with any proofreader's proof

? corrections legible, unambiguous and correct, e.g. insertion marks correctly placed (5.2, 5.5, appendix 13)

? corrections consistent in style with rest of book

? all corrections essential

minimize cost of corrections by adjustment where possible, if author agrees (5.3)

warn author if likely to exceed correction allowance

see that corrections are correctly colour-coded (5.4)

check that all queries have been answered

see that something has been done about overmatter, short pages

check that all cross-references have been completed

note any changes that will affect index, e.g. spelling of proper names, material moved from one page to another

? any turned material correctly orientated (foot at right-hand side)

delete any running heads on turned pages

? footnotes correctly placed on short pages
? note to designer: e.g. page nos. for design problems; illustrations needing correction, resizing or better position; where index should start; position of separately printed illustrations
? note to production dept: e.g. request for further revise; large corrections for which you think typesetter should pay; persistent typesetting faults
? any offprint lines included and correct
write to author after dealing with proofs, describing any changes made by you and saying what happens next

Half-title and verso
check book title, series title, series editors, list of other books
? recent changes in series editors, titles of books in production

Title page
? book title, subtitle, author's name and qualifications or affiliation correct and consistent with jacket/cover
? should a translator or artist be mentioned
? '[Second] edition' etc. needed
check publisher's name, symbol, address

Verso of title page
? publisher's addresses correct
? copyright holder(s) and date(s) complete and correct
? publication date correct
? any earlier publishing history complete and correct
check and insert CIP data, Library of Congress catalogue card number if required
? ISBN(s) complete and correct; has a paperback been decided on or cancelled since copy-editing stage?
? notice about performing rights etc. needed
? printer's name and address correct; it must include name of country

Contents list
? page nos. correctly inserted
? other preliminary material correctly inserted
check headings against text for discrepancies in wording, capitalization, punctuation, etc.
check chapter titles against subheadings in endnotes
make sure index and its page number have been included

if more than one index, see that titles are given correctly and in the right
order

if no list of illustrations, position of a general map or separately printed
halftones should perhaps be included

Lists of illustrations, etc.

? page nos. correctly inserted

Illustrations

? none missing

if not yet included, make sure position of all is marked

give designer list of illustrations that need correction or other attention

if typesetter will not be able to make corrections, give designer the artwork
and a photocopy showing the corrections, to send to artist

? scales and magnifications OK

? halftones the right way round and with the right caption

Separately printed halftones

? have they been proofed

? where will they be bound in

insert 'facing p. 000' at foot of first page of batch, if position not given in list
of illustrations or contents list

Paste-up

check that corrections on marked proof will not affect layout

transfer corrections from paste-up to marked proof

Index proof

see that corrections are clear

? any entries still without page refs. or personal initials

check page no. of first page against contents list

check that correct 'continued' lines included

Revised proof

check that all corrections marked on earlier proof have been carried out
accurately

answer any queries

recheck half-title, title page, verso of title page

check that correct page no. inserted in contents for index and any other late
material

Camera-ready copy (5.7)

mark any corrections on a photocopy, not on the c.r.c. itself

check that all earlier corrections have been made

recheck half-title, title page, verso of title page

? complete

? unnumbered pages are in correct position

? halftones the right way round

Jacket/cover proof (5.8)

check book title, author's name and qualifications or affiliation, series title,
   etc., against prelim proof

check consistency of caps./l.c. in title and subtitle everywhere

check blurb for accuracy, consistent style

check any contents list against the prelims

? correct credit for any pictures included

? credit for jacket/cover design included

? ISBN correct

? bar code included

? does spine wording read in right direction

jacket must state country in which printed

Proof of spine wording for blocking die

? author's name correct

? title correct

? name of publisher correct

? all in correct position

Appendix 2
Book sizes

	Trimmed page size in millimetres	Untrimmed page size/board size in millimetres	Trimmed size equivalent in inches (to nearest $\frac{1}{16}$)
Standard sizes			
Metric crown octavo	186 × 123	192 × 126	$7\frac{5}{16} \times 4\frac{7}{8}$
Metric crown quarto	246 × 189	252 × 192	$9\frac{11}{16} \times 7\frac{7}{16}$
Metric large crown octavo	198 × 129	204 × 132	$7\frac{13}{16} \times 5\frac{1}{16}$
Metric demy octavo	216 × 138	222 × 141	$8\frac{1}{2} \times 5\frac{7}{16}$
Metric demy quarto	276 × 219	282 × 222	$10\frac{7}{8} \times 8\frac{5}{8}$
Metric royal octavo	234 × 156	240 × 159	$9\frac{1}{4} \times 6\frac{3}{16}$
Metric royal quarto	312 × 237	318 × 240	$12\frac{3}{8} \times 9\frac{3}{8}$
A5	210 × 148	216 × 151	$8\frac{1}{4} \times 5\frac{13}{16}$
A4	297 × 210	303 × 213	$11\frac{5}{8} \times 8\frac{1}{4}$

Appendix 3
Abbreviations for states in the USA

For completeness, the list includes US overseas territories.

The two-letter abbreviations in the third column are those specified by the US government for use with zip-code addresses.

Alabama	Ala.	AL
Alaska		AK
American Samoa	Amer. Samoa	AS
Arizona	Ariz.	AZ
Arkansas	Ark.	AR
California	Calif.	CA
Canal Zone	C.Z.	CZ
Colorado	Colo.	CO
Connecticut	Conn.	CT
Delaware	Del.	DE
District of Columbia	D.C.	DC
Florida	Fla.	FL
Georgia	Ga.	GA
Guam		GU
Hawaii		HI
Idaho		ID
Illinois	Ill.	IL
Indiana	Ind.	IN
Iowa		IA
Kansas	Kans.	KS
Kentucky	Ky.	KY
Louisiana	La.	LA
Maine		ME
Maryland	Md.	MD
Massachusetts	Mass.	MA
Michigan	Mich.	MI
Minnesota	Minn.	MN
Mississippi	Miss.	MS
Missouri	Mo.	MO
Montana	Mont.	MT
Nebraska	Nebr.	NE

Nevada	Nev.	NV
New Hampshire	N.H.	NH
New Jersey	N.J.	NJ
New Mexico	N.Mex., N.M.	NM
New York	N.Y.	NY
North Carolina	N.C.	NC
North Dakota	N.Dak., N.D.	ND
Ohio		OH
Oklahoma	Okla.	OK
Oregon	Oreg.	OR
Pennsylvania	Pa., Penn., Penna.	PA
Puerto Rico	P.R.	PR
Rhode Island	R.I.	RI
South Carolina	S.C.	SC
South Dakota	S.Dak., S.D.	SD
Tennessee	Tenn.	TN
Texas	Tex.	TX
Utah		UT
Vermont	Vt.	VT
Virginia	Va.	VA
Virgin Islands	V.I.	VI
Washington	Wash.	WA
West Virginia	W.Va.	WV
Wisconsin	Wis.	WI
Wyoming	Wyo.	WY

Appendix 4
Phonetic symbols

The following table shows the most commonly used phonetic symbols and diacritics, including those from the 1989 revision of the International Phonetic Alphabet. When phonetic characters in a typescript are not clear, it is often helpful to send the typesetter a photocopy of this table, ringing the symbols used by the author and identifying them by the reference numbers in the table. Diacritics (14d to 17j inclusive, below) can appear in varying positions in relation to the phonetic symbol. It must be clear to the typesetter what the correct position is in each case. Symbols 5f and 11g are currently recommended for two sounds for which an alternative pair of symbols 5e and 8j are sometimes used. Only one pair of symbols should be used (5f and 11g *or* 5e and 8j).

	a	b	c	d	e	f	g	h	j
1	a	ɐ	ɑ	ɒ	æ	ʌ	ɓ	ɓ	ʙ
2	β	c	ɕ	č	ç	ҫ	ƈ	d	ɗ
3	ɖ	dʒ	ð	e	ɔ	ɛ	ʒ	f	ɡ
4	ɠ	ɢ	ɢ	ɣ	ɤ	h	ħ	ɦ	ɧ
5	ɥ	ʜ	i	ɨ	ɪ	ɪ	j	ʝ	ǰ
6	ɟ	ʃ	k	ƙ	l	ɬ	ɫ	l	ʟ
7	ƛ	m	ɱ	ɯ	ɰ	n	ɲ	ŋ	ɳ
8	ɴ	o	⊙	θ	ø	œ	ɶ	ɔ	ω
9	p	ƥ	ɸ	q	ɗ	r	ɾ	ʈ	ɹ
10	ɺ	ʀ	ʁ	s	š	ʂ	ʃ	t	ƫ
11	ʈ	ʧ	ɿ	θ	u	ʉ	ʊ	v	ʋ
12	w	ʍ	x	χ	y	ʎ	ɣ	z	ž
13	z	ʐ	ʒ	ʔ	ʡ	ʝ	ʕ	ʖ	|
14	ǂ	‖	!	ǀ	ˈ	̆		⊥	⊤	⊢
15	⊣	ʼ	¯	`	´	˵	˶	ˇ	ˆ
16	´	`	↑	↓	~	¨	ˌ	ˌ	ˑ
17	˷	□	˥	˩	ˍ	+	×	›	‹

Source: International Phonetic Association.

Appendix 5
The Russian alphabet

				Trans-literation					Trans-literation
А	*A*	а	*a*	a	Р	*P*	р	*p*	r
Б	*Б*	б	*б*	b	С	*C*	с	*c*	s
В	*В*	в	*в*	v	Т	*T*	т	*m*	t
Г	*Г*	г	*г*	g	У	*У*	у	*y*	u
Д	*Д*	д	*д*	d	Ф	*Ф*	ф	*ф*	f
Е (Ё)	*E (Ё)*	е (ё)	*е (ё)*	e (ё)	Х	*X*	х	*x*	x or kh
Ж	*Ж*	ж	*ж*	ž or zh	Ц	*Ц*	ц	*ц*	c or ts
З	*З*	з	*з*	z	Ч	*Ч*	ч	*ч*	č or ch
И	*И*	и	*и*	i	Ш	*Ш*	ш	*ш*	š or sh
Й	*Й*	й	*й*	j or ĭ	Щ	*Щ*	щ	*щ*	šč or shch
К	*К*	к	*к*	k	Ъ	*Ъ*	ъ	*ъ*	`` or ″
Л	*Л*	л	*л*	l	Ы	*Ы*	ы	*ы*	y
М	*M*	м	*м*	m	Ь	*Ь*	ь	*ь*	` or ′
Н	*Н*	н	*н*	n	Э	*Э*	э	*э*	ė or é
О	*О*	о	*о*	o	Ю	*Ю*	ю	*ю*	ju or yu
П	*П*	п	*п*	p	Я	*Я*	я	*я*	ja or ya

The use of a prime ′ rather than an apostrophe avoids confusion with a closing quotation mark.

Appendix **6**
Old English and Middle English letters

Name	l.c.	Capital	Approx. sound	Remarks
ash	æ	Æ	h*a*t	There are two forms of italic lower-case ash – *æ* and *œ*. The former is preferable, but it does not usually matter, provided the typesetter is consistent
eth	ð	Ð	*th*is	But used interchangeably in OE and ME
thorn	þ or þ	Þ	*th*in	Typesetters sometimes read thorn as *p*, so identify them if they are rare or look like *p*
wynn	ρ	Þ	*w*ynn	But *w* more often used in printed texts, to avoid confusion with thorn
yogh	ȝ	ȝ		In OE usually printed as *g*. In ME both yogh and *g* were used, *g* being equivalent to the stop (*get, go*) and yogh being used for the sounds *y* (*ȝeer* 'year') and *h*, or rather *gh* (*kniȝt* from OE *cniht*). (Yogh sometimes appears in ME texts as a scribal error for *z*, e.g. *ȝeferus* = 'Zephyrus'.)

7 is used in OE as an ampersand. In a text there would need to be a capital version (7) as well as a lower-case one (7), but in quotations one form is used throughout, to save expense.

Appendix **7**
French and German bibliographical terms and abbreviations

FRENCH

Abbreviation	Full form	Meaning
ap(r). J.-C.	après Jésus-Christ	AD
av. J.-C.	avant Jésus-Christ	BC
c.-à-d.	c'est-à-dire	that is to say
ch(ap).	chapitre	chapter
Comptes Rend.	Comptes Rendus	Proceedings
conf.	confer (Lat.)	compare
exempl.	exemplaire	copy (of a printed work)
inéd.	inédit	unpublished
in pl.	in plano (Lat.)	broadsheet, flysheet
l. c.	loc. cit. (Lat.)	in the place cited (*not* lower case)
liv.	livre	book (usually in the sense of a division of a volume)
m. à m.	mot à mot	word for word, *sic*
p. e.	par exemple	for example
pl.	planche	full-page illustration
rel.	relié	bound
s. d.	sans date	no date (of publication)
s. l.	sans lieu	no place (of publication)
sq. (sqq.)	sequens (Lat.)	following
s. (ss.) suiv. }	suivant	following
t., tom.	tome	book – may be a volume or a division of a single volume
v.	voyez, voir	see
vol.	volume	volume

GERMAN

Abbreviation	Full form	Meaning
a. a. O.	am angeführten Ort	loc. cit.
Abb.	Abbildung	fig.
Abt.	Abteilung	part, section
Anm.	Anmerkung	note
Aufl.	Auflage ⎫	edition
Ausg.	Ausgabe ⎬	
Bd., Bde.	Band, Bände	vol., vols.
bes.	besonders	especially
Bl.	Blatt	leaf or perhaps fascicle
br., brosch.	broschiert	sewn, in pamphlet form
bzw.	beziehungsweise	respectively, or
ca.	circa	circa, about
d. h.	das heißt	that is to say, viz
d. i.	das ist	that is
ebd.	ebendaselbst ⎫	ibid.
	ebenda ⎬	
Erg. Bd.	Ergänzungsband	supplementary volume
Evg.	Evangelium	gospel
geh.	geheftet	sewn, in fascicle form
Hft.	Heft	part
hrsg.	herausgegeben	edited by
Hs., Hss.	Handschrift, Handschriften	MS, MSS
K., Kap.	Kapitel	chapter
Lfg.	Lieferung	instalment, issue, part, etc.
m. E.	meines Erachtens	in my opinion
m. W.	meines Wissens	as far as I know
n. Chr.	nach Christus	AD
Nr.	Nummer	no., number
o.	oben	above
o. ä.	oder ähnlich	or something similar
o. J.	ohne Jahr	no date (of publication)
o. O.	ohne Ort	no place (of publication)
R.	Reihe	series
s.	siehe	see
S.	Seite	page, p., or pp.
SA	Sonderabdruck	offprint
s. a.	siehe auch	see also

German (*cont.*)

Abbreviation	Full form	Meaning
s. o.	siehe oben	see above
sog.	sogenannt	so-called
s. u.	siehe unten	see below
u. a.	unter andern	among others
u. ä.	und ähnlich ⎫	and such like, and so on
u. ä. m.	und ähnliches mehr ⎭	
u. s. f.	und so fort ⎫	etc.
usw.	und so weiter ⎭	
V.	Vers, Verse	verse, verses
v. Chr.	vor Christus	BC
verb.	verbessert	revised
Verf., Vf.	Verfasser	author
vgl.	vergleiche	cf.
z. B.	zum Beispiel	e.g
z. T.	zum Teil	in part

Other bibliographical terms

Abhandlung(en)	article, essay or transactions (of a learned society)
Auswahl, ausgewählt	selection, selected
Beiheft	supplement
gesammelte Werke	collected works
Herausgeber, herausgegeben von	editor, edited by
Teil	part
Übersetzung, übersetzt von	translation, translated by
Verlag, im Verlag von	publication or publishing house, published by
Verlagsrecht	copyright
Zeitschrift	journal

Appendix **8**
Mathematical symbols

Symbol	Description
′	Prime
″	Double prime
( )	Parentheses
[ ]	Brackets
{ }	Braces
⟨ ⟩	Angle brackets
⟦ ⟧	Open brackets
∞	Infinity
∝	Proportional to
°	Degree
!	Factorial sign
| |	Modulus
‖ ‖	Norm
‖	Parallel to
⊥	Perpendicular to
⩾	Greater than or equal to
⩾̸	Not greater than or equal to
>	Greater than
≯	Not greater than
≫	Much greater than
⋙̸	Not much greater than
⪌	Greater than or less than
≻	Has a higher rank or order
⊀	Has not a lower rank or order
⩽	Less than or equal to
⪇	Not less than or equal to
<	Less than
≮	Not less than
≪	Much less than
⋘̸	Not much less than
⪋	Less than or greater than
±	Plus or minus
⊕	Direct sum

Appendix **8**

Symbol	Description
$\mp$	Minus or plus
$=$	Equal to
$\neq$	Not equal to
$\cong$	Equal or nearly equal to / isomorphic to
$\approx$	Approximately equal to
$\equiv$	Identically equal to
$\sim$	Equivalent to / of the order of
$\nsim$	Not equivalent to / not of the order of
$\simeq$	Asymptotic to
$\not\simeq$	Not asymptotic to
$/$	Solidus
$\div$	Divide
$\nmid$	Does not divide
$\times$	Multiplication
$\otimes$	Direct multiplication
$\backslash$	Set difference
$\Rightarrow$	Implies
$\Leftarrow$	Implied by
$\Leftrightarrow$	Double implication
$\longleftrightarrow$	Double arrow
$\Rrightarrow$	Converges to
$\longrightarrow$	Tends to the limit
$\leftrightarrow$	Does not tend to
$\uparrow$	Tends up to the limit
$\downarrow$	Tends down to the limit
$\vec{A}$	Arrow over letter
$\tilde{A}$	Tilde over letter
$\hat{A}$	Hat over letter
$\bar{A}$	Bar over letter
$\leqslant$	Contained in, or equal to
$\subset$	Strict inclusion
$\nsubseteq$	Not contained in
$\subseteq$	Inclusion
$\nsubseteq$	Is not contained within
$\supset$	Contains
$\not\supset$	Does not contain
$\supseteq$	Contains
$\nsupseteq$	Does not contain

Symbol	Description
$\cap$	Intersection
$\cap$	Large intersection: $\bigcap\limits_{i=1}^{\infty}$ in display $\cap_{i=1}^{\infty}$ in text
$\cup$	Union
$\cup$	Large union: in display $\bigcup\limits_{i=1}^{\infty}$ in text $\cup_{i=1}^{n}$
$\angle$	Angle
$\sphericalangle$	Spherical angle
$\wedge$	Vector product
$\vee$	Sum of two sets
$\exists$	There exists
$\nexists$	There does not exist
$\forall$	For all
iff	If and only if
$\in$	Belongs to (is an element of)
$\notin$	Does not belong to (is not an element of)
$\varnothing$	Null set / empty set
O	Of order (used thus: $O(x)$)
o	Of lower order than (used thus: $o(x)$)
$\vdash$	Assertion sign / logical entails
$\neg$	Logical negation
$\int$	Integral sign: in display $\int_{-\infty}^{\infty}$ in text $\int_{-\infty}^{\infty}$
$\oint$	Contour integral
$\oint$	Contour integral (clockwise)
$\square$	D'Alembertian operator
$\sqrt{}$	Square root
$\sqrt[3]{}$	Cube root
$\sqrt[n]{}$	n-th root
∂	Partial differentiation
$\triangle$	Triangle
Δ	Increment or finite-difference operator
∇	Nabla or del
Π	Product sign: in display $\prod\limits_{n=1}^{\infty}$ in text $\Pi_{n=1}^{\infty}$
Σ	Summation sign: in display $\sum\limits_{n=1}^{\infty}$ in text $\Sigma_{n=1}^{\infty}$
$\aleph$	Aleph
$\wp$	Weierstrass elliptic function
$\&$	Conjunction of statements
$\circ$	Composition
$\mathcal{C}_L$	Centre line

Appendix **9**
Hebrew

These notes apply to short extracts of classical Hebrew matter (typically, biblical text) appearing as interpolations, e.g. quotations, within text primarily using non-Hebrew alphabets. Modern Hebrew uses the same characters; but slightly different conventions and nomenclature may be employed.

Hebrew, like Arabic, is written from right to left. This may cause difficulty when the Hebrew copy is broken at a line end. Continuous Hebrew words which are interrupted in the copy at a line end:

2   1

הבל הבלים

4   3

אמר קהלת

should appear as

4   3   2   1

הבל הבלים אמר קהלת

when set in the same line. A phrase appearing continuously in copy on the same line as:

5   4   3   2   1

בראשית ברא אלהים את השמים

for example, will become:

3   2   1

בראשית ברא אלהים

5   4

את השמים

when turned over in setting.

The Hebrew alphabet consists of twenty-two characters, all originally consonants. Five of these have a different form when in the final position (i.e. at the left-hand end of a word). Notice close similarities between certain characters (*beth* and *kaph*; *daleth* and *resh*; *he, heth,* and *taw*; final *mem* and *samekh*; etc.), which may present difficulties, especially when dealing with handwritten, or even printed, copy.

Three of the consonants, ה (*he*), ' (*yodh*) and ו (*waw*), came to be used also as vowels, but most vowel sounds either remain unwritten ('unpointed' text) or are rendered as modifications of the consonantal characters which precede them ('pointed' text). Hebrew words and passages may occur in print in either pointed or unpointed form. The style of pointing usually encountered is that known as Massoretic, commonly used in biblical matter, but other styles have existed and may, rarely, be required in scholarly books. Points are used to modify characters for other purposes than indicating vowels, e.g. to double, or harden, a consonantal sound. The only character that is sometimes found modified in unpointed copy is ‭ש‬ (‭שׂ‬ = *sin*; ‭שׁ‬ = *shin*).

HEBREW ALPHABET

Name	Form	Final	Transliteration	Numerical value
ʾaleph	‭א‬		ʾ	1
beth	‭ב‬		b	2
gimel	‭ג‬		g	3
daleth	‭ד‬		d	4
he	‭ה‬		h	5
waw	‭ו‬		w	6
zayin	‭ז‬		z	7
heth	‭ח‬		ḥ	8
teth	‭ט‬		ṭ	9
yodh	‭י‬		y	10
kaph	‭כ‬	‭ך‬	k	20
lamedh	‭ל‬		l	30
mem	‭מ‬	‭ם‬	m	40
nun	‭נ‬	‭ן‬	n	50
samekh	‭ס‬		s	60
ʿayin	‭ע‬		ʿ	70
pe	‭פ‬	‭ף‬	p	80
sadhe	‭צ‬	‭ץ‬	ṣ	90
qoph	‭ק‬		q	100
resh	‭ר‬		r	200
sin, shin	‭ש‬ ‭שׁ‬		ś, š	300
taw	‭ת‬		t	400

Points which may be added as modifications to the consonants are as follows:

located above the character ·
located medially, within the body of the character · : ָ
located below the base line . : ֱ ֵ — ָ ִ

Below the base line ֽ or ֑ may be combined with ַ , ֶ , or ָ

Numbers are represented in Hebrew by alphabetic characters; there are no separate numerals.

Hebrew does not make any distinction between upper and lower case. In classical Hebrew the punctuation marks most frequently encountered are the period, similar to a colon, and the hyphen, used for linking words and placed in a slightly raised position. In addition certain accentual or pause signs are very occasionally required:

located above the characters ∴ : • ı: <
located below the base line ı ʌ ҁ ɹ ɺ

Note that some of these signs are identical in form with points listed above, but when used in this role they may need to be positioned slightly differently in relation to the alphabetic characters.

A number of systems exist for transliterating Hebrew into Latin characters. A common and well-established one is shown in the accompanying table. Vowels are usually added when pointed text is given in transliterated form; the *shewa* ְ , a tonally colourless short vowel, is often indicated by a superscript lower-case ^{e}.

Words in Hebrew characters may not normally be broken or hyphenated at line ends. When transliterated words are thus broken, the hyphenation should follow the syllabic structure of the Hebrew, dividing only before a consonant.

Aramaic (the third original language of the Bible, in which passages of Ezra, Jeremiah and Daniel are written) is represented in Hebrew characters.

Appendix **10**
Arabic

The following notes are intended to provide some guidance for copy-editors unfamiliar with Arabic who have to deal with it in a typescript, whether in Arabic script or in transliterated form.

Arabic script, no matter whether it is handwritten or typeset, is a cursive one, written from right to left. Only consonants and long vowels are normally shown in the script; there are orthographic signs to represent the short vowels (see below), but they are not usually shown except in the Koran, school books, and old or difficult texts (script in which the short vowels do appear is referred to as 'vocalized'). There are no capital letters.

The table shows the twenty-eight letters in their traditional order, with their names, their various forms, and their transliteration according to two different systems: (1) a commonly used one and (2) the British Standard system (BS 4280: *Transliteration of Arabic Characters*). It will be seen from the table that there are two classes of letters:

those which can be connected both to a preceding and to a following letter; they have four possible forms
those which can be joined only to a preceding letter; they have only two possible forms

In addition to the twenty-eight letters there is a 'hybrid' letter, formed from *hā'* with the two dots of *tā'* added. ة (independent form) or ـة (joined to a preceding letter). This represents the commonest feminine ending, which is pronounced either *-a* or, in specific grammatical contexts, *-at*.

The glottal stop, *hamza*, is a sign rather than a letter. It usually has *alif*, *wāw* or *yā'* as a 'bearer'; however, it can also occur without a bearer. With or without a bearer it can take all three vowel signs, just as if it were a consonant (e.g. إنّ *'inna*).

Name	Form				Translit-eration	
	Independent	When connected to				
		Preceding letter only	Preceding and following letter	Following letter only	(1)	(2)
alif	ا	ـا				
bā'	ب	ـب	ـبـ	بـ	b	b
tā'	ت	ـت	ـتـ	تـ	t	t
thā'	ث	ـث	ـثـ	ثـ	th	ṯ
jīm	ج	ـج	ـجـ	جـ	j	ǧ
ḥā'	ح	ـح	ـحـ	حـ	ḥ	ḥ
khā'	خ	ـخ	ـخـ	خـ	kh	ḫ
dāl	د	ـد			d	d
dhāl	ذ	ـذ			dh	ḏ
rā'	ر	ـر			r	r
zā'	ز	ـز			z	z
sīn	س	ـس	ـسـ	سـ	s	š
shīn	ش	ـش	ـشـ	شـ	sh	s
ṣād	ص	ـص	ـصـ	صـ	ṣ	ṣ
ḍād	ض	ـض	ـضـ	ضـ	ḍ	ḍ
ṭā'	ط	ـط	ـطـ	طـ	ṭ	ṭ
ẓā'	ظ	ـظ	ـظـ	ظـ	ẓ	ẓ
ᶜain	ع	ـع	ـعـ	عـ	ᶜ	ᶜ
ghain	غ	ـغ	ـغـ	غـ	gh	ġ
fā'	ف	ـف	ـفـ	فـ	f	f
qāf	ق	ـق	ـقـ	قـ	q	q
kāf	ك	ـك	ـكـ	كـ	k	k
lām	ل	ـل	ـلـ	لـ	l	l
mīm	م	ـم	ـمـ	مـ	m	m
nūn	ن	ـن	ـنـ	نـ	n	n
hā'	ه	ـه	ـهـ	هـ	ḥ	ḥ
wāw	و	ـو			w	w
yā'	ي	ـي	ـيـ	يـ	y	y

VOWELS

In vocalized script

1   The *short vowels* appear (placed above or below the consonants they fol-
    low) thus:

> *a* – oblique stroke above (called *fatha*)
> *i* = oblique stroke below (called *kasra*)
> *u* = small *wāw* above (called *damma*)

Examples: كَتَبَ *kataba*; مِن *min*; رَجْل *rajul.*

2   The *long vowels* appear thus:

> *ā* = *fatha* followed by *alif*
> *ī* = *kasra* followed by *yā'*
> *ū* = *damma* followed by *wāw*

Examples: كَان *kāna*; دِين *dīn*; رَسُول *rasūl.*

In unvocalized script, *fatha*, *kasra* and *damma* are not shown, so *short vowels*
are not indicated at all; *long vowels* have only *alif*, *yā'* or *wāw* to indicate their
presence.

DIPHTHONGS

There are two diphthongs, which appear thus in vocalized script:

> يْ *'ay* or *ai*
> وْ *'aw* or *au*

In unvocalized script these are represented only by *yā'* or *wāw.*

OTHER SIGNS

The sign ˝, called *shadda*, is used to indicate doubling of a consonant, e.g.
كلّ *kull.*

The sign ˚, called *sukūn*, placed over a consonant, indicates that the consonant has no following vowel, e.g. مسْجد *masjid.*

The sign آ, called *madda* (it is *alif* surmounted by a wavy bar), is used to
represent the sequence *hamza* + short *a* + *hamza*, or *hamza* + long *ā*, e.g.
قرآن *qur'ān.*

The use of the 'dagger *alif*' is another way of writing the long vowel *ā* in
certain words, e.g. ذلك *dhālika.*

In classical Arabic a final *n*-sound (*-un*, *-an* or *-in*) denotes an indefinite noun or adjective. This is called 'nunation' or *tanwīn*, and it is denoted by doubling the vowel signs, with the addition, in the case of *a*, of an *alif* (e.g. فَرَساً *farasan*).

PUNCTUATION

Arabic uses a turned comma, a colon and a turned question mark. *Guillemets* may be used for quotation marks.

NUMERALS

Arabic numerals, unlike the script, read from left to right. They are:

0	I	2	3	4	5	6	7	8	9	10
٠	١	٢	٣	٤	٥	٦	٧	٨	٩	١٠

ARABIC QUOTATIONS

Problems may arise when run-on Arabic-script quotations appear in English text. If the quotation turns over in the typescript, thus:

the words كمـا تتكم²¹

تسمع كذلك⁴³ occur again later

it is helpful to number the Arabic words and say 'Arabic to appear 4 3 2 1 if set on one line.' Similarly if the quotation appears on one line in the typescript, thus:

the words   تسمع كذلك تتكلم كمـا⁴³²¹   occur again later

number the Arabic and say 'If Arabic turns over, set 1 / 4 3 2 or 2 1 / 4 3 or 3 2 1 / 4.'

TRANSLITERATION

Though the table shows only two systems, others do exist and may be used by authors. They should use one system consistently; but they often fail to do so, and oddities should be watched for. For example, if you find in a typescript both components of any of the following pairs:

t	and	th
ǧ	and	j
ḥ	and	kh
ḏ	and	dh
š	and	sh
ġ	and	gh

it would be as well to query whether elements from more than one system have been used.

If the British Standard system (or any other which includes underlined characters) is used, and transliterated words are to be set italic, you will need to make clear to the typesetter where both underlining and italic occur together.

Hamza is usually represented by an apostrophe (its 'bearer' being ignored); an initial *hamza* is not usually transliterated. For *'ain*, some authors use an opening quotation mark, instead of superscript 'c': in typescripts where this is the chosen style you should watch out for confusion between transliterated *'ain* and *hamza*.

The definite article, *al*, is not usually capitalized except when it occurs at the beginning of a sentence; so it is an acceptable style for book or article titles beginning with the definite article to start with lower case.

A hyphen may be used to separate two grammatically different elements within a word; for example, where an Arabic word consists of a preposition + noun/pronoun, or the conjunctions و *wa* or ف *fa* + noun/verb, the transliterated form may have a hyphen between the two. So وقال, 'and he said', is represented by *wa-qāla*.

The transliteration of modern Arabic names is complicated by the fact that such names have often acquired modified spellings. For example Najib may appear as Naguib, Husain as Hussein, while 'Abd Allah, 'Abdallah and 'Abdullah are all accepted forms of the same name.

Appendix **11**
Islamic and other calendars

ISLAMIC

The Muslim calendar is based on a lunar year of approximately 354 days, i.e. eleven days less than a solar year. The Islamic era was established by the Caliph 'Umar and takes as its starting point the flight of the Prophet Muhammad from Mecca to Medina on 16 June 622. Unlike other lunar calendars, however, the Islamic one does not intercalate a thirteenth month at calculated intervals to keep the lunar months in alignment with the seasons. Thus each Islamic month circulates through the seasons in roughly thirty-three years. There is a conversion table in J. L. Bacharach, *A Middle East Studies Handbook* (Cambridge University Press, 1984), pp. 8–15, which also provides a detailed explanation of the Islamic calendrical system, a list of the Islamic months, major festivals, etc.

One small problem not directly mentioned by Bacharach arises out of the official adoption in Iran some sixty years ago of the solar (*shamsi*) year of 365 days. Although the solar calendar continues to take the *Hijra* (or Hegira) of the Prophet as its starting point, each solar year begins in March, at the Spring Equinox, so that a conversion to AD dates involves the addition of 621 years for the first nine months of the *shamsi* year and 622 for the last three months, e.g. 1350 *shamsi* ran from March 1971 to March 1972.

If Islamic dates stand alone they should be identified, e.g. AH 1382, s. 1341. But it is best to ask the author to provide both Islamic and Western dates; and in that case it is clear from the form of the Western date which calendar is being used: 1341/1962–3, 1382/1963.

Turkey adopted the Western calendar in 1926.

CHINA

For most practical purposes the Western (or Gregorian) system has been in use in China since the foundation of the Republic in 1911, though the traditional Chinese year is still used, for example in calculating festivals. This traditional year is a lunisolar one in which an attempt is made to have a 'civil' year that keeps in step with the sun, and months that remain in step with the moon. Since neither a true lunar month nor a 'tropical' year contains a whole number of days (approx. 29.53 and 365.24 respectively), this involves some day-juggling, including the insertion every few years of an intercalary month. The Chinese New Year's Day usually falls in late January or early February – at all events never later than about 17 February.

In the absence of a commonly agreed single starting point, such as the birth of Christ or the flight of the Prophet, the expression of dates in the Chinese systems of the imperial era tends to be complicated. Two systems were used. The first involved a recurring cycle of sixty years (the sexagenary cycle), each year being designated by two characters, the first being one of the ten 'celestial stems' (*t'ien kan*) and the second one of the twelve 'earthly branches' (*ti chih*), each combination of characters occurring once every sixty years. Each of the twelve earthly branches is further associated with a symbolic animal; these animals are rat, ox, tiger, hare, dragon, serpent, horse, sheep, monkey, cock, dog and boar.

The second system – the *nien-hao* or reign-title system – comprises the name (strictly the 'throne-name') of the ruler and the number of the particular year of his reign. For the earlier emperors (down to the second century BC) no more is involved than the name of the ruler and the relevant year of his reign. From 163 BC onwards (i.e. at the height of the Former Han), the *nien-hao* system became much more complicated. Reign titles no longer necessarily corresponded with the duration of the emperor's reign or with his personal name. For ritual and astrological reasons an emperor could – and commonly did – adopt several *nien-hao* in the course of his reign, and these periods were not always the same length. This practice was particularly common in the T'ang (AD 618–906) and Sung (960–1279) dynasties. From the Ming dynasty (1368–1644) onwards through the Ch'ing (1644–1911) the *nien-hao* remained unchanged throughout a reign; for example the K'ang-Hsi period of the Ch'ing lasted from 1662 to 1722 and the Ch'ien Lung period from 1736 to 1795.

Because the duration of the Chinese and Western years is reasonably close, and the two begin and end more or less simultaneously, the difficulties of correlation associated with the Islamic year, for example, are mostly avoided. However, dates expressed only in the traditional Chinese system do remain a source of difficulty even to modern Chinese readers; so Western dates should also be given.

JAPAN

After the Meiji restoration of 1868 the calculation of dates is comparatively simple. The system parallels the later (Ming and Ch'ing) Chinese system of a single *nien-hao* or reign-title – as in the case of China this is not identical with the emperor's own name – that runs throughout that reign. There have been four reign-periods since the restoration:

Meiji	*starting in*	1868
Taisho		1912
Showa		1926
Heisei		1989

Thus Meiji 14 would be 1881; Taisho 6 would be 1917; Showa 22 would be 1947; and Heisei 2 would be 1990

For dates in the Tokugawa shogunate of 1603–1867, and certainly for earlier periods, Western as well as Japanese dates should also be given.

THE FRENCH REVOLUTIONARY OR REPUBLICAN CALENDAR

Inaugurated officially by the vote of the National Convention in 1793, the French Revolutionary or Republican Calendar took as its starting point the foundation of the first Republic in 1792. The year was divided into twelve months, each of thirty days, with five or six extra days at the end, which were intended to be celebrated as festivals. The beginning of the year was the Autumn Equinox (22 September), and the names of the months, invented by the poet Fabre d'Eglantine, reflected the progress of the agricultural year:

Vendémiaire	Germinal
Brumaire	Floréal
Frimaire	Prairial
Nivôse	Messidor
Pluviôse	Thermidor
Ventôse	Fructidor

The Republican Calendar was abolished on 1 January 1806, on Napoleon's orders. It is, however, widely used by historians of the French Revolution, though equivalent dates should also be given where necessary. The *Oxford Companion to French Literature* contains an excellent table showing the Republican Calendar.

Appendix **12**
Electronic typescript information sheet

Author: _____

Title: _____

In order to assess the practicalities of using your disks/tapes for producing the above book with Newnham University Press, we need to have the following information. Please return this form along with a sample disk/tape and a hard-copy printout as soon as possible.

1 **Your machine**
Make and model: _____
Approximate date of manufacture: _____
Name of word-processing software, with version number if applicable:

_____

Type of operating system (indicate which): MS-DOS / PC-DOS / UNIX
(or a derivative) / other _____

2 **Your machine's output**
Your floppy disks are (indicate which): 3", 3.5", 5.25", 8"; single/double
sided; single/double density; soft/hard sectored
Your files are in (indicate which): ASCII/word-processor format.

3 **Your text**
Please supply a hard-copy printout of your text along with the sample
disk/tape.

4 **Special characters**
Are there any special characters you require for your text that you *cannot*
produce on the printout (e.g. Greek, mathematical symbols, other unusual characters)? If so, please list what these are below, indicate how you
have keyed them and give a reference to an example on one of your printout pages, plus an estimate of how many times they occur throughout the
book and whether they are needed in the notes/bibliography as well as in
the text.

Special character required	How it is keyed now	Examples on pages	Used in text only or also in notes, references?	Approx. how often used
_____	_____	_____	_____	_____
_____	_____	_____	_____	_____
_____	_____	_____	_____	_____
_____	_____	_____	_____	_____
_____	_____	_____	_____	_____
_____	_____	_____	_____	_____

Typesetter's report:
disk/tapes can/cannot be used (and why)

disk/tapes will be more useful if author does the following:

Appendix **13**
Proof correction symbols

Instruction	Textual mark	Marginal mark
Leave unchanged	_ _ _ _ under characters	(✓)
Remove extraneous marks	Encircle marks to be removed	✗
Delete	/ through character(s) or ⊢—⊣ through words	♂
Delete and close up	⌢/ through character(s) or ⊏⊐	♂ (with close-up dots)
Insert in text the matter indicated in the margin	⋏	New matter followed by ⋏
Substitute character or substitute part of one or more words	/ through character or ⊢——⊣ hrough word(s)	New character or new word(s)
Substitute ligature e.g. æ for separate letters	⊢——⊣ through characters affected	⌣ e.g. a͡e
Substitute or insert full stop or decimal point	/ through character or ⋏	⊙
Substitute or insert comma, semicolon, colon, etc.	/ through character or ⋏	, / ; / ⊙ / (/) /
Substitute or insert character in 'superior' position	/ through character or ⋏	⌐ under character e.g. ⌐/
Substitute or insert character in 'inferior' position	/ through character or ⋏	L over character e.g. L
Substitute or insert single or double quotation marks or apostrophe	/ through character or ⋏	⌐ ⌐⌐ and/or ⌐ ⌐⌐
Substitute or insert ellipsis	/ through character or ⋏	. . .
Substitute or insert hyphen	/ through character or ⋏	⊢–⊣
Substitute or insert rule	/ through character or ⋏	Give the size of the rule in the marginal mark ⊢1 em⊣ ⊢4 mm⊣

Instruction	Textual mark	Marginal mark
Substitute or insert oblique	/ through character or λ	Ⓛ
Wrong fount. Replace by character(s) of correct fount	Encircle character(s)	⊗
Change damaged character(s)	Encircle character(s)	✕
Set in or change to italic	——— under character(s) Where space does not permit textual marks, encircle the affected area instead	⊔⊔
Change italic to upright type	Encircle character(s)	⊔
Set in or change to capital letters	≡≡≡ under character(s)	≡
Set in or change to small capital letters	═══ under character(s)	═
Set in or change to bold type	〜〜〜 under character(s)	〜
Set in or change to bold italic type	〜〜〜 under character(s)	⊔⊔
Change capital letters to lower-case letters	Encircle character(s)	≢
Change small capital letters to lower-case letters	Encircle character(s)	≠
Close up. Delete space between characters or words	⌒ linking characters e.g. a⌣scribe	⌒
Insert space between characters	| between characters	Y Give the size of the space when necessary
Insert space between words	Y between words	Y Give the size of the space when necessary
Reduce space between characters	| between characters	⋀ Give the amount by which the space is to be reduced, when necessary

Instruction	Textual mark	Marginal mark
Reduce space between words	⌢ between words	⌢ Give the amount by which the space is to be reduced, when necessary
Make space appear equal between characters or words	⎮ between characters or words	⋎
Close up to normal interline spacing	(each side of column) linking lines	
Insert space between lines or paragraphs	───(or ─)	Give the size of the space when necessary
Reduce space between lines or paragraphs	──) or ⊂─	Give amount by which the space is to be reduced, when necessary
Start new paragraph	⌐	⌐
Run on (no new paragraph)	⌒	⌒
Transpose characters or words	⊔⌐ between characters or words, numbered when necessary	⊔⌐
Transpose lines	⊏⊐	⊏⊐
Transpose a number of lines	─── 3 ─── 2 ─── 1	Rules extend from the margin into the text with each line to be transposed numbered in the correct sequence
Centre	⌈ enclosing matter ⌉ ⌊ to be centred ⌋	[ ]
Indent	⊏	⊏ Give the amount of the indent
Cancel indent	⊢⊏	⊐
Move matter specified distance to the right*	enclosing matter to be moved to the right →	⊏

Instruction	Textual mark	Marginal mark
Move matter specified distance to the left*	enclosing matter to be moved to the left	
Set line to specified measure*	⊢[and/or]⊣	⊢→
Set column to specified measure*	⊢——→	⊢→
Take over character(s), word(s) or line to next line, column or page		The textual mark surrounds the matter to be taken over and extends into the margin
Take back character(s), word(s) or line to previous line, column or page		The textual mark surrounds the matter to be taken back and extends into the margin
Raise matter*	over matter to be raised under matter to be raised	
Lower matter*	over matter to be lowered under matter to be lowered	
Move matter to position indicated*	Enclose matter to be moved and indicate new position	
Correct vertical alignment	‖	‖
Correct horizontal alignment	Single line above and below misaligned matter	placed level with the head and foot of the relevant line

* Give the exact dimensions when necessary.

Extracts from BS 5261 Part 2 1976 are reproduced with the permission of BSI.

Complete copies can be obtained by post from BSI Sales, Linford Wood,

Milton Keynes MK14 6LE; telefax 0908 320856, telex 825777 BSIMK G.

424

Glossary

The entries are restricted to words, and meanings, that a copy-editor is likely to meet fairly frequently. In order not to introduce more technical terms, the definitions are perhaps oversimplified; books on printing and binding, for example, will explain the various terms and processes more fully.

Alphabetical order is letter by letter.

acknowledgements a list of copyright owners and other people to whom the author is indebted.

affiliation an author's university or other post; used in this book to mean also any degrees or honours given below the author's name on the title page and jacket or cover.

AH *anno Hegirae*, in the year of the Hegira, i.e. from the flight of Muhammad (mid AD 622 by the Christian reckoning; see appendix 11). Used to identify Muslim dates.

angle brackets ⟨ ⟩.

apparatus criticus materials for the critical study of a document, usually variant readings.

art paper coated paper used for printing fine-screen halftones (q.v.).

artwork an illustration or typeset material suitable for reproduction.

ascender the part of such letters as d and h which extends above the height of the letter x (see fig. G.1). *See also* descender.

ASCII abbreviation for American Standard Code for Information Interchange; one of a number of standard binary codes used to represent a character in a computer (others include ISO7, the International Organization for Standardization 7-bit code; and EBCDIC, the Extended Binary Coded Decimal Interchange Code).

author–date system a system of bibliographical references, in which a particular work in the list of references is referred to in the text etc. by author's name and date of publication, e.g. 'Smith, 1990'. See section 10.2.

a/w artwork (q.v.).

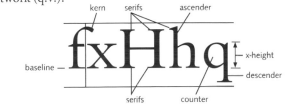

Fig. G.1 Type nomenclature.

bastard title (or **half-title**) the first printed page of a book, preceding the title page and containing the title of the book.

b.f. bold face (q.v.).

bleed *to bleed* is to extend an illustration beyond the trimmed edge of a page; *the bleed* is the amount by which the illustration extends beyond the trimmed size to allow for variations in trimming, normally 3 mm or $\frac{1}{8}$ inch.

blind blocking *see* blocking.

blocking impressing a design or lettering on a book cover. (The US term is 'stamping'.) The blocking may be in ink or metal foil, or it may be *blind blocking*, to produce a recessed surface without the addition of ink or foil.

block quotation a displayed quotation.

blow up to enlarge photographically.

blue, blueprint contact dyeline proof made on paper from film, one method being called an Ozalid.

blurb a description of the book for the jacket, cover, half-title or publicity material.

boards sheets of strawboard, millboard, etc., used in hard-cover binding. Also heavy paper or light card used for paperback covers.

bold (face) a type with very thick strokes, a thickened version of another typeface.

BP before the present (1950). Used in prehistoric dates.

brace may be a curly bracket } or ⌒ ; used mainly in tables.

bracket to a typesetter a bracket is a square bracket; a round one is called a parenthesis or paren. *See also* angle brackets, brace.

brass a brass die used for blocking (q.v.); also used loosely to mean any blocking die. Brasses are wholly or partly cut by hand and are considerably more costly than Chemacs and other machine-cut blocking dies.

break off to begin something on a separate line rather than running it on within a paragraph, e.g. subheadings and index subentries.

breathing one or other of two signs in Greek to show the presence or absence of the aspirate (see section 14.1).

broadside page a landscape page (q.v.).

bromide (1) light-sensitive paper used in photographic reproduction; (2) a positive photographic print.

bulk thickness of a book, estimated in advance in order that the jacket, cover and blocking die can be designed with the right spine width; also thickness of a sheet of paper.

bullet a large dot used for ornamentation.

caesura a pause in a line of verse, usually near the middle.

camera-ready copy, camera copy material ready for photographing, usually for reproduction by litho. It should not be marked, except lightly with a pale blue pencil; so mark any corrections on a photocopy. *See also* draft c.r.c., text c.r.c.

cancel reprinted leaves (e.g. four-page cancel) to be substituted in bound copies and sheet stock, when a serious error is found after a book has been printed.

c. and l.c. capital and lower case; better to use 'caps. and l.c.'

caps. capitals.

caps. and s.c. capitals and small capitals (q.v.).

caps. and smalls capitals and small capitals (q.v.)

caption wording set below an illustration; also called a legend or underline.

caret an insertion mark.

case a 'hard cover' for a machine-bound book, consisting of front and back boards and spine. *See also* lower case, upper case.

cased bound in hard covers by machine.

cast-off a calculation of the number of printed pages that the copy will occupy when set in a given typeface and measure.

catchword, catchphrase (1) a word or phrase from the text, repeated at the beginning of a textual note or a gloss at the foot of the page, (2) a word or phrase, such as a headword in a dictionary, used as the running head.

chapter opening the beginning, or first page, of a chapter.

character a letter, figure, symbol or punctuation mark.

Chemac a kind of copper die, used for blocking (q.v.).

CiP Cataloguing in Publication (see section 7.5.6).

clothbound bound in hard covers. As non-woven material is sometimes used in place of cloth, this kind of binding is best described as hard covers or hardback.

club line the first line of a paragraph at the foot of a page. Also called an orphan.

collate (1) more correctly to *conflate*, i.e. to transfer corrections from one proof to another, say from a proofreader's proof to the author's corrected proof; (2) to gather the signatures (q.v.) of a book in the correct sequence; (3) to check the signatures to ensure that they are all there and are in the right order.

colophon (1) an account of the book's production, or a printer's imprint, at the end of a book; (2) a publisher's device on a title page.

colour-coding of corrections see section 5.4.

composed typeset and paged.

composition cost the cost of setting, paging and proofing a book.

compositor formerly a craftsman skilled in making up and correcting pages in metal type; still sometimes used to describe an operator of modern type-setting systems.

compuscript use 'electronic typescript'.

contraction an abbreviation which includes the first and last letter of the full form of the singular (e.g. Dr, Mme, St); it is not followed by a full point.

control codes those internal word-processor or computer codes control-ling the putting of characters into varieties of typography, e.g. into bold, italic, etc.; these codes are not usually visible on the printout.

copy raw material such as typescript, photographs, rough drawings, etc.

copy-preparer a person employed by the typesetter to translate the designer's typographical specification into instructions on the typescript.

corrigenda a list of corrections printed in a book, as against a separate erratum/errata slip (q.v.); however, an erratum slip may be called a corri-genda slip.

c.r.c. camera-ready copy (q.v.).

credit a picture credit is an acknowledgement of the source of a picture, e.g. the photographer or a picture library.

Cromalin a proprietary system for dry proofing (q.v.) four-colour subjects without the need for printing.

cropping 'cutting down' or masking an illustration, such as a photograph, to remove extraneous areas. Better called masking (q.v.), to avoid the risk of the cropping being done with a sharp instrument. *Crop marks* are placed on the back of an illustration or on an overlay, to show what is to be omit-ted. (The term 'crop marks' is also used to describe the variable growth of crops visible in aerial photographs, which often indicates the presence of an archaeological feature.)

cross-head a centred heading or subheading.

cut lines shadow lines on a proof created in photocopying by the edges of separate pieces of camera-ready copy (q.v.) that are fractionally higher than the board on which they are pasted.

descender the part of such letters as g and y which extends below the base-line or foot of the letter x (see fig. G.1). *See also* ascender.

desk-top publishing producing printed material on authors' or publishers' computers or word processors specially equipped to produce paged text that includes illustrations.

diacritical marks accents, dots and bars above or below letters etc.

diaeresis two dots placed over a vowel, to show that it is pronounced separately, e.g. naïve, Brontë. *See also* umlaut.

digitize to convert a letter or other character into a series of photoelectronic impulses which can later be used to produce the image of the character.

displayed set on separate lines, and distinguished from the text by being set in a smaller or larger size or by its position in relation to the margin (e.g. indented or centred). Displayed matter is usually preceded and followed by a little extra space. Examples of displayed matter are headings, long quotations and mathematical equations.

double-page spread, spread (1) an illustration or table extending across a pair of facing pages or 'opening'; (2) a layout or proof showing a pair of facing pages.

draft c.r.c. author-generated copy submitted to the publisher, that will be read and assessed for content and design, probably copy-edited, and returned to the author for correction, before being used as camera-ready copy (see section 1.2.3).

dry proofing a method of producing a colour proof by the use of toner powder rather than ink.

d.t.p. desk-top publishing (q.v.).

dummy a dummy book, which may or may not be bound, made up of the correct number of signatures (q.v.) of the paper to be used for the book, to show the thickness or 'bulk'.

duotone a two-colour halftone produced from a single-colour original. The two negatives are made at different screen angles and to different contrast ranges.

eadem the feminine form of *idem* (q.v.).

edition one or more printings (or impressions) of the same version of a book in the same kind of binding. The term 'new [or second] edition' should not be used unless the text has been changed so much that libraries which already have the book will need to buy the new version. Issues with only minor corrections are called reprints or impressions. The same text issued in a different binding or at a lower price may be called a paperback edition or cheap edition.

electronic typescript a typescript submitted for publication in electronic (disk or tape) form.

elision the running together of pairs of numbers, e.g. 38–39 becomes 38–9 and 213–218 becomes 213–18.

ellipsis three points used to indicate an omission.

em the square of any size of type, i.e. a 10 pt em is 10 points wide, though the width of a 10 pt letter M will depend on the set (q.v.); 12 pt (or 'pica') ems are used to measure the width of the text area on a page, irrespective of the size of type in which the page is set. If copy is set to '24 pica ems' or '24 picas' it is approximately 101 mm or 4 inches wide, since 72 pts = approx. 25.33 mm or 1 inch.

em rule a rule occupying the full width of the square of any type size. For the use of em rules see section 6.12.2.

en a measurement half the width of an em (q.v.). *See also* en point, en rule.

endmatter the material that follows the text proper, e.g. appendixes, bibliography and indexes.

endnotes notes which follow the appendixes or text (or, more rarely, the relevant chapter) rather than appearing at the foot of the relevant page of text.

endpaper a folded sheet, one leaf of which is pasted to the front or back cover of a hardback book. The other leaf, known as the flyleaf, is pasted along the folded edge to the first or last page of the book.

en point a point set midway along the width of an en, so that the point will appear with space either side of it; it may be medial or low.

en rule a rule half the width of an em rule (q.v.). For the use of en rules see section 6.12.1.

epigraph a quotation in the preliminary pages or at the beginning of a part or chapter.

erratum (or **errata**) **slip** a slip of paper containing a list of corrections and pasted into, or placed in, a copy of a book.

estimate an estimate of the cost of producing a book; an estimate of length is called a cast-off (q.v.).

e.t.s. electronic typescript (q.v.).

even small caps small capitals (q.v.) without full capitals.

even working a multiple of the number of pages that will fill one sheet of paper of the size to be used for printing the book. Usually a multiple of 32 octavo pages.

extent the length of a book in terms of the number of pages.

extract a term used by some typesetters to refer to a displayed quotation.

face *see* typeface.

festschrift a collection of articles published in honour of someone.

figure (1) an illustration printed in the text; (2) an arabic numeral.

film advance *see* film feed.

film feed the distance in points by which the film in a phototypesetter is advanced between lines. Also called film advance or line feed.

filmsetting or **phototypesetting** typesetting by photographic means.

floating accents accents that can be positioned over any letter.

flush left, **right** adjoining the left or right margin.

flyleaf *see* endpaper.

fold-out or **pull-out** a folded insertion in the text, which, when unfolded, extends beyond the normal page size. Also called a throw-out.

folio (1) a sheet of typescript or leaf of manuscript; (2) a printed page number; (3) in book sizes 'folio' traditionally indicates a sheet folded in half, i.e. twice the size of quarto.

font *see* fount.

foredge the outer edge of a book, opposite the spine.

foreword introductory remarks about a book or its author, usually written by someone other than the author.

format the trimmed page size; the term is loosely used to distinguish between different styles of binding, or to describe the style of production. *To format* is to arrange data or a book in a particular format or style, according to specific instructions called formatting codes.

foul proof an obsolete corrected proof.

fount the characters of one size of the same typeface, including alphabets of capitals, small capitals, lower case, figures, punctuation marks, etc.; sans serif founts have no true small capitals. A titling fount consists of capitals, figures and punctuation only. The proof correction *wrong fount* indicates that a letter of the wrong design or wrong size has been included in the text.

Fraktur a specific German fount; often used as a generic name for any 'black letter', 'gothic' or 'old English' face. Occasionally used in mathematics.

frontispiece an illustration facing the title page; usually, but not always, a halftone (q.v.).

full out adjoining the left or right margin. If a passage starts full out it is not indented.

full point a full stop.

function calls *see* control codes.

galley originally a flat metal tray, with raised edges on three sides, used for holding metal type; *galley proofs* were proofs taken on a long slip of paper from the type while it was still in the galley, though the term is now used for any proofs not yet divided into pages.

global search and replace the facility of a computer program to find all examples of a word or group of words in a file and replace them with an alternative.

gloss an explanation of a difficult word, either in the margin or in a note.

gravure photogravure (q.v.).

guillemets special quotation marks (« ») used in French and some other languages. See *Hart's Rules* (39th edn), p. 100.

gutter (loosely) the inner margins of a book; really the inner, folded edge, also called the back.

half-title (1) the first printed page of a book, preceding the title page and containing the title of the book; (2) a subsidiary title page (often called a part title or part-title leaf) used to introduce each of the parts into which the book may be divided; the recto contains the number and title of the part, and the verso is blank or may contain a map or introductory note.

halftone a process by which various shades of grey, from black to white, are simulated by a pattern of black dots of various sizes (except in photogravure, q.v.). One method of breaking the picture into dots is to photograph it through a screen. Screens of various gauges can be used to suit the paper on which the halftone is to be printed: for offset litho printing a screen of 85 lines per inch is suitable for printing on newsprint (q.v.), a screen of 120 for uncoated cartridge paper, and a screen of 150 for art paper (q.v.).

hanging indention the first line of the paragraph starts at the left margin, and subsequent lines are indented.

hard copy copy sent to the publisher on a medium that is 'hard', i.e. paper, as opposed to the 'soft' medium of electronic disks or tapes.

hard hyphen a hyphen that is an integral part of the word and remains wherever the word appears in the line.

hard return the space and, sometimes, the indention resulting from the author or keyboarder's pressing the 'return' or 'paragraph return' key, as opposed to the 'soft' return resulting automatically from the continuous keying of text.

Harvard system a version of the author–date system of bibliographical references; loosely, the author–date system generally.

headline a running head (q.v.).

histogram see section 4.4.

hot-metal typesetting a form of typesetting in which type was cast from molten metal, as distinguished from hand-set (and therefore cold) metal type or phototypesetting etc.

ibid., *ibidem* 'in the same place' (see p. 243).

idem or *id.* 'the same', used to mean the same (male) author as before. The feminine form is *eadem*.

idiot tape unformatted tape with no line-ending commands.

imperial measurements a non-metric British series of weights and measures, such as ounce, pint, inch and acre.

impose *see* imposition.

imposition the arrangement of pages of type etc. in such a way that they will appear in the right order and with the correct margins when the printed sheet is folded.

impression a number of copies printed at any one time; a new impression is a reprint with only minor corrections (if any). *See also* edition.

imprint the publisher's or printer's imprint is their name and address, which is usually given on the verso of the title page.

indention, indentation beginning a line further from the margin than the rest of the passage. *See also* hanging indention.

index locorum in classical books, an index of passages cited

indicator a note indicator is the number or symbol in the text which indicates that there is a footnote or endnote to the word or sentence.

inferior a subscript (q.v.).

insert a small group of pages (often halftones) inserted so that half appears, for example, between pp. 4 and 5 of a sixteen-page signature, and the other half between pp. 12 and 13. *See also* inset.

inset a small group of pages (often halftones) inserted in the middle of a signature, e.g. between pp. 8 and 9 of a sixteen-page signature.

inset map a small map inserted in a corner of a large map.

insetting (1) the placing of the signatures (q.v.) of a book one inside the other; (2) *see* inset.

interfacing sometimes used to mean the process of 'translating' an author's disks or tapes to the typesetter's system.

ISBN International Standard Book Number (see section 7.5.4).

ISSN International Standard Serial Number (see section 7.5.5).

italic characters that slope to the right. True italic is a specially designed typeface *as here*; sloped roman is created electronically from roman characters.

justified setting setting in which the space between words is varied from line to line, so that the last letter or punctuation mark in each complete line reaches the right-hand margin.

kern (1) the part of certain characters that projects beyond the body of the type (see fig. G.1); a feature of certain italic or sloping types. Now also (2) to adjust the fit of adjacent characters by programming the phototypesetter, (3) letter fit.

key to 'type' text into a typesetting machine. *See also* key in.

keyboard (1) the rows of keys on a typesetting machine; (2) to key (q.v.).

key in to key in illustrations is to indicate their approximate position by a note in the margin of the typescript.

landscape the shape of an illustration or book is referred to as 'landscape' when its width is greater than its height; a *landscape page* is a page on which tables, illustrations, etc., are turned to read up the page, so that their foot is at the right-hand side of the page. *See also* portrait.

l.c. lower case (q.v.).

leaders a series of dots leading the eye from one column to another, e.g. in old-fashioned contents lists.

leading the spacing between lines of type, so called because strips of lead were added between lines of metal type.

leaf two pages which back on to one another.

legend a caption (q.v.).

lemma (1) a headword or catchword such as a quoted word or phrase, at the beginning of a textual note (pl. lemmata); (2) in mathematics a preliminary proposition used in the proof of a mathematical theorem (pl. lemmas).

Letraset a system of dry transfer characters, used in preparing artwork.

letterpress the process of printing from a raised surface.

letterspacing the addition of small spaces, usually between capitals or between small capitals, to improve their appearance. In German and Greek texts, lower-case letters may be letterspaced for emphasis.

ligature two or more letters joined together and combined as a single character, e.g. ff, fi, ffi, ffl, fl, œ.

line drawing a drawing which consists of black lines, shading and solid areas, but no greys. Grey may be simulated by using a suitable tint (q.v.).

line feed the distance between the base lines of successive lines of text.

lining figures arabic numerals of equal height, usually the same height as capitals (see p. 144). *See also* non-lining figures.

literal a mistake made when setting type; used mainly of mistakes affecting only one or two letters. US term is 'typo'.

litho, lithography a planographic process in which ink is applied selectively to the plate by chemically treating image areas to accept ink and non-image areas to accept water. *See also* offset lithography.

loc. cit. abbreviation of *loco citato*, 'in the place cited'. (See pp. 243–4.)

logarithmic graph see fig. 4.2, p. 93.

lower case the small letters as distinct from capitals and small capitals (q.v.).

M *see* em.

machining printing.

macros term used for the pre-formatted disks or tapes sometimes provided to authors for keying their text directly, resulting in electronic typescripts containing all the design information required.

make-ready adjustment necessary to ensure that an even impression will be obtained from every part of the printing surface.

make-up the making-up into page of typeset material. It also includes the insertion of running heads, footnotes, tables, illustrations, captions and page numbers.

marked proof the copy of the proof on which the typesetter marks any corrections and queries, and which should be returned to the typesetter, once the author's and any other corrections have been added.

masking indicating the unwanted areas at the edge of an illustration such as a photograph, either by means of an opaque cut-out overlay or by lines marked lightly on a transparent overlay or on the back of the illustration.

Matchprint a dry proofing system (q.v.).

measure the width to which a complete line of type is set; usually expressed in picas (12 pt ems).

mechanical (US) camera-ready copy (q.v.).

modem (modulator/demodulator device) a device that converts telephone transmission into digital form and vice versa.

N *see* en.

net book a book with a fixed UK price.

newsprint a cheap paper used for printing mass-market paperbacks, newspapers, etc.

non-lining figures arabic numerals which have ascenders and descenders. Also called old style figures. (See section 6.10.1.)

non-ranging figures non-lining figures (q.v.).

octavo a page one-eighth of the size of a traditional sheet.

oddment a printed sheet containing fewer pages than other sheets in the book.

offprint a printed copy of a single article from a book or journal; also called a separate or, less accurately, a reprint.

offset offset lithography (q.v.).

offset lithography the commonest printing method, in which the flat image is printed on to a rubber-covered cylinder (blanket) from which it is transferred to paper.

old style figures non-lining figures (q.v.).

op. cit. abbreviation of *opere citato*, 'in the work cited'. (See pp. 226–7, 243–4.)

opening a pair of facing pages, also called a spread or double-page spread. *See also* chapter opening.

original a photograph, drawing, etc., provided as copy for an illustration, as distinct from a proof etc.

orphan the first line of a paragraph at the foot of a page. Also called club line. *See also* widow.

overlay a transparent flap covering the front of a photograph or other illustration (see p. 87).

overmatter typeset material that exceeds the allotted space.

overrunning the rearrangement of lines of type caused by a correction which makes a line longer or shorter. The insertion of a word in the first line of a paragraph may mean overrrunning as far as the end of the paragraph, i.e. taking a word or two from each line to the next and altering the word spacing accordingly.

Ozalid a method of making photographic copies, used for making paper proofs from film.

pagehead a running head (q.v.).

pagination page numbering.

paperback a book bound in flexible board covers.

paren a parenthesis (q.v.).

parenthesis a round bracket; to typesetters a 'bracket' is a square bracket. *See also* brace.

part a group of related chapters, with a part number or title or both; this part heading often appears on a separate leaf that is sometimes called a part title (see p. 59).

paste-up (1) a paged layout with proofs of the text pasted in position, and the size and position of the illustrations shown by outlines drawn on the layout, as a guide to the typesetter; (2) camera-ready copy (q.v.) assembled for platemaking.

perfect binding an unsewn adhesive binding.

perfecter a printing press that prints both sides of a sheet of paper in one operation.

period US term for a full stop.

permission permission to reproduce copyright material.

photogravure the process of printing from a surface in which ink is contained in recessed cells of various depths. Gravure halftone 'dots' are all the same size, the variation in shade being effected by the different amount of ink in each cell.

photolithography the process of printing from a photographically prepared metal plate on which the non-printing areas are protected from the greasy ink by a film of water. Offset lithography (q.v.) is the commonest printing method.

photomechanical transfer, PMT a process for converting halftone or line originals to final-size bromides (q.v.) for inclusion in camera-ready copy (q.v.).

photo-offset offset lithography (q.v.).

phototypesetting typesetting by photographic means.

pica a measurement, 12 pts, i.e. approx. 4.21 mm or $\frac{1}{6}$ inch.

plate (1) an illustration printed separately from the text, on a separate sheet, e.g. a letterpress halftone printed on art paper; now used loosely to identify halftones that are numbered in a separate sequence; (2) any one-piece printing surface, such as a lithographic plate which prints the whole of one side of a sheet.

PMT a photomechanical transfer (q.v.).

point (1) as a measurement, approx. 0.35 mm or $\frac{1}{72}$ inch; (2) a dot, e.g. a full stop ('full point').

portrait (1) the shape of a book or illustration is referred to as 'portrait' when its height is greater than its width; (2) if a table is 'set portrait' it is set upright on the page and not turned. *See also* landscape.

preface a personal note by the author about the book.

prelims preliminary pages, which contain half-title, title page, contents list, preface, etc. (see chapter 7). The US term is 'front matter'.

press proof the proof that is read last before printing, and authorizes printing.

print run the number of copies printed.

proof a photocopy or roughly printed copy, for checking and correction.

pull-out *see* fold-out.

quarto (1) a page one-quarter of the size of a traditional sheet; (2) a size of stationery, 10 × 8 inches in Britain, 11 × $8\frac{1}{2}$ inches in the USA, now mostly replaced in Britain by A4, an international size, 297 × 210 mm.

quotes quotation marks, inverted commas.

ragged right unjustified (q.v.).

range to align.

ranging figures lining figures (q.v.).

rebind the binding of a second or subsequent batch of printed sheets.

recto a right-hand page. *See also* verso.

reduction the amount by which an illustration is to be photographically reduced before reproduction (see section 4.0.1).

references (list of) bibliographical references.

register (1) the accurate superimposition of colours in multicolour printing; (2) the exact alignment of pages so that they back one another precisely.

registration marks pairs of marks, often a cross in a circle, to show the relative position and exact orientation of two pieces of artwork that are to be superimposed, or to ensure accurate register (q.v.) in colour printing.

reissue a book that is republished after being out of print for a time.

reprint (1) a number of copies reprinted from the same setting of type, with only minor corrections; also called a new impression (*see also* edition); (2) loosely, an offprint (q.v.).

retouching handwork on photographic prints or transparencies, to remove blemishes, to obtain more accurate colour reproduction, etc.

reverse left to right to reproduce an image so that it is reversed like a mirror-image.

reverse out to reverse black to white when making a plate or block, so that the final appearance is of white printed on black (or another colour) rather than black on white.

revise the revised, or second, proof.

rotary press a printing press in which the printing image, as well as the impression surface, is cylindrical.

rough the author's rough sketch, or any drawing that will have to be redrawn.

royalty a payment to an author (or someone else) for every copy sold.

rule a continuous line, e.g. in a fraction or at the top and foot of a table.

run *see* print run.

running head the heading set at the top of each page except over chapter openings, deep or turned pages, in most non-fiction books and some novels. Also called a headline or pagehead.

running text continuous text, as against displayed equations, note form, footnotes, etc.; used in such phrases as 'chemical symbols should be spelt out in running text'.

run on (1) continue on the same line, rather than starting a fresh line or new paragraph. (2) Chapters run on if each one does not start on a fresh page.

sans serif a typeface with no serifs (q.v.).

s.c. small capitals (q.v.).

scatter proofs proofs of illustrations, with the illustrations placed close together and in random order.

screen *see* halftone.

script a typeface based on handwritten letterforms; used in mathematics.

section (1) a signature (q.v.); (2) a subdivision of a chapter.

semi-bold a typeface with strokes midway in thickness between ordinary roman and bold.

separate an offprint (q.v.).

serif a small terminal stroke at the end of a main stroke of a letter (see fig. G.1).

set *to set* words is to produce the photographic image of the characters that make up those words. *The set of a letter* is its width.

set-off the accidental transfer of ink from a freshly printed sheet on to the back of the next sheet.

SGML Standard Generalized Mark-up Language, a computer-assisted technique for marking up documents for storage, retrieval and processing.

sheet a printed sheet; the term is usually used of sheets which have not yet been folded, and which may comprise one or more signatures.

short-title system a system of bibliographical references which employs a shortened form of the book title after the first mention (see section 10.1).

sig signature (q.v.).

signature (1) a folded section of pages in a book, i.e. one sheet or part of a sheet. Some people prefer the term 'section' but I have used 'signature' in this book to avoid confusion with the second meaning of 'section' (q.v.). (2) The identification letter(s) on the first page of each signature.

SI units Système International d'Unités. For a list of the fundamental units see section 6.8.

sizing deciding the reduction or final size of an illustration original.

sloped roman sloping characters created electronically from roman ones.

small capitals capital letters similar in weight and height to a lower-case x. They are not generally available in bold, italic or sans serif type; but the typesetter will be able to simulate them by setting smaller capitals (e.g. 7 pt capitals in a 10 pt context): they will align at the baseline, but will be lighter than the surrounding characters.

small type type intermediate in size between the main text and any footnotes.

soft codes those codes added by the keyboarder, visible on the printout (therefore also called 'visible codes'), which can be searched for and replaced by a typesetter's control codes for the feature required.

soft hyphen a hyphen that occurs only when a word must be broken when printed on a set text-line measure, as opposed to the 'hard' hyphen (q.v.).

solid if type is set solid, it is set without additional space between the lines.

solidus an oblique stroke, /.

sort a single character of type. *See also* special sort.

spanner rule where a table has two levels of heading above the columns, a spanner rule is inserted above the group of lower-level headings covered by each upper-level heading (see fig. 9.2, p. 218).

special sort a character that the typesetter does not have in stock; more generally, a character that cannot be keyboarded with the rest of the text, or a character not included in the standard fount of type.

specification the designer's typographical specification lists the typeface and sizes, style for headings, etc.

specimen sample page(s) set to show the various type sizes, headings and other typographical complications. (See section 2.3.)

spread *see* double-page spread.

s/s same size; an illustration so marked will be reproduced the same size as the original.

s/t small type (q.v.).

stet an instruction that the characters with a row of dashes or dots below them (see first correction in appendix 13) are to remain unaltered or to be restored if already deleted or altered.

strip in, strip up to combine two pieces of film or paper; to insert corrections or illustrations in camera-ready copy or phototypeset material.

stub the left-hand column in a table, which identifies the rows in the same way as the column headings identify the columns (see fig. 9.2, p. 218).

subheading a heading to a section of a chapter or of a bibliography.

subscript a small letter or figure set beside and/or below the foot of a full-size character. Also called an inferior. *See also* superscript.

subtitle an explanatory phrase forming the second part of a title.

superior a superscript (q.v.).

superscript a small letter or figure set beside and/or above the top of a full-size character. Also called a superior. *See also* subscript.

swash letter an ornamental italic character, usually a capital.

symposium (1) a conference; (2) a volume of papers presented at a conference.

T_EX a typesetting programming language designed to enable keying of complicated mathematics; pronounced 'tech'.

text area *see* type area.

text c.r.c. author-generated camera-ready copy of the text of a work, to which the publisher will add running heads and page numbers, preliminary matter and the like.

text type the size of type in which the main text of the book is set.

throw-out a fold-out (q.v.).

tilde the diacritical sign over an n in Spanish to indicate the sound *ny*, i.e. ñ; the sign is also used in mathematics.

tint usually a *mechanical tint*, i.e. a ready-made dotted, hatched or other pattern, available in various densities, which can be applied to an illustration. Also a solid panel in a second colour.

tip in to paste a plate or fold out to the adjoining page.

transliterate to transcribe in letters of another alphabet.

transpose to change the order of letters, words, etc.

ts typescript.

turned a turned table or illustration is one which is turned on the page so that its left-hand side is at the foot of the page.

turnovers the second and subsequent lines of a paragraph, entry in an index, etc. Also used where a long line of verse runs over on to a second line. The term is used in phrases such as 'turnovers indented 2 ems'.

two-page spread a double-page spread (q.v.).

type area the area occupied by text and footnotes on a page; it should always be made clear whether the area does or does not include the area occupied by the running head and page number.

typeface originally the printing surface of a piece of metal type; hence the design of that surface.

u. and l.c. or **u./l.c.** upper and lower case, i.e. a mixture of capitals and lower-case letters rather than all capitals or all lower case.

umlaut two dots placed over a German vowel (a, o or u), to show a change in sound. Unlike French accents, umlauts must be included, even when the vowel is a capital. *See also* diaeresis.

unbacked printed on one side of the paper only.

underline (1) a caption (q.v.); (2) an instruction to the typesetter that characters underlined in the typescript are to be underlined rather than italic.

unit system a counting method used in phototypesetting systems to measure the width of the individual characters and spaces being set.

unjustified unjustified lines have even word spacing and a ragged right-hand edge. *See also* justified setting.

upper case capitals.

Vancouver system a system of bibliographical references used in many biomedical journals (see section 10.3).

verso a left-hand page. *See also* recto.

virgule a solidus (q.v.).

virus a 'bug' in computer hardware or software that corrupts a user's data or, in extreme cases, causes total machine failure.

w.f. wrong fount, *see under* fount.

white line a line of space the same depth as a line of words.

widow the short last line of a paragraph at the top of a page. Typesetters try to avoid widows by making a pair of facing pages one line longer or shorter than the rest.

word break, word division splitting a word at the end of a line.

word-wrap a computer word-processing function whereby a new line of text is started automatically when the existing line has insufficient space to contain a new word.

working *see* even working.

wrap-round a small group of pages (often halftones) wrapped round one signature of the text, so that half the group appears before the signature, and the other half, say, 32 pages later.

wrong fount *see under* fount.

x height the height of the letter x. The x height of a lower-case alphabet is the height of a lower-case x, i.e. a lower-case letter without ascender or descender (see fig. G.1).

Select bibliography

For books relevant to science and mathematics and to classical works, see sections 13.10 and 14.1 respectively. For lists of abbreviations for journal titles, see p. 257. For books on music, see section 14.3.8.

BRITISH STANDARDS

1629: 1989. *References to Published Materials*

1749: 1985. *Alphabetical Arrangement and the Filing Order of Numbers and Symbols*

2979: 1958 (1983). *Transliteration of Cyrillic and Greek Characters*

3700: 1988. *Preparing Indexes to Books, Periodicals and Other Documents*

4148: 1985 (1990). *Abbreviation of Title Words and Titles of Publications.* To be used in conjunction with the ISDS word list

4280: 1968 (1983). *Transliteration of Arabic Characters*

4754: 1982 (1989). *Presentation of Music Scores and Parts*

4755: 1971 (1989). *Presentation of Translations*

5261. *Copy Preparation and Proof Correction.* Part 1: 1975 (1983). *Recommendations for Preparation of Typescript Copy for Printing.* Part 2: 1976. *Specification for Marks for Copy Preparation and Proof Correction, Proofing Procedure,* at present under revision. Part 3: 1989. *Specification for Marks for Mathematical Copy Preparation and Mathematical Proof Correction and their Use*

5605: 1990. *Citing and Referencing Published Material*

BOOKS

General

Anderson, M. D. *Book Indexing,* Cambridge Authors' and Publishers' Guides, Cambridge University Press, 1971; revised 1985

Achtert, Walter S., and Joseph Gibaldi, *The MLA Style Manual,* New York, Modern Language Association of America, 1985

Book Production Practice, 2nd edn, London, British Printing Industries Federation and Publishers Association, 1984

Carey, G.V. *Mind the Stop,* 2nd edn, Cambridge University Press, 1958; now a Penguin Reference Book

Chicago Manual of Style, 13th edn of *A Manual of Style,* University of Chicago Press, 1982

443

Copinger and Skone James on Copyright, 13th edn, London, Sweet & Maxwell, 1990

Gowers, Sir Ernest. *The Complete Plain Words*, 3rd edn, revised by Sidney Greenbaum and Janet Whitcut, London, HMSO, 1986; now a Penguin Reference Book

Greenbaum, Sidney, and Janet Whitcut. *Longman Guide to English Usage*, Harlow, Longman, 1988

Harris, Nicola. *Basic Editing: A Practical Course*, 2 vols., *The Text* and *The Exercises*, London, Book House Training Centre, 1991

Hart's Rules for Compositors and Readers at the University Press, Oxford, 39th edn, Oxford University Press, 1983

MHRA Style Book: Notes for Authors, Editors and Writers of Dissertations, 3rd edn, London, Modern Humanities Research Association, 1981

Miller, Casey, and Kate Swift, *The Handbook of Non-Sexist Writing for Writers, Editors and Speakers*, 2nd British edn, London, Women's Press, 1989

Names of Persons: National Usages for Entry in Catalogues, 3rd edn, London, International Federation of Library Associations, 1977

Oxford Dictionary for Writers and Editors, Oxford, Clarendon Press, 1981; now also available as a paperback called *The Oxford Writers' Dictionary*

Rees, H. *Rules of Printed English*, London, Darton, Longman & Todd, 1970

Right Word at the Right Time: A Guide to the English Language and How to Use It, London, Reader's Digest, 1985

American usage

Schur, Norman W. *British English, A to Zed*, New York and Oxford, Facts on File, 1987. (Explains how US usage differs)

Success with Words, Pleasantville, N.Y., Reader's Digest, 1983

Webster's Dictionary of English Usage, Springfield, Mass., Merriam–Webster, 1989

Australian usage

Australian Government Publishing Service, *Style Manual for Authors, Editors and Printers*, 4th edn, Canberra, 1988

Murray-Smith, Stephen. *Right Words: A Guide to English Usage in Australia*, 2nd edn, Ringwood, Vic., Viking, 1989

Index

Alphabetization of subentries ignores prepositions such as 'in' and 'of'. Page numbers in bold indicate a main section on a particular subject in the text or an appendix. Quick checklists of copy-editing are also indicated with bold pagination. Page numbers in italic indicate a reference to an illustration which may appear on a different page from the text. Definitions of words used in publishing can be found in the Glossary on pp. 425–42. Abbreviations: c.r.c.=camera-ready copy; e.t.s.=electronic typescript; WP=word processor.

Index

Index

448

Index

Index

Index

Index

Index

Index

Index

Index

Index

Index